PRAISE FOR *GET RICH PLAYING GAMES*

"A must-read... The first book on the videogame business that's both insightful *and* entertaining."
Ed Zobrist
President, Sierra Online

"Finally, a book that shows you how to make all your dreams come true – and make serious money doing it!"
Brian Fargo, Founder
Interplay and InXile Entertainment

"A home run... touches on all the bases necessary for creating a winning strategy for success in the videogame field."
Bill Gardner
President and CEO, Eidos

"There's a fine line between getting rich and losing your shirt in the videogame business, so arm yourself with the essential weapons to succeed: This book's a cruise missile!"
Charles Bellfield
Vice President, Marketing
Codemasters, Inc.

"Reveals the secrets of playing to win... and how to do it making great games!"
"Wild Bill" Stealey
Lt. Colonel, USAF Retired
Founder, MicroProse Software and Interactive Magic

"Full of sound advice and priceless resources for those looking to change the face of gaming."
Nolan Bushnell,
Founder, Atari, Chuck E. Cheese's and uWink

GET RICH PLAYING GAMES

BY
SCOTT STEINBERG

SCOTT STEINBERG'S
GET RICH PLAYING GAMES

Published by P3: Power Play Publishing
4045 Five Forks Trickum Rd.
Suite B-8, #244
Lilburn, GA 30047
www.p3pub.com

ISBN 978-1-4303-2028-9

FOREWORD

Curiously, today's videogame business has founded itself on sequels and hits that cost literally millions to develop, produce and market. But don't be fooled by what you see on TV or in the movies.

The real truth of the matter is that there are many ways to make money in the field… even if you don't have a ton of cash sitting around burning a hole in your pocket. In fact, sometimes capital is a poor substitute for creativity and passion – something the game industry desperately needs more of, especially now!

Hoping to strike it rich and see your name up in lights, even without technically ever having played in the big leagues? Allow me to share a trade secret I've learned during my years at the sector's forefront: Plain and simple innovation is what drives the field ever forward, expands it and helps it to uncover new markets and attract new customers. And there's nothing stopping you from tapping into its potential, right now, this very minute.

Case in point: Currently, there are over 15 million hardcore gamers and 285 million casual gamers. Nonetheless, bizarrely, most of the industry's output focuses on the former audience, leaving literally hundreds of millions of potential buyers (not to mention the vast majority of the market) out in the cold.

Because of this, there are huge opportunities lurking on the sidelines right outside of the mainstream gamer demographic just waiting to be tapped. And a fortune presently sits there untouched, ripe for the taking by those with the insight, talent and wherewithal to deliver innovative products and services destined to engage players' attention and spark their passion for interactive enjoyment.

In other words, you're more likely to land a high score if you take the road less traveled… So if you have an idea for a new version of a hit product like *Madden*

NFL, DON'T attempt to do it! Remember: *Madden* took hundreds of millions of dollars' worth of programming hours and hundreds of people supported by a solid business infrastructure to produce and market. Even if you were to develop a competitive product, simply marketing it alone would cost millions – and then you've still got to go head-to-head with the #1-selling game in its category.

The lesson to be gleaned from these scenarios, not to mention years of real-world experience, is as follows. If you really want to score big, instead of attempting to follow in others' tracks, do things your own way, be smart about your business and look for low-hanging fruit. Doing so can potentially even be as effortless as targeting openings in markets that already exist with lower-cost games that, with better gameplay (or a little tweaking), could easily become tomorrow's best sellers.

In addition, I'll also say this: It further pays to know your core skill set, inside and out, and educate yourself thoroughly in those areas you don't. Combining multiple talents and abilities – as well as possessing the know-how to gauge situations from several perspectives – is vitally important if you ever want to break the bank to boot.

Ask yourself… Are you a programmer? An artist? What about a level planner or mod-making expert? Imagine how much more capable you'd be as a combination of all. Many of today's most acclaimed producers possess greater talents than simple job titles convey. As insiders know, the ability to visualize ideas as tangible graphic representations or edit soundtracks on the fly to better convey desired moods, for example, can add to any game design.

Furthermore, when it comes to choosing topics to base products or services around, be sure to think about areas in which you have unique knowledge and can therefore specialize.

For example: Ever worked at a gas station? How about a restaurant? *Diner Dash* is a best-seller – and it's merely a game about a girl waiting tables. Who knows… perhaps a title featuring a gas station and its overworked attendants is the next big thing? Maybe even being a barista at Starbucks – open as the market's become today, the sky's the limit. Consider: There are books filled with games that were popular in pubs 200 years ago that have yet to be converted into interactive form... and they're already proven to have been played and enjoyed by millions.

In my opinion, the mother lode you should be questing for isn't just a game, but a new game type unto itself. To be specific, one that has not been done before... and something that new technology allows for the first time. People forget that way back when, even *Tetris* was once such a property.

Similarly, *Dance Dance Revolution* and *Guitar Hero* struck a chord with fans by turning everyday concepts like dancing and guitar-playing into best-selling titles based on entirely new experiences. Nintendo's Wii is doing the same thing as we speak as well, with its motion-sensing controllers rapidly giving way to new types of interaction and virtual experience. Frankly, the types of controllers and activities associated with these outings will likely give way to an entirely new era of entertainment and record-breaking profits alone.

Then again, when it comes to financial success, not everything has to be about software itself... Sometimes, new business models are just as important.

Can an MMO game make sense selling spells for a nickel? What about *Halo* selling bullets for a penny? Is there million-dollar potential in cell phones with built-in GPS abilities that allow for location-based play based on treasure hunts in Manhattan or live whodunits that sprawl across the entirety of San Francisco? Who knows, but these days, such ideas don't seem so far-fetched, and both brazen entrepreneurs and old-world media titans are waiting with bated breath alongside one another to find out.

The main point I'm trying to get across being simply this. The world consistently hungers for new and fun experiences – and no matter how and where they're delivered, it's always willing to pay for the good ones. Knowing this, as game enthusiasts, developers, fans, marketers and executives, not to mention fiscally-responsible individuals, it's our job to champion the cause of innovation and help bring it to market.

Take what you will from the following manuscript, full as it is of sound advice and priceless resources for those looking to change the face of gaming as we know it today. Ultimately, the most important thing is that no matter how future ventures pan out, we always have as much fun taking part in them as our customers   and probably more, if anyone's counting.

Nolan Bushnell
Founder of Atari, Chuck E. Cheese's and uWink

AUTHOR'S NOTE

So you want to be rich, right? Congratulations – you've come to the right place!

But before starting down the golden road, let's be up-front. As you'll soon see from the following collection of assorted essays, how-to articles, interviews and editorials, there's only one constant when it comes to commercialism. Specifically: For any lone, individual gamer or software development/publishing company, there is no one surefire path to profitability.

Certainly, the advice and insight contained herein presents a singular record of several men and women's quest for, and achievement of, record financial gain and stardom in the $13.5 billion videogame field. (An industry that brings in more than Hollywood, for those counting... Although astute readers will note that a $600 PlayStation 3 and $60 game do cost more than a $10 ticket and concessions, even if a large popcorn will set you back, what, $125 now?)

However, you should never lose sight of the most important maxim: Despite what you may think, in most cases, for these and countless other would-be entrepreneurs with IPOs dancing in their eyes, it's seldom really about the cash. Those who break the bank gaming generally do so because of a passion they share for this groundbreaking creative medium and rugged determination to pick themselves up and succeed no matter the cost. Even if that means risking everything and losing it, then suffering the pain and ignominy of living to tell the tale.

What's more, learning to write your own chapter in the pages of interactive history is half the fun. Therefore the best professional lessons I, or anyone else, can ever provide you are simply don't stop believing, never quit trying and remember the people and ideals you came up with – not to mention never lose sight of what inspired you to greatness in the first place.

Being a good sport, though, and not the sort predisposed to sentimental dross, I'll also do you one better. I'll give you some personal advice, distilled over nearly three decades' worth of fascination with one of the globe's most captivating entertainment fields.

Forget the parties. Forget the celebrities. Forget the wine. Forget the women. Forget the limelight. Forget the distractions. Getting rich off electronic entertainment isn't about staying up late rabblerousing, sleeping in and then sitting at home in your underwear playing *Gears of War* against sexy gamer girls all day. What I've learned is that it seems to be a function of the following seven variables, a canon I like to call "The Winning Game," in almost every single case:

1. Hard Work – Sorry, there's no 9-to-5 jobs for would-be millionaires in gaming. Days, nights, weekends… Get ready to put in the overtime. Focus your energies on the most important tasks (those that deliver the fastest payout, the most headlines and the biggest long-term gains) and do them till it hurts. However, always make sure you're working to your own benefit first. I know very few well-to-do slackers, but the ones I do know generally got that way off the fruits of someone else's labor.

2. Passion – To truly strike it rich, you've got to love what you do. This enthusiasm (or lack thereof) won't just shine through in your work – it'll also inspire others who'll eventually rally to the cause. Never forget that for every one person offering encouragement behind any PC or videogame project, 1000 more will tell you that you're a madman for trying. In other words, if you don't stick up for yourself and be your own most outspoken evangelist, no one else will. Stand tall, stand proud and never let bitterness or resentment take hold. Most importantly, be a believer – positivity begets results, negativity failure. Remember, opportunity is what you make of it.

3. Timing – Playing to cultural trends or commandeering various fads for your own purpose is always a plus. But also knowing when it pays to be first (or second, if it means letting an adversary get there first and thereby experience initial headaches or growing pains for you) to market is also crucial. As is, for that matter, realizing when it's best to hold a game back, or postpone production until the social climate or political atmosphere best supports your new virtual venture. Likewise, understanding when chance has passed you by, and being brave enough to kill an underperforming or ill-timed project, no matter how much it means to you from a personal standpoint, is further the mark of a great leader.

4. Persistence – I've spent 13-plus years grinding to get where I'm at; others take even longer just to make the first step. Success seldom happens overnight, and the greatest fallacy the media has perpetrated on an unsuspecting public is that you only get one chance in life to shine. Win or lose, to crack the vault, you've got to be willing to be in the game for the long haul, and make mistakes – frankly, that's how people learn. Sometimes you're up, sometimes you're down. Either way, just keep playing: The world has a funny way of making sure everything comes out OK in the end.

5. Ingenuity – Book smarts, street smarts, inborn savvy, whatever… no matter which school of thought you subscribe to, you've got to think fast on your feet, because pitfalls lie at every turn. Self-made videogame moguls are generally hyper-intelligent and, in some cases, borderline savants. Others, just astute businessmen. So, at minimum, you've got to be at least aware of, if not sharper than, all the sharks swimming around out there with so much moolah involved. (Classic example: Despite selling millions of copies of his iconic game the world over, even brilliant and visionary *Tetris* creator Alexey Pajitnov went years without seeing royalties once upon a time.) Whether through college courses, tradeshow appearances or simply browsing the local library's stacks, educate yourself: Knowledge truly is worth more than gold.

6. Resilience – Like the Boy Scouts say, be prepared. The world is a harsh place, and despite what everyone claims, things *will* change on your way to the top. Friends just as easily as competitors may leave your body (as well as budget) beaten and bruised. Partners split; companies declare bankruptcy; legal hassles and development woes can sink the best of AAA games. Throughout it all, the truly rich man is he or she who best learns to weather the storm. Remember, cash remains king. Guard yourself against the vagaries of a cruel world by learning to stack it fast, and prioritize stockpiling that life-saving lucre.

7. Showmanship – Like 19th century circus magnate and legendary huckster P.T. Barnum, most videogame industry wizards understand a single, fundamental truth: Appearance is everything. Out of sight, out of mind... Fickle as the public's attention span may be, you've got to learn to court it. A product or person who goes unpublicized is seldom one who captures the world's imagination. What's more, human nature being what it is, most people tend to take things at face value, making the way in which you present yourself all the more vital. Teach yourself how to play the game right, and no matter the reality of your situation, you'll be able to catapult yourself to untold heights.

And that, my friends, is truly money in the bank.

ACKNOWLEDGEMENTS

To Trip Hawkins, for opening my eyes and allowing me to "see farther." To Josh Levetan and Paul Scigliano, for helping an unknown get his foot in the door. To The Humble Guys for giving the gift of swagger. To Kris Ramac, Eric Knipp and Bjorn Larsson for raising the bar.

To Florence de Martino, for taking a chance on a total stranger. To Elliot and Olivier Grassiano, for being just crazy enough to import their very own pet American intern. To "The Nature Boy" Ric Flair for the cocksure attitude. To all the fellow editors, executives, acquaintances and peers without whose support and generosity none of this would have been possible.

To my dear pal Ronnie, who too often went without. To my good chum, Chris Zimmerman, who spent many a night letting me indulge my habit. To my parents, Karen and Richard, for their lifelong care and encouragement. To my sisters, Jamie and Lisa, for always being there when needed. To my wife Karyn, for years of playing best friend, therapist and yin to my yang all rolled into one. To every videogame enthusiast who's ever dreamed of making it big in the biz.

But, most importantly, to those who never made it – and those who realize that, as long as you don't give up the good fight, there's time to make it still.

Dedicated to All Videogame Developers and Publishers That
Ever Were and Will Be: A Priceless Source of Inspiration to Us All

TABLE OF CONTENTS

INTRODUCTION

I blame *Dragon's Lair* for ruining my life.

Released in 1983, the pioneering laserdisc arcade game – a groundbreaking fanta-sy adventure featuring cartoon-quality visuals and a storyline starring bumbling knight Dirk the Daring's quest to rescue ditzy Princess Daphne from evil dragon Singe – actually gets a bad rap. And who could blame critics? The title, whose action was limited to simple pattern-memorization sequences (you merely hit left, right, up, down or sword to dodge traps, slay monsters and otherwise advance the video reel) wasn't exactly the pinnacle of playability.

Nonetheless, its gorgeous hand-drawn sequences – created by master animator Don Bluth (*An American Tail*, *The Secret of NIMH*) – left this formerly chubby lit-tle lad awestruck. Laugh all you want… Sitting there next to classics like *BurgerTime* and *Defender*, dazzling with its stunning graphics and belly laugh-inducing sense of humor while competitors could barely eke out enough blocky pixels to portray a walking hot dog, it might as well have been the Holy Grail of high technology for me. And, in turn, for all the @&$! quarters it was fed (this, even after I swiped a well-thumbed copy of 1984 book *How to Win at Dragon's Lair*, which got read, oh… 8 million-odd times), the game left an indelible, Chuck E. Cheese token-shaped mark on my soul – and personal sense of showmanship.

You see, the outing – co-developed by Gary Goldman and Rick Dyer, who also deserve to burn in the virtual fires for their contribution to my downfall – wasn't just a game to me. It was an ear-ringing, mind-numbing wake-up call, standing so far ahead of its peers (even with the great industry crash of '83 helping to some-what thin the competitive ranks) that, in essence, no other form of stimuli effec-tively existed within a radius of 200 feet to my young, impressionable mind if it was anywhere near in the vicinity.

The lesson learned: Appearance is everything, and if you're going to do it up, you might as well go big. And so, standing there wide-eyed on the sticky, soda- and gum-riddled floor of a nameless boardwalk gallery where the machine was first viewed, my life as an innocent effectively ended. Right then and there, an obsession with the fabulous, fantastical game industry, and scaling its loftiest heights, effectively began.

Bad timing, though: Being that I wasn't exactly well-connected, $999,999 short of a million and, you know, barely out of my He-Man underoos and Keds at the time, it would be nearly 15 years before I'd begin to apply the insights this titan among games bequeathed. In the meantime, my mind was left to fester during over a decade's worth of Trapper Keepers, wedgies and pop quizzes, and wonder... Why were other kids so fascinated with Transformers, G.I. Joes and these mysterious creatures known as girls while all I could ever dream of was playing, making and marketing interactive entertainment?

To put it in perspective: When I was in grade school, others loved Garbage Pail Kids and 5th period French; me, I spent days dreaming of *River Raid* and *Tutankham*. Come junior high, while classmates spent weekends playing basketball with friends or flirting with members of the opposite sex, my best pal was the NES, and the furthest I ever got wasn't to second base – it was the outfield in *Bases Loaded*. Circa high school, buddies started to come around, and dreamed of careers in game design... somehow I was the jerk who wanted to grow up to be the fat cat CEO sitting on top and deciding what they'd publish. And by the time college rolled around, well... I'd just had enough entirely – instead of attending class at all, I practically locked myself in my dorm room and refused to come out until I'd mastered *Warcraft II* and *Shadow of the Comet*.

Throughout this process, one thing remained constant: No one would give me a break to save my proverbial behind. And so, despite being willing to work virtually as slave labor, by the time I was 17, I'd already begun having to actively call up companies and offer to beta test crap games for free just to get a foot in the door. Thankfully, a few years later, after being rejected by dozens of publishers, going headfirst into a windshield in a freak car accident, and hobbling to E3 the day after without even press or biz credentials, I finally caught a lucky break. Courtesy of the good folks at French publisher Microids, I was off to Paris for a magical, star-studded (read: unpaid) internship, during which I had the good fortune to quickly rise through the ranks, sign a hit title (*SHOGO: Mobile Armor Division*) and rocket off into Z-grade semi-stardom.

So I can sympathize… All your life, you've probably heard about the American dream, and what it's like to go to school, work hard and raise a family like most honest, respectable citizens. Unfortunately, as with most members of Generation X and those who came after, you've probably also grown up knowing deep down that you'd happily sacrifice all for a shot at living out your *Space Invader-* or *Street Fighter-*filled dreams. And, ironically, that those who most deserve a chance at computerized acclaim are sometimes those least likely to ever get a proper crack at living the fantasy.

Bearing this in mind, if you're willing to accept life's harsh realities and pass up a run at the big time in favor of safer, smarter choices, then congratulations: I applaud your conviction, and wish you nothing but the best. You've been able to accomplish what thousands across the world haven't – recognizing the joy that comes from truly knowing peace of mind. But if you're willing to put your hopes to the side, to do what millions of respectable, God-fearing people across the globe agree is intelligent and right, then I must also kindly ask that you stop reading here. Because what follows is a roadmap to ruin as much as it is riches… a descent into depravity and obsession as much as a chance to achieve unfettered mastery over your domain.

The truth is, there is no set formula for 'making it.' Only by putting it all on the line, and living to learn from one's mistakes, no matter how catastrophic, can success in the videogame business, or any other field, ever be truly achieved. If there is one thing I've learned in decades of questing it's this: Suffer you will, before you see the light of day, or even promise of a first digitally-funded paycheck.

4

Nonetheless, without risk, there can be no return. And victory, of course, goes to those willing to seize the day. Just be warned: From here on out, there's no turning back – once the bug bites, and you understand the rules of the game, you can't turn it off. Accomplishment, as they say, can be habit-forming… and the second you've tasted it, like brilliant puzzler *Bust-A-Move*, it's sure to become an all-consuming addiction. Consider yourself warned.

Still with me, bucko?

Then perhaps you've got that hunger… that drive… that *fire* to succeed that burns so hot you can't sleep at night – or perhaps you've just been sucking down the Red Bulls and playing too much *Metal Slug Anthology*. Either way, I'm here to tell you that dreams *do* come true. As you'll see illustrated by the life lessons of several one-of-a-kind personalities I've had the distinct pleasure of working with and interviewing herein, making wishes reality is generally just a function of experience, timing, brashness and enthusiasm.

So listen up, because I'm going to share something all those self-avowed experts won't: Once upon a blue moon, long before the limousines and primetime specials, they were all starry-eyed hopefuls just like you. What's more, the high life doesn't come easy. Weekends in Vegas and parties at the Playboy mansion? Try nights in cramped Motel 6s and frolics at the local McDonald's. Screw it though – you're smart enough to be in it for the love, not the money, right?

This being the case, do yourself a favor and heed the advice Infogrames founder Bruno Bonnell once gave to me. When asked if he missed the good old days of the gaming biz, he said, "You can't see the way forward if you're always looking back." And so, for those of you determined to hit it big, I invite you to come along with me on an odyssey of self-discovery and shameless pursuit of personal betterment. Never forget: Experience and understanding are the most valuable assets you'll ever possess… and nobody can ever take them away from you.

Although, in fairness, the chance to sip drinks with *Super Mario Bros.* creator

Shigeru Miyamoto or trade war stories with Insomniac Games founder Ted Price is nothing to scoff at either. And hey, if anyone's got a spare *Dragon's Lair* machine, take time out to pause from your self-reflective musings and have a laugh on your old friend.

Would you believe, in all these years of gaming, despite owing an entire career and lifetime of fun and excitement to the coin-op – not to mention likely having deposited enough cash in these units to equal the down payment on a Porsche – I'm still too cheap to shell out for one? Then again, maybe that's why, 25 years later, they're still selling tens of thousands of pixel-perfect conversions on PlayStation 2, PlayStation 3, Xbox 360, Nintendo DS, Game Boy, PC and damn near every console or disc player known to man.

But heck, what do I know anyway?

Like millions of fans throughout every known hemisphere, deep down, yours truly simply still remains that same teary-eyed tyke sitting stunned by that first great flashing marquee and sizzling soundtrack at heart.

Scott Steinberg
"The Hardest-Working Man in Gaming"
www.scottsteinberg.com

Said a photographer to music and fashion mogul Russell Simmons once: "Your pose looks too much like an ad."

"I don't think you understand," Simmons replied calmly. "*Everything* I do is an advertisement."

DEVELOPERS

HOW TO MAKE YOUR OWN VIDEOGAME

Fun fact: Most so-called gaming experts don't know the first thing about the business beyond what they see on their PC or high-def TV screens.

So, after critiquing countless titles for more than 300 media outlets and counseling dozens of publishers on how to improve their products, I decided to do what any sensible entrepreneur would: Put my money where my mouse is.

Two years, hundreds of sleepless nights and one hair-brained scheme later, the impossible became reality: My independently produced, developed and conceived PC boxing sim, *Heavyweight Thunder*, arrived on store shelves circa 2005. And, with the help of several lifelong friends, I managed to build software production company Overload Entertainment into a thriving venture.

Here's how you can found tomorrow's Atari out of your home office, too.

DON'T PLAY AROUND

Dream big, but think small, and never let your reach exceed your grasp. Everyone's got a great idea for a game, but sensible ones are much rarer. Start by creating a concept document defining every detail of your ultimate fantasy project. Then begin chopping inessential features. Save grand ideas for sequels. After all, three guys in a basement tinkering on hand-me-down PCs can only accomplish so much.

KEEP IT SIMPLE, SILLY

Gaming isn't just for geeks anymore. Most titles are purchased by everyday people shopping at mass merchants who can't tell a peashooter from a plasma launcher. Increase your chances of success by creating a product that speaks to their interests. Choose concepts audiences will instantly recognize and relate to. (Football, poker and racing are in; extraterrestrial Nazi-hunting psychic vampires, out.) Art-school projects are amusing, but they don't sell.

HANDLE YOUR BUSINESS

Talk about an expensive hobby: Games cost roughly $5,000 to $30,000,000 (around $15-20 million on average for next-gen consoles, infinitely less on PC) to produce, so budget accordingly up-front. Spend no more than six figures initially. Licensing will also run you extra in terms of percentage-based royalties. Registering trademarks takes an additional $10,000 or so, too. That said, always keep some "play money" in reserve; hidden expenses (voice-acting, language translation, etc.) are common as well.

CASH AND CARRY

Why risk your savings when you can gamble with someone else's? Venture capital's an excellent source of funding... if you can produce a game prototype and sample packaging. Seeing is believing, so always approach investors with something tangible; it makes a lasting impression. Can't find a backer? Do what the best of us must at times: Beg friends and family members for seed money.

ORDER OUT

Forget developing the next *Oblivion* in your home office. Games typically take half a dozen or more people to produce. Unless you're keen on paying health benefits, hiring programmers/artists/musicians, and otherwise overseeing a bunch of professional slackers, hire an external development team. Sites like Gamasutra (www.gamasutra.com) can connect you with independent contractors all over the world. Hint: Search for firms sporting proven experience making the type of the title you've envisioned.

GET WITH THE PROGRAM

If you're lucky, partners will have the resources on hand to handle all the grunt work, including constructing characters and environments. If not, you'll need tools like Adobe's Photoshop (available from www.adobe.com) or Alias's Maya (www.alias.com) to help participate in the process of building virtual worlds. Ready-made software engines like GarageGames' Torque Game Builder and

Engine – selling for only $100-$150 at www.garagegames.com – also offer an easy way to cut corners.

ENCOURAGE COMMUNITY SERVICE

Many joystick jocks are self-righteous loudmouths. And even more are simply outspoken and passionate about their hobby. Either way, they're a blessing in disguise. Why? You won't find a more vocal bunch on the Internet – or a better way to get word out about your game online. Employ newsgroups, user forums, websites, press releases, screenshots, demos and video trailers to spread the message. Enthusiastic as gamers are, they'll also willingly test and provide feedback on software prior to release, just for the privilege of a hands-on sneak peek.

AIM FOR A HIGH SCORE

If you've made enough noise about a title, international distributors will already be calling. But when it comes to selling your game, overseas firms, especially those located in countries where the American court system can't touch them, can be unpredictable. It's rare you'll ever see royalties. Instead, negotiate a healthy, guaranteed advance from publishing partners. Don't pawn off all rights to your game onto a single company either; you can negotiate sales licenses for each individual country separately.

GET STARTED EARLY

So much for retiring to a life of *Gran Turismo*... there's still work to be done. Software errors need patching, features updating and fans reassurance that there are better things to come. Strike while the iron is hot; begin work on add-ons or follow-ups ASAP, so you remain hungry and motivated. As fast as the interactive entertainment industry moves, there's no time to waste. The game, as they say, is always afoot!

GETTING YOUR GAME SIGNED

Allow me to share a little secret with you: I'm a glass half full of beer kind of guy. I want to see people succeed – most notably game developers, who pour their heart and soul into every project. After all, the more great titles that find their way onto store shelves, the happier consumers are, the larger the profits generated and, naturally, the better things become for our beloved industry as a whole. But having been to several Game Connection, E3 and Game Developer's Conference events, I find myself in an uncomfortable position.

Personally, I've acted as a talent scout since '98, helping companies from Microids to Atari and DreamCatcher pick smash hits to acquire dating all the way back to Monolith's *SHOGO: Mobile Armor Division.* Embassy Multimedia Consultants further does extensive work on the product acquisitions end for multiple clients as well, advising private and publicly-traded corporations alike on which titles to buy and how to market them. Heck, I even purchase and self-publish the occasional game myself, dipping into my own pocket when the occasion merits. However, if what I've seen recently is any indication of the current state of the development community's approach to publisher outreach, well… all I can say is that not much has changed in the last decade, and it's no wonder so few original products are finding their way to retail channels.

Now don't get me wrong. I'm not denying that there presently exists a pervasive climate of mistrust, in which a largely hit-driven business model has pushed major players into a situation where they favor sequels and franchises in a perceived effort to minimize risk. But as creative sorts who prefer artistry over accounting and mostly rely on the large cash subsidies publishers provide for their livelihood, developers would do well to remember that interactive entertainment is a serious business. New intellectual property (IP), familiar IP, movie licenses, whatever… From the perspective of many executives, what eventually goes into the box is simply pure product. Therefore what you're really looking at is a simple game of risk and return, with those able to garner the most trust and deliver the most cost-effective content reaping the largest rewards.

This being the case, salesmanship is just as important on the back end as it is the front. In other words, initial product pitches are equally (arguably more) crucial than the ones you'll eventually use to woo end-users. Essentially, if you're looking to get your new game project signed, as with any customer, you'll need to court the suits – only harder, as you're asking them to part with hundreds of thousands, or even millions, of hard-earned dollars. If the notion strikes you as disingenuous, take a step back, breathe deeply and consider. Remember that many of these people aren't actual gamers, and yet control not only your destiny, but also those of the employees and co-workers who've entrusted you with preserving their stability and sole source of income. Trust me: You don't want to see the sell-through figures, or success rate, associated with the vast majority of titles that fail to make it to retail. Let alone, for that matter, what happens to a company as well as its people and products when it gets dissolved.

The ultimate point of my little rant being this... Far be it from me to deny that greed, hubris and ambition are factors that weigh equally heavy on any publisher's decision to add a product to its portfolio as a title's actual quality level and content. But, as a software developer, if you want to have a shot at getting your first break, keeping your company chugging along or even changing the overall status quo, it's high time that you learned to play the virtual mating game a little bit better. Following are a few simple tricks that will help you cut to the chase, deliver more compelling presentations and maximize chances of finagling that star-studded deal you dream of. Not to mention (true story), saving me the trouble of yet again watching team after team's dreams get systematically flushed down the toilet as executives casually dismiss one concept after another over a leisurely continental breakfast.

Understand Your Audience

This first, most important point can't be stressed enough: Do your homework, and always know to whom you're speaking before opening your mouth. If you're pitching a $3 million sci-fi first-person shooter, it doesn't make much sense to hold a publisher of budget-priced casual puzzle games captive for an hour does it? That's a serious waste of their time – and yours. Likewise, asking for initial funding for a concept from a publisher who specializes in buying near-complete or finished goods? Not the smartest use of your day.

Therefore always research potential partners before proposing a meeting, let alone sitting down with them. A simple search of the Internet won't just reveal their history, size and scope of access to needed resources. It'll also give you a good look at their current and future lineups, letting you know what type of product or pitch best resonates with corporate heads. And, for that matter, give you a sense of just how successful they are at functions like advertising, marketing and public relations – since, naturally, you don't want to pick just any partner, but rather the right one for the job.

A few hours' of Web browsing, email and/or phone calls is all it takes to get a sense of who would make a good fit as a publishing partner in various territories. Several more is also enough to come up with an individually-tailored sales presentation for all possible collaborators. (Sorry, as in dating, one size does not fit all – you wouldn't approach every woman with the same tired pick-up line, right?) By being choosy and focusing your outreach efforts, you won't just save time and money, but also maximize chances of success. Not to mention connect better with companies who enjoy shared interests. Ask anyone who's unsuccessfully marched their adventure game through 50 action-, arcade- and racing-focused publishers – quality trumps quantity every time.

Dress for Success

I realize – it's hot, you're nervous and uncomfortable, and besides… you work out of your back bedroom anyhow. But please, if you're going to show up and ask for $10 million with a straight face, at least clothe your product and presentation (not to mention yourself) to look the part.

You've heard the expression "first impressions are everything," yes? Well that goes double in sales meetings. Your product, not to mention you yourself, are, essentially, what you are perceived to be – so if there's one area I wouldn't skimp on, it would be visual presentation. Screenshots, sell sheets, video trailers, boxes, websites, etc… Supporting assets should all be of the highest caliber, and presented on the best possible machine/setup manageable. The same goes for product demos – I'd rather see a spectacular-looking 10-minute hands-on teaser than dozens of lifeless levels or examples of physics-driven technology in motion. Never forget, it's all about context: You've got just seconds to capture observers' attention, and even less time to leave a lasting impression. Impact is everything. Ask yourself: If the publisher reps are likely seeing 25+ titles in one day, what's to make them remember yours?

Sales presentations should further be short, sweet and to the point: Gamers have notoriously limited attention spans… If you can't quickly pique my interest, what's to make me think you'll grab theirs? Also worth noting while we're at it: Such pitches are best delivered by the most charismatic and well-spoken member of your development team, who should be able to bullet-point key features with brief overviews. Oh, and showing up with bed-head, unshaven, in a t-shirt and shorts is ill-advised too – we all know appearances aren't everything, but taking the time to compose yourself is a simple sign of mutual respect.

Show and Tell

Less talk, more action – that's what publishing partners really want to see. You can trot out the biggest, fattest, coolest sounding design document in the world, but if you want to be the beneficiary of a five-, six- or seven-figure check, hoo boy… Brother, you better be able to put a playable demo where your mouth is. (Especially since we're sure as snot not reading a 50-page essay on the spot, let alone while swamped back at the home office…)

Part of the reason for doing so is showing you're capable of delivering on claims;

part of it is helping partners visualize exactly how the end-product may turn out. On the one hand, we all know things have a tendency to change during extended development cycles – having a clear-cut vision for a title up-front helps. On the other, if you're going to ask someone to entrust you with life-changing sums of money, you've also got to have the goods to back it up. So do yourself a favor: Prototype every concept you're determined to sell in, and show up to meetings with playable code in-hand. Don't believe me? Ponder the words of *LocoRoco* creator Tsutomo Kuono, who unsuccessfully pitched the cult hit PSP smash to Sony twice before they finally gave it the green-light the third time around. The reason, as he told audience members at 2007's Develop conference: "It's very important to make a demo and show something that moves."

What's more, if you really want to be proactive, highlight several applications for the same technology in various settings. For example: Those routines you've coded that let a psychic hero toss huge boulders around with their mind might work equally well, if not better, in a comic book/superhero-style context – or a magic-infused medieval outing. That way, maybe the initial idea you'd intended to create doesn't get off the ground, but for little immediate cost, you exponentially increase the chances a publisher finds a product that's potentially to their specific taste, and offers a much-needed contract. A little extra effort is all it takes to give yourself that extra edge, or at least ensure you're harder to dismiss outright.

Dare to be Different

Great minds think alike – especially when they're trying to capitalize on successful commercial trends. A recent big theme is Nintendo DS titles… Next year, it could just as likely be social networks and MMOs. Either way, publishers aren't stupid: With a flood of similar product coming down the pipeline, succeeding at retail involves more than simply trotting out titles for a popular platform. Certainly, there may be more price points and options for us to choose from, but acquisitions experts are still looking for games than give them an edge over the competition.

Meaning that saying "OK, let's do a DS title" isn't enough. You've also got to figure out how to do one with a minimum of one to two immediately-recognizable unique sales points (USPs) that set it apart from the competition. Thus, instead of presenting a basic touchscreen-enabled strategy game, maybe you do one that's housed in a contemporary setting like the Middle East, or come up with the first offering based on aerial combat. Choices of subject matter or features don't need to be complex or visionary – just interesting enough to immediately separate the title from the rest of the pack at a glance. Otherwise, you run the risk of being lumped into the has-been category, or worse, going head-to-head with several products being shopped around by rivals, any one of which would satisfy prospective corporate buyers' needs.

As above, prototyping a range of concepts helps in this regard – heck, just swap out art assets if you're feeling lazy. That way, you can see what connects with acquisitions experts, and/or quickly pursue a different concept if you should find out someone's doing your original idea already. As Sun Tzu explains in seminal tome *The Art of War*, the trick isn't going head-to-head with an opponent, but rather learning to strike where your enemy isn't. You can still capitalize on irrational thirsts for products on certain platforms or in certain genres… Merely make sure you're offering different ways to quench them in unique flavors before guzzling that corporate Kool-Aid.

Think Fast

Development times, release dates, projected costs, company background, manpower, track record with similar titles, budget breakdown, relationship with platform manufacturers… Acquisitions and executive teams are going to walk into any meeting looking to ask dozens of relevant questions pertaining to any new development. Do you have the answers ready on the tip of your tongue, and in printed materials they can take away and reference later? If not, you'd better rethink your strategy: It always pays to be prepared.

Being able to think fast on one's feet is also a virtue: The one rule of publisher meetings is to always expect the unexpected. A good way to practice would be to stage faux meetings with internal staff where one or more individuals in the room assumes the role of the publisher representatives – and plays devil's advocate. Smart publishing concerns always keep at least one guy in the room when meeting developers to do just that. (Often myself… maybe it's shaved head and earrings, or imposing midget-like stature.) It's further imperative you handle any and all questions with grace and calm – many developers get visibly hot under the collar when you challenge a statement, never a good sign. And if you or an associate don't have an answer handy, don't be afraid to say you'll follow up… and make sure you do so in record time.

What's more, keep the focus on your own titles – never reference another successful game unless hard-pressed. Rest assured everyone else is comparing their products to or aping the market's current best-sellers. A good basic litmus test for general viability is whether or not your game has enough of an identity to stand on its own, with no prior knowledge of the topic, genre or play style required to comprehend it. If publishers, whose business it is to hock games, can't figure out where a title fits in the marketplace without your prompting, how's a media/trade member to create buzz surrounding it or consumer to decide whether it's worth adding to their collection?

Stay Hip to Cultural Contexts

Why yes, you have built a very nice bocce or badminton simulation. And indeed, the graphics on that cel-shaded piñata-smashing title of yours positively have to be seen to be believed. But, you know, before making me sit through a 20-minute demo, perhaps it's best to understand whether the subject matter even makes sense for the territory in question.

There's only one thing worse than hashing it out with an Eastern European developer for ages as to why their latest "smash hit" works in Prague and not Peoria. And that, of course, is when said blockbuster features an absolutely great theme and premise, but either play centered on intensive stat-crunching or artwork straight out of the Sunday funnies. One word, people: Localization. I realize that the last thing you want to do is tweak your title, at added cost, to make it more marketable in certain countries, especially once the product's finalized elsewhere in the world. Nevertheless, if nothing else, at least take the time to research whether or not region-specific updates may be necessary just to show a given title… and to what extent. You do yourself no favors (and in many cases burn goodwill) spending large amounts of time attempting to present prospective partners with product they know at a glance that they can't use outright.

Here's a thought too: At some point during the development cycle, why not bring in a native of each key distribution territory, and solicit their honest opinion? It's at this stage where you're most able to implement any needed changes in terms of alternate play options and graphic sets, and will be most willing to make the adjustment. After all, I fully understand: Following a protracted 12- to 16-month development cycle and smashing commercial reception throughout the German-speaking world, I'd be loath to start from scratch and rework that critically-acclaimed cycling manager too. But if you want to crack the US market, remember… Sometimes, change is good.

Be Ready to Negotiate

Believe me, I know… You've sacrificed blood, sweat and tears – not to mention the better part of the last decade and your marriage – to get your dream naval warfare title out the door. To you, the game represents years of heartache and passion; unfortunately, to most publishing firms, it's just another commodity to be jazzed up, repackaged and splayed across a shelf. In short, everyone's coming to the meeting armed with their own agenda, and unless you're willing to be flexible, talks will quickly dissolve, or reach a stalemate.

The bottom line: Don't arrive at the bargaining table unless you're willing to negotiate, and open to seeing things from the publisher's perspective. This doesn't necessarily mean accepting less money than anticipated, but it may mean adjusting royalty figures or expectations in terms of marketing and promotional commitments. Fun fact: Everyone's goal is always to maximize return while passing the most possible risk onto the other party. And so, if you want to have any hope of getting signed, let alone landing a deal whose terms are even close to favorable, you have to leave yourself room to maneuver. Deals are always a subtle process of give and take. Offended easily? Perhaps this isn't the right business to be in – you'd be amazed the proposals various game-making and –manufacturing entities will attempt to float past one another.

Still, leave yourself several outs and options, and it'll be easier to wrangle a deal that'll satisfy both parties in any transaction. Publishers aren't necessary the evil entities they seem to be – like most of us, they're just looking for a leg up, and development partners willing to play ball. Ultimately, recall that the goal is finding some contractual path equivalent to meeting in the middle. (Or, better yet, slanted heavily towards your end of the spectrum…) However, that's hard to do when you refuse to do anything but stand unmoving atop an indefensible position.

THE SECRET
TO MAINSTREAM SUCCESS

Call it a landmark industry moment.

Much as I love to hear the sound of my own voice – I'm an executive (and male, at least last I checked), after all – for once, I'll spare you the rhetoric: We all know casual games are serious business.

Titles like *Cake Mania* and *Diner Dash* have made millions online, are quickly invading the DS and PSP, and, per the International Game Developers Association's 2006 White Paper, the biz will surpass $2 billion in revenue by 2008 in America alone.

Now, given that it's my day job as an author, marketing/publishing pro and head of Embassy Multimedia Consultants to keep my ear to the ground, this has the old spider senses tingling for several reasons:

1. The rise of the casual gaming market obviously speaks to its increasing maturity… and therefore the inevitable dawn of several issues ranging from troubles with standard development/publishing practices to the need to juggle the pressures of a rapidly expanding audience base.

2. Marketing has thus far consisted solely of cross-promotion of content across in-house properties and online distribution partners/portals, highlighting the glaring need for both wider-reaching and more targeted efforts in the space. And, for that matter, even more innovative advertising and promotional campaigns than executives are used to… Unlike in the traditional gaming world, they must now speak to end-users potentially wholly unfamiliar with interactive entertainment.

3. The "gold rush" mentality that seems to have gripped publishers in the

wake of the business model's proven viability. Fortune 500 companies seem convinced they can simply take the same mindset and approach that serves them so well on the PlayStation 3 and Xbox 360, transfer it to this new platform and meet with immediate success. Ask insiders though, and you'll hear instant snorts of derision.

That being said, it strikes me as obvious that there's a wealth of potential lessons to be learned from the biz.

Need I remind you: Most outfits currently operating at the top started out small, pushing product the retail industry once wouldn't touch out of spare bedrooms and garages on budgets that'd make most CFOs blush. Learn how to walk a mile in their shoes, and imagine how successful you'd be when backed by the resources and manpower of a major corporation.

With this spirit in mind, I opened our famed Rolodex, and reached out to a few notable acquaintances. Let their own words serve as a warning to some, a surefire roadmap to fame and fortune for others:

PAUL THELEN

CEO of Big Fish Games, which offers a new game *every day* and publishes popular franchises such as *Mystery Case Files* and *Travelogue 360.*

"My favorite analogy is that the same people playing casual games are those who 50 years ago would have been knitting or building model airplanes. Casual games and hardcore games are played for very different purposes. When a person knits of crafts, they focus their attention on the task, feel satisfaction from being good at it, and – when finished – feel an almost addictive sense of relaxation. It's the same effect casual games have on audiences today.

Economically, hit casual games still take the lion's share of industry dollars. It's a more honest gaming industry: The try-before-you-buy and ad-supported models force developers to focus on making great games before all other facts. [Unlike] with traditional games, recognized brands and heavy-handed marketing can't turn a fundamentally bad title into a success. These business models will change and the demographics [behind casual gaming] shift over time. But with baby boomers starting to enter retirement age, with lots of time/disposable income on-hand, I expect growth to continue for some time.

Important to note – casual games are different than core ones; they have more similarities with the e-greeting business or scrapbooking industry. Potential moguls' greatest barrier to entry is arrogance: If someone thinks they know what will sell, they'll be wrong almost 99% of the time. Remember: Our audience is 25-65 years old and 75% female.

Conversely, cloning is an unfortunate fact of life – it makes the industry stagnant and ultimately hurts customers. The only rule is there are no rules: Success requires a balance between taking risks on innovative games (most of which fail, but the occasional gem makes up for 10 flops) and tried-and-true offerings. Never forget, innovation drives every big success – there needs to be some risk-taking to differentiate oneself in a world of thousands of competitors. The only way to increase chances of success is to have a laser-like focus on customers' wants and needs."

ROMAIN NOUZARETH

Founder of Boonty S.A and President & CEO of Boonty Inc., owners and operators of popular international casual game portals Boonty.com and Café.com.

"Circa 2001, we saw there was a gap between free Java games and the more advanced titles found on CD. We felt that if we marketed a great catalog of games at the right price with a simple distribution method, people would buy. We were right, and growth continues thanks to the following factors:

• Instant gratification via digital distribution
• Broadband penetration
• The try-before-you-buy model
• Great content
• Distribution on most of the world's major online portals

Casual games cost $50K-$300K to develop. Still, as with other entertainment sectors, the market's hit driven – many games don't sell. I still think opportunities exist, but only for high-quality content and new business models. I also believe there's an opportunity for brands to emerge: Ask any woman on the street about a search engine – she'll tell you Google or Yahoo. We're hoping Café.com will be the answer when she's asked about online game portals.

Nowadays though, there are too many sequels, copycats and games offered for free, making it hard for the business to grow. I think a better way's based around a mix of digital distribution, the "free to play, pay for value" model, advertising, multiplayer connectivity and social interaction. To succeed though, you need to have a good user base, pick the right distribution partners and select the best content.

Our audience isn't just the standard 60% soccer moms most companies in the industry attract. Interestingly, we discovered that a casual game works similarly in the US, Italy or Japan. If localized, marketed, promoted and distributed properly, it works almost anywhere – and provides a good way for developers to monetize content. When a game is only available in English, you cut yourself out of 70% of the market.

Even so, there's no real recipe for success. But I'd tell aspiring entrepreneurs to focus on the following: Simplicity, quality, innovation, forgiving gameplay and appealing to the largest user base."

JAMES GWERTZMAN AND JOHN VECHEY

Director of Business Development and Co-Founder/Director of PopCap.com, respectively, for PopCap Games, creator of landmark titles such as *Bejeweled* and *Bookworm Adventures*.

James: "I wouldn't say the economics of casual gaming vs. traditional gaming are necessarily more or less favorable – just different. Even our most expensive games cost us 20X less to build than a typical big-budget console game. They also lend themselves better to viral marketing techniques.

On the other hand, we're targeting a broad audience not used to paying for games – a casual title is generally considered a hit if it sells 100,000 units at $20 apiece. Ironically, however, even though online distribution is very efficient (no boxes to print and ship), because our distribution partners essentially end up paying for customer acquisition they earn a larger revenue share… in general, developers see a smaller percentage of that final sale.

Growth in the sector will come from two directions: New users, and existing customers. The casual game industry's famous for having only a 1-2% conversion rate on average – that number's actually better than it sounds, since only 10% who play a free web game download the deluxe version. So for every 1000 people who play that game free online, only 1-2 people actually buy it. There's a LOT of room there for improvement, and we're all getting better at it."

John: "The biggest differentiating factor with casual games is their cross-platform nature. *Bejeweled* is still *Bejeweled* on a mobile phone, iPod or Xbox 360. If you took *Grand Theft Auto*, it would be a drastically different game on all those devices.

But opportunity cost is a stumbling block. The biggest hang-up for startups in the casual space is that for everything you do, you're not doing [10 others]. It's even worse when you're starting out since you don't have the frame of reference, budget or experience to know when to cancel a title, or how to pick your next project. Regardless, I think it's anybody's industry still. We haven't had a big round of acquisitions, everyone is partnered up for the most part, and we all know each other. We're the Wild West before railroads; the industry's only going to get crazier.

Interestingly, the casual game industry has yet to take advantage of user-generated content. I predict it will become more prominent. The big buzzword right now is "community." What most companies don't understand is you don't just create it. It's taken Pogo 10 years to build their user base – they didn't just plug it in one day and [attract millions of people]. Growth comes from nurturing your customers and adding features people want – you can't just set out to do something giant outright and think it'll work.

JOHN WELCH

CEO and Co-Founder of PlayFirst, publisher of smash hit offerings including the hugely influential and record-breaking _Diner Dash_.

"The future of casual gaming, at least from our perspective, is to [jump from] publishing casual games to become a leading multiplatform company focused on "mass-market interactive entertainment.""

While content will still include popular games like _Chocolatier_, it will also include titles with more perspective, and television programming with more game-like interaction between the network and members of the audience themselves. It will require a mastery of game design, Internet technologies and new business models, plus a deep understanding of the mass-market consumer. Companies who can bridge gaming, Hollywood and technology will be especially well-positioned.

Going forward, there's a lot of opportunity. I wouldn't describe it as "social networking" so much as "optionally social play." Here's a real-world example.

Some people go to a bar to meet new people – they might not even have a drink. Others go to have a good time with their friends. Still more go to grab a bite to eat, maybe watch the game on TV. Same place, shared experiences, very different goals. Multiplayer game experiences are similar – some enter for the interaction, others for the game itself. We're just at the cusp of this with casual games. The next frontier is innovating at the intersection of content, community and commerce to deliver compelling social gameplay with zero entry fee and numerous ways to earn revenue.

Personally, I don't care about competition from traditional videogame publishers; I'm looking to what Hollywood is doing, as well as what innovative Silicon Valley software entrepreneurs are cooking up with small, lightning-fast teams. The pace of innovation will only accelerate. The pace of producing more and more non-differentiated single-player games isn't sustainable – and about to cause a lot of people a lot of heartache.

I will say that the Internet is key, and developing and distributing product to consumers online is a whole new ball game. What you see today will tell you how to be successful today – except your product cycle isn't instantaneous and the market is moving quickly."

CONQUERING THE MMO MARKET

We've all heard the hype: Massively multiplayer online games, a.k.a. MMOs – persistent virtual worlds that players can simultaneously mix, mingle and/or adventure within 24/7 alongside literally thousands of fellow users – are the next big thing.

No surprise there... Selling 100,000 copies of a standard full-price title in its initial production run, which can last mere weeks, is still big news to many game publishers. (Although, in fairness, many can expect to garner additional sales and revenue when products are re-released at budget prices, through OEM channels, via online vendors, shipped overseas or relaunched as value-minded compilations.)

On the flip side, massively multiplayer Internet-only outings can generate just as much retail action through the release of boxed goods, while at the same time enjoying longer virtual (and overall) lifecycles. Plus – more pointedly – producing extended, ongoing income in the form of paid subscriptions or microtransactions at little added development and manufacturing cost. The difference between approaches, naturally, being as vast as it is compelling from a commercial standpoint... and irresistible to explore.

Picture the situation faced by those dealing in standalone retail product.

You ship your latest award-winner for $49.99-$59.99. Following, there's perhaps just a six- to eight-week premium shelf life period in which to capitalize on this expensive, years-in-the-making title, which dozens, more likely hundreds, of peers contributed to. Maybe you succeed, maybe you fail, and the title's quickly reduced in price or pulled from retailers altogether; hopefully, at some point, you see some recurring back-catalogue revenue. Considering that you've spent $10-20 million and invested heaven knows how many man-hours up-front, it's hardly a tempting or risk-averse proposition by even the greenest executive's measure.

Now envision you could sell the same title in-store just as long, yet also at full sticker price online for months to come – or give it away free via digital download, thanks to a more flexible business model. And, what's more, get to see around $9.99-$14.99/month, every month, on average from users in recurring revenue in exchange for a little customer support and new content, or $3-4 in regular, bite-sized purchases of virtual items and enhancements. Suddenly, what was once a potentially lucrative, but hit-or-miss income stream becomes not only consistently predictable and profitable... the trickle becomes a raging torrent. And that's before you count the additional onrush of capital created by peripheral income-generating activities, such as the public sale and trade of virtual goods and characters.

To put things in perspective: Market leader *World of WarCraft* tops 9 million subscribers worldwide. Alone, it swells owner Vivendi's coffers to the point that the corporation could literally fund the start-up of an entirely new, fully-functional standalone game publishing subsidiary *every single month*.

Sounds like an incredible deal, right?

Not necessarily – infinitely more expensive, trickier to maintain, more upkeep-intensive and likelier to implode than single-player-only experiences, these cyber-space realms can cost tens of millions initially *and* on the back-end to build and support. And that's before you count the grief, public outrage and aggravation associated with inevitable outages and downtime.

Nor, as the failure of countless titles from *The Sims Online* to *The Matrix Online* and, most recently, *Vanguard: Saga of Heroes* to ignite the gaming world illustrates, is success guaranteed, whatever your firm's past track record in the industry. Note that this maxim holds true even for the most pedigreed and well-funded of intellectual properties: Anyone remember *Asheron's Call 2* (the now-defunct sequel to a much older forerunner which is actually still profitably running) or *Need for Speed* spin-off *Motor City Online*?

Bearing this in mind, before rushing out and attempting to capitalize on one of the hottest trends since in-game advertising, take a second to stop and ponder the following hints, tips and advice. Certainly, the analysts at DFC Intelligence predict big things for the sector, saying it will be worth over $13 billion by 2012. But as we at Embassy Multimedia Consultants counsel clients both new to and familiar with this rapidly-growing market, it always pays to know the rules before getting in the game…

Defy Expectation – "Most MMOs follow the narrow framework defined early in the market's history by *Ultima Online* and *EverQuest*," explains Richard "Lord British" Garriott, creator of the *Ultima* franchise and NCSoft's *Tabula Rasa*. "There's no feeling of a dynamic world; no real sense of accomplishment beyond leveling up."

Translation: We don't need another *World of Warcraft*, or similarly-styled, grind-heavy sword and sorcery romp – ditto for sci-fi themed escapades as well. That market's already sewn up thanks to an immense number of current offerings from *Dark Age of Camelot* to *Anarchy Online*, *The Lord of the Rings Online*, *EVE Online*, *Gods & Heroes*, *Age of Conan*, etc. (Notice a trend here? We call that overstaturation.) What's more, consumers tend to form long-standing bonds with specific games, heightened by these products' sense of familiarity and community. Attempting to convince them to part from their present obsession, after endless months of character-building and relationship-forming, just to try a largely carbon-copy alternative isn't the easiest, or most cost-effective, task.

Instead, when developing your next blockbuster, focus on more uncommonly explored, yet just as interesting topics. Although still in the minority, publishers like Sony Online Entertainment with *The Agency* (spies); Netamin with *Ultimate Baseball Online* (sports); and Flying Lab with *Pirates of the Burning Sea* (I'll give you one guess) are leading the way. Bonus points if you maximize marketability by picking a topic that extends the title's appeal to non-traditional gaming demographics such as women, casual shoppers and seniors. See Nexon's *Audition* (dancing), Linden Labs' *Second Life* (human interaction), Sulake's *Habbo Hotel* (kickin' it with friends) or *Kaneva* (social networking) for inspiration, with even

Sony's *PlayStation Home* initiative speaking to the popularity of this growing practice. In other words, making niche titles for limited audiences with tired play mechanics based on already well-exploited trends won't do wonders for your bottom line. Dare to boldly go where rivals aren't: In one fell swoop, it'll let you raise your profile, recognize greater financial upsides, improve game quality and face reduced competition.

Put Profits First – Here's a simple equation even all us non-bean-counting types can understand: Less development cost + smaller overhead + fewer licensing fees + lighter manpower = greater payouts, minimized risk, faster profitability and exponentially increased ROI.

It's the reason why outfits like Worlds Apart Productions (creators of *Stargate: Online Trading Card Game* and other computerized collectible card game outings – now known as SOE Denver) have operated for years successfully on skeleton crews, yet still produce top-notch product. And, of course, browser-based offerings from small outfits such as *Kingdom of Loathing* can quickly become lucrative. What's more, the phenomenon further explains how relatively low-key titles with little-to-no marketing expenditures such as *RuneScape* can be amongst the most successful (featuring 5.6 million players, 1 million of whom are paying subscribers) MMOs in existence.

The takeaway here being that massive budgets and expansive universes filled with endless surprises aren't everything. To improve chances of success, simply devote as much attention to your business plan as the actual game itself. Before building a title, determine a break-even point and core set of goals, then staff accordingly and stick religiously to assigned budgets and design plans. Don't let feature creep or, worse, hubris – always estimate conservatively when forecasting revenues, subscriber bases, rate of customer retention, etc. – stand in the way of common sense. Ultimately, what you need to focus on is building a polished, high-quality product of manageably limited, but infinitely expandable scope that drives word-of-mouth sales, the single biggest contributor to any given MMO's success. And above all else, ensures the flexibility to accept multiple revenue streams and dynamically adapt your strategic approach as needed. When it comes to virtual worlds, anything and everything can, and will, often change on the fly.

If you have to start small, so be it: Build a solid core game than can operate with fewer members then use a low, but steady stream of subscriber income to expand slowly and organically. If you need to achieve larger payouts and recruit customers faster, focus on promotions (e.g. online campaigns, demo discs, mailers, contests, etc.) that directly put the title, or a means of interacting with its assets (i.e. fan site kits, playable mini-games or teaser trailers) in front of the most possible buyers. Always look for alternate income channels, as companies like K2 Network (whose games are free to play, yet generate a healthy income on small power-up and item purchases) or virtual miniatures seller Octopi have done. And whatever your size or ambition, as a rule of thumb, anticipate that costs of customer support will far exceed initial expectation – players can and will be demanding.

Either way, do the research and take the managerial steps necessary to ensure your reach doesn't exceed your grasp, and you'll already be ahead of 90% of the competition. "Our goal is to grow organically, profitably and healthy," confirms Funcom product director Jorgen Tharaldsen. "And [of course] deliver the best possible games where people can enjoy themselves and have fun, regardless of their nationality or background."

Nurture Your Community – Remember: Most players play not for actual in-game content itself, but rather to chat, canoodle and interact with others just like themselves.

That said, a top-notch (but not, by definition, necessarily technically cutting-edge or audio-visually astounding) hands-on experience and the associated community it inevitably attracts is the most effective sales tool you've got, and means of driving continued growth. Therefore you'd best treat end-users like royalty. Why? Well, quite frankly, they're the ones paving your simulated streets in gold.

Or, as *A Theory of Fun for Game Design* author Raph Koster is kind enough to point out on his website, "Glory is the reason why people play online; shame is what keeps them from playing online. Neither is possible without other people being present."

To wit, the fine art of listening, responding to and providing encouragement for your customer base can't be underestimated. Just ask *Star Wars: Galaxies'* creators, who sparked a storm of controversy with their undesired "enhancements" to the title in 2005. Nor should one fail to recognize end-users' inherent ability, or motivation, to "break the system," whether intentional or not... As makers of pioneering MMOs dating all the way back to 1987's *Habitat*, which saw a months-in-the-making treasure hunt designed to take the user community weeks to solve cracked in minutes, can attest, expect the unexpected and be ready to deal with it when it inevitability happens.

With this in mind, it's imperative that you invest heavily in customer support, keep your ear to the street and recruit designers who remain active and willing participants in their own simulated worlds. Not to mention continuously arrange a spate of in-game events and activities such as tournaments, political rallies and even celebrity appearances, to keep users coming back. (Real-world gatherings such as fan faires and conventions too...) Putting consumers' needs first and being able to respond speedily and effectively to any situation that affects their happiness and satisfaction is crucial, as is perpetually enhancing the quality of their ongoing play experience. Never forget that an MMO is less a game, more an active commitment – everyone, including you and your social life/checkbook, needs to be in it for the long haul.

Promote User-Friendliness – Bad news: If you're an MMO maker, you're already playing to audience that's a subset of a subset. Think PC gamers with an interest in the subject matter that possess specific minimum hardware/Internet configurations who are willing to try new things, outlay regular amounts of cash and spend multiple hours each week getting up to speed with and enjoying your product. If it helps, imagine each step required to play your title, from its initial purchase to installation, configuration, character generation and active play as another gateway through which gamers must pass. And it's only natural that there will be a steady rate of attrition, or customer loss, along the way at each checkpoint.

Game developers want to know why more people aren't getting hooked on the hobby. The short answer: We're not making it easy for them. So if you want to increase chances for success, it has to start at the earliest phase of development. As in, going all the way back to when you're choosing a topic, determining how to present it to the world and deciding how players will interact with your simulated universe.

Want to really see an MMO take off? Create one with a mass-market theme, lower the system requirements, make it possible to play in bite-sized sessions and show people how they can jump right in and begin playing in minutes. It's the difference between enjoying a best-selling novel that's been adapted into an hour-long TV special or actually picking up and thumbing through the original, 600-page book. Most gamers want to get right to the good stuff, not sit around reading every last tome or scroll you've crammed onto a 3D bookcase or pimping out their new superhero or paladin by endlessly tapping their mouse to wail on generic thugs or low-resolution rats. That's why hardcore players – a small subset of your audience – should have the option to delve into games in detail, while the majority of players should, by default, be given the choice to skip the minutiae.

Certainly, customizability is mandatory: The end-user must be made to feel as if they have ownership of their virtual experience by being allowed to personalize everything from avatar look/feel to assigned quests/missions and in-game controls. But you also have to truly put that power in their hands, and make it – like actually jumping in and seeing where a title's fun really lies – easy to access and appreciate. Sadly, most who do include such features still hide them behind a dizzying array of menus, toggles and keyboard inputs... Not to mention game designs which instantly infuriate players by immediately forcing them to download 30-minute updates the initial time they're loaded. You know what they say about first impressions, right?

Oh, and just because "massively multiplayer" is the watchword, shouldn't mean it's the only game in town. Counterintuitive as it seems, don't force players to automatically have to interact with other subscribers. Instead, create a large subset of compelling adventures they can accomplish alone. Then let them choose to reach out to the virtual world at large for help, advice or just to recount war stories when ready. Newcomers need a little time to get adjusted, and we all have moments where we want to just cut loose, feel like a one-man army, raid a few wyvern's nests, and not have some foul-mouthed teen named "j00m4Ma69" tagging along to ruin the experience. In plain English, it's their fantasy: Let players individually decide when they're ready to allow someone to rudely intrude on it.

"It's always tricky to communicate to potential users that making a game that's friendly to everyone, even casual players, doesn't need to necessarily preclude depth or challenge," confesses *EverQuest II* senior producer Scott Hartsman. "Lots of hardcore gamers, even developers, hear 'casual-friendly' and think 'no thanks.' The truth is that it's actually possible, and highly recommendable, to make a game that has interesting things to do for people across the spectrum."

In essence, the sooner we all stop making MMOs the old-fashioned way, and start simply making sense, the easier it's going to be to expand the medium, and enjoy unfettered success.

Besides, lest you doubt the upsides, recall: Given aforementioned financial forecasts, if, by following these suggestions, you manage to seize even .005% more of the market, well… Per going rates on online auction houses, that still buys one heck of a level 60 dark elf necromancer.

CREATING HITS

By Steve Allison
Chief Marketing Officer, Midway Games
www.midway.com

In the past several months there has been some interesting banter about changing the way games are marketed as we enter the next generation, particularly when it comes to new IP (intellectual property). But is this really the case? According to our numbers, the actual success rate of new IP over the past four years is just 7% In other words, 93% of new IP fails in the marketplace. So while the 90-plus review scores and armfuls of awards create the perception that titles like *Psychonauts*, *Shadow of the Colossus*, *Okami* and other great pieces of work were big successes, the truth is that they were big financial disappointments and money losers.

The call for a change in marketing has come primarily from a few developers who have seen their games passed over by the marketplace or by their competitors and decided to reboot their projects a couple of times. Yet I've never seen a highly anticipated game with a truly powerful concept hurt by a product delay. I've been through a few with the *Unreal Tournament* franchise and the launch of *Neverwinter Nights*. These were truly anticipated releases that were destined to be big whenever they shipped and have publicity all along the way, however long it took. But let's face it: Not all games are as highly anticipated as these. If a game loses its momentum because of delays it will be because the concept itself is weak, or because bad timing has made the product either less relevant or allowed a rival developer to get to market first with a similar idea.

So with a success rate of less than 10% percent for new IP, it is not the way we market and launch games that needs revisiting in the next generation. No, it is development that needs reflection, refinement and change. It is development that must evolve in all its various facets, from inception to execution. It is the conception and creation of new IP that must be redefined in this new generation so that we can all pull together to beat the 93% failure rate – even as we face significantly higher development costs – by reaching a common understanding that the potential success of any game is wholly dependent on three key factors, in the following order of importance: The true commercial power of the game's high-level *concept*, the *timing* of the game's release, and finally, the quality of the game's *execution*.

1. The Most Important Thing to Get Right is the Concept.

Games should have an elevator pitch that makes avid gamers *and* average mass market consumer who plays games say "I've got to get that" or "Bad ass!"

One very important truth is this: 16-35 year-old males [in this day and age] are not attracted to the things our PD (product development) guys naturally tend to come up with. Why? Because working at a publisher day in and day out, particularly in development, we all get trapped in the hardcore gamer's mindset. It's really important to understand that our customers on next-generation home consoles – PlayStation 3 and Xbox 360 – are 90% male, and that's not going to change anytime soon. Therefore, the games that have the highest commercial potential are those that provide an outlet for them to live out their alpha male fantasies, to do the things they truly want to do but never could in real life.

In other forms of entertainment, the audience is content to sit back and passively take in the experience. With interactive entertainment, our customers actually want to do things they see in other forms of entertainment or in the news. They want to lead a rock band; become a pro skateboarder; be LeBron James; stride onto the field with their favorite NFL team; save the world from tyranny during World War II; drive a car in ways that would be completely reckless in real life; lead an elite counter-terrorist unit against threats in Las Vegas or New York; rise to power in a Scorsese-like crime saga; or, to use an example that's very close to home, step into

Chow Yun-Fat's shoes in a John Woo movie. In general, when you test concepts with our target customer, these are the types of things they dream about. What holds the greatest attraction for them in video games is this: Culturally-relevant fantasies established by current events, recent cultural trends or forms of entertainment that appeal to their age group.

Want to be certain that you have a powerful concept? Don't take internal debate or internal polls as proof of commercial viability. Instead, really get to know your audience. Test your concepts with them. Be sure your audience loves the game premise and key features in an elevator pitch of no more than one page. If you need more than that in order for an average 16 year-old to get it, you've got too much story and an insufficiently powerful concept. The most successful concepts are going to be those our audience fantasizes about doing, but could never otherwise do without the videogame arena to do it in.

Conversely, what doesn't our audience fantasize about or respond to? Desolate, post-apocalyptic wastelands. Werewolves. Vampires. Mechs. Exo-suits. Cybernetic enhancements. Magic dogs. So if your next game is set in a post apocalyptic world, starring a cybernetically-enhanced vampire hunter, you may make hardcore gamers say "Bad ass," but you're facing an uphill battle when it comes to the larger segment of the market who simply say "Meh... another one of *those* games."

What's both funny and fascinating is what happens when an obtuse concept like the ones above come in from various parts of our company. One of the higher-ups will suggest a refinement like "Let's take out the post-apocalyptic future and set it in the present day." All of the sudden, there's a revolt because "the suits" are wringing the innovation out of [some poor developer's] game concept. That's simply not the case. Innovation doesn't come from the setting. It comes from what you do within a powerful concept. Trust me, there's nothing innovative about cybernetic enhancements.

There is one exception. The name recognition of highly successful developers and individuals can be a powerful commercial draw in its own right. But that's a select group of talent: Blizzard; BioWare; Epic Games; Bungie; id software; Rockstar North; Will Wright, Shigeru Miyamoto; Hideo Kojima and a few others. The next game from any of these studios or individuals is enough of a powerful concept to be bankable even if the concept is otherwise obtuse. By repeatedly succeeding both critically and commercially, these studios or individuals have earned the near-undying trust of consumers. That trust gives them the right to a level of creative freedom that other studios or individuals will not be able to justify to the suits from a commercial perspective, no matter how well they execute.

The only time one of *those* games will attract a broad segment of our audience is if it comes from one of the aforementioned superstar developers. People like Kojima or Miyamoto and studios like BioWare or Bungie can show up at E3 with a game about cybernetically-enhanced magic dogs battling exo-suit-wearing werewolves in a desolate post-apocalyptic wasteland, and they'll get the benefit of the doubt from the press and from gamers. Other developers – no matter how talented they are, or how much acclaim they've gotten from the press – can only claim to be at this level when they have won the confidence of gamers through repeated commercial success.

2. Timing is the Second Most Important Factor in the Sales Potential of a Game.

No matter how cool your idea may be, understand that great minds think alike. Being first to market on key features or powerful concepts can make you top dog. Missing your window will make you irrelevant. Because an incredible feature that a developer is working on is never unique for long: Multiple teams are usually chasing the same general idea or feature breakthrough.

In Hollywood, where you'll see three Wyatt Earp movies or three asteroid flicks from three different studios in the same release season, you don't want to be the last one to hit the theatres. The last one will be irrelevant, and the same is true for games. Just look at the number of musical instrument and karaoke singing games that are flooding the market. Joining *Guitar Hero* and *SingStar* are *Boogie* from EA, Harmonix's *Rock Band* and I'm sure several others. Timing to market is going to make or break these games at retail, because all of them are expected to be well-executed.

Whenever execution on an innovative feature is expected to be a key driver of a game's success, timing to market is a huge factor. Our *Stranglehold* team is working on an incredibly tough feature they call "Massive D," which allows pixel-level destruction of the environment. It's very impressive and nobody has delivered this before in a videogame, especially the way they are doing it. However, we're not alone. We also know of about four or five other next-generation games based around a similar feature, like EA's *Battlefield: Bad Company*. But with *Stranglehold* strategically timed to [arrive ahead of them], we're assured of being first ever to market with this eye-catching technology.

If *Stranglehold* were to come out twelve months late with Massive D as one of its major selling points, there would still be people who'd think it's cool. But the sales impact of a genuinely innovative feature has much greater impact than a mere commodity feature, as Massive D will be in 2008.

This is a fact of life. Developers who get it and want to be recognized as pioneers have to grasp the paramount importance of being first to market on technology and gameplay mechanics – while still being motivated to execute them well.

3. Execution is Only the Third Most Important Factor In A Game's Success. Yes, Third.

This doesn't mean that we shouldn't strive to make great games. Nor does it mean that a great concept gives developers the license to make a crappy game. It simply means that execution alone is no guarantee of commercial success. The developers who understand this will thrive in the next-generation home console business. The ones who don't will fall victim to the realities of the shifting marketplace.

The average reader of this piece, especially one working in the gaming business, will say, "Wait a minute. A great game whose review scores average 90 or higher can ship when it's done and it'll still be a great game." Or they'll say, "Whatever the concept may be, a great title is all about the game mechanics." Unfortunately, this is not true. A great game is one that is a commercial success. Period.

Consumers review games with their wallet, and you don't get to sell them a million units at full price unless a bunch of people love your work – especially at $59 a pop. Sure, your craftsmanship may be amazing. But if your concept is not a powerful and relevant male fantasy, executed in a timely fashion, at a level that delivers on the promise of your core idea, you've probably just delivered the videogame equivalent of an art house film.

An art house game certainly proves that your development team is really talented, but it also demonstrates you're really not in tune with the audience. This kind of creativity is only fine as long as your art house game was built on an art house budget. But an art house game made on a blockbuster budget – especially the sums of money required to be competitive on Xbox 360, PS3 and high-end PCs – is fiscally irresponsible.

The truth is that there is no correlation between review scores and commercial success. If there were, "great" games like *Beyond Good & Evil*, *Ico*, *Okami*, *Psychonauts*, *Shadow of the Colossus*, *Freedom Fighters*, *Prey* and Midway's own *Psi-Ops* would all have been multimillion-unit sellers. The aforementioned games are all games that average review scores of nearly 90% out of 100, some even higher. The reality is that none has sold more than 300,000 units at full price in the U.S. and a couple of these less than 250,000 units [throughout their] lifetime, even with bargain pricing. In today's home console business, a true next-generation game costs between $12 and $25 million dollars to produce, which sets the break-even point at 1 million units (and in some cases even 2 million units) depending on how high the budget has gotten.

What happens all too often in the videogame business is that we get art house movies made at blockbuster budgets. These games inevitably fail to find an audience large enough to support their costs, and nobody is happy. The developer thinks they were destined to sell 5 million units because they scored a 90 on average. The publisher is mad for spending so much on a game that had no broad appeal despite a very talented team and a large budget.

Let's be clear: It is not the amount spent on marketing that determines how many units of these games are sold. A game's sales potential is entirely determined by the strength of its overall concept, while the difference between its sales potential and its final tally is determined by its execution. And given the phenomenal execution of *Psychonauts*, *Ico*, *Psi-Ops* and the other art house games listed above, their failure can be ascribed to a misguided concept, poor timing or both.

4. One More Thing – Develop Vertically With Concept, Timing And Execution In Mind.

Begin by developing your game vertically, not horizontally. In other words, don't just take the design document and start building levels 1 through 20 because that's the way that the lead designer mapped out the game progression. By first taking the time to build a single level to the quality of a finished product; by rapidly prototyping all new gameplay mechanics; by prioritizing the riskiest and most innovative features, you take the unknown and make it completely known. You'll also know how long it takes to make a level of finished quality; whether the gameplay ideas and features are working properly and, most importantly, whether they're fun. And if there's anything that's not working, you can cut it sooner rather than later.

If you've got a truly powerful concept, it should help generate a specific, quantifiable set of features. Focus on that. Don't develop a laundry list of features to merely functional status – which means they work, but they still need tons of additional work to actually be fun – then move on to yet other features. You won't even know if your ideas are genuinely fun until you develop one vertical slice, or several, depending on the ambition and challenges of your project. Don't be wedded to a paper design document: That's not your game. Game development is an iterative process, and only by iterating early and often will you discover the best version of the game that is hidden inside your concept. Keep refining your game by constantly scaling it back and rebuilding it around the genuinely fun elements that emerge during the vertical slice process.

If, during this process, a feature turns out to be just OK and not great, it's decision time. If it's essential, keep at it. If it's a nice-to-have, but not a must-have, drop it, or, better yet, save it for the sequel. On the other hand, if nothing is fun or true to the concept after this extended pre-production period, kill the project and move on

The key to good game development is to prove what is both fun about your game and critical to its success – but let the rest go. One or two elements, done spectacularly, are exponentially more likely to yield a blockbuster than 15 average features. Look at [recent] hit *Gears of War*. Its feature set is not very deep at all, but it does what it does exceptionally well: Stop-and-pop gunplay with use of cover, executed to perfection, with best of breed visuals and core technology.

If you do this type of pre-production correctly, the actual production process should be shorter; major levels can be built efficiently via outsourcing to specifications determined during pre-production; and the development schedule can be projected with less error, making your game's time-to-market more of a known quantity. And when you've got the concept and timing in the bag, thanks to your well-engineered pre-production process, everything else about your game's development now comes down to good old-fashioned execution, based on things that you've already proven with your vertical slice.

If developers follow the process I've outlined above, they'll create a product that can achieve the biggest sales possible based on the potential of its concept. Meanwhile, marketing can begin its process around the near-final quality vertical slice instead of a design document and a prayer. Everyone is on the same page. Everybody wins. The stakes are so high in the next-gen landscape that marketing or publishing leadership needs to be involved all along the way so that concept, timing and execution are clear from start to finish.

EXECUTIVES

JUMPSTART YOUR CAREER

Fast-paced, ego-driven and competitive as the videogame industry is, I probably shouldn't be telling you this… but then, that's never stopped me before. So here it goes: You – yes, *you*, no matter your level of interest, experience or familiarity with the business – possess all the basic skills and know-how it takes to win big in the gaming business.

Think I'm pulling your joystick?

Recall: World-renowned designer Sid Meier (*Pirates!*, *Civilization*) started out a simple computer/IT grunt. Sales legend J.W. "Wild Bill" Stealey, a former Air Force pilot, founded MicroProse, one of the most successful gaming companies of the '80s/'90s, after randomly bumping into him in an arcade. Former Microsoft honcho Peter Moore, one of the biz's most respected figures and a staple fixture both on TV and in print, actually began his career as a physical education (PE) teacher. And Video Games Live founder Tommy Tallarico, who lives in a theme park-like mansion and travels the world playing sold-out concerts for thousands of international fans at venues as diverse as the Kennedy Center and Hollywood Bowl? Long before the fame and fortune, he started out homeless and sleeping under a pier.

And if you believe it can't happen to you, well… Sorry, my friend – you've got your wires crossed. I should know.

At 17 I was just another overweight, lonely geek dreaming of stardom, beta testing games like *Blood Bowl* and *Alone in the Dark 3* pro bono just to feel like part of the industry. Two years after: Your average, everyday college kid and dedicated fansite owner desperately seeking a summer job, who'd been rejected by nearly every game company on the east coast.

But despite possessing no programming, graphic or design skills, by the time I was 20, I'd landed my first internship, working for multimillion-dollar, decade-old software publisher Microids out of Paris, France. Three weeks after arriving, was named head of international public relations. And three months following, when I departed back for America? Dubbed VP of Product Acquisitions – and enjoying the prestige of a having a hit title already under my belt. Since then, it's been nothing but start-ups, self-published software hits, book signings and radio/TV appearances – proving, yet again, that literally anyone can make it, if they just know where to concentrate their talent and effort.

The good news then: Today's your lucky day. Rather than retread the same tired ground – seriously, the amount of books, articles and podcasts now devoted to breaking into the gaming biz practically dwarfs Koei's catalogue of *Dynasty Warriors* re-releases – I'm here to tell you how to get where you'd truly like to go: Straight to the top.

Want to slap hands with legends like Shigeru Miyamoto, Will Wright and Trip Hawkins? Build an electronic empire? Someday day see your latest title's name sitting up in lights alongside best-sellers like *Halo 3, Metal Gear Solid 4* and *Splinter Cell: Double Agent* as the next interactive smash? Here's how to send your career, as well as both personal and job prospects, skyrocketing…

ARTISTS

Great art is nothing without an audience: Get your work in front of as many people as possible. While publishing an online portfolio's a great start, equally vital is learning to establish a singular, marketable identity.

Concentrate on mastering a particular style of visuals to generate a dedicated fan base. Next, continue to cultivate your following through cost-effective promotional vehicles such as newsletters, virtual gallery viewings and other self-engineered publicity campaigns designed to push their buttons. For instance: Anyone can give away free desktop wallpaper featuring spoofs of popular characters in unexpected situations. Or, for that matter, contribute stunning graphic sets or concept sketches to the dozens of complimentary game mods, or fan-made updates, for chart-topping outings such as *Half-Life 2* and *Unreal Tournament* that are being casually constructed in their spare time by legions of loyal fans as we speak.

More than anything else, it pays to be inventive, and prolific – from web-based comics to indie game box covers or even just eye-catching finishes to your favorite fansite, don't hesitate to leave your mark on any colorful venture that's bound to capture the public's imagination.

TIP: Afraid potential employers won't see what you're getting at? Paint a picture for them. Anybody can send in a resume or email off a few slick pics. Instead, improve your chances of being noticed by taking the time to visit with prospective patrons at various industry events – putting a face to a name makes you harder to dismiss. And hey, should you leave behind a snazzy, well-produced keepsake (services like CafePress, Lulu.com and BookSurge make it easy to self-publish books, mice, mugs, etc. at minimal costs) that's bound to look great on someone's shelf – and serve as a ready reminder – to boot, so much the better. After all, as you well know… it's all about making an impression.

DESIGNERS

Go against the grain – to a point. While it pays to avoid clichés (hel-lo, World War II shooters and sci-fi real-time strategy epics) and pick story topics, underlying premises, art styles and control schemes that the market has yet to embrace, always stick with a base concept that both hardcore gamers can instantly comprehend the value of and casual shoppers immediately recognize. It's one thing to be ahead of the curve (and there should always be a minimum 1-3 key innovations you hang each new creation's hat on, both from a design and PR standpoint) – another to be out in left field completely.

Similarly, reach for the stars… But also know when to stop grasping at empty space. The best videogame projects generally begin with a detailed design document and fully mapped-out production schedule. While it's inevitable projects can, and *should*, evolve as team members contribute new ideas and insight though, a wise man knows when his ambition exceeds his resources – and when to save killer ideas for a token sequel.

True: If everyone were to accept their limitations at face value, we'd never see bar-raising outings like the original *Doom* or boundary-busting MMOs such as *World of Warcraft*. But chances of batting one out of the park are 10,000 to 1, as even experienced vets will tell you. So instead of swinging for the fences – and most likely whiffing – just set out to create the best game you can using a concise, well-researched plan of action, and *given the time, money and manpower provided.*

As any pro ballplayer knows, base hits, when taken cumulatively, can be just as important as home runs. Don't try to force a blockbuster: Let the process evolve naturally, if and when it happens, as a result of team chemistry.

TIP: There's no substitute for good, old-fashioned playtesting. Never show your work to peers or the general public before it's ready – you only get one chance to make a first impression. Nonetheless, don't be afraid to put the product in people's hands either. Even in the old days, when one-man crews were the norm, great games seldom sprung forth fully born from the womb of a lone designer's imagination. They're often created as the direct result of outside influences, subtle or otherwise, on a single craftsman or team's initial creative vision.

EXECUTIVES

If you've ever worked a full-time job at a videogame developer/publisher, or any other commercial firm for that matter, then surely you're aware: Sadly, corporate advancement isn't necessarily tied to smarts, personality or performance. The secret to success in the boardroom: Making sure your voice is respected – and, more importantly, heard.

In other words, first you've got to make yourself a standout commodity, not just another cog in the wheel... Hardly an easy task when you're just one of several dozen faceless marketing execs or middle-managers. The solution: Learning to live without fear, cultivate political allies, inspire by example and master the art of timing. Or, in plain English, knowing when to speak up, when to shut up, whom to speak to and how far to push it with the things you say and do, regardless of established process or convention... then simply having the guts to back any given play up, and smarts to spin it to your favor.

Naturally, be sensible about your approach: Cutting your boss out of the loop or misappropriating corporate resources to fuel a snappy side-project, say, isn't always a smart way to go about getting what you want. But, not that I'd insinuate anything, what's wrong with innocently asking the CEO if you could just buy him or her a cup of coffee sometime and hear their thoughts on the rise of casual, or massively multiplayer, online gaming, thereby putting yourself on a first-name basis? Or seeing if that friend of yours – you know, the software engineer – wouldn't mind helping you prototype that sweet idea you've had for months for a side-scrolling shooter on your lunch break? Heck – how about just dipping into your own pocket and buying some of the guys in the development trenches a pizza here and there during crunch time to help keep morale high, and over a deep-dish pie, innocently inquiring about that feature you'd love to see them introduce?

Genius – hardly. Simply be spontaneous: Whatever people expect from the average worker bee, dare to go above and beyond it.

TIP: Strategize, and always think long-term. Ask yourself: How is what I'm doing good jointly for myself, the individual in question and the entire corporation as a whole? Learn to incentivize behavior based around this – people react faster, more often and with greater alacrity when there's something in it for them. Can't wait to get certain projects up and running? Grease the wheels and watch how easily they turn.

JOURNALISTS

Pick better subjects – and learn to play the hype game. Translation: Choose topics and headlines designed to generate the most interest, controversy and/or mass-market appeal. After all, it's no coincidence the first thing you see on any newspaper, website or magazine are sensational headlines. Or that Mario Armando Lavandeira, of PerezHilton.com fame, went from being a virtual nobody to Internet sensation almost overnight.

Having written literally thousands myself, it pains me to say it: No matter how slick and polished your game-related news clips, reviews and previews, it's nigh impossible to stand out when hundreds more on the same themes and products from an equal number of faceless copywriting drones are published every single day. Meaning that if you want to establish yourself as a singular voice, you need to start speaking in one – and delivering equally one-of-a-kind stories to an eager audience. Thankfully, those who take the time to craft unique or gonzo pitches don't just stand a better chance of building a following amongst readers. They also put themselves in a better position to potentially get a clip published by eager editors constantly on the lookout for scoops. (Hint: Go with features to generate the most bang for the buck/visibility…)

Equally important: Controlling the rights to your own content, and learning to market yourself as much as your narrative. Tempting as a fat paycheck may sound to a starving artist, by giving up a byline, bio or personal stake in any given piece in exchange for an article's high-profile placement in a national publication and/or a one-time fee, you're literally writing yourself out of the story.

TIP: Be serious about your business. Thrilled as many penmen are just to be getting paid to diddle around on their Xbox 360, let alone get compensated for their wit and charm, they forget that contracts were meant to be negotiated. You never know when 10 seconds' chatter can result in a 50% pay increase, or the right to republish your story in another outlet, thereby doubling the productivity of any given day's work.

MUSICIANS

Every closet rock star dreams of getting in the groove. The ones who're really ready for the big time know that it's a combination of savvy marketing and raw talent that'll finally help them hit that high note. Creating music on the fly isn't the challenge it used to be: Utilities like Pro Tools and the free Audacity can turn even the most tone-deaf DJ into a smooth operator. What's really tricky is getting people to hear the message behind your music.

Recognize: Game tunes, at odds with other forms of harmonic composition, don't just need to be clever and catchy. These little ditties often have to accurately reflect various in-game/story event progressions, or help set certain moods. Typically, they serve a unique function – and must be snappy enough to attract the user's attention and stand up to multiple, looping plays, all without distracting from the on-screen action they're meant to supplement. As a result, if you want to capture audio directors' attention, you won't just have to exhibit unfettered genius in your work. It also pays to show range, forethought and versatility – especially if you plan to work with a firm who publishes everything from puzzlers to platform-hopping romps.

Ultimately, make yourself stand out by circulating tracks as much as possible throughout the gaming community, and in new and creative ways. Quick example: Designing concept albums inspired by various videogames for free online giveaways, performing a virtual concert in *Second Life*, or creating an unofficial downloadable "mixtape" to be enjoyed in the company of various specific interactive outings. Alternately, look for opportunities to pair tracks with complementary and striking visualizations – e.g. by scoring the soundtrack of a dazzling homebrew demo or title sequence of a popular independent game offering.

TIP: Tag any composition you make with a signature sound effect or calling card of some sort – a nom de plume, special shoutouts, certain instrumental tricks… whatever makes you instantly memorable to the listener. Then create a portal (i.e. a MySpace page or Facebook profile) where fans can easily find you and draw attention to it. Needless to say, you'll never play to a packed virtual house if software promoters don't know where to send all those Jagermeister- and Cool Whip-filled contract riders...

PROGRAMMERS

Be sure to avail yourself of every learning resource and industry contact. Sites like Gamasutra, GPWiki.org and GameDev.net, not to mention organizations such as the International Game Developers Association (www.igda.org), are your best friend here. One's skills must constantly be kept current, regularly expanding your knowledge base and experience is crucial, and when it comes to staying ahead of the curve, it always pays to keep your ear to the ground.

Next, do what you do best: Grind out code like a cryptographer on crystal meth. But don't make the mistake of thinking you're the next John Carmac; today's games are built by dozens, sometimes hundreds, of individuals laboring for years on end. Just as valuable as the signature courses and curriculums you'll find at schools such as Carnegie Mellon, Digipen and The University of Southern California? Learning how to work as part of a team, mastering abstract thought, honing your problem-solving skills and developing the discipline needed to successfully cope with and work the endless overtime hours nearly all game projects require.

Also crucial: Stop thinking like an artist, and start thinking like an engineer. The simplest, most expedient solution is often the best, and the most successful programmers know to improve chances of success by breaking projects of any scope down into manageable, milestone-based goals.

TIP: Short on cash or time? Focus on innovation – not invention. Yes: We're all occasionally blown away by technically-astounding titles like *Company of Heroes* and *Crysis*. But from a software publishing executive's perspective, when it comes to pricey, risky, budget- and time-sensitive creative projects like games, sometimes it's easier, more rewarding and better for your overall career prospects to avoid reinventing the wheel. In other words, if you can't do something new, concentrate on doing it *better*. Off-hours tinkerings offer a ready vehicle (and one in which you're free to experiment, with no outside influence or constraints) for your wilder and more revolutionary impulses. Note: Rapid prototyping is the easiest way to tell if you're onto a winner.

VIDEOGAME ADVERTISING 2.0

Greetings from 30,000 feet! As I type this, I'm halfway to Denver, en route to Europe by way of Los Angeles (don't ask)... but more importantly, also 75% of the way through the latest issues of half a dozen leading industry publications including *Play* and *Game Informer*.

Being a consummate marketing professional – and not particularly intrigued by *The Queen* or those little packs of trail mix the airline's currently trying to pass off as meals – this disturbs me. Not so much because I'm sure I paid for a stale piece of chicken somewhere in that exorbitant last-minute ticket price, and don't have a spare Nintendo DS handy either. Rather, it's because breezing through the bulk of each publication simply involved zipping past nearly every single featured advertisement within.

Let me preface the following by saying I have every impetus in the world, and certainly more incentive than the average consumer, to pause and admire the corporate-sponsored view. It's my job to keep abreast of current promotional and sales strategies in order to stay ahead of the competition. Therefore, when an ad proves even remotely unique or engaging, I stop and notice.

So as someone who buys games regularly, makes a point of following emerging trends and has a vested interest in any biz-related outreach, the thought suddenly strikes me as chilling. I wonder: Could it be that, as game makers and marketers, we continue to pour hundreds of thousands of dollars, sometimes millions, into advertising vehicles that consumers and biz observers alike are finding increasingly more off-putting and outdated? Loyal readers of past books like *Videogame Marketing and PR* can, of course, deduce by now that my answer leans much towards the affirmative.

Mind you, there's plenty we could be doing to improve presentation and delivery as is. Exhibit A: *PC Gamer*'s March 2007 issue, flush with page after page of promotional spots sporting less of what actual enthusiasts look for (e.g. large, high-quality in-game screenshots) and more of what they don't (obscure, oversized pieces of artwork or eye-scrunching stat readouts). Exhibit B: The fact I've just wandered through one of the country's largest airports and seen only a single, solitary banner reminding me that instead of spending my next layover idly skimming *War and Peace*, I could be enjoying a quick brainteaser or shootout via mobile phone. And, of course, Exhibit C: The realization that I've just unpacked a copy of *Final Fantasy III* – hence my grouchiness about that missing DS – and can't find anything inside telling me where to purchase, oh, the other dozen-plus titles in the series.

The upshot being that, perhaps, we as an industry need to start getting with the program a little quicker and looking ahead as to how the advertising and product messaging we produce should better be evolving alongside the consumer. Rather than bore you with the usual, albeit insightful suggestions (i.e. recommending marketing mainstream-friendly titles where women and casual consumers really do shop or, you know, actually creating in-game ads that don't interfere with the physical play experience), I'm taking a different tack, though. What follows is simply a short rundown of several hip, proven methods of getting the word out about new products and services that are already working for other businesses, and could do just as well for ours. Not to mention, hopefully, a wakeup call to start paying much more attention to them:

CUSTOM PUBLISHING

I recently read a definition of custom publishing that went a little something like this... "Simply defined, custom publishing is a targeted publishing program delivered to key audiences with a goal of increasing brand perception, improving brand loyalty and influencing or improving the overall decision making process."

In other words, forget courting the eyes of the media and hoping to increase consumer awareness via various methods of PR outreach, which can produce unpredictable and sometimes even damaging results. Instead, why not create your own darn articles and/or corporate-owned print or online publications, brand these items as desired and deliver them to consumers where you know they'll already be at the time and place of your own choosing?

Confused? Think about the magazines you always find in every 747 seat back during any airborne business trip. It shouldn't come as a surprise to note that these are all paid for by the airline itself, painstakingly sculpted to get certain core themes/messages across and strategically delivered to a captive audience of millions.

Note that editorial content in the form of a custom publication can take several guises. Think brochures, catalogues, magazine inserts, websites, free POP giveaways or even advertisements disguised as articles in proper newsstand periodicals. What's more, content is completely controlled by the custom publication's sponsor. Certainly, copywriting agencies may be given leeway to pen their own writer-suggested articles around various broad/narrow requested topics. However, the funding party does have ultimate say over what does or does not eventually appear in the publication – and gains greater ability to influence its readership's eventual perception and impressions of any highlighted product or brand.

This "advertorial" approach works on multiple fronts. Advertisers are happy, because they're getting crucial selling points across in the manner and method they choose. They also gain a nice marketing vehicle through which to shout out trade partners, sell more goods and fuel increased consumer loyalty. (Say, by rewarding frequent shoppers with a free magazine subscription.) Consumers benefit by virtue of increased entertainment value – after all, people buy magazines for articles, not ads. What's more, even targeted advertorials are more fun to read than pure advertisements and keep you engaged longer than goofy photos or short, catch-phrase driven copy. In addition, they also provide an opportunity to speak to and connect with consumers on a casual, one-on-one level and may even be perceived as meaningful souvenirs.

Better still, custom publishing pieces aren't just able to be enjoyed by a single reader. They're often passed on to friends, laughed along to online with buddies during coffee breaks at the office, or read at length over the toilet. Ask yourself: When was the last time you enthusiastically handed a friend a copy of Sony's *MotorStorm* inside cover spread or referred them to a banner ad for *Supreme Commander*?

According to a recent study conducted by the Custom Publishing Council and Publications Management, companies spent an average of $1,129,649 on custom publications in 2006 – an 18.4% increase from the year before. (The biz's largest year-on-year growth rate on record…) What's more, additional research says eight out of ten CMOs believe custom media should be an integral part of the marketing mix for any business, with 78% saying it's the future of marketing, period. Roper Public Affairs further discovered, on investigation, that 85% of consumers surveyed view custom publications as a preferred source of information, mostly because of their contents' highly-targeted nature.

Take it from experience too. We at Embassy Multimedia Consultants have already worked on everything from nationally-circulated articles to mailers, newsstand inserts, full-blown magazines, websites, micro-sites and more for dozens of clients including Sony, Microsoft, The Academy of Interactive Arts & Sciences, DreamCatcher Interactive, Nokia, Toys R Us, Nyko, Sam Goody, XM Radio, Major League Baseball, Sony Online Entertainment, Suncoast Video and ADV Films alone. So while game industry staples such as Electronic Arts, UbiSoft, IGN, IDG and Future Publishing are all starting to dip their toes more into these waters with single-/two-page advertorials or entire one-off publications, it's about time more game publishers considered doing a proverbial cannonball.

INTERACTIVE OUTREACH

It's one thing to voluntarily sit through a TV commercial, shoo away a pesky video trailer or scream in frustration after the 15th pop-up window touting the latest and greatest new FPS unceremoniously storms its way onto your screen. Another entirely to kick back, relax and allow yourself to become immersed in an online multiplayer puzzle game that lets you happily square off for hours on end against newfound friends worldwide that just so happens to be sponsored by Dodge or Samsung.

That's right, ladies and gentlemen, welcome to the future of advertising... It's not making people sit through half-assed viral spots or brainstorming methods to slap your logo on a banner located far off in the background environment of a new *Need for Speed*. It's finding ways to build entire titles around specific brands, or place your messaging front and center in exchange for an overt value trade-off, i.e. giving the consumer something complimentary they'd otherwise have to pay for. You don't have to believe me, though – just scroll through an ever-growing list of immensely popular casual amusements out there ranging from *LEGO Bricktopia* to *Teen Titans: One on One* and even Comedy Central's oh-so-classy *South Park*-endorsed *Brown Noise Pooblast*.

The 3 million-plus copies Burger King recently sold of its exclusively-branded Xbox 360 titles – *Pocketbike Racer*, *Big Bumpin'* and *Sneak King* – can't spell it out clearly enough. Consumers don't mind being marketed to directly as long as such initiatives are tied to actual pieces of engaging content, have a compelling reason for being there and don't interfere with the hands-on experience. Heck, even I don't mind sitting through the odd Acuvue contact lenses commercial, if, as I recently discovered, it means getting to play WildTangent hits like *Blasterball 3* for free online via my Web browser versus paying $19.99 for a full, downloadable edition.

The lesson being that ads shouldn't be static experiences that the consumer believes serve no purpose other than to make someone else money... Buyers need to feel as if the messaging itself is smartly wrapped around an intriguing product (say, an addictive desktop/console diversion or Web-based amusement). Alternately, it's also acceptable to work it in as a play component included for sake of real-world continuity – such as when *Splinter Cell* hero Sam Fisher whips out a

Sony Ericsson phone. Or, failing both of these instances, a trade-off buyers are willing to make in exchange for something of tangible value, i.e. pro bono or discount access to a cool game they wouldn't otherwise be able to afford or enjoy.

I'm a huge fan of publishers keeping their names and games on people's lips – a real problem in an industry where it takes 1-2 years on average to build a finished product. But even so, simple tricks such as designing Flash games based around core properties to keep interest high between sequels or offering free utilities like Rockstar's *Beaterator* that keep users coming back to your site, even during slow months, can work wonders for business in terms of influencing consumer perception. Shoot, just release a level editor or building designer such as CDV did with *City Life* and watch a community flourish, breathing new life into aging properties… and, possibly, depending on how savvy you are, fueling cheap content for later bundles and expansion packs.

Remaining at the forefront of people's minds is everything, given that we operate within an industry that's all about the newest and hottest products. And, naturally, there's no better way to do so than by making them want to constantly see more of what it is you're selling. (Especially if it provides a way to screw around for 15 minutes in the office when they should be doing work…) The upshot: If you build it, they will come. Provided, that is, there's a compelling reason – i.e. instant gratification, the joy of creating something from scratch, an activity people can bond over, or ways to happily fritter the day away shooting aliens instead of filing TPS reports – to do so.

EMPOWERING CONSUMERS

Recently, I sat down and had a chat with Greg Fischbach, founder of Acclaim Entertainment, to get a 20-year industry vet's thoughts on where videogame marketing and PR was headed. Now serving on MumboJumbo's board, one of the first things he happened to mention in a humorous anecdote involved his prior tenure overseeing Activision back in the '80s. Specifically, the story concerned how the company used to issue fans collectible sew-on badges for mailing in photos of themselves hitting high scores on specific games. Some of you may recall this specific promotion; coming of age in the Atari 2600 era and being the proud personal owner of *Oink!* and *River Raid* patches, I certainly did.

Which only goes to prove a point – not only was such a marketing scheme, which basically provided enthusiasts tangible rewards for their continued participation, interest and brand loyalty, hugely successful. Here we sit two decades later, and it's still coming up in passing conversation. The kicker: There's no reason modern-day advertisers couldn't be devising similarly compelling frequent-shopper plans or even online-based initiatives that deliver just as much value. Hilariously though, people act as if Xbox Live's Achievements system (players are awarded points and virtual badges of honor that essentially give them greater standing and bragging rights in the online community) is ultra-revolutionary. Looking back, is it really so hard to see that game buyers like interactive, competition-driven promotions that offer the chance to hone their skills, socialize with peers and walk away with some perceived payout for their efforts?

MMOs and casual games are adept at exploiting this knowledge. Online portals like Pogo.com and King.com are flourishing – and amongst the "stickiest" websites on the Internet. Massively multiplayer titles such as *Eve Online* and *Second Life* generating incredible user traction. Frankly, there's no reason whatsoever a traditional PC/console publisher couldn't tap into the market with similar ventures. Building community- and new content-fostering features into games from the very beginning represents a smart step forward. Even simply releasing mod-making tools and encouraging consumers to utilize them (as well as building supporting social hubs) or creating mail-order programs, print/online newsletters or official newsgroups and forums would be a help. It's not like a fansite-based giveaway wherein you issue some basic graphical assets then hold a contest rewarding end-users with prizes for the best designs would even be particularly expensive or hard to execute.

The bottom line: It's now imperative that you find ways to continuously court the consumer, put the power to influence product perception in their hands and make them feel like they're a member of your extended family. If it sounds troublesome, remember... As key influencers – the folks who directly fuel the buzz behind specific products and services throughout their demographic by constantly chatting them up – these people are essentially your ambassadors to the public at large. Or, in other words, the most effective champions for your brand that money can buy, enjoying greater influence than even the most powerful advertising campaign.

To put things in perspective: When I consider buying a new game, I always check how it's scored with key magazines and websites like *GameDaily*. But ultimately, before plunking my hard-earned cash down, I scan the net to see what people are saying, and ask friends for their personal opinion. Frankly, an individual with similar interests and outlook's bound to give me better purchasing advice than a critic who inherently comes at a title from an entirely different philosophical and experiential context.

As one high-level game industry exec recently confirmed, it is common knowledge now that roughly nine of ten males research games on the Internet before buying them. This being the case, a few banner placements on IGN.com and pages in *PSM* will only get you so far. The lesson to be learned here... If you really want to craft better game advertising and positively influence public perception, you have to create ongoing outreach programs that basically make players themselves walking, talking billboards.

BECOMING A BETTER MARKETER

As much as insiders relish spending hours debating the medium's artistic and intellectual value, if there's one sign gaming has truly come of age, it's this: The amount of outsiders flooding into the business. Film directors, venture capitalists, television networks, futurists, authors, politicians, music moguls, heads of state… With overall industry sales now topping $13.5 billion, the entire world – not just 18-34 year-old males – is finally sitting up and taking notice.

That said, as many newcomers as one sees passing through Embassy Multimedia Consultants' doors, one subject bears repeating – making and marketing videogames isn't rocket science. The trick being that you simply need a solid frame of context to approach the twin problems of not only building high-quality product, but also finding ways to help it make sense to everyday consumers. Meaning as follows: Your chances are greater than ever to hit it big and score with products that not only rack up millions in sales, but also those that resonate with insanely wide demographics. One simply needs to understand how developing and promoting these goods differs from those produced by other industries.

In other words, what works for *Halo* isn't guaranteed to fly in Hollywood; what goes for Gucci not necessarily *Grand Theft Auto*. Following are just a few tips sure to help you become not simply a better game promoter and businessperson, but also learn to evangelize interactive brands with the best of them:

Familiarize Yourself with Your Target Market

As with many industries, gamers are clearly divided into two camps – casual users, or those with a passing knowledge of the hobby, and hardcore players, who spend endless hours voraciously consuming new/classic titles. Needless to say, each is essentially its own self-contained society, and speaks a different language…

Learning how to communicate with both, and tailor game concepts and surrounding messaging to reach these differing users, is crucial. Therefore it pays to spend time going hands-on with associated products to ensure you're familiar with each form of vernacular and always plot a two-pronged marketing approach. In other words, don't target *Game Informer*'s audience with the same tactics as *Glamour*'s: When it comes to choice of game subjects and promotional vehicles, one size does not fit all. And just as you wouldn't try casually talking cinematography with aspiring film students who worship at the altar of director Stanley Kubrick, don't attempt to coddle diehard joystick jocks by telling them how great an arcade game *Gears of War* is. (Hint: It isn't.)

Choose Better Topics

Let's level for a second: Yes, titles like *S.T.A.L.K.E.R.* and *Enemy Territory: Quake Wars* often connect with thousands of tech-savvy geeks worldwide. But, as the success of the casual gaming space popular with women age 40 and up, as well as seniors – with nontraditional demographics proves, there's an entire market out there waiting to be tapped. Ask yourself: Why is Nintendo's Wii the fastest selling next-generation console? Simple – it's immediately accessible and appealing to all ages. Therefore, always remember that the titles you choose to invest in control your financial destiny... and that there's no better way to improve marketability, not to mention ROI, than by setting your sights on the broadest possible range of end-users. Any time you have a smashing idea for a game, just try this simple test. Consider whether a mother of three from Nashville walking into Wal-Mart will see it and immediately understand what you're getting at. Because, truthfully, it's ultimately going to wind up sitting there next to titles featuring instantly recognizable themes like *Nintendogs* or *Madden NFL 08*. And if everyday buyers can't make sense of it in 2-3 seconds, what chance does it really have of moving off the shelf?

Go Broad or Go Home

Massive ad spends are all well and good, but in the PC/videogame space, success hinges on your ability to think minute. A hip and highly computer literate bunch, gamers don't simply see a 30-second TV spot and think to themselves: "SOLD!" Realize: The average purchase price of game systems and goods hovers around $400 and $50, respectively (more if you factor in high-end PCs) – quite costly for a large portion of this demographic. What's more, dozens of alternatives to any given platform or game exist. (Try scanning store shelves to see how many sci-fi first-person shooters there are alone.) Countless channels are further available to source more information on titles ranging from websites to newsgroups, TV shows, magazines and even chatty friends. Therefore it can't be repeated enough – you've got to hit influencers from several angles, using multiple, highly-targeted vehicles to reach them. Bottom line: As a general rule, several smaller impression-generating tactics that play out over an extended timeframe will serve you better than a single, larger attention-getting gimmick. Never mind quick hits; it's all about building familiarity, and establishing context, over a greater period of time. At the very least, you can expect that casual shoppers, as Internet-addicted and socially-minded as they are, will hear about a product from more than one source of information.

Enlist Enthusiasts

Consumers are savvier than ever… Sticking a two-page spread in *Games for Windows: The Official Magazine* or simply shoving billboards touting a comple-mentary product into the latest high-resolution racing simulation isn't necessarily going to make a true believer out of anyone. What's more, it can be a costly proposition. Instead, give gamers the tools they need to tout your brand in a man-ner that's valuable and constructive to both parties. For example: Build an online portal that lets users create profiles, engage in ongoing discussion, find new oppo-nents or exchange custom-created maps and characters. Design a level editor into your product so they can swap new missions and weapons. Even just providing excitable groupies the graphic files they need to construct a fansite makes a difference. It's all about interactivity... The more ways buyers have to enjoy your game and surrounding assets, the more they'll become personally invested in the title, the greater value they'll garner and more time they'll spend in front of it. And, of course, the more hours they'll essentially put in working as evangelists to help tout the party line.

Educate Yourself

Face it – there's a simple, underlying reason we're even having this discussion to begin with. Specifically, the fact that, thanks to the dawn of new technologies and platforms like Web 2.0, social networking, digital distribution and massively multi-player gaming, the business is literally changing daily. No joke – even 20-year boardroom veterans are constantly finding themselves having to relearn their craft. (Seriously: How many CEOs do you know that really understand the mentality of working hand-in-hand with influential blogs like *Kotaku* and *Joystiq*?) Therefore the importance of books like *Videogame Marketing and PR*, *The Videogame Style Guide and Reference Manual* and *The Indie Developer's Guide to Selling Games* can't be understated. At the very least, it's an absolute must you attend conferences like E3, Leipzig Games Convention and GDC to keep up with trends, network with peers and get a sense of what the competition is doing. The upshot being this: If you really want to learn how to improve your game marketing skills, make products fly off the shelf and rack up millions in revenues, it pays to invest in your continuing education – and take an active interest in the biz.

FIVE TIPS FOR BETTER GAME MARKETING

1. Don't Overcomplicate Matters – Just because it's high-tech doesn't meant it has to be high-concept. You've got less than 2-3 seconds to capture an audience's attention – and are competing with hundreds, sometimes thousands, of other products. People have to be able to look at your game at a glance and immediately understand the key value it offers – so all you developers scheming on the next sci-fi shooter starring 100 foot-tall MCs fighting alien zombie Nazis on remote snowy worlds circa 1100 B.C. had best think twice.

2. Make it Pop – Call it human nature: We're suckers for visual appeal. Never forget – like first impressions, presentation is everything. So don't step out if you're not dressed for success. Boxes, ads, sell sheets, websites, videos – art assets should be of the highest quality, because that's the public face your showing. If there's one place you shouldn't spare expenses, it's here. Sound disingenuous? Hit the club and see how many gorgeous girls you spend hours staring at versus nondescript wallflowers.

3. Get to the Point – Time is money: Enthusiasts aren't going to sit around reading sales copy like it's the next *New York Times* best-seller. Keep text short, sweet and catchy, and focus on no more than 5 or 6 essential messages you're trying to get across. And always state them in plain English that anyone can understand – don't assume any prior knowledge on the part of the reader. Main text should come in 150 words or under, and features should be bullet-pointed. Remember, less is more: Mobile phone games are marketed in 150 *characters* (read: letters and spaces) or less.

4. Attract Attention – Borrow a page from rapper Paul Wall's playbook: Get the Internet going nuts. It costs next to nothing to throw up a catchy website, issue a bunch of slick screenshots, pump out some gameplay videos and offer admirers the base material needed to build their own fansites. Then rinse and repeat. Don't be afraid to use Google to research and reach out to media as well. Persistence pays: The more noise you make, the more attention you'll attract. If you force them to sit up and take notice, eventually, the right people will come knocking.

5. Be Honest and Forthright – Fans deserve your attention, and respect real talk. Always support them before, during and after launch, and keep things on the level. You want an interview? No problem. Some features you'd like added? Done. Looking for some copies to give away for contests? No problem, just tell us where to send. A can-do attitude won't just endear you to buyers, who you're asking to cough up hard-earned money. It'll also enable real-time dialogue with them, letting you keep your ear to the street, and see the next big thing coming before it arrives.

POWER PR

Today's deep thought: As you've no doubt surmised – and like countless game industry outfits including everyone's favorite scapegoat, Take 2 Interactive, already know from experience – the power of the press can be enormous.

The funny thing is, as many aspiring public relations (PR) gurus as I've met in a decade-long career as a serial entrepreneur, consultant and interactive entertainment's most prolific writer, many still don't know how to successfully interface with the Fourth Estate. At best, it's a painful annoyance, creating major roadblocks that will prevent your business from ever being the focus of positive news stories, front-page mentions or widespread public recognition. At worst, it can cripple any chance you have at achieving fame and fortune, or send a former empire into a crumbling tailspin.

Oh, and if you still need added incentive, even more good news... Editors are known for their strong opinions, and aren't shy about expressing them. Trust me: There are gossip columnists who'd blush at some of the behind-the-scenes chatter surrounding certain companies and individuals spread across insiders' telephone lines and instant messenger windows on a daily basis. After all, if you want to judge a certain firm or personality's current standing, there are few better barometers than listening to the latest buzz echoing over the grapevine. And as the sleuths constantly hot on the trail and self-appointed overseers of all things buzz-worthy, the media's often an inquisitor's first port of call.

Accordingly, this means several things for computer and videogame developers, publishers and service providers hoping to project a better public image and establish credibility in the minds of both the media and consumers. Specifically:

• The eyes and ears of the world are constantly upon you – hence you've always got to be on your "A" game.

• How you present yourself is almost, and in many cases more, important than the actual facts surrounding any situation.

• Understanding how to work with, and alongside, the press isn't just a key part of any game business' ongoing responsibilities – at the end of the day, it's one of the core determinants used to ultimately determine public perception, and thus financial success.

• Would-be industry captains can no longer afford to treat PR as an afterthought.

• Every person you hire is, by extension, a company ambassador – their every word and action reflects positively or negatively upon your firm or brand.

In the interests of helping interactive entertainment industry players of all sorts and sizes – yes, even all you garage developers toiling around the clock to build the underwater basket-weaving simulation of your dreams – I've compiled a handy tip sheet to help you master several public relations basics.

Don't take my word for it as a former international PR director, game publisher, and lean, mean writing machine, though. The following advice also comes from several of the industry's biggest names, who were kind enough to share their thoughts and insights...

BE AN EXPERT

PR is nothing if not a glorified form of salesmanship. And as we're all aware, you can't effectively sell a product you don't know. Not only does it pay for PR reps to be gamers – it also pays for them to be the enthusiastic kind, who's happy to stay late, put in extra hours behind the controller, ask development team members probing questions or do whatever else it takes to better understand the titles they're promoting.

Remember that passion, says Dean Bender, co-founder of Bender/Helper Impact, is what defines a successful gaming PR rep from an ineffective one. Not only will this passion translate into being able to better think on your feet, respond to any questions the media might ask and achieve results with greater expediency. It also means you'll know exactly how to craft messaging, the best way to sell this messaging in and when/where to place stories to achieve maximum coverage.

He further points out that enthusiast media are a savvy bunch – you've got to be able to talk the proverbial talk, if you want to be taken seriously. Thankfully, getting up to speed is easy, even for beginners… Just ask. Executives, producers and even members of the press are human too (at least, the ones who bathe on a regular basis), and are generally happy to help with your education. As in any PR-related initiative, it's the effort that counts – just showing you care will aid your cause more than any fancy press release or painstakingly-negotiated exclusive.

PLAN AHEAD

Opinions differ on how long it takes to plot out a proper PR campaign – some say a year, others 6 months or less. But one theme's consistent across the board from all respondents surveyed: It's that you can't effectively promote a title without first having clearly-defined objectives and a master strategic plan in place. Essentially, you have to know what type of product you're promoting, who the potential audience for it is, how to speak to them and what goals/expectations are realistic for the game in question.

Start by determining a product's release date. Then define its top selling points – the three to five features that make the game different from the 10,000 competitors already out there on the market. Come up with a way to get these messages across in 30 seconds or less (oh sure, like you really listen in-depth to most cold calls or read beyond the first paragraph or two of any press release). Build a list of media outlets you'd like to connect with and decide on a dissemination strategy for each. Then create a tactical approach designed so that coverage breaks at carefully cultivated times, e.g. right before your sales team approaches retailers or so that print coverage arranged 90 days in advance coincides with the arrival of online stories. And for heaven's sake, make sure you have a steady supply of assets and chat-worthy tidbits designed to keep people talking throughout the entire period leading up to and on through the product's launch.

All you MMO providers will have to go a step further as well, says Sony Online Entertainment PR manager Katie Hanson. This means having something new to reveal or discuss every three months or so. The logic here: If you're trying to maintain a sustainable revenue source, you also have to keep generating sustain-able buzz surrounding it.

And sure, glitches will certainly arise that are bound to throw even the best-laid plans off-track – i.e. embargoed stories getting out, bad reviews popping up, etc. But being able to confront all with poise and grace, not to mention react smartly on the fly, is what separates the true greats from the simply played out.

SEIZE THE DAY

Director Woody Allen once said "70% of success in life is showing up;" I couldn't agree more. Just taking the time to recognize the value of public relations and making an attempt at outreach will put you way ahead of the pack. There's a rea-son many independent and even major game development and publishing studios fail to get decent media coverage – it's that they don't even try.

Certainly, pros like Bethesda Softworks VP of PR and Marketing Pete Hines believe that focusing on enthusiast media, thereby reaching a readership you know is buying games already, is an important part – possibly even the centerpiece – of any game-related promotional venture. But even he recognizes the importance of making overtures to any and all consumer media publications such as *Maxim*, *Rolling Stone* and *Wired*. (If in doubt, compare circulations: For example, *Electronic Gaming Monthly* boasts 600,000 to *Playboy*'s 3 million-odd readers.)

Ironically, as someone who's writes for both regularly, I'm frankly stunned by the lack of pitches and emails I get on a steady basis – even if my blood pressure's thankful for it.

Even if you can't afford to throw fancy junkets or have celebrity talent attached to your titles, it's still possible to earn just as much coverage as those companies who do. If nothing else, merely shooting journalists (whatever their background) a simple email or giving them an occasional call on a regular basis when there's something new and noteworthy to discuss is crucial. Naturally, you don't want to be pushy or inundate anyone's inbox with spam. But the old maxim holds: "The squeaky wheel gets the grease." Staying top of mind is imperative.

At any time, for any reason, from an editorial standpoint, holes can suddenly open up in single pages or entire sections of magazines as advertisements and stories fall in and out... So when in doubt, never forget. I can't tell you the number of times an obscure Japanese import's made it into North America's biggest publications just because someone randomly shot me a note at just the right time.

Want an easy way to get your message out? Try **GamesPress.com**: It's free to broadcast assets to 22,000+ game journalists worldwide. You can even order fully-customized, user-friendly online pressrooms that go up in as little as 4-6 weeks, can be maintained by a junior associate and offer automated fulfillment of tasks like screenshot, fact sheet and release date delivery.

Persistence pays, as does diligent follow-up. Just make sure when pitching you've taken the time to craft ideas for the specific outlet, know the right editor to speak to and where stories would fit in the publication. Can the blanket sales routine too: One size does NOT fit all. That goes double when dealing with consumer media – you'll get farther devising a timely, tangential hook (say a featured musical track, celebrity or bonus item on the disc) to tie games to. The proven trick to nailing a story every time: Finding an approach that helps titles make sense not just as attractive products unto themselves, but also in an overall cultural context for the outlet's specific readership.

KEEP IT REAL

Surprise, surprise… In all these years working for virtually every videogame book currently in existence as well as a host of consumer outlets, I've yet to meet a PR person who wasn't my "friend."

No shocker there: I do use AXE body wash, and the most successful public relations representatives know that the business is entirely based on relationships. It's no secret that you should always cultivate a connection with the people you work with – especially members of the media, since, as in all walks of life, "you are who you know." But let's run a reality check. Like all editors, at the end of the day, I come to events (yes, even those flashy red carpet premieres at five-star hotels we all love to indulge in) and conduct personal outreach to do business, not slap hands and quaff free drinks.

As Funcom product director Jørgen Tharaldsen so sagely puts it, it pays for PR reps to be honest, friendly, welcoming and knowledgeable and truly mean what they say. Moral of the story: Don't be the sort of shill who comes off so greasy you'd spontaneously combust if someone suddenly took a drag off a lit cigarette. Like many members of the press, I can spot a snake oil salesman at a glance, and I remember any shady overtures made, as well as sly, seemingly offhand remarks. Body language is important too: Sure, you're all smiles when we're shaking hands, but I notice when you immediately turn away, attempt to escape conversation in seconds or your eyes light up when the next self-styled big fish enters the room.

The lesson to be learned here: Keep things on the level, act like a decent, respectful human being and always be on your best behavior around press. Actually care about them as people, not just tools to an end. Answer all questions with candor, and be reasonable when managing product expectations. And understand that you'll ultimately be judged by your actions and ability to deliver – not how fun you are to hang out with, or how lavish a party you can throw.

Most of all, treat all members of the media equally… from broadcaster to blogger, it's a level playing field out there, and you can't afford to play favorites. You never know where that person you unwisely slagged off in public will wind up either. I got started in this biz running a fansite out of my college dorm room – and still deal with some of the same folks who stiffed me back then today.

Above all else, be supportive. (Hint: If a writer's started a new venture – e.g. a strategy guide company – you'll probably get further supporting them in it with extra info, unique developer access and introductions to top internal decision-makers than offering still more free trips and meals.) And never, ever let friendships get in the way of business: The importance of maintaining a professional relationship, and the proverbial separation of church and state, can't be underrated.

Never take anything personally (i.e. a scathing review or highly-critical editorial) either. Everyone's entitled to their opinion – how would you react if you were told yours is wrong? And hey, you never know when a higher-up's stepped in and changed something, or a situation's otherwise out of an editor's control.

Oh, and if you do have a problem with something someone's written, don't expect to change something that's already in print. Call the writer and have a friendly, positive discussion explaining that you understand their point, clarify where you're coming from and ask for feedback so that things won't play out the same in the future. Never try to browbeat someone into taking a story back. The better solution: Suggest ways (say, the introduction of a new article that might cast your product or client in a better light) to meet in the middle, so everything evens out in the end.

GET THE JOB DONE

Most importantly, if a journalist asks for something – a screenshot, an interview, a meeting, Sly Stallone's autographed jock strap, whatever – make sure you respond promptly, and do your best to deliver.

They'll understand if the request falls through, so long as you've shown them enough respect to make the effort. Most members of the media are hard workers who'll do anything within ethical limits and the bounds of reason to make a story happen... As a sign of mutual appreciation and understanding, it's expected you will too.

Always remember: Gaining an editor or freelancer's trust is easy, but it only takes one dropped ball to ruin your reputation with a journalist irrevocably. No story equals an unhappy writer, which equals wasted time, lost money and a teed off bunch of folks all around. The upshot being that you've always got to be prepared to deliver assets, playable code or whatever else media need on-demand.

My favorite snafu...? When I'm pestered non-stop to mention a title in print then told due to budget limitations, there's a shortage of review copies. After wondering why all the wasted effort and ill-will generated to begin with, my answer: Compare the cost of one sample review unit of a piece of software with even a 1/3-page ad in any major newsstand publication. You don't like found money? Fine – there's 50 other savvier developers/publishers who do.

It sounds like common sense, but really... Do your job to the best of your ability (be honest – you know when you're selling yourself, and others, short), and success will come. Ultimately, it's by being reliable that you'll install the highest level of confidence in your abilities and make yourself an indispensable resource amongst those you work with on both sides of the PR and media divide.

As Alex Josef, CEO of Pacific Media Partners so wisely explains: "Clients and employers need to know that they can count on you to handle things and represent both themselves and their products in the best possible light."

Frankly, I couldn't have put it – or summed the whole point of this entire long-winded discourse up – any better.

SELLING CASUAL GAMES

Face it – with development costs escalating, retail shelf space shrinking and conversion rates topping out at 1% or 2%, casual game creators can't afford to play around. Attracting consumers is no longer enough. Even when you hold a virtual monopoly on distribution, it's also crucial that you court key retail publishers and online portals.

So ask yourself: "What differentiates my game from the thousands currently at market?" Because if you can't answer that basic question in seconds, sorry . . . it's game over. With literally dozens of similarly-styled alternatives to choose from, there's nothing stopping execs or end-users from picking proven performers over your latest masterpiece.

Thankfully, the following tips won't just make your titles sell better and stand out more prominently. They'll also help you build buzz, increase awareness and generate headlines worldwide:

Don't Get Fancy

Can the high-concept ventures: Games should be simple, straightforward and make immediate sense to consumers in an everyday context. You've got less than three seconds to catch a buyer's attention. To maximize sales potential, position product around familiar themes, such as food, fashion, music or art. Added bonus: The simpler the subject matter, the greater the international viability of a games— and the easier it is to localize. One need only look to proven hits like *Cake Mania*, *Dream Day Wedding* and, of course, the 85 million unit-selling *The Sims* series (the best-selling franchise ever on PC) to see this phenomenon in action.

Expand Your Horizons

Pick topics with broad appeal. Think horizontal: Before developing any new game, ponder all potential audiences, which of their needs it can meet and how to instantly communicate that value to as many people as possible. From artwork to surrounding text and in-game features, assets should universally support and reinforce this core messaging, helping you reach a wider audience and increase return on investment accordingly. This being the case, maybe that futuristic turn-based strategy/shoot-'em-up hybrid starring the music of Pantera isn't such a safe bet compared to alternatives like a globetrotting adventure or IQ-building brainteaser after all.

Add Tangible Value

Two ways to succeed in business: Innovation or invention. Choose one. Either way, risk-taking is essential: Daring ideas move the medium forward. Likewise, it's not cloning that is killing the market—it's developers' inability to innovate with each passing release. (Risk-averse publishers actually *prefer* proven formulas with measurable sales potential.) Bottom line? Regardless of how you choose to add value to the space, you should include at least one new meaningful feature with every debut. Additions can be as simple as introducing a new setting (Victorian times vs. modern-day) or gameplay twist (say, branching storylines depending on the player's actions). Note: Better graphics don't count.

Stay Open-Ended

Avoid the use of territory- or company-specific imagery. By all means—create billboards, jumbotrons, blimps, signage and other in-game vehicles through which content can be cross-promoted or advertisers hyped. Just design such opportunities so that any supporting material can be inserted globally, as partners will want to reserve the right to individually brand these placements. Bottom line: All those buildings plastered with banners featuring silly in-jokes and pictures of your coworkers? Probably not a wise insertion…

Evangelize Your Wares

Promote, promote, promote. Incessantly. Create a striking website and supplemental assets ranging from screenshots to in-game videos. Then court the media. Budget tight? **GamesPress.com** lets you quickly reach 22,000+ journalists worldwide at zero cost. Throughout development, regularly issue news and updates to whet fans' appetites. The more noise you make, the better your chances of attracting additional buyers and trade partners. Need motivation? Consider how many hundreds of titles are released daily – then how many your mother actually knows by name. I rest my case.

WHO WANTS TO BE A MILLIONAIRE?

Let's speak frankly for a second. As many years as I've been in the business of interactive entertainment, not a day goes by that I don't reflect on how blessed I am to be doing something I love. Counseling software/hardware developers, publishers and investors, acting as a product talent scout and writing about the industry is its own reward – there's no substitute for working with the most talented and creative people in the world.

But let's not kid ourselves either: The game industry is just that – first and foremost, a business. And while money isn't everything, as any successful entrepreneur can tell you, it sure does open doors. That said, Embassy Multimedia Consultants takes great pains to, above all else, ensure that our clients get their financials right first. In other words, we not only want you to see you relish your work, garner widespread acclaim and recognize constant personal growth. We also want you to get paid what you're worth – and enjoy the increased leverage, greater stability and better bargaining power that such success inevitably affords.

It's not about rocking a new Porsche or spending summers sunning oneself in the Hamptons. Rather, for a developer, putting food in the mouths' of dedicated employees and holding enough influence to control the use of original intellectual property (IP), and therefore one's own destiny. For a publisher, being able to deliver on promises to shareholders and investors, and ship the kind of first-rate titles today's discerning fans demand. And, of course, for an individual, establishing the means to make one's dreams reality by starting new companies, developing groundbreaking technologies, or just gaining the kind of life-changing, real-world business education you can't put a price on.

My own personal advice for would-be tycoons:

• **Get Rich Slow** – Learn what it's like to operate lean and mean, and the responsi-

bilities that come with earning large sums of money. Stay humble, stay hungry…
It's one thing to see huge windfalls, another to avoid pissing them down the drain.

• **Invest in Yourself** – Cash spent on cars, penthouse offices and vacations is fun
while it lasts – but it seldom lasts long. Instead, try building a stable, self-fueling
financial foundation for yourself. It'll continue to feed your personal and professional ambitions long after success, and the glamour, inevitably fades.

• **Control Your Destiny** – Do it yourself, or don't do it all. Working for someone
else is the best way to learn any craft, but you'll never truly master it without col-
oring outside the lines. Simple logic dictates that any employer will have their
own, not your, best interests at heart. Remember: With great risk comes great
reward.

That being said, given the sensitivity of this subject, you deserve feedback straight
from the horse's mouth. And so I recently reached out to a few acquaintances that
just happen to have enjoyed fame and fortune by virtue of their past and current
efforts in the gaming industry.

The mission: Speak to each, to gain firsthand insight into just what it takes to not
only break the bank in our beloved field and realize the dreams of millions of
aspiring moguls worldwide, but also enjoy a long and fruitful reign at the top.
Listen closely to their words. If time truly is money, well… consider yourself
about to enjoy several tens of thousands' worth:

NOLAN BUSHNELL

Founder of Atari and the Chuck E. Cheese's restaurant franchise. Now head of uWink, an innovative food services chain which combines high-quality dining with even higher-caliber interactive entertainment.

"The most obvious advice for anyone looking to hit it big in gaming – be sure you go where no one else is. Entertainment is all about new experiences: Iconic properties like *Star Wars* and *The Matrix* stood out from the crowd when initially released, and wound up creating entire genres and sequels as a result. These days, people to tend to forget that even *Madden* was novel once.

The mistake many companies make is to try to do sequels in categories they don't exclusively own. Ask yourself: What is the essence of a first-person shooter, and nowadays, in that category, what do you have to do to set yourself apart? Step back and assess the odds, and you'll see the probably of success in that space is probably less than 1 in 10,000. That's not what I'd call a good investment.

Regardless, it's possible to be extremely successful with almost no money starting out. Look at properties like *Line Rider* that are tremendously popular, yet had virtually no financial backing. You just have to right-size your approach based on who you are and how much money you have in the bank. Thankfully, it's a fertile field out there: The Internet has dropped the barrier to market entry tremendously. Using online sales and digital distribution, you can easily bypass the bottleneck of shrink-wrapped retail product.

Persistence is always a good predictor of success, as is the ability to successfully read the market. Being flexible enough to change to meet its needs creates a synergy that's unstoppable. You really have to believe in your product because no one else will. But mostly, I'm finding that today's biggest sign of impending victory is not just a good game, but one that's linked to a new technology or economic model. Just look at MMOs and the sale of virtual items, or products like *Guitar Hero II*.

Oh, and something I've learned from experience: When creating new ventures, you really need to stay with the areas where you're most comfortable. Don't think you can replicate your previous successes in another field – as good as you think you are, you need to realize that sometimes, you just managed to capture lightning in a bottle."

JOHN ROMERO

Co-founder of seminal game developers id Software and Ion Storm, as well as founder of Monkeystone Games, one of the earliest providers of games for mobile devices. Currently a co-founder of upstart MMO provider Slipgate Ironworks.

"In the past, everything was about new technology… Whenever you had a computer that could do X, and saw a game that could do Y, as long as it was fresh and compelling, it was going to sell a lot of copies because it was new and exciting. But at present, there's a ton of competition in every area from casual gaming to hardcore. Nowadays, at any point, you have to take a harder look at what's out there, do a lot more thinking, and consider the future of the space before committing to any project. The trick is to either launch something eye-opening before others get to the table, or step up to the plate with something innovative, but not too out of left-field or crazy.

Anyways, if all you care about is getting rich, you probably aren't going to make it, because you're too wrapped up in the money, and not likely to put enough love into your game. That said, to stand out, you really have to look at what space you want to hit and find a niche you can monetize quickly that's not a one-shot. (For example, not console games, which you just put out and hope to sell over a 3-4 month period if you're lucky). What you're really looking for is something sustainable like a subscription-, episodic- or item-based model as MMOs have shown which can generate insane cash compared with traditional channels. But you have to build a really strong brand behind it.

A few guys out of a garage can always make it – you've just got to do it really smart, do something people didn't expect or do something in an established market. For example: If you have just a few guys tinkering away after work who do an MMO (which would be really hard, I'll admit) and do it right, where there's just enough technology and compelling content, even a low base of subscribers will carry you to success. And then if you just grow organically, reinvesting money back into the company, product and people, you've built yourself a money-generating machine.

The most important thing game industry execs should understand though is this: Don't put a game out before it's finished. Quarterly goals aside, it's always better to take 2-3 months to polish a title than waste 2-3 years of effort. As for my secret to longevity in the industry – stay optimistic. There are too many guys who've been doing this 20 years who are massive downers… There are a ton of success stories who are 40+ years old. Myself, I worked all through the '80s trying to be a great game programmer and never hit it big. When the 8-bit era died, I felt I'd wasted 10 years: Suddenly, we hit it. Things come together… Keep working hard and create the right team. If you've got a small, passionate group, that's a great place to be. Even if you're not successful, it's worth more than a pile of cash.

I can tell you that working at Monkeystone was the most fun I've had working in the game industry, from 1979 on up to today. If you have fun making a title, it'll be reflected in the product. And if you're having fun creating that game and have the right team, well then… the sky's the limit."

KENZO TSUJIMOTO

Founder of Capcom, one of the largest and most storied publishers of computer/video games. Helped grow the company from a small, but scrappy maker of Japanese arcade games into the thriving multimillion-dollar international concern it is today.

"Our industry is very fast-moving. There's a major upheaval every five years so. Companies have to prepare for this. I've been doing it for 30 years now – there weren't even semiconductors when Capcom was first founded. When these changes come around, companies have to be ready. Many weren't. We were, which is why we're still around.

Our company is always looking at how to stay trendy and keep up with consumers' lifestyles. In the past, when you talked about interactive entertainment, you'd think of those crane games. Now the value these products contain doesn't always have to be physical in nature: A lot of what the consumer takes away from a game isn't tangible… it's just the satisfaction of having had fun. As this has come into play and technology has progressed, we've put an emphasis on creating complex games that entertain and excite in new ways. We're always thinking about advanced entertainment, and that's what pulls us through.

The chief difference between American and Japanese game publishers: In the United States, publishers are very successful – they're run by professional management. They focus on money, not making great games. On our side, we always operate under the assumption that there's a high possibility of losing money, but that's just our style. American publishers make games so everyone can play. The Japanese – especially Capcom – favor the hardcore gamer.

We're just lucky to have some great and talented people who are making games, however. And as creative people, they like to make something new whenever possible, not do the same things over and over again. They look for new ideas, and I've given them a lot of freedom to operate in this regard. Still, the thing to keep in mind is that whether you remake old titles or create new ones, as long as you come up with a great product, it always pays in the end."

SID MEIER

Visionary software creator responsible for more than 25 games including the best-selling *Civilization*, *Pirates!* and *Alpha Centauri* franchises, which have sold in excess of 10 million copies. Co-founder of Firaxis Games; often called "the father of computer gaming."

"I have to say up-front that, from a development perspective, we have no idea of knowing off-hand which games will be hits: Some strike a chord with consumers, some don't. Many we thought would be huge successes weren't, and vice versa.

But I will say that we're extremely proud of every title we've produced, and that, as a designer, picking titles with broad appeal is important if you hope to sell. It's not just that you can mine them to find juicy nuggets of fun. It's also that these topics are more interesting to work on, produce better results and offer players reasons to come back and replay the games, offering greater value.

Companies often mistakenly make technology the focus of a product – cool tech is a great way to support great gameplay, but without the latter aspect there, titles just won't resonate as well with players or be as long-lasting. And play quality is just as important today, if not more so, as it was 10-15 years ago. Developers really have to be true to their passion, and get excited about what they're doing – if they don't have fun making a game, no one else is likely to either. Some initial financial successes have allowed me to enjoy a rare degree of freedom in terms of trying new things; I think it's a grave error to try and follow the latest trend or hot genre.

To really achieve success too, you also have to be careful to stick with what you know. Tempting as it is to consult at this point or run a company, I found what I enjoyed most was making games, not managing people. I like to think that's reflected in my work. I always think about the audience I'm designing for (say, for handheld platforms versus the PC) and the technical capabilities of the medium as well, so I can deliver a compelling experience that's an interesting fit for the system. I'd like to think that you can't go wrong with this approach.

The key thing to remember though is that every game we make here is fun and accessible, even those based on deep or complex topics. You want players to feel good about themselves at the end of the day. If they're able to jump right in and have a good time with a game, it's a good sign you're onto something special."

JOURNALISTS

BREAKING INTO GAME WRITING

By Dan Hsu
Editor-in-Chief, Electronic Gaming Monthly
http://egmshoe.1up.com, www.1up.com

Be Lear-ned

English, writing and journalism are all great degrees to pursue. They'll give you a huge advantage, but aren't necessarily mandatory – we've hired plenty of great writers who don't have any of those credentials. Having a college degree, period, is definitely a good thing as well, but also not mandatory in most cases. (Keep in mind, everything else being equal, an employer is more likely to pick a candidate with a degree over one without one because Mr. BA is probably more disciplined.) But unless you're some superstar genius writer, I'd say some college education is a must.

Japanese (as a minor or something you learn on the side) wouldn't hurt, just so you can be useful when covering Japanese games or trade shows (or even reading Japanese magazines and websites), but depending on the outlet you want to work for, it may not matter that much these days. At *EGM*, for example, only a couple of guys have a very basic, rudimentary understanding of Japanese. If we need something translated, we'll freelance that out to someone more qualified, or we'll consult one of our Japanese correspondents. We have no need to hire a Japanese-fluent editor.

OK, I'm Lear-ned... What Now?

Submit work to a fansite first. That's how you can gain some experience and get some feedback from others... perhaps even get noticed by a bigger outlet. You won't get paid, but you'll get published a lot sooner than if you wait around for someone to hire you. Some professional editors (including James Mielke from *1UP.com* and Greg Sewart, formerly of *EGM*) got their start on the fan side of things. If I'm not mistaken, James was recruited by *GameSpot* after they read some of his reader reviews. Greg used to write for *Gaming Age*.

Or try blogging! We've already been eying a few of you out there who have some serious game-writing potential. But please, don't be annoying in trying too hard to get people (especially me) to read your work. Just let it come naturally. If you're doing a good job, you'll slowly gain your own audience. Maybe someone at *1UP* may even notice your blog and then feature it on the front page one week, thus getting you lots of eyeballs all at once. Just hang in there.

Going Pro

OK, maybe a professional organization is looking for writers, freelance or other-wise. Or they're looking for an intern. When submitting samples to a professional magazine or site for job consideration, custom tailor your work for that outlet! Look at what they do (style, length, etc.) and write specifically for them. It'll show that you're actually serious about this. For example: Why submit a 5000-word review to *EGM*? We don't ever publish any reviews that big. But if you can say a lot in a 100 words, that'll show me what you're capable of – at least, for our mag-azine.

Take a look at *GameSpot*, who has a very defined, professional style. Along the same lines, don't go submitting them your funniest, *Maxim*-ish, totally off-the-wall reviews. It doesn't match their way of reporting.

Of course, if you're already an established writer with published samples, that's good to show off too. But I don't necessarily like judging a writer's ability from those, because I never know what other editors have reworked that piece before publication – so I like raw, fresh samples. But that's just me, and including published work with raw samples is the best combination. This way, I can see how you write off the cuff, prior to any edits, and I know someone else out there digs your stuff enough to print it. Hey, if you're good enough for the *Charlotte High School Daily*, maybe you're good enough for *EGM*.

Before you turn in any work for evaluation though, for God's sake, spell check! Proofread! I can't believe how many well-written cover letters I receive, only to notice one tiny error that kills the whole thing for me. I mean, if you can't be perfect in your one submission to *EGM* for a job, how can I expect you to take day-to-day duties seriously? After all, you have all the time in the world to perfect and fine-tune your samples and cover letter, and if it has just one grammatical error, well then, forget you. I even had one guy write the name of our magazine incorrectly in his cover letter! Guess how quickly I threw that one out. Too bad, because he had potential otherwise. But I have way too many qualified candidates to waste time on someone who can't even get something like that straight. If it's too difficult for you to get your "its" vs. "it's" or "your" vs. "you're" straight, then it's time you looked for a different line of work, my friend. Or apply at one of those smaller mags where such things don't seem to matter as much. Zing! (I probably just jinxed myself...)

So I mentioned gearing the writing samples toward the outlet you're interested in, because we all have different styles (read *EGM* vs. *PSM*, for example). This counts toward the little details, too. Let's take two fictional applicants. Corky gives me reviews on a 5-point scale. No problem. Benny gives me the same level of writing, but he uses *EGM*'s 10-point scale, and gives me some "good, bad, and XXX" (see *EGM*'s reviews) text to boot. Who do you think impresses me more? Benny, cause he's taken the extra little effort to make sure I know he reads and understands our magazine. Remember: Employers not only want to know that the skills are there, but that you WANT the job. That ambition goes a long ways in my book.

(We're not hiring, by the way, so don't be emailing me, trying to prove how ambitious you are! On that note, don't just randomly stop by the office, either. We've had people do that, thinking they're showing us how gung-ho they are, but if you stop by for an interview without ever scheduling that interview, you're only scaring us.)

Bling It In

So how much does a game-writing job pay? Obviously, this depends on where the job is. Most gaming mags in the U.S. are based in the San Francisco or Los Angeles areas. You'll be commanding a higher salary in these two spots because the cost of living is insane compared to Normal, USA where you're probably from. I'm just guessing, but I'd assume *Game Informer* (based in Minnesota) would pay slightly less on average. But I'm also willing to bet that you'd come out ahead over there because you're not getting raped on your rent (and other daily living costs like gas, insurance, food, etc.) the way you are in the San Francisco Bay Area. So take that into consideration.

Most starting positions are Staff Writer, Assistant Editor or Associate Editor... and those titles can mean different things depending on the outlet. For the Bay Area, you may be looking at anywhere from the low to high $30,000 range for an entry-level salary. When I started as Associate Editor at *EGM*, I was in the mid $20,000s, but that was 8 years ago. And in Illinois.

If you're an experienced writer (and I don't mean that you like writing in your *Hello Kitty* diary every night), you'll be commanding a higher salary, natch. But it's rare that you'll get hired right into a higher position without previous gaming magazine experience. For example, when *EGM* moved from Illinois to San Fran, a bunch of people couldn't make the transition (families, homes, etc.), so I had to rehire about half the positions. For all the non-entry spots (Art Director, Managing Editor and so on), I was only looking at experienced folks who've worked on magazines before, preferably gaming ones. Turned out I filled those two specific spots with ex-*Next Generation* (remember that mag?) staffers.

Besides Writing...

That brings me to another point: Gaming mags aren't just employing writers and editors (though I suspect that's what most of you are interested in). We also need layout people: Production Artists, Graphic Artists, Art Directors, Associate Art Directors, etc. In some ways, even though everyone wants to be a game reviewer, the art jobs are more competitive. This is because you can hire an art person with a non-gaming background. So while my News Editor will have to be someone who's knowledgeable about the videogame business (and has gaming magazine experience), my Art Director doesn't. He or she just needs layout experience. For example, *EGM*'s Associate Art Director came from *Wired* magazine. Even though he plays games, he's not a "true" hardcore gamer like the writers/editors on staff. (Though he did beat *Ninja Gaiden*, which is pretty tough to do...)

And beyond that, our company employs marketing folks, salespeople, and lots more (circulation and production departments, etc.). So really, you may have an "in" through other avenues... or if you simply want to be involved in this business on some level and don't care whether you're a writer or not.

Note that gaming magazine jobs are great springboards to other fields. Just in the last few years, Dan Leahy (*GameNow*), Todd Zuniga (*Official PlayStation Magazine*), Greg Sewart (*EGM*), Joe Fielder (*EGM*) and Kraig Kujawa (*EGM*/*Official PlayStation Magazine*) have all gone from editors to game designers.

Advice City

Back to the writer/editor gigs: Game knowledge is obviously a must. In fact, *EGM* used to make game-playing part of the interview! After I interviewed with the Editorial Director at the time, he sat me down with one of the *EGM* editors so I could prove that I really did know how to play videogames. They hooked me up with a game that wasn't out yet: *Alien Trilogy* for PSOne, if I recall. I beat the first level while chatting with the editor, so that was that. I must say... Walking through the *EGM* offices and seeing game systems and televisions on everyone's desks, then playing an unreleased game as part of my interview (this was no stuffy corporate environment), I was pretty much on cloud nine and was surprised I was able to interview well at all.

Not-so-quick side note: This game-playing test actually worked one time. We had this qualified writer – some dude who wrote for a paper in Iowa with apparently great samples. The Editorial Director interviewed him then sat him down with another editor and me to play some games. Hoo boy... Good thing we did. It was the funniest thing, and we still bring it up when we tell stories around the campfire. This interviewee didn't even know how to hold a PSOne controller properly. We gave him *Ridge Racer* and quickly explained the controls. Then he asked – I kid you not – "How do you hit the gas button and steer at the same time?" Turns out, he had both thumbs on the d-pad: Left thumb for pressing left, right thumb for pressing right. No joke! He had no thumbs left for any other buttons, you see. Try to envision this radical new way of holding a controller and you'll know why we still laugh about it to this day. Writer from Iowa: If you're reading this... well, what the heck did you think we did at *Electronic Gaming Monthly*?

OK, I'm spending entirely too much time on this, but it's my party and now I'm on a roll making fun of this guy. So then he's picking his *Ridge Racer* car and selects Manual Transmission. We were like, "Are you sure? You may want to take Automatic." (Obviously, he doesn't have the job now, but at this point, we were having too much fun watching him play games, so we kept him going.) He took MT, so OK. Next thing: The race starts, and he's gunning the engine in first gear, redlining it to hell. Us: "Try shifting. You picked Manual, remember?" The guy jams on the shift button and goes straight from first to fifth gear. So now he's only about 100 feet off of the start line and going about 40 MPH in fifth gear. It was awesome. First guy I've ever seen not even make the first checkpoint on the first track of a racing game.

Then we scrounged up the easiest game we could find: Puzzle game *Bust-A-Move*. Easy, right? Just aim the damn ball and match three of a color. Well, we play some two-player to see how badly we can smoke him. Ten minutes after we first started playing and about 20 matches later (well after we've explained how to play this game), he asks, "How come my bubbles aren't popping?" It turned out that matching-three-balls-of-the-same-color thing, which we taught him already, just went over his head. For real.

Back on Track

Sorry about that sidetrackin'. If you've been hanging in there, you get this prize – probably the most useful tip I can give you (besides spell check/proofread): Write a good cover letter. This includes the actual body of an introductory email that may contain a separate, proper cover letter as an attachment. Whatever is the first thing I read from you, if it doesn't catch my attention right away, I'm throwing it out (I have way too many interested, qualified candidates to put any effort into making any one work). To me, it's more important than the resume, and I'll tell you, it's the only reason I got the *EGM* job (the Editorial Director liked my cover letter – he didn't even read my resume).

Remember how I said earlier that one tiny error can kill the whole thing for me? That's because with your submissions, we assume you spent a lot of time making sure everything's perfect; that these are the best pieces of work that we're going to see from you because you want to impress. So a bad cover letter means you're probably not capable of writing any better than that for day-to-day work, under deadline strains, with 10 other projects waiting for you. Of course, if you cheat and get someone else to write an awesome cover letter for you, you're setting yourself up to disappoint the magazine later, so don't go there (but getting feedback from your friends or teachers or whoever isn't a bad idea… you can always learn from others). Make it the best you can so the magazine knows what you're capable of. And again, don't forget Mr. Spell Checker.

Freelancing

I'll tell you it's much easier for a new writer to get a PC freelance gig than with a console magazine. Reason: You need special equipment to play pre-release console games. For example, at *EGM*, we have special "debug" PlayStation 3s, Xbox 360s, and Wiis to play the discs that the companies send us for preview and review. Those discs won't work on your Wal Mart PlayStation 2s, you know.... Most people don't have these machines, but pre-release PC games usually do install on any PC (it's an open platform, after all). Therefore a PC gaming magazine is in a better position to send out their discs for other people to pre/review.

Now, certain people in the know have "modded" systems that make them act like debug systems. But that doesn't mean you're all ready to freelance for *EGM*. We're not going to send out these highly confidential discs to just anyone out there, just because they sent us a few good writing samples (same with PC magazines). If these discs get lost or pirated somehow, we're liable. So we're never going to send this stuff out to anyone we don't know, PC disc or otherwise.

Classic catch 22, eh? We're not going to give you freelance work if we don't know you, and we can't know you unless you're already in the business. But some people have figured out ways. Some freelancers I know, for example, have made a name for themselves by working hard and being persistent, working and writing for whatever outlets they can (fansites, for example). After a while, they may get invited to industry events, and that's how you can establish contacts with some of the professional magazines or websites.

One of our Copy Editors and regular contributors, Greg Ford, for example, was writing for a fansite and did various small-time work until he was invited to a Sony press conference. There, he met me. A year later, he sends me his resume and reminds me he was the guy I met at the Sony event. I didn't hire him at the time (I was at *Gamers.com* and didn't need anyone then), but then a couple of years later when I went back to *EGM*, I was looking for a new Copy Editor... I remembered him and looked him up. Now he's a full-time editor at Ziff-Davis and one of our regular reviewers on the side.

That said, please don't be stalking us! "Making contacts" or "trading business cards" is a lot different than "being annoying" and "borderline obsessive." Just remember: It's still a professional business, so treat it like one, and you'll get places.

Bottom Line: Start off small. Patiently work your way up. Be ambitious (but not annoyingly so). And be really mindful of every single piece of work you submit and every letter, word and sentence you type, whether it's something for a fansite, your blog or an email to a potential employer. Stick with it, and you may get there some-day. Good luck.

REPORTING TIPS

Excerpted from
The Videogame Style Guide and Reference Manual
www.gamestyleguide.com
by David Thomas, Kyle Orland and Scott Steinberg

The style of game reviews ultimately depends on the editorial direction and philosophy of the publication running them. There are, however, some general guidelines to keep in mind when crafting game evaluations.

Avoid first- and second-person references in your reviews. Keep your writing squarely focused on the subject matter. Remove yourself and the reader from the review.

> Example: The boomerang is used to defeat the boss found in the third dungeon.

> Wrong: I defeated the boss in the third dungeon with the boomerang.

> Wrong: You defeat the boss in the third dungeon by using the boomerang.

Remember that each player's experience with a game in unique. Avoid generalizing about experiences or features that might be unique only to your playthrough. For instance, avoid using the phrase "hours of gameplay" to describe the longevity of a game, since different players will spend different amounts of time with the title.

Craft the review to the audience. Avoid use of jargon like "boss" or "1-up" if the readers might not have a deep familiarity with gaming.

Use specifics as often as possible. Avoid abstractions. The more specific details included, the more likely you will engage a reader with your writing.

Example: The lock-on targeting feature allows players to spend less time aiming and more time trying to figure out how to defeat the enemy troops.

Wrong: The game's targeting system is well-designed and fun to use.

Ask yourself: How did the game make you feel while playing it? Frustrated? Angry? Powerful? Overwhelmed? Useless? Make those feelings come through for the reader.

Avoid cleverness and word games. Get to the heart of the matter. Be quick about it.

Keep your reviews concise. Time spent reading about videogames is time that your reader could be spending playing videogames!

The easiest games to write about are the ones that are very good or very bad. The hardest games to write about are the mediocre and/or nondescript games.

Unless specified by your assigning editor or formal publication policy, don't separate your review into distinct sections. (Paragraph one covers graphics, paragraph two deals with gameplay, etc.) Instead, weave all these elements into a single, compelling critical narrative.

When editorial policy calls for giving a game a review score, be fair. Not every game produced is an A, and most probably are not even a B. In a world where C is average, dole out the praise sparingly. Puffing up the score for an average game is not fair to the game or the reader.

Be bold. Be brave. Say something interesting. Ask yourself: What makes your review stand out from the hundreds of other reviews being written at this very moment?

HOW TO WRITE BETTER REVIEWS

Start Off Strong – The importance of a controversial, funny or simply offbeat intro can't be understated: It pays to be punchy. The first few sentences set the tone for your article – if you can't hook readers with a quick overview of what's on the menu, it's a safe bet they won't stick around for dessert. Gamers aren't known for their attention spans, after all...

Cover the Bases – Don't assume the reader knows anything about games – help frame everything in a broader cultural context. Serious enthusiasts may get what you're saying, but let's face it... Like virgins at a video shoot, they're in the minority. Mass appeal is everything: If you really want to people to feel what you're getting at, make sure they know what the heck it means to begin with.

Stick to the Facts – Make like an action movie director: Can the b/s, and cut to the chase. People ultimately read reviews for one thing: The straight dope on the product. Instead of wasting time with cute stories or personal anecdotes, give 'em the facts – they want to read about the game, not your depressing social life.

Do You – As a rule, your personality and point of view should shine through in any article – otherwise, what's to make your opinion stand out from the other 50 million out there? That doesn't mean you should go off-topic or make yourself the subject of the piece... Just, as in real-life, give people a reason to listen when you speak.

End on a High Note – The last paragraph of any article should sum up the entire piece quickly and concisely. No matter how well-worded or entertaining the article is, it always pays to summarize, and restate, your key points. Don't be afraid to have fun with it, however – an entertaining kicker's essential. It's the last thing a viewer will read, and the last to stick out in their mind. Besides, as any entertainer will tell you, it always pays to leave an audience hanging...

GAME WRITING BASICS

Following are answers to the most commonly asked questions I'm posed concerning how to write about games for living.

Everything you need to know to make your dream of sitting home on the couch jabbering away on Xbox Live, chomping down cookies while making dough (Get it: Cookies, dough… oh, never mind) lies herein:

Q: How'd you get started in the industry?

A: Living in a city that wasn't a hotbed for game development, and not possessing many leads within the business at the time, like many folks interested in breaking into the industry, I didn't have much choice in terms of a career path. I wanted into the game industry badly, so I did the only thing I knew: I took my experience writing for fansites and small-scale professional outlets, and attempted to parlay that into work with larger, more respected outlets.

Thankfully, because of my experience writing for little to nothing and tireless passion for scamming free games, I'd already been published, and invited to various events courtesy of several publishers: Luckily, I was able to take the contacts I made there by simply shooting the breeze with various editors and apparently convince someone I'd be good for the occasional article. These far-sighted and generous (OK, desperate maybe? Who knows…) individuals have my respect and gratitude to this day.

Moral of the story: Don't be discouraged – opportunity is what you make of it. Get out there and start writing, and take advantage of every chance you have to network. You may wind up working long hours (or even years) for free and little to no recognition at first, but all that effort will eventually pay off in spades.

Q: Is it hard finding enough work to fill up the day?

A: That all depends on who you ask – but honestly, no matter the freelancer, it's generally a feast or famine situation. You always have too much or too little… Never just enough. Thankfully, it all evens out in the end.

Two points to note here: 1. The more work you do, the more that comes your way and 2. Sometimes, the hardest thing isn't finding more work, it's saying no – I literally grind 12-14 hours a day, 7 days a week. Hint: That's not what you'd call healthy.

Q: How do you go about approaching an outlet that you've never written for before?

A: Fancy stuff, let me tell you (note the sarcasm) – I just make contact and keep it brief: Shoot them a note or drop them a phone call and simply explain who I am, who I've written for and why I'm so witty, naturally, in about a paragraph (or under a minute, in case of a conversation) or less.

Then I just follow up religiously, at respectful intervals (say, every 2-3 days) until they provide an answer one way or not. There's no trick to it, and you shouldn't be afraid to approach people or make cold calls. After all, the worst someone can say is "no," and being married well… Let's just say you get used to that.

Q: Is the market for game freelancers growing or shrinking, in your view? Has it gotten easier or harder to find work since you've started?

A: The market's certainly growing, and it's easier to find work thanks to the explosion of blogs, video distribution sites and other online outlets: There's more places to write for than ever, and with greater frequency, even with print media in the midst of what I suspect will be a permanent decline. But at the same time, there's also more competition than ever – so good luck finding steady gigs, let alone publications that pay a decent rate. Thousands of people want in, and the market's completely oversaturated. But hey, let's be honest: For richer or poorer, nothing beats playing *Halo 3* for a living.

Q: Do you miss the camaraderie of the office, or do you enjoy working in solitude?

A: I prefer solitude, but it's just a personal quirk – I work best in complete silence. But working alone can definitely drive you a little stir crazy: I'm happiest when I'm on the phone, as any freelancer should be – the gig's more about schmoozing than writing. Besides, the dog's not been laughing as much at my jokes lately…

Q: Is it hard staying focused without the structure of a 9 to 5 job?

A: No, but then, a true freelancer's a walking ad for ADD. I remember virtually anything a prospective client says in passing, yet strangely, I'm lucky if I remember my own name half the time…

Q: Are you looking for a full time game journalism job? If not, how long do you think you'll be able to keep on freelancing?

A: Alas, no – frankly, if I wanted to be serially abused, overworked and underappreciated, I'd just start dating again. Happily, thanks to the kindness, forethought and goodwill of gaming editors, some of the smartest, hardest-working and most vastly undervalued individuals in the business, I've been privileged enough to enjoy 10 years of horrendous jokes, and (knock on wood) am still going strong… Let this be a lesson to you: A. Sanity and political correctness are no prerequisite to success and B. If you want to get anywhere in life, in terms of self-employment vs. corporate solidarity, it generally pays best to go it alone.

THE VIDEOGAME FREELANCER'S BIBLE

Shocker: Once upon a time, long ago, I wasn't the gorgeous, silver-tongued author and marketing/publishing/PR guru you all know and love. (Or as full of self-aggrandizing b/s, but hey, I digress…)

Nay, before all the glitz and glamour, I was just another starry-eyed fansite owner dying to break into the biz. Just one catch – being based on the East Coast, lacking insider contacts and disinclined to pack and move cross-country, game industry jobs weren't exactly easy to come by.

So, circa 1999, after several months writing semi-professionally for websites such as *Online Gaming Review* and *The Adrenaline Vault*, I did what any fresh-faced newbie would do and took the plunge. I quit my cushy day job and went full-time freelance, using contacts I'd acquired by attending the occasional media event.

Pissing into the wind, some might say. Me? I'd go with "spraying a fire hose filled with raw sewage into an oncoming tornado." To keep it brief: I had no savings, no sense of how tough the business really was and no way of comprehending the stumbling blocks ahead. Amusingly, my timing couldn't have been better either: If you were out of the industry at that time, be glad you missed the dot com bust.

Thankfully, ignorance means nothing to a young, twenty-something male – in retrospect, second to getting married to a certain special lady, it was the best decision I ever made. The resulting years of struggle and hardship taught me invaluable lessons about marketing, sales, public relations, accounting and countless other aspects of running a small business you won't come across in the average day job. And, of course, many other crucial elements of the gaming industry and career development in general. The end result: I've gone on to found several successful businesses, pen three books and contribute to 300+ outlets from CNN to *The New York Times*, including virtually every videogame magazine in existence.

That said, I remain a realist: Let's skip the hype and cut to the chase – if you're reading this, chances are you want in. Can't say as I blame you: All things considered, getting paid to travel the world, play games months in advance of release and rub elbows with the industry elite is nice work if you can get it. It certainly doesn't hurt that the vast majority of editors, fellow freelancers, marketing/PR reps and developers I've encountered are some of the hardest-working, most intelligent and interesting people you'll ever meet.

Still, while several manifestos outline the path to getting a job writing about games for a living, they're nonetheless somewhat incomplete. The kicker being that none tell you what you fully need to know to truly DIY, or Do It Your-Darned-Self, as a home-based scribe hoping to make a long and successful career of hustling slang by the word or project.

Therefore listen up, because I won't say it twice. Couple the aforementioned resources with the following advice, gleaned from years in the proverbial trenches, and you'll be ready to start cashing in on your passion for playing *Pokémon*. So easy literally anyone can do it, so hard it can break the best of men, either way, the future's yours. It's high time we got some new blood in this business. Read up, soak up, then step up and make ol' pappy Steinberg proud:

GETTING STARTED

1. The first and most crucial thing you need to do is build a writing portfolio – read: get as many published clips as possible. This may mean writing for free for ill-paying, off-brand magazines, newspapers, websites or weeklies. So be it: I'm not too proud to admit I've offered services pro bono in the past just to toe a door open. Creating opportunity is everything; when things seem tough, or like you're not making any headway, redouble your efforts. Breaking in is a killer, but these things tend to steamroll; build an established background, and it'll be that much easier to approach top editors and gain additional gigs. Key takeaway here: The more you work you pump out, the more that comes rushing right back in.

2. Looking for leads? Try the local bookstore – simply taking the time to flip through the pages of certain publications and send the editors an email got me dozens of placements in the past. Get to know each outlet as well: All are basically larger entities consisting of smaller, self-contained departments headed up by specific overseers. The trick is simply pitching the right idea to the right editor. Either way, no one's going to come to you with their hand out – you'll be the one having to suggest story topics. Bearing this in mind, take the time to come up with several custom-tailored suggestions before approaching these individuals as well. (And remember that magazines generally operate on 60- to 90-day lead times, so stories must be relevant for 2-3 months from the date you submit.) It's a pain, but it does keep your name top of mind, and give you some control over the topics you work on. Hot tip: If there's one thing publications in every field are consistently looking for, it's feature stories.

3. Persistence pays. Except in the case of dating, 'no' does not mean 'no,' typically – coming from most editors, it just means "not now," or "possibly later, if you manage to actually catch my attention." Follow-up is essential too: If an editor says "write back in a week," take the time to do it. If they don't respond to queries (the most common outcome), wait a respectful interval, e.g. 2-3 days, then reach out again. If it helps get your mind right, consider: In all my years of scribbling, I can count the number of writing ops that fell into my lap on one hand. It's murder out there, sure, and you'll fight to gain every inch of ground, but that just makes victory all the sweeter. Most people give up and accept things resignedly; don't, and you'll see how rewarding it can be.

4. Always treat others with respect and dignity. They teach you this in pre-school; sadly, not everyone remembers it, and after a certain amount of wining and dining, many writers get a fat head. You're a freelancer; never forget that everyone's a potential friend. If you're genuine, and not just some corny dweeb trying to fleece them, they'll recognize this. Ensuring, of course, that even if these folks don't help pay the bills, at least you'll have someone to snicker and pass notes with at the next boring press demo.

5. Never lose sight of this maxim: You are who you know. Most of the time, it's a multi-way street. In other words, you need editors to assign work; PR people to help make a story happen; experts to provide the commentary that links it all together; analysts to offer hard data; and so on. Assembling most stories requires interacting with several individuals and getting them to two-step as deadlines approach, guaranteeing that those with the best, most reliable social network come out ahead. Mastering the art of knowing whom to call in a pinch is one of the single most important attributes you'll need to survive out there.

STAYING AFLOAT

1. Treat your career like a business, because that's exactly what it is: Your reputation precedes you – never forget to act professionally, or with integrity and respect. John Q. Public might not sound like much on paper, but your name is your brand: Always meet assigned deadlines, live up to your word, deliver solid work and watch your career and repute grow. Mind you, editors are gossipy sorts; all it takes is one blown deadline or drunken brawl to tarnish your sterling reputation across several outlets.

2. On the flip side, don't be overly sensitive either: Fellow freelancers are, by definition, competitors. It's inevitable that at some point, whether by design or serendipity, you'll be perceived as taking food out of their mouths, and catch hate as a result. So be it: Real chums will always treat you as such, and peers who respect one another can simply sit down and discuss any difference of opinion. Want to be Mr. Popular? No sweat – you can always apply for a job handing out tax refunds.

3. Customer satisfaction is crucial; clients work nights and weekends – if you plan on keeping up, you may very well have to too. Going the extra mile in terms of both effort to make a story better and expedience (remember: editors live harried lives, and the less callbacks and edits they must make, the happier they'll be) is also imperative. Essentially, if you're going to convince sponsors to assign something out of house at added cost, you'd best do everything in your power to make their lives easier, thereby proving you're a justifiable go-to guy/gal. Fun fact about human nature too: People don't like change. It may be hell getting there, but once you're in, as long as you maintain these high standards, chances are you're there to stay. Pardon the pun, but freelancing is not a game. Dependable, hard workers get ahead, others don't – end of story.

4. Don't get depressed: The first 6 months are the toughest in your freelance career, as you struggle to establish a reputation and build a client base. Certainly, ups and downs are frequent afterwards. And experienced freelancers know that it's always either feast or famine. Just remember: It all evens out in the end. The easiest way to save yourself untold heartache? Keep a 6- to 12-month savings cushion in the bank, restocking and adding to it as opportunity permits. Interesting trend you'll note as well. There's a shakeout every few years, whereby those who've failed to save for a rainy day fall by the wayside. The bonus being that those left standing afterwards appear all the more able – and survive to dine on the scraps – when the smoke eventually clears. Moral of the story: Freelancing is not a sprint, but rather a marathon.

5. ABC – Always Be Closing. Networking is crucial, as is having the moxie to walk up to potential contacts and freely speak your mind. You have to be outgoing. A good freelancer's as much a schmoozer as he/she is a writer. Trade secret: In the videogame biz, do a great job with your stories and most people will be amazed that you're simply making deadlines and actually giving them what they asked for. But getting in the door is the real challenge, not doing the work – attend events, and don't be afraid to approach people, make cold calls or whatever else it takes to nudge it open. Should you need incentive, just ask yourself: If there are a million other jealous guys/gals out there vying for the same few dozen opportunities, were you to keep silent, what would make you stand out from the crowd to a prospective backer?

GOING THE DISTANCE

1. Philosophically, here you have two choices. You can try to get in good with a few publications and do a lot of work for them. Alternately, you can do less work for a larger number of clients. I recommend the latter; in the former event, if someone goes under, it can be problematic, because you've been leaning too heavily on them. The best job security you can have is a lot of clients; one goes kaput, no biggie – you've got 15 more lined up. Sure, some folks love the prestige of being known as "*Hotwired*" magazine's exclusive guy or head correspondent for "*The Bollywood Reporter.*" Me, I wouldn't want my career to be defined by a singular gig that can, and will, eventually fizzle. Take it from experience: In a best-case scenario, even the most established magazines undergo proverbial regime changes as editors constantly join and depart, taking their stable of writers' fortunes up or down with them. Nothing is static, least of all a writing job.

2. Save grand, involving pieces of work for clients you trust. Freelancing is a business, plain and simple, and time is by far your most valuable (and limited) resource. Days and weeks wasted on a project that goes unpaid for are unrecoupable and, last I checked, compelling a read as it may be, you can't eat an unpublished essay on the artistic merits of *Ico*. Granted, it's nice to do 3000 words of insightful counterculture prose for your favorite underground fanzine that's always on the cusp of going bankrupt – I still get a kick out of it today. But if the local newspaper that's been around as a stable business for 100 years asks for a 1000-word review of *Forza Motorsport 2* for a similar or slightly less asking fee, go with the latter, unless you can afford to take the hit. Seeing a story in print is nice: Actually getting to see a check for your work is what will afford you the freedom to write day in and day out and eventually explore more artistic endeavors at your leisure as time and chance permit.

3. Embrace diversification. An experienced writer can summon up artful prose about anything from vacuum cleaners to vegetables when pressed. So why limit yourself to just games? Books, movies, music, half-dressed supermodels – surely there are other, related topics you love. Take the time to explore them: It won't just heighten your stability, expand your portfolio, increase your knowledge base, provide future points of reference and make you more marketable, not to mention a more talented penman overall. It'll also help ensure a steady stream of incoming work – and the more aspirin, or copies of *Quake*, you'll eventually be able to afford.

4. Don't tie yourself too heavily to trends. Cultural phenomena such as these tend to be cyclical, which guarantees huge popularity swings. While being known as an expert in one field can help increase your visibility and land you a lot of work quickly, it can also send you sinking down with the ship. Convergence, for example, may seem a hot topic now, but it also was back in 1983, before the fad went into a 15-year death cycle. My advice? Do yourself a favor that's equally good for your self-esteem and resume: Like any good entrepreneur, teach yourself to be a jack of all trades.

5. Stay positive, and maintain your sense of humor. As in any highly competitive field, even the most able-bodied workers are subject to the vagaries of the marketplace. Trust me on this one: You're never out of the game if you keep actively playing.

Still there? Bully for you!

That stubbornness won't just serve you well in your future career as a superstar videogame freelancer extraordinaire, sipping cocktails and shaking hands with Z-grade celebrities, or at least getting the odd free *Super Mario Bros.* keychain.

With any luck, it'll keep you hacking away on copy long after I've quit spewing these snarky monologues and settled down to a quiet life of *Super Street Fighter V Turbo: The Director's Cut* and *Tony Hawk's Project 367.*

PARTING THOUGHTS

EXPERT INSIGHT

Finally, we come to the end of this volume – and, naturally, I've saved the best for last.

Who better to tell you how to stack chips, make waves around the world and dominate the field than those very iconic individuals who've survived their meteoritic rise to the top and, along the way, gained dozens of stories to share?

And so, without further ado, ladies and gentlemen, I give you the game industry's best and brightest: Let their words serve as a guidepost, as well as warning, to would-be jet-setters and entrepreneurs.

Moral of the story: Be careful what you wish for. Heed the following advice, and you just might get it…

TRIP HAWKINS
Founder, Electronic Arts, 3DO and Digital Chocolate

Q: As one of gaming's most well-known figures, what do you credit as the secret to your success?

A: Passion, determination, practicality and bold ideas backed up by tons of analysis. And I can hang with the best of the ponytails and the suits.

Q: Any major gaffes you've made on your journey to the top, and lessons learned, that you'd care to share with readers?

A: OMG, that would require another entire book! Icarus comes to mind when I think of 3DO. You have to become self-aware and figure out early which people, ideas, and opportunities are a waste of time. To my surprise, great companies like Apple and EA turn out to be built from executive teams where 50% of the executives are mediocre or worse, but you just don't realize it at the time. My biggest mistake in life is having an emotional desire to be optimistic about human nature and wanting to trust people even when I don't really know them. It's okay to have these kinds of feelings, but if you are self-aware and paranoid, you will waste less time and get into less trouble.

Q: Where are the big bucks in gaming these days?

A: For future growth, three words: Mobile, social, casual.

Q: Ways individuals operating in the videogame field can help themselves stand out?

A: Figure out where you need to be to learn what you need to know, and go there and volunteer to work for free. Very few people demonstrate insightful analysis, have legitimately interesting new ideas or go sufficiently out of their way to demonstrate passion. I've flown to countries without appointments. I've shown up in building lobbies without appointments. You need to put yourself on the line. And then you had better have something to say.

Q: The trick to picking hits is?

A: I have a strong personal commitment to learn the history of all media, all media titans, all media companies and all media platforms... and also to be a constant historian and critic observing popular culture across all media. A wonderful Disney consultant once said to me, "Creativity is the rearranging of the old in a new way." Many great new things fit that model, but you have to know all the history of what has come before so that you have reference points and know how to mash an old idea into a new medium. If it is your passion, then you can develop experience and insight because you are living and doing it. But just because you play games does not mean you know how to make one, any more than attending a Green Day concert would make me know how to succeed as a rock star. Finally, to quote from a story on the TV industry that happens to apply to games: "And never forget: All hits are flukes."

Q: How can one train and educate themselves in order to maximize chances of striking it rich in the gaming business?

A: In formal education, you need to go as far as you can go in every disciplinary direction that is available, from management to marketing to finance to art to engineering to design. When you find your boundaries, you will know what you should do and you will have context for the other areas as well as the know how to speak the language.

Q: Any fallacies about the typical game mogul's lifestyle you'd care to clear up?

A: How hard you have to work. For most successful people, they are doing what they do 24/7.

Q: Things folks should watch out for on the path to success?

A: It's important that you stay true to yourself and stay humble. None of us is more important than anyone else.

Q: The one thing every hopeful game industy titan should remember?

A: As I've always said, keep it "simple, hot, and deep..."

RICHARD "LORD BRITISH" GARRIOTT
Creator, *Ultima* and Founder, Origin Systems

Q: What's the secret to your success?

A: For me, it was timing. I had a very unique opportunity that was created by getting into the business early. Computers were far more simple than they were today. That allowed me the opportunity to not just deal with one specialty, but rather become a master of sorts at all trades (i.e. programming, art, design, sound).

That unique background is very hard to achieve today. It takes much more of a concerted effort for someone to really figure out how to put a game design together and really understand the impacts of changing any part of that equation. How it's implemented, what the cost would be... it's an infinite array of tradeoffs you have to make – almost too much for one man to handle anymore.

Q: But surely timing wasn't entirely the reason for *Ultima*'s popularity?

A: Oh no, that was just a unique trait that allowed me to grow as a game creator. If you look more specifically at the success of the game, the key was innovation. It's funny because I stumbled into success more than planned my way to achieving it.

If you look at the early *Ultima*s, and by that I mean *1* to *4*, or even *Akalabeth* (what I like to think of as *Ultima 0*), there really wasn't much of a game to them. *Akalabeth* was basically a dungeon crawl where you hunted monsters and collected treasure. There really wasn't much game there. There was no end or winning condition, even.

Over a period of time, from *Ultima*s *1* to *3*, even though I'd succeeded with the first of the games, instead of creating what I call a cheap sequel, I did something different, as opposed to my contemporaries. If you look at the early *Wizardry* titles, they actually outsold the original *Ultima*s. But *Wizardy 2*, the sequel to *Wizardy*, came out as essentially just an expansion to the first game, with new weapons, spells, and stuff, but it was primarily the same game engine.

In contrast, the early *Ultima* engines were very primitive, so I started throwing away the large quantity of code I'd written between games due to the fact I'd learned so much in the intervening time and felt I could go so far beyond it. So I'd write each new game over from scratch and create a better engine. It's just kind of a fallout of the process.

But if you look at the sales curves of the early *Wizardy* games versus the early *Ultima*s, each sequel tended to sell to a subset of the people who'd bought the previous edition, whereas each successor to *Ultima* was actually outselling its predecessor by a substantial margin. And if you look at those, you can actually say *Ultima 2* was a much better game than *Ultima 1*, whereas *Wizardy 2* was just a different game from *Wizardry*, if you follow my drift.

That habit of maximizing innovation was important to the franchise's staying power. I think you can see that even today, with some other great companies (for example, the folks at id Software): With each new *Doom* or *Quake*, it's a substantial revamp of existing technology. If you're going to do first-person shooter games, for example, you need to push the technological boundaries. That particular truth of our industry is interesting and is created because we're building on top of technology, since we're advancing so quickly.

If you look at the movie industry, which has been around for 100 years, save for instances like *The Matrix* where technology has begun to play a role, films are judged solely on creative content and the quality of the storytelling, pacing... a wide range of qualities that have little to do with technological innovation. In the games industry, technological innovation is still one of the predominant ways to ensure the success of your product – and an unfortunate one at that.

Q: So you believe for someone to stay relevant, they have to keep reinventing themselves?

A: Yes, definitely. If you look at the first three *Ultima*s, it was a maximization of technology. *Ultima 4* was a new kind of reinvention, in that by the time I'd had four successful games out there (counting *Akalabeth*), while all had gotten successively better from a technological standpoint, they hadn't improved from a story-telling or content standpoint. You know, technology improved, you could talk to characters, but up until *Ultima 4*, the actual craft did not much improve.

In fact, if you look at almost all old role-playing games, the storyline is pretty much the same. You're the hero. Your goal is to defeat the bad guy, because you're told to do so. And what you do as a player is pillage and plunder, because that's the game's instructions, with the ultimate goal being to gain enough power to fight the bad guy, who generally has been doing nothing during the tenure of the game. He's been waiting there the whole time waiting on you to get enough power to knock him down.

So the storylines are what I'll call morally ambiguous at best. Just not well-crafted in the sense of giving you a compelling reason to participate in the proceedings. *Ultima 4* was for me the first opportunity to craft real storytelling. And that's just one example of ways outside of core technological advancement you can reinvent yourself.

Other games that have done a good job along similar lines exist too. I thought *Medal of Honor* was brilliant as far as advancing level and mission design went. Things like *American McGee's Alice* did a great job of creating an atmospheric environment. *Myst* too... it created a very compelling universe to play in. There are lots of ways to be innovative – sadly, many products are simply what I describe as "me too, plus one feature."

Q: Roughly how much has the *Ultima* franchise generated?

A: Right now, upwards of $100 million. *Ultima Online* currently generates $25 million a year to this day.

Q: Of that, how much did you see?

A: Nowhere near that much, but several million, certainly. Back in the pre-Electronic Arts days, I got a large portion of royalties. I go back to the freelance era – the first few *Ultima*s I created on my own ticket. I hired the teams myself... even paid their salaries when I ran Origin.

Q: The best thing the money bought you?

A: The biggest fringe benefit of that success for me has been to have the opportunity to explore the world, which has been a passion since youth. It spawned a lot of the creative energy which went into the *Ultima* series. I've now traveled the globe... been to Antarctica and the South Pole twice, deep diving in a submersible almost ten times. I've visited an undersea wreck that had never been discovered and brought up chests of gold and silver coins, the threshold of space via the Russian space program. In my mind that's a part of the lifestyle we try to create for players in the virtual sense. But to do it in the real world's a costly endeavor.

Q: Biggest drawback of the loot?

A: The expectations which get built around you. There's an inertia that builds behind you, and people are always wondering what comes next. There's a lot of pressure... you can't really back off and work on a game that people won't expect to be epic and have an epic level of success. It actually interferes with your willingness to take risks or do small projects.

Q: Was establishing a character like Lord British crucial to your success?

A: It was a big part of it... crucial, I don't know. There's no question that it substantially increased the level of success and gave the franchise longevity, though. It also lended a lot of credence to the fact that I'm just as much a player and want to live in these virtual worlds as much as anyone else. And the moniker sticks - it's helped me become more memorable than other equally successful game creators.

Q: Did it ever cause an identity crisis?

A: In Austin, I'm commonly recognized as Lord British ahead of Richard Garriott. Funny thing is, my father is a NASA astronaut. There's times we'll be in a science circle and people will recognize me ahead of him. But then there are times at game conventions when they'll recognize him ahead of me.

WILL WRIGHT
Creator, *The Sims* and Co-Founder, Maxis

Q: You've already had a lifetime's worth of hits. To what do you accredit your success?

A: Luck's a big factor. It's hard to predict what's going to be fun to someone else. It's much easier to figure out what I would enjoy playing and design that. Execution is also extremely important. A lot of the credit goes to the teams I work with, who bring so much to each product.

Q: How has success in the game biz enabled you to indulge your passion for nearly any project?

A: Two ways. First, the money side… it gives me the financial wherewithal to do it. That has more to do with having been in the industry in the early days and co-founding a company than anything else. Second, the contacts it's helped generate. Now that the industry has mainstream acceptance, it helps people see crossover potential in other fields. It helps you get in the door at places you normally wouldn't.

Q: Can success in the field of interactive entertainment be a stepping stone to Hollywood?

A: Well, it's not like Hollywood is that grandiose. It actually matches the stereotype exactly. But now that people are looking at how games have skyrocketed, yes, I'd imagine so.

Q: When you got into the industry, did you see it as a springboard for future ventures like robot hobbyist group Stupid Fun Club, *Spore* and other initiatives?

A: Truthfully, I didn't see gaming as a vehicle to get elsewhere. It sort of just happened as I grew personally. In the beginning, I just loved gaming... a job in the industry seemed a match made in heaven. Seeing trends and figures that show that games will outgrow movies at some point though, I'd think that such an evolutionary step has to happen in the future.

Q: Must an artist have certain notoriety before they can take chances like you always do with your games?

A: Anyone can produce interesting stuff on a shoestring budget. It just depends how much money you need. Investors like to see a proven track record.

Q: Any advice for developers who'd like to follow in your footsteps?

A: Be patient. Hit games can take years. It's easy to get sick of them. Maintain your passion... it's the biggest indicator of eventual success.

DENNIS "THRESH" FONG
Co-Founder, Xfire / "The Michael Jordan of Videogames"

Luckily for those of you who haven't had an original thought since *Pac-Man* was all the rage, even everyday scrubs can score big off this industry. Just ask Dennis "Thresh" Fong, former *Quake* champion, serial entrepreneur and winner of John Carmack's Ferrari. "Gaming was just a hobby... I never realized I was any good until I started winning tournaments and money started rolling in."

While hardly likely to give the average oil tycoon a run for his checkbook, make no bones about it... Fong *has* prospered. Riding the Internet boom, he sagely used his newfound fame as a launching pad for businesses like Gamers.com, FiringSquad.com and gamer-friendly instant messaging client Xfire, which MTV Networks bought for $102 million circa April 2006.

Want to follow in his footsteps? Good luck, says Fong, who advises, "This industry changes every six months... you've gotta stay ahead of the curve." He describes the situation for aspiring armchair entrepreneurs as a volatile one. "For people today, it's easier and harder to break into the business like I did. Gaming's become more mainstream... lots of professional leagues exist now. At the time my fortunes changed for the better, there weren't. I was once undisputed champion... now there are many."

Indeed, clawing your way into the big time doesn't take much, what with so many new paths one can take. Where once there was only Twin Galaxies'-sponsored tournaments, players can now sign up to become part of bustling organizations like the Cyberathlete Professional League or Major League Gaming. Even Yahoo! offers card and board game competitions that reward top-ranking players with cash and prizes. All told, between upstart confederations like the Global Gaming League and event-based competitions offered at expos such as QuakeCon and the World Cyber Games, there's ample room for advancement.

Don't count on getting rich quick, though – with so many contenders currently in the mix, competition for top slots is fiece. Considering the potential payoffs, however ("The Ferrari I won still sits in my parking lot looking real pretty" affirms Fong), I'm confident at least a few of you will try rising to the challenge. Go get 'em...

TOMMY TALLARICO
Founder, Video Games Live

Q: How'd you fall into this gig?

A: I've been playing piano since I was 3 and composing music since I was a teenager. I grew up on videogames but never thought to put my two greatest loves together until I moved out to California when I turned 21. I moved out in 1991 with no money, no place to stay, no friends or family, no job... nothing! I was literally homeless and sleeping under the pier at Huntington Beach. The first day I was in California I picked up a newspaper and got a job selling keyboards at Guitar Center. I started the next day and the first customer to walk in the store was a producer at a new videogame company called Virgin Mastertronic (which later turned into Virgin Games). I was wearing a TurboGrafx-16 t-shirt and we struck up a conversation about games. I went down to the studio and was hired the next day as the very first games tester. It was then that I decided what my career was going to be.

Q: How did you first get sign-off to start making music for games? And at what point did the whole virtual audio thing snowball?

A: I wanted to help change the way people thought and felt about videogame music. I didn't want it to be associated with child-like bleeps and bloops; our generation had grown up and we were still playing games. I wanted to create thematic film score music, rock, blues, electronica and all the music I would normally listen to. At the time you had to be a computer programmer in order to do music for games. I barely knew anything about programming so I had programmers build me systems in which I could play my MIDI keyboard into the actual game systems. I then convinced the programmers and bosses to give me an unheard of amount of cartridge space so I could use samples and other tricks to create the best possible audio experience. It all worked out great for my career and the games I worked on. Titles like *Global Gladiators*, *Cool Spot*, *The Terminator*, *Aladdin* and the *Earthworm Jim* series were all getting lots of attention for their audio, which helped me prove my theory that game audio should be taken a lot more seriously.

Q: What's the secret to making great in-game audio then? Is it different from composing songs for traditional mediums?

A: Let's say you've got an adventure-style game where you're trapped in a cave, looking for an exit. You might have a two-minute looping ambience in the background until the character pulls a lever to open a stone door. Then you would quickly fade out the ambience and play a four-second music sting, like a harp glissando or string crescendo, then quickly fade in a 30-second loop of suspense music while the character walks down the corridor behind the door. When the hallway opens into a big room – where 30 guys are waiting to attack – you could hit with a big orchestral cue.

We've come so far in the last 10 to 15 years. The biggest difference was the creation of CD-ROM as a storage medium. We were no longer limited to creating MIDI files and attaching sounds to them. We could now use live musicians and create real music which could be recorded and produced. This change came in the mid-'90s. We went from bleeps and bloops to live orchestras. It took the film industry 50 or 60 years to get where we are today, but the technology is changing so quick, we're actually surpassing the film industry now... using multiple streams and interactive 5.1 crossfades, things that movies aren't even capable of giving you, because it's a linear experience.

That's what keeps this all exciting to me, and I've worked on over 250 games. What keeps me excited is that every year, there's something new that no one's ever done before, that the technology allows for. It's really exciting for me, because I'm a videogame player too... not just a composer.

Q: The craziest or most expensive production you've ever arranged to put together for use in an interactive outing?

A: For *Advent Rising*, I used a 72-piece Hollywood union orchestra with an Emmy award-winning conductor (Mark Watters). We recorded on the Paramount Pictures stage with Academy Award-winning recording engineer and mixer Armin Steiner.

We then went to Salt Lake City to record members of the Mormon Tabernacle Choir and a full childrens' choir. We mixed and mastered the music in the most prestigious studios in Hollywood and had a full team of orchestrators and copyists working on the scores. From the voice-over side, we also had the talents of Orson Scott Card helping to write the dialogue as well as some of the top union talent for the acting. After everything was said and done, we spent around $400,000 on the audio, which (when compared to the entire game budget) isn't a lot of money for such a high-quality production. In the end we released the *Advent Rising Soundtrack* CD as well.

Q: You created the Video Games Live events. What was the inspiration, how successful has the tour been, and do you think we'll see more of this stuff in the future?

A: Over four years ago my partner (and fellow videogame composer) Jack Wall and I wanted to bring the greatest videogame music and visuals to an audience not only made up of gamers, but non-gamers as well. At that point there had never been a videogame concert in North America and we felt strongly that the time was right for something like this to start happening over here. The Dear Friends concert came out a few years later and really helped us to prove our concept to the right people because that show did so well initially. It was very important to us to come out of the gate as big as possible, which we did by putting on the biggest videogame concert in the world on the most prestigious stage in the world. On July 6th, 2005 we premiered Video Games Live at the Hollywood Bowl to over 10,000 people with the LA Philharmonic Orchestra.

It was an incredible accomplishment for us in a number of ways. Not only were we able to prove the concept and have a great number of people show up, but, more importantly, we turned on many non-gamers to the beauty and emotion of videogame music and their visuals. We got amazing feedback from people like grandmothers who brought their grandkids saying things like "WOW!! I never knew that videogame music was so emotional and amazing. I now understand why so many people are into this." That was always one of our goals from the beginning and to see it happen before our eyes was very special for us.

The split second right before Jack and I walked out on the stage for the first time I looked at Jack and said, "What the heck have we done?!" It was such an emotional and incredible feeling to know that after four years of hard work, sacrifice and many bumps in the road that the dream had now become a reality. Not only was it the first time any of that music had ever been performed in North America, but having the entire industry there to support us was very special. My friends like *Metal Gear* series creator Hideo Kojima and *Sonic the Hedgehog* creator Yuji Naka traveled halfway around the world just to be there for us. Everyone from Nolan Bushnell (founder of Atari) to the *Halo* guys (Marty O'Donnell and company) were there on hand to take part in the celebration. We had over 50 well-known industry people there, so at the end of the show, I brought them all up on stage and introduced them to the crowd. It was amazing!

Please check out www.videogameslive.com to get all of the latest info.

Q: Are your days of showing up at E3 with strippers on each arm over? Why so/not? And any cute stories you'd care to share from one of those occasions?

A: Oh hell yes! That was strictly a publicity stunt I pulled at the first two E3s because...

a.) I wanted people to pay attention and get my name out there.

b.) Back then there seemed to be a LOT of suits and not enough personalities.

Developers were still pretty much looked down upon and most of the time not even mentioned.

I thought I would be wacky and dress up like a flashy idiot with a big entourage which included tons of hot scantily clad girls, bodyguards... and, of course, midgets. It was strictly just a marketing ploy to get people to ask... "Who the hell is that?"

Most people laughed and got the prank and others took exception and thought I was being serious or something. The fact that you knew about it and asked me the question over 10 years later proves my point that it must have worked.

I've learned from the entertainment industry that reinventing yourself (or the products you work on) is a very important way to stay at the top of your game and always be a topic of discussion for people, which is important when you are always trying to network and be involved with the next coolest thing.

As far as "cute" stories go, we were at the first E3 and had the 17-person entourage going. I had girls on each arm and bodyguards all around me. In one of the booths a *Star Wars* stormtrooper would jump out and try to startle people in a tunnel. As we walked in the stormtrooper jumped out and without hesitation one of the bodyguards (without even looking) stiff-armed the guy out of the way... The bodyguard dude didn't even flinch. It was pretty funny and no one was hurt but I did actually hire real bodyguards so they were just carrying on business as usual. Suffice it to say that when the Empire came a-knockin, I was prepared.

Q: How can others make a name for themselves creating game music and/or break into the industry?

A: Well that's easy... Just show up at E3 with a crazy outfit and a bunch of strippers and midgets!! Seriously though, there are three simple things which will REALLY help out anyone looking to get into doing audio for the videogame industry.

1. Join the Game Audio Network Guild (G.A.N.G.) at www.audiogang.org. It's a non-profit organization established to educate the masses in regards to interactive audio by providing information, instruction, resources, guidance and enlightenment not only to its members, but to content providers and listeners throughout the world.

2. Attend the Game Developers Conference (www.gdconf.com) and E3 (www.e3expo.com).

3. Buy the book *The Complete Guide to Game Audio* by Aaron Marks.
Similar to Hollywood and the music industry, talent is important... but it's not the most important thing! Networking goes a very long way in helping to achieve your goals.

Q: Do you need tons of expensive equipment, studio time, or access to any special connections to start composing?

A: Not really. Technology and equipment is so advanced now that you could have a complete digital studio at your fingertips for under $10,000 thanks to computers, software and plug-ins. The same quality would have cost millions of dollars in a studio less than 10 years ago.

Q: What are the perks of your job?

A: Again I would have to say that the pleasure I get when I accomplish something that no one has ever done before is the greatest perk and feeling. Ptolemy once wrote of Alexander the Great, saying: "His failures towered over other men's successes." This has always been a saying I've kept with me. Even if you dare mighty things and fail, it still may be a great accomplishment. Being defeated is often only a temporary condition... Giving up is what makes it permanent. Nothing I have ever tried to accomplish has ever been easy, so when something positive eventually happens it makes it all worth the time, effort and sacrifice that was put in.

Q: Rumor has it you live in a theme park ride of a house: Do tell...

A: Yeah... think Michael Jackson's Neverland, except replace the young kids with strippers and midgets. Seriously though, I've always prided myself on being the kid who never grew up. I love the fact that I have Peter Pan syndrome and I'm damn proud of it. I like to surround myself with all the things I ever wanted. If you can picture giving a 10 year-old lots of money to build his dream estate... that's pretty much my place. Spider-Man rooms, magic Houdini bathrooms, a full arcade, movie theatre, game rooms, cartoon cels, indoor waterfalls, dinosaurs, castles, Egyptian tombs, pirates and baseball rooms are just some of things that inhabit my lair. Oh yeah... my music studio is there as well.

I like to be surrounded by things that help me create and remember the feelings and thoughts I had as a kid. At its core, the videogame industry is all about having fun. I like to surround myself with as much fun as possible, especially in the place I spend 90% of my time. It inspires me.

Q: How lucrative can game music be as a profession?

A: You can make anywhere from $50,000 to $1 million a year depending on how hard you work, how good a businessman you are and how good the projects you work on end up selling.

GREG FISCHBACH
Founder, Acclaim Entertainment

"This business goes through cycles – at times, there aren't enough suppliers of game product to meet demand for certain platforms and titles. Then, when there are finally enough providers, the market switches to a licensing model, where the brands themselves are needed to get product onto the market... And, in many ways, become more important than the content itself. Right now: Licenses are strictly a marketing vehicle – content is the most important thing.

One thing I see that's troubling is how the mainstream videogame industry somehow went off on this bent where it began to think greater realism and more buttons meant better titles. It's begun to limit the audience. If you look at a phenomenon like casual games, the user interface is incredibly simple – anyone can pick up and play these titles, and the mouse used to control them has what, two buttons? The problem is that marketers have always looked at their traditional audience as well-educated 18-24 year-old males. That's OK – they're a part of the market. But what we're starting to find out now is that maybe casual gaming is the bigger part of the pie, suggesting that companies should start to design titles that are more accessible.

Looking back over Acclaim's history, I'd say one of the smartest things we did was to be the first company to move into licensed games – it gave us a real edge and the ability to strengthen our marketing dollars. It's easier to sell something consumers already recognize, and saves millions, since the product already has brand recognition to support it. We were also the first game publisher to be platform-agnostic – a decision based on economic modeling, the method all smart companies should use when making the decision to go exclusive or not.

I would also advise prospective publishers to have a solid green-light process in place that fosters dialogue between various departments including sales, branding, product marketing, development and finance. All areas have to be involved, no matter if your company is 25 or 2500 people, and everyone has to buy into ideas being considered for approval. Teamwork is everything – you need to invest in your people, because when they're motivated and trust in one another, it's amazing what you can accomplish.

As for pitfalls I'd caution people about, let's start with this – sometimes being first to market with a certain concept can be very profitable, but sometimes, being cutting-edge is very dangerous. From a marketing standpoint, *BMX XXX* brought more visitors to our website in the 3-month period before its launch than any other product in our entire history. You'd think we'd have been shipping millions; instead, thousands were more accurate. There was a complete disconnect with mass merchants: They just weren't ready for such an edgy product.

Likewise, review scores don't always tell the tale. Our inline skating game did great with critics – I think we sold 3 of those as well. And fun games don't always sell the most: Our *ATV Quad* game played poorly, yet kept selling out at Wal-Mart… we couldn't stock them fast enough. The lesson here is that there's no sure formula for guaranteeing a hit.

Otherwise, unless you're really of a large size, I'd caution publishers to stay out of the next-generation console market. It takes too long to see returns, and a small company can't sustain the potential losses. Right now, young and hungry publishers need to reach out to fresher parts of the business to find success and look for newer, better market segments and revenue streams. I think it's a strategy casual and mobile publishers are proving is quite viable."

LORNE LANNING
Co-Founder, Oddworld Inhabitants

Q: You guys came out of nowhere with *Oddworld*... Was the company a pipe dream, or...?

A: [Co-founder] Sherry McKenna and I were working for a special effects company, where we had no creative input. I wanted to be a storyteller and own my own intellectual property, and knew videogames were the medium of the future. It's all about creative control.

Q: And the money to do this came from where?

A: Venture capital. We ran into a guy who saw how much money the publisher Rocket Science had raised and wanted to write his own get rich quick story.

Q: You must've been wishing on the right star, eh?

A: It's all about who you know. And smart business negotiation... But there was also some random, dumb chance to it.

Q: So you attribute your breakout star power to luck?

A: I think luck is something you create. Timing was everything for us, but we knew that money was going to be coming into the technology business in coming years. Because we did our homework, setting out to get some of that money was much easier. You have to understand the market before you can master it.

Q: Then *Oddworld*'s grand reception was no surprise to you?

A: Heh. I always say it's pleasant to have success, but when you borrow a million dollars to make an entertainment product, you really have to plan on succeeding. We were even ready to walk away from our initial investment proposal if we didn't get what we want, because we were so confident in our capabilities.

Q: But not everyone can afford to be that ballsy...

A: Hey, I believe being creative and innovative is safer than taking the "me too" route most game developers do.

Q: Your best suggestion for anyone who'd care to break the bank via gaming, then?

A: [Hitting it big] has more to do with work ethic than any approach. You can't have low standards. If someone thinks they can do great work that'll blow people away on a 9 to 5 schedule, they're getting into the wrong business. It's like the Olympics... Don't train your ass off, and you'll never win a gold medal.

BRUCE HACK
CEO, Vivendi Games

Q: Vivendi controls quite a large number of big-name properties. Any secrets you can share for successfully managing and leveraging so many brands?

A: Franchise planning is critical. VU Games' brand strategies are developed through quantitative and qualitative information; we assess market opportunities by geography, platforms and genres, and then place what we believe are well-educated bets on our key properties.

Q: Forget new franchise entries, though. Rumor has it even your older titles still do big numbers...

A: Yes, VU Games has a wealth of internally owned intellectual property like *Warcraft*, *StarCraft*, *Diablo*, *Crash Bandicoot* and *Spyro*, which are hugely important to the future success of our company. Mining our vast library of more than 700 titles is a priority for VU Games.

Q: Every enthusiast out there thinks they can run a videogame company better than you. But what are some of the challenges you face running the business on a daily basis that the average gamer would never dream of?

A: Games are expensive and risky, often take two years to complete, aim at global markets which differ substantially in taste, and are in no short supply. All that said, I welcome any idea a fanboy or fangirl wishes to send my way.

Q: What's your company's publishing strategy in a nutshell?

A: Our publishing strategy is global – based on consumer tastes by region, platform and genre. We believe we can make nearly any game demanded by the market. Some of our franchises, such as *Crash* and Spyro, appeal to younger audiences. Others, like *Diablo* and *SWAT*, appeal to a very specific demographic – usually males 18-30.

ED BOON
Co-Creator, *Mortal Kombat*

"One thing you should never, ever do if you want to market a hit title: Set out to copy a game that's already out.

Saying 'let's do *Gears of War*' in a different setting, for example, doesn't work. The whole point is that *Gears of War* is different – that's what makes it so amazing. A game that's novel has a way better chance of monopolizing sales charts and headlines. It may sound like a smart bet to clone something popular and add a slight twist at first, but if you go that route, you're screwed to begin with.

So many companies play it safe – and I can understand that, given that game development now requires such huge investments. There's this perception that the only way you're guaranteed to succeed is by doing something that's worked before. But formulaic titles never turn out to be as big a sensation as you'd hope. You have to set out trying to do something big to accomplish something big, so to speak.

As for maintaining some sort of longevity when it comes to hitting it big in this business and staying at the top, the trick is to do something different with every new game that helps to revitalize the franchise on which it's based. I've seen a lot of game sequels where designers and marketers do the same thing over and over... they all do well at first, but sell fewer and fewer units with each successive iteration.

Developers and publishers are afraid to change. But the only way to win big is to gamble big and take risks. Novelty is important. People like to lump games into categories, e.g. another World War II shooter or fantasy role-playing game. So if you don't have a game with an immediate, original hook, it's instantly discounted.

As for when you're working with an existing property like a movie or TV show, marketing and PR need to play a huge role in your publishing plan. Programmers and artists aren't trained to promote these types of titles. However, conversely, when it comes to original IP, I'd like to think that marketing and public relations people would take the time to ask creators about their games and get to know each product.

Striking gold when it comes to achieving commercial success with games is elusive, though. It's honestly like winning the lottery – it's a combination of luck, hard work and timing. If there was a set formula for topping the charts, everyone would be using it."

DON BLUTH
Co-Creator, *Dragon's Lair*

"Coming from a background in movies and storytelling, we knew that there was something magical about a tale in which a character goes through incredible hardships, but somehow triumphs at the end. That's the secret to success *Dragon's Lair* hooked into. Nowadays, videogame companies are recognizing this and hiring professional writers to come in and pen their scripts. But blending a fun element with a story that grabs you right away is an essential concept for gaming success that *Dragon's Lair* picked up on way back when.

Even so, when we were doing the game, we didn't have an idea that it was going to be successful from the start. We just thought we were making another title that would make a little money. So everyone was just animating and the super caution that's always present when you're animating for a feature film went out the window, and everyone just started having fun. The animators would try new things and there was a spirit of adventure that permeated the air. Everybody was just trying to make themselves laugh. Playtime was what it was all about, and at the end of the day, this relaxed atmosphere translated into the final product – much to its benefit."

JANE JENSEN
Creator, *Gabriel Knight* and Co-Founder, Oberon Media

Q: A lot of women love your games – is there a trick you can share to successfully designing titles for or marketing interactive games to them?

A: It's hard to stereotype a gender, because some women do like traditional action games. But it's generally true of the studies I've seen, especially for older women, that what they don't like is violence, intense competition, things that take a long time to get into and, in general, 'twitch' games. They do like story, character, an interesting setting, and a relaxed pace.

Q: How do you design products that appeal to the mass market's tastes?

A: For me, it's not really a choice. I design games that I would like to play, and being a woman in my early 40s, I tend to have the same likes and dislikes as the demographic I'm trying to hit. I love puzzle games and a good story and personality in any game.

Q: Are women more prone to certain genres – say, adventure or action? Why so?

A: Yes, adventure games always had a very high female ratio at Sierra – much higher than any other genres of games at the time. And puzzle games like *Bejeweled* have as high as an 80% female audience ratio in the downloadable game market today. Female gamers shouldn't be underestimated.

Q: Do you believe the industry provides enough content to address these topics?

A: Not traditional publishers like Activision or UbiSoft. However, the online downloadable market is a completely different story. On places like RealArcade or Microsoft Zone or Yahoo! Games there are many titles aimed at the female market, and they've done very well.

Q: Critics and designers largely lament the relatively small number of girls that are passionate about gaming. Could it be they just haven't figured out how to market the message, or are women just not the game-playing sort in general?

A: Women and girls are absolutely game players. *The Sims* is a great example of how strong that demographic could be. There's just not great product available in most game venues so women tend to ignore gaming as something that they're not interested in, [creating an opportunity smart game makers can capitalize on].

Q: If given free range to design a product that appealed strictly to women, what would it be about, what would gameplay involve, etc?

A: When I founded [casual gaming giant] Oberon Media, we dedided to squarely target that downloadable games market. I focused on puzzle games, but injecting more story and character work into them with the goal in mind of appealing, if not strictly to women, then particularly to women. Women don't have 3 hours an evening to get into something heavy like an RPG. They want something that's fun and relaxing to play for an hour after the kids are in bed or on their lunch break – the digital game equivalent of a crossword puzzle or solitaire. At the same time, women also tend to be big readers and want to get emotionally involved with characters and a gripping storyline. An adventure game is just a more interactive version of a novel [at heart].

Q: Anything to say to game manufacturers who spent years foolishly ignoring this market, and those who still have yet to realize what a moneymaker it can be?

A: I think there's going to be much more attention paid to the female market in the future. The downloadable game market is growing like mad and is very profitable. It's a nice vindication that women DO like to game.

Q: Why is it you feel the titles you've worked on personally resonate so strongly with both genders?

A: I think any good writer can hopefully appeal to a wide range of people. Many good female novelists do not appeal ONLY to women. I write in more of a mystery and thriller genre, which does have a pretty good crossover rate. And then I don't tend to put in gameplay that I don't like, so I guess that makes it more accessible to women like me.

Q: Will any lessons learned in terms of the female market be applied to your upcoming project(s)? How and why so?

A: I'm just doing what I've always done. What I have learned is that you can build the right product, but if you can't get it to the right audience, there's a problem. I think the real challenge is in marketing and sales. If we build a game women will like, how do we let them know about it? That's where we have a real mountain to climb.

JONATHAN "FATAL1TY" WENDEL
Professional Gamer

"The secret to anything is practice. Even though I'm playing games for a living, it's just like a full-time job. You have to put in your hours. There's a lot of travel involved too. I've visited so many places that I can hardly remember them all. Germany, Singapore, Australia... I just got back from Dallas, and was in Los Angeles the week before. Now I have to return almost immediately after. In the last 4 weeks, I've been away on business trips equally as many times.

If you want to make it big though, you have to be smart with spending. Any cash I earn is invested right back into my company. I want to sponsor teams and events... host my own LAN party. Helping others make their dreams come true and growing the gaming community is what's most important. You'll never make it big if you don't care about your fans. In the past, top gamers wouldn't even give normal people the time of day. I've got 200 emails from fans in sitting in my inbox right now… I always do my best to answer every one.

As for gaming tips that'll help you climb the ranks? You have to understand the pro mentality. I study opponents, learn how to counter them. It's all about perform-ance under pressure. There's this internal drive that compels me to win. Like how Tiger Woods dominates his sport, that's how I have to do mine. No matter what I do, I dedicate my focus to one thing and one thing alone: Being the best there is.

There are downsides to success, though: It's like how [Andre] Agassi trained all the time as a kid…. he missed out on his entire childhood. By doing this, I effec-tively threw away any hope of having lived the life of a normal teenager or twen-ty-something. But I'm blessed to be a part of the professional gaming circuit. It'll make one hell of a story to tell my grandchildren. And while I intend to keep com-peting, if it all goes away tomorrow, it's no big deal… I've earned enough to see me through 4 years of school without student loans!"

BRUNO BONNELL
Founder, Infogrames

"We, as an industry, sell dreams. You have to respect that.

Still, I'm a firm believer in market share. And a company is a living body – noth-ing about it should ever be set in stone.

Let's say you buy an Accolade or a Legend. If a studio isn't performing up to stan-dards, you can always change your mind, change the management, etc. Failing that, you can also incorporate people into other parts of your organization.

Shutting down an operation is a purely pragmatic decision – in many cases, a stu-dio, as much as we're fond of it, just may not be delivering the necessary level of quality in its products we demand. I may have been too hasty in the past in acquiring minor studios like Accolade and Gremlin. But from the point of view of learning experiences, all of these milestones were very important.

I'm a big fan of [Sun Tzu's literary classic] *The Art of War* – it's my secret to success. As the book teaches, one shouldn't fight an enemy on their strengths. For example, Electronic Arts – in the sports arena, I can't match them face to face. There are a lot of people in the videogame business you just can't go head-to-head with in certain categories. But you can be smart, and attack in areas where they don't expect.

I'm a strong believer in different corporate identities too. Say you go to a club, and you're a good looking man, but blonde. Other good-looking men can also be at the same club who are bald or have brown hair. Some women will prefer you; some women will prefer the other men at the club. The reason for the analogy is that business as a whole revolves around freedom of choice, and therefore it's nothing but a competition. Never forget, everyone is a rival.

The future of interactive entertainment is clearly headed towards easier user interfaces and more accessible games. People want to play what they want, when they want.

Remember the old days of radio in the U.S.? People listened to music all day long, and programming was formatted. Then we became surrounded by music. The videogame business has been similarly insulated. Now we can download on-demand, and play outdoors. Consumers are pushing towards having much more freedom in terms of their gaming experience – that's why mobile and online gaming is growing.

A second evolution is also going to happen in the space where games have traditionally been seen as an art form. In the past, game designers have viewed making their creations as something like producing an opera… they want to produce something epic, titles that offer 30-40 hours of in-depth (and sometimes open-ended) play. Consumers are moving towards a desire for something more complete, and more exciting. It's as if they want to make the move from opera into pop music.

A new generation of consumers is growing that wants quick, fast-paced entertainment that's instantly gratifying. After all, dancing along to a pop song is more fun than watching a 3-hour opera, isn't it? The problem is that in the past, the critics in our game industry have largely been opera specialists. This is going to change going forward."

HOWARD SCOTT WARSHAW
Designer, *E.T. the Extra-Terrestrial, Yars' Revenge*

"People joke about [Atari 2600 mega-flop] *E.T.* being the worst game ever, but keep in mind – to this day, it's still on people's lips. So if you subscribe to "there's no such thing as bad press" school of thought, then *E.T.* is a huge success. There are literally thousands of games that never come up in conversation anymore. Besides: Even after returns it still sold over a million copies. And the game was done in five weeks, start to finish. No other game had been done in less than five months before that (and usually much longer).

I wouldn't buy the rumor about millions of copies being buried in the desert either. No one has ever presented any solid evidence or a single copy (or piece thereof) from that hole. Here's my take on it: It didn't happen.

Here are two reasons why:

1) Burying stuff out in the desert is expensive. Running truckloads of carts, bulldozers and all that cement into the middle of the desert costs a lot of money. If you were a financially failing company, would you spend a bunch of extra money getting rid of an old product or would you recycle the plastic and components to save money while making new products that might sell? It doesn't make any sense.

2) I was pretty tied into the Atari grapevine. If a project like this was going on, I'd have heard about it and I would have grabbed a photographer and flown the two of us out to the dumpsite and got a picture of me standing on top of the heap. That would have been irresistible. Ultimately though, I'm just glad I don't have to store them in MY garage.

Anyhow, after two decades of answering questions about this development I have pretty much covered everything, but there is one moment I never shared before. The project started with a secret phone call to my office.

Once I agreed to do it, I was given two days to get myself and a design to the executive terminal of San Jose airport where a Learjet would be waiting to take me and the design to director Steven Spielberg. And there it was. I was blown away with flying on private jets and riding in fancy limos on the way to see such an iconic figure. The limo from Burbank airport to Warner Bros. studios had a TV, a phone (hey, this was 1982), a full bar and a sink. I had never seen anything like this. I thought it was just soooo cool.

The chief legal council for Atari tried the sink. When nothing flowed, he seemed seriously put off and disappointed. Of course, I'm loving every moment of my trip and it really shocked me that his experience seemed tarnished by the sink. It really struck me, and I remember hoping I would never become that jaded, a [trap potential rich kids] would do well to avoid.

Since leaving Atari, I have been all over the place. I got a real estate broker's license and tried that for a while (hated it), taught classes in everything from Object Oriented Programming to life skills for pre-teens, wrote two books, worked in industrial robotics, did some commercial photography and even got back into videogames for a while. Sometime around the mid-90's I began producing videos and that is truly my passion. Capturing people revealing themselves on camera and delivering that to an audience is irresistible to me.

Laugh if you will, but remember – I also made [huge hits] *Yars' Revenge* and

Raiders of the Lost Ark. Even if you hit it big once, not everything you do will be a success. If you're smart, you'll remember that – and not let the failures get to you."

MARK REIN
Vice President, Epic Games, Makers of *Gears of War*

"There's no secret to succeeding in this business besides making what you love. Make sure you love to play and are passionate about any game you're working on, and hope that there's a ton of people out there who agree. You should always listen to the fans and other game developers, but ultimately, a successful product has to be one you enjoy. If you love it, chances are others will too.

The main thing, though, is just to be smart about what you do. Epic's succeeded because we're financially independent, and have spent sweat equity to develop our own intellectual property. That way, we've been able to self-fund titles and take games to publishers from a position where we have ultimate creative control. Of course, that said, luck plays a huge role in any game [industry] enterprise.

I would also warn you not to let other people get in the way of your ideas and to always think about products' commercial viability. As a developer, you want to make something that you adore, but also that a publisher can sell. I guess the key is to have a product that people are interested in and want to talk and learn more about, then giving them the means to do just that.

You also have to be smart about how you handle your business once you've achieved some measure of success. The most intelligent thing you can do: Reinvest in your own studio and people. A lot of the money we make at Epic goes into our employee bonus plan – we put a high value on our team. You can do well too by creating your own IP, hiring the best people and treating both with the utmost respect. That said, developers too determined to hold onto their

IP or obsessed with making certain visions become reality can sometimes wind up going down with the ship...

But if there's one piece of advice I'd say game makers and marketers should take away above all else, it's this: You can't build a successful title based on someone else's expectations. There's no way to second guess what the market wants or reviewers will respond to. All you have control over is your own game. Make what you want, the way you want, and chances are, everything will fall into place."

MORGAN WEBB
Co-Host, G4's *X-Play*

Q: How'd you get started in the gaming industry?

A: I have enjoyed games all my life, starting with classics like *Combat* on the Atari 2600 and later *Zelda*, *Phantasy Star* and tons of *Contra*. Now I have to say my favorite games are first-person shooters, but I also have a soft spot for RTS titles and RPGs. I officially got my start in the gaming industry on *X-Play*. They needed a woman with a passion for playing games, and I wanted to play games all day. Sometimes these things just work out.

Q: Any thoughts on climbing the corporate ladder?

A: I got my start in broadcasting doing computer help and tips on a live daily show called *The Screen Savers*, and it was hard to gain credibility with viewers. They assumed I was just a mouthpiece who had no idea what I was talking about, and they had no qualms about telling me so via email and message boards. Over time the viewers started to accept that it was possible for a woman to have an interest in and understand technology. I suppose the challenge was partly my own fault. I chose technology as a field partly because it included few women. I enjoy challenging stereotypes.

Q: How can other folks, especially women, looking to make a name for themselves as advocates of gaming get a start in the media or television business?

A: Before we attempt to force women into the gaming industry, we need to get more female gamers. It's a natural progression. Publishers can help: We need to start outreach when women are young, to get them hooked early. Most games aimed at younger girls are cheesy and terribly made, such as *Mary-Kate and Ashley: Sweet 16 - Licensed to Drive*. The mechanics were so bad I just imagine girls putting it down in frustration and assuming they were just bad at games. These games do a disservice to the industry.

AL LOWE
Creator, *Leisure Suit Larry*

Q: How'd you get started in the gaming industry?

A: Growing up in the countryside in the '50s outside of St. Louis, I was a musician, and wound up getting a masters degree in education. What background would better suit someone for this biz? (Note the sarcasm.) I guess it helped that I was a geek before that term even existed; the type of guy who jumped up and fixed the projector when it didn't work.

When it came to computers, I started out thinking I'd explore the lucrative field of management software for music festivals: I actually wrote a 20-program suite. Thankfully, I started making adventure games and things just snowballed. The key takeaway being that background doesn't matter, talent does: Nobody in the game business gives a damn if you have a degree if you can't perform. If you're looking to break in, you need to train yourself to be good at some aspect of game creation, which, on a happy note, can now be self-taught by working on a Web-based game or mod.

Q: How can developers or designers make themselves stand out in today's next-generation game industry?

A: Back in the old days, one person with a vision could do something spectacular. Today, it costs too much to take a chance on people – games are so expensive, publishers can't afford for them to fail. Nowadays, everything's done based on focus groups or testing: Games get watered down because they're designed by committee.

So don't go the traditional route if you can avoid it. The Web's the way to make a name for yourself. In fact, I think the retail game business is in serious trouble. The rise of independently developed games is imminent, just as it was for indie music and films. Either way, you have to be an auteur – a successful scriptwriter, for example, makes a movie in his or her own vision. If you rattle off the most successful games in history, very few are designed by committee.

Q: Is there any consistent predictor for how successful an interactive title might be?

A: Unfortunately, you just can't predict success – good games don't necessarily always sell, nor bad games fail. But having a great game does help. Ultimately, the success or failure of most hinges on whether they're effectively handled by a visionary: Someone must take the responsibility at the end of the day and make sure the concept isn't tampered with or diluted from its original form. Honestly, the best games are made by a team that fits in one room (if you can't fit, you're too big).

Some general advice, though:

• Avoid doing everything yourself – we're long past the point and era where major hit games could be designed in this fashion.

• Skip out on going to work for a large corporation filled with nameless cogs powering the machine; you'll never be heard from again.

• If you can, limit yourself to a small group. A handful of talented people can produce something truly great.

• Only attempt projects you can handle: For a tiny team, this would not include first-person shooters and MMOs.

• Don't attempt to create titles in large, bloated genres. These categories are filled, and have been done to death.

Q: Why did *Leisure Suit Larry* succeed – and might its titular hero ever stage a triumphant comeback?

A: Because people can relate: Every guy has put himself on the line at one time or another and failed, and been put down for it. The loveable loser has been around as long as comedy itself – I just put a new spin on the stereotype, that being quirky humor and borderline naughtiness.

The truth is that Larry was the perfect character for his time, just as adventure games were the perfect titles for their time. Unfortunately, more people recognize him than a "leisure suit" these days, and it's kind of hard to tell a joke that folks aren't in on…

BILL KUNKEL
Co-Founder, *Electronic Games* Magazine and Author, *Confessions of the Game Doctor*

Q: To what do you attribute your success in the videogame industry?

A: Durability and flexibility. If you last long enough and continue to stay abreast of the industry, you'll come back into vogue. It's like any other form of show business… Remember, John Travolta was doing "Look Who's Talking" flicks before

Tarantino rescued him with "Pulp Fiction."

Genuine veterans, people who have paid their dues in this industry, will similarly go in and out of vogue. The trick is being able to stay alive during the slumps. That's where the flexibility comes in; the more skills you possess (journalism, marketing, design, art, programming, etc.), the more scenarios become available for remaining plugged into the culture, even when you're not at the top of the food chain. Games are tech-driven and even a short time out of the loop can make it almost impossible to get back in.

Q: Any lessons you've learned scaling to the top of the biz others would do well to remember?

A: Never sell yourself short. Put a value on yourself and, if it's realistic, stick to it. Someone once taught me that hungry people make mistakes. Even if you are hungry, never let them know.

Q: If someone wanted to get rich off gaming, where should they focus their energies these days?

A: There are so many areas to exploit, from garage band-level creations that sell to mobile systems and online sites to $20 million games... But the real money is always at the same place – at the top.

Q: If I wanted to set myself apart from the average rank and file, how would I do so?

A: Wear your underwear on the outside? Do a good and consistent job? Honestly, if you're waiting for the industry to make you a star, good freaking luck. Look at guys like Tommy Tallarico and CliffyB; they marketed themselves to the point where their name had value in an industry that does anything it can to keep the creators largely anonymous.

Q: Is there a trick to developing hit titles or picking hit games to publish?

A: If it was a trick, people would establish that they could perform it, lease the secret and then retire. Tricks only happen in cheat codes and in magic shows.

Q: The most common misconception about those who succeed?

A: That they were lucky. Luck, as Branch Rickey once observed, is "the residue of design."

Q: The one thing every game industry mogul should remember?

A: Life'll kill ya.

SHIGERU MIYAMOTO
Creator, *Mario / Donkey Kong / The Legend of Zelda*

Q: Most of the smash hit franchises you're known for aren't just huge moneymakers – they're also 20 years old and still generating massive returns to this day. How do you continue to pump out the blockbusters?

A: Well, if you look back at [franchises like] the *Mario* and *Zelda* series, we don't really update those games until we have some type of new capability or technology to apply to them. We don't take the same engine and just create a sequel. Every time we create a follow-up to a title, we rebuild the game, recreate its systems and create an entirely new game. I think that's one of the biggest reasons we continue to innovate and do so well.

When I think back on how an iconic character like Mario is different from an iconic character like Mickey Mouse, to maintain that popularity, it has a lot to do with the way they're presented. When new technology and enhancements occur, and the character is presented again alongside them, they appear to stay fresh. Whereas with a character that's pure 2D animation, you're stuck within the confines of that medium and so it doesn't retain the freshness, even though you create new versions, because you're basically retaining the same elements as before. I think I've been very fortunate that over the years, as I've created new games, I've been able to keep the characters fresh [and sales figures high] by keeping the experience fresh.

Q: What makes Nintendo a continued family favorite – and why will it win this generation's console war?

A: I'm not sure there is a war – it's the media who's calling it that. When you look at the situation in different terms, we don't see this as being a "next" generation for us – we see it as being a "new" generation. We've said this before; it's very easy for a company to look at an existing market, think about what it wants, and create a product to try to serve consumers in that market.

But when you do that, you only capture the attention of a portion of that market, and you never get beyond that. That's why we're looking at a new market. We're trying to find out what it is people desire that they're not getting elsewhere and going in that direction with the Wii. We're demonstrating that we've created a product that goes beyond the boundaries of what people expect from a videogame and bringing in new consumers. Whoever gives the people what they want; that's what'll determine who the winner is on tomorrow's battlefield...

Q: What do competitors like Microsoft and Sony miss about salesmanship that Nintendo seems to comprehend so well?

A: What they really haven't done is attempt to expand beyond their core user base. Nintendo is looking at a much broader market. Our motto for some time has been to target people from ages 5 to 95 and everyone in-between – people will all types of interests. If we can really go after this mass market, and manage to create a meaningful impression, it's better for the industry as a whole.

Nintendo has been talking for a long time about its direction, and it should be apparent that we're moving in a very different direction than everyone else. I don't feel like a part of any next generation. We're entering a new generation. Microsoft and Sony are doing the same things. We're doing different things. And because of that, it's not even a competition.

Q: With costs and associated risks higher than ever in the videogame business, what's the solution to saving the industry from itself?

A: I think the answer is "Wii," naturally. As you've seen with Nintendo DS, we've sold a very large number of systems and attracted a new audience. Similarly, with Wii, by making these new types of interfaces, even people making the same types of games year after year are being inspired by the opportunities this new control scheme creates. We're filling them full of new ideas that they can then take and incorporate into their own game design. As they wind up creating new videogame experiences that people are able to experience and play, the audience for these titles is going to expand and attract new users. As long as we continue to expand the overall videogame audience, I think that will prove the solution to our industry's current problems...

Q: Any advice you'd be willing to share with aspiring designers hoping they can come anywhere close to filling your storied shoes?

A: My design philosophy is that you have to take the overall game environment, including the player him or herself, and use that to really capture people's attention. The thing about an interactive environment like a videogame is that it's fun and interesting because people voluntarily enter the interactive space and have an experience there of their own accord. It's not somewhere you go just to look at flashy images on-screen; it's that interactivity that makes things interesting. Because of that, in my game designs, I have to try to think up ways to not only make the game design itself interesting to encourage people to enter that interactive space. I also have to think up ways to make the image of people playing games interesting, because it's something that entices other people to play the game.

TODD HOLLENSHEAD
Co-Owner and CEO, id Software

Q: Should you go into this industry planning to achieve overnight success? If not, what are some more realistic expectations people should have?

A: Well, I don't think that there's any proven formula that says that if you do these X number of things that you're going to have a massive success. And everybody who has had success, there are a lot of different factors you can credit that success to, as well as different approaches. At id, our track record speaks for itself: Not everything we've done has been a great success. We've had projects we've had to cancel, game design directions that we experimented with that didn't work out, months of the company's effort that was wasted, huge negative returns on investment from an economic standpoint.

But obviously, we are game-focused. We don't think for our titles it's about a movie license or big-name actor, not that we haven't worked with these sorts of people before. That's not the core of the experience we're trying to create; we think it's the game itself that matters. So that then is really our formula for success: To have an exacting standard of quality and make sure that you put play itself first and foremost. You always have these competing philosophies about how long you should take, what your technology window is… Those definitely have to be taken into account, but for us, game quality has always been paramount, and the way we've always approached every project.

That won't always work if you're an Electronic Arts who has a title like *Madden NFL* that comes out every August and have to waste millions on tie-ins and licensing, or gearing products to launch timed with movies and other franchises. It's not to say that that's a wrong approach – it's just not the right approach for every title.

Q: Is there some background or insight you'd like to share with developers, financiers or publishers looking to achieve a similar track record as yours?

A: Generally, most publishers that have been successful in the business know that there are competing priorities, and sometimes those priorities have to be different depending on what the project is. Timing may be far more important on one title than for another. For us, we don't lose any sleep, or marketing leverage, over trying to synchronize with specific events or licenses. If a game's release date slips for us, it's not a big deal. But if we ship a bad game, then we've wasted all the time and effort we put into making that IP and trying to make it successful. And if it's the sequel to one of our franchises, like *Wolfenstein* or *Doom*, then we've diluted the brand – not to mention cost ourselves in terms of sales down the road when we go to work on another project.

I think most publishers understand that, but, because of a shareholder-driven focus on quarterly returns, priorities in retrospect tend to get out of whack. At the end of the day, shipping May 15th vs. March 31st isn't a big deal in the grand scheme of things, even if it causes a publisher to miss a quarterly number. Unfortunately, the market's not sophisticated enough to take that into account. I think people have to be a little bit more Warren Buffett-ish about it, and try to court more long-term investors versus those just jumping on the bandwagon because of momentum behind the stock. When we have tough conversations with most publishers about games, they understand the financial commitment, but they always worry about what Wall Street or their shareholders will think. In that case, you really have people involved in the decision-making process who aren't helping you to make better choices. That I think is the big issue on the decision-making side for publishers.

And I think that for financiers, they need to remember that anything great requires a great deal of time to come to fruition – and sometimes, seeing it through to the end requires more patience. Sometimes it also requires a greater investment to reap a more meaningful long-term reward. You can look at a lot of examples in the industry, such as [legendary designer] Will Wright: *The Sims* was like a sandbox experiment, and it's the biggest game franchise of all time now. But if he wasn't given the time and freedom to make the game, and develop it to its fullest potential, look at what the opportunity cost could have been...

There are a lot of people in the industry who don't get the same sort of long leash he does, and it's to the detriment of the games they work on.

Q: Common mistakes developers often make when it comes to the business side of videogames include?

A: Probably the number one mistake the business people at developers make – and I'm probably going to catch hell for saying this – is that they go and figure out what their schedule is based on information from programmers. Generally, bugs are what take the longest to fix, but biz people on the development side are constantly misguided by their programmers. Not intentionally, mind you, but programmers, coming from an engineering standpoint, have a very difficult time conceiving of the unknown, unexplained problems that inevitably come up on the production side that can cause them to have to totally rework various features or in-game elements.

So the businesspeople get bad information, end up making statements to publishers in terms of delivery timing that end up not being true, and don't apply the proper level of discretion in terms of leaving themselves a way out if schedule forecasts are inaccurate. The thing about software development is that, especially when innovating technologically, you're trying to push the envelope and fix problems that haven't been solved before. So you really don't know what it takes to correct them. And until you're in optimization mode, you're really just making wild guesses about what the schedule will be, and if you present what's really a guess to somebody as fact because they want you to have that confidence that what you're telling them is true instead of just admitting that there's some uncertainty, well... You get into a situation where you postpone very hard conversations until the point in time in development where it's worst to have them, so you just compound your misery.

Q: id Software has always played to the hardcore gamer with most of its concepts – thankfully, you always back them up with superior technology. For the benefit of all these developers focused on similarly-themed sci-fi or run-n-gun outings,

please tell us once and for all. From a business standpoint, should so many people be trying to do the same things you folks do?

A: Certainly, I'd be dishonest if I said that having John Carmack and his technological skills wasn't a huge factor in our success. So I don't think that game development is just taking some genius kernel of an idea and figuring out how to make it work with minimalist goals in terms of implementation. We do things a little bit differently: We are a technology-centric company – John always thinks about where he can get the most impact from a technology standpoint that'll make a casual audience go wow... something that immediately stun anyone, even if they're not a gamer.

Whatever you do, you can't simply copy the greats and hope you'll succeed – you have to make some sort of impact. There are people who've licensed our technology who haven't overwhelmed people visually that have done huge business. Look at the Infinity Ward guys with *Call of Duty* and Valve with *Half-Life*; games that were built off of technology licensed by id, years after the first id game came out using it, so the sheer technical wow factor was lessened. What made these games successful was that the developers innovated in their own ways, whether through scripting, atmosphere, whatever... There are copycat games out there that can achieve some measure of success, but to have the breakout hits, you really have to push the envelope somewhere. It doesn't have to be everywhere... you don't have to try to innovate everything at once. That's a flaw a lot of developers have: They see something cool, and their eyes get real big, but their appetite exceeds their ability to execute. They want to cram in every gee-whiz technical feature; you just have to pick your spots where you have your core competency and execute as well as you can.

Q: Any famous last words for people hoping to break in and master the business, then barnstorm the charts?

A: Breaking in is tougher than it used to be, just because the financial requirements to get a full-blown PlayStation 3, Xbox 360 or PC title done are a lot more than they were back in the *Doom*, *Wolfenstein* or even *Quake* days. It's not easy to get a game out. But I think that the studios that keep their ego in check and are willing to learn as they work can be successful. Guys like Croteam with *Serious Sam*, or Remedy with *Max Payne* or DICE with *Battlefield 1942* – there's a lot of blood, sweat and tears that went into making those games, before any of these guys got any notoriety at all. They slaved away in obscurity until they had something that was really impressive to show that could move them foreward. To me, it's better to show someone something that's great that you've been working on when it's ready, rather than talk about what it is you don't have yet, and then have to figure out how you're going to have to put it together.

SCOTT MILLER
Founder, Apogee and 3D Realms

Q: From *Kingdom of Kroz* to *Duke Nukem 3D*, *Max Payne* and *Prey*, you've got quite the knack for churning out hits. What's the secret to your success?

A: Self-education.

This started in the mid-'80s when I really poured my focus into learning how to run a business, and I began my lifelong quest to learn everything I could about business and marketing. Even 20+ years later, I read no less than 50 books a year that relate to making games in some way. Just yesterday, I finished *Crafty TV Writing*, and went through half a highlighter doing so, as the book is filled with knowledge we in the game industry can put to great use.

One of the books that influenced me the most was *Positioning: The Battle for Your Mind*. This marketing book, along with others by the two authors, radically altered my worldview on how to make a product that sold itself, rather than needed to be sold. Positioning is a cornerstone of how 3D Realms makes successful games, and was applied to *Duke Nukem*, *Descent* (back when Apogee first kicked off this brand with Parallax Software), *Max Payne*, *Prey* and even our more recently-announced title, *Earth No More*.

I read about 100 books a year, about 80% non-fiction. I'm passionate about self-education. Practically everything I learn ends up being useful to designing games and running a business. And because this has worked out so well for me, it's my best recommendation for anyone else.

Q: What game industry lesson(s) do you wish you'd learned sooner?

A: That everyone makes mistakes. The key is not to repeat them. Mistakes are part of learning, same as the successes. When I'm asked this question, I always have trouble searching for a good answer though, because I never live in the past, I never have regrets and I stay focused on what I need to do to keep climbing.

Q: Where does the real money lie in gaming now?

A: For developers, it's always been the same: You need to own your own IP. This single thing gives a studio everything it needs: Clout, leverage, profits, control and the right to exploit the IP in other markets. This is why publishers so thoroughly resist allowing any IP ownership to studios they work with. Look at the richest, most successful independent studios, like Epic, id, Valve, 3D Realms, Gearbox and Remedy, and they all own IP. This is not a coincidence.

Q: In this era of 100-man production teams, is there a way for someone working in the development or executive trenches to make themselves stand out?

A: I believe people who excel will always rise to the top, unless they work at a company that doesn't appreciate talent. Executives, in particular, need to know games. I can't count the number of industry execs I know or have heard about that do not play games. I wonder if there are movie execs who don't watch movies?

Q: The trick to developing hit titles or picking hit games to publish?

A: The trick is differentiation. You cannot make a clone and expect to have success. And yet the play-it-safe, cover-your-ass mentality of most publishers is just the opposite. If you pitch a project that cannot easily be compared to an existing hit, you might as well be pitching an un-hittable screwball. Publishers will just about always pass on a game concept that isn't basically a clone of a recent success.

And yet differentiation is a core principle of positioning. What it means is that you need to develop a product that has something substantially unique about it, that sets it apart in a meaningful, yet compelling way. For example, with *Duke Nukem*, we created a talking hero while every other game had a silent hero. With *Max Payne*, we created slow-motion gameplay. With *Prey*, we created a story revolving around Cherokee mythology, and also added other never-before-seen gameplay elements, like deathwalk, gravity effects and portals. So, the trick is to zig when everyone else is zagging. Think of it this way: If you're following someone else, by definition, you can't be a leader.

Q: Essential skills every would-be game industry player should possess?

A: Just to give an answer I'm sure will be unique, I'll say this: Learn how to write. Seriously – everyone should take journalism, creative writing and technical writing classes. Luckily, I did, and it has helped me to no end. And even beyond those classes I've read several dozen books on writing in various forms (that self-education thing again). This knowledge helps me tremendously with something I do most of the day: Communicate. When people you deal with cannot write well, it's a helluva problem to have to fight through.

Q: The most common misconception about those who succeed in the game business?

A: That we all have sports cars! Seriously though, I can't speak for anyone but myself, but for me success just means I need to keep trying harder. I never want to let myself, or those around me, down.

Q: Once you do break the bank, what stumbling blocks should you watch for?

A: If you have a lot of cash at your disposal, it's all too easy to go on a spending spree, and buy companies, services, equipment or super-nice offices that you really don't need. You see this time and again when companies hit a new plateau of success, and then burn it up before they know it.

Q: The one thing every budding game industry mogul should remember?

A: Failure is always nipping at your heels. What will you do to outpace it?

TOMONOBU ITAGAKI
Head of Team Ninja and Creator, *Dead or Alive*

Q: To what to attribute your continued critical acclaim and chart-topping commercial performance, as well as status as a proven hit-making videogame creator?

A: Success is simply an outcome of our entire development team's hard work. If anything can be said about my success, or that of the *Dead or Alive* and *Ninja Gaiden* series so far, it's that we didn't focus on being "successful." Instead, we just focused on making the best games possible.

Q: Got some tips you'd care to share for those who'd like to climb the same heights you've scaled?

A: It's important to be in the right place at the right time. But it's also crucial to maintain mutual respect amongst those you work with. In today's competitive game market, it's almost impossible to create a mega-hit title without a group effort – so you've got to be [a team player].

Q: People tend to glamorize the game development lifestyle – what's it really like for you?

A: First of all, our day is not 9-5. On the average, my team members all work 20 hours a day. And, in many cases, 7 days a week during crunch times that can last as long as 6 months. Altogether, I have about 150 guys working day and night.

Q: After all this time and so many smash titles, how do you stay motivated?

A: As many milestones as I've seen in my game development career, I continue to strive to create ultimate games for gamers. They're the ones who keep raising the bar – and pushing me forward.

CHRIS TAYLOR
Founder, Gas Powered Games and Creator, *Dungeon Siege* and *Total Annihilation*

Q: What are qualities, in your mind, that a visionary game designer absolutely has to possess?

A: I would say it's important to understand state-of-the-art gaming technology – but also know the difference between something that looks good and plays good. To understand that videogames are for entertainment and not a sugar-coated IQ test. Lastly, it doesn't hurt to have a sense of humor about this whole business of making videogames, because it really is quite a ridiculous job.

Q: With titles like *Supreme Commander* and *Dungeon Siege*, how do you constantly continue to breathe new life into aging genres?

A: We start out by immersing the player in gigantic 3D worlds. We also use open-ended systems so that the player has the freedom to develop their characters or units any way they like. It's important to focus games on what we consider to be the most entertaining aspects, things like exploration and combat. We also present players with the most important decisions, the ones that have the largest impact on how the in-game experience plays out.

Q: Since development team members are encouraged to keep their head in the clouds, how does any work ever get done around your offices?

A: We try and think of this job as fun. That way we are never at work, and so it follows logically that no work is ever done. Simple!

BRAD MCQUAID

Co-Founder, Sigil Games Online and Co-Creator, *EverQuest*

Q: The secret to hitting it big with massively multiplayer games would be...?

A: Massively multiplayer games require large teams and quite a bit of development time, due to their scope and scale. Entertaining thousands of players in one world for month after month, even year after year, necessitates a very large and detailed world, full of entertaining things to do. *EverQuest* took almost three years to develop before commercial release, and the team grew to almost thirty people. And years after release, [Sony Online Entertainment] still has a very large team and significant budget keeping the franchise updated and interesting, as well as working on expansions.

Q: How else do MMOs differ substantially from standalone counterparts?

A: They are a very different animal, requiring not only large development teams and budgets but also significant amounts of network infrastructure as well as customer service. I guess that's the key [to success]: Customer service. Ultimately, we're not simply making games, we're also running a service, and this does require some very different approaches.

Q: In what ways do you design entire worlds as opposed to levels?

A: Levels are usually associated with single-player games, which are meant to be played from beginning until end. Massively multiplayer persistent games don't really end, and must provide content that entertains players long-term. A large world, lots of areas to explore and quests to complete, as well as something to fall back on (character development, socializing and adventure) do tend to make our games more worlds than a series of levels.

Q: What makes your titles so darned addictive, leading people to coin phrases like "EverCrack?"

A: Three primary areas of focus: Character development, community building and an immersive world. Players build up their characters over time and also acquire experience, knowledge and possessions. And because of the social and interdependent nature of these games, players also develop relationships with other people. Both of these aspects create an ownership that compels players to keep playing over a long-term period, all the while exploring and experiencing a very immersive 3D world.

Q: Let's settle the issue once and for all: Was your original smash hit game so huge just because it was one of the first MMORPGs to market?

A: Actually, *EverQuest* was probably the third MMORPG to market, following *Meridian 59* and *Ultima Online*. And while I do think timing had a lot to do with the game's success, I also think there were many other factors, including its cooperation-centric gameplay, true 3D world and emphasis on character development and game balance.

Q: When setting out to develop blockbuster games, do you and your associates do anything out of the ordinary to get in the creative spirit?

A: We have a very casual working environment and we do a lot of brainstorming and outside of work get-togethers and activities. It's really a fun environment, but there's also a lot of work, and game developers often work many, many hours towards the end of a project.

MARC ECKO
Founder, Marc Ecko Entertainment

Q: From the beginning, you've set out to change the gaming industry's status quo. Why so?

A: Because it needs changing. Consumers don't care about everything that goes into making a game – they only care about the final product. What the industry is producing now is good for people already in it, but it's not good enough if they don't understand what the consumer wants – product that speaks to phenomena in the broader pop culture pool. Not just "games for gamers."

Q: Why is the time right to strike hard in the business – and strike it rich?

A: It's the Wild West out there. We are on the eve of a new platform cycle. Film and gaming will blur. How we consume entertainment is evolving faster than our capacity to understand its impact on us. It is a crazy exciting time, and I'm just glad to be part of it.

Q: Why is it we don't see more individuals of your stature recognizing its potential?

A: It's not that these people aren't out there doing games… it's the level of commitment shown towards creating a credible end-product that is sometimes questionable. I could easily slap my rhino logo on a game, add a dose of sex and violence, and call it a day, but I want to create properties that can stand on their own and be recognized for their rich, original content. That's where success truly lies.

Q: What's the message you're trying to get across to peers, game industry heads and haters alike?

A: If I can make a game, the person reading this can make a game. Hopefully my efforts will open up opportunities for more outsiders. Just because you're categorized as an outsider or you don't know how to program a game doesn't mean that your point of view isn't worthwhile. And just because they continue to put sh*t product on the shelves doesn't mean that you have to keep buying. It's time for a change of pace.

VINCE DESI
CEO, Running With Scissors, Creators of *Postal*

Q: How have you managed to get ahead in the videogame business?

A: By knowing my goals as well as my strengths, and assembling a great team to support my weaknesses.

Q: Any mistakes you've made on your journey to the top?

A: Being too cautious when I could afford to take greater risks.

Q: Where's the true payout these days in gaming?

A: Where it always has been from the very beginning: DISTRIBUTION!

Q: How can someone make themselves a bankable commodity in the game biz?

A: The best thing any individual can do to succeed in the game industry is to focus on a specific mission/goal/talent and then relentlessly pursue it. And, if that isn't clear, don't just go out there and pretend you're a programming designer/artist/modder/marketing genius/publisher or anything that you are not.

Q: The best way for those just getting started to make a name for themselves?

A: Make a game that gets banned in 12 or more countries.

Q: Is there any rhyme, reason or methodology to making hits?

A: There's no trick or secret other than having a clear vision and the will to deliver the vision into a finished product. The ultimate commercial success of the product is based on numerous key factors all coming together and working in a favorable way. If charting success was as easy as defining a theory or creating hit games and a plan to implement them as well, then 99% of the crap that's out there today wouldn't exist!

Q: Vital skills every aspiring game industry hustler needs to possess?

A: A knack for communication and honesty! Not to mention knowing what you're *not* capable of – and finding a way to overcome your weaknesses and what you are missing.

Q: What's the most common misperception about those who realize success in the interactive entertainment biz?

A: That they somehow were more talented than others and that their games were inherently of an excellent design.

Q: Let's say you do strike it rich: Any potential pitfalls big spenders should watch for?

A: Don't invest your own money. Once you've proven you can be successful with your own money, the next time around, find an investor. Because, honestly, lightning doesn't usually strike twice... and there's no reason to lose your ass.

Q: The single most important thing every hopeful game tycoon should remember?

A: You're nobody without your customers and fans!

BRIAN FARGO
Founder, Interplay and InXile Entertainment

Q: How have you managed to make such a name for yourself in the gaming field?

A: I think more than anything that I have been both a gamer and an opportunist. Being successful takes the ability to spot a trend or hole in the marketplace and fill it with the right title. Anyone can be creative for creativity's sake, and there have been many great games that didn't sell well because they don't fulfill any [market need]. It's also important to be nimble and move fast on opportunity when it arises. I've had countless successful games or ventures that had I moved just a week or month too slow I would have lost out. People don't appreciate the sense of urgency you have to have if you want to be successful.

Q: Major errors you've made climbing the career ladder others would do well to avoid?

A: Probably my biggest mistakes have been in spending too much time with employees that don't buy off on the program. There is a certain vibe and mantra that each company has and your fellow workers all need to subscribe to, and when they don't, you have to swap them out for people that do. I spent countless hours trying to get people to come along and in the end we lost a lot of time and missed out on great opportunities.

The other thing to be wary of is trying to grow outside your core business too quickly. In the beginning of a company you look for every possible opportunity, but then with success, you then need to filter out all of the possible opportunities. There is nothing wrong with expansion, but it's a matter of how may things you should take on at one time.

Q: With development and publishing teams being so huge nowadays, how can someone hope to make themselves more than just another nameless gear in the system?

A: I can comment on the things that would impress me for standing out – and most of them are obvious things that people don't do. A full 50% of standing out would just be good old follow-through and professionalism. This industry lacks in that department, and whenever I see people on top of it I am impressed.

People need to return phone calls, keep organized by writing everything down, and they need to communicate the status of projects even if nothing is happening on them. Sounds simple, but most people don't do this. If I see 700 messages in someone's inbox, I know they are disorganized. Development is a bit different in that you need technical skills and gameplay philosophy skills in addition, but you still need to possess the basic attributes that a professional executive needs to have in order to stand out as well.

Q: A key point wannabe industry players should never forget would be?

A: The first thing every mogul should remember is the consumer who buys the games and the people in the industry who helped work with them along their way to the top. It's too easy for success to breed contempt for the people who helped make you successful in the first place.

I've seen certain individuals lose track of the fact that there are people using their hard-earned dollars to buy a game and that these fans expect a certain quality level. I hate to see some of the junk I've seen shoved out knowing it will sell well because of a license or because of its high concept. Not all games come out as "A" quality, but you at least have to do your best to try.

And any mogul should strive to be a great person, and that means returning phone calls and helping give advice to others who also seek to be successful. Once again, it's too easy for success to make people behave poorly… It is always so much more impressive when people are benevolent with their new-found mogul-ness.

Q: Any thoughts on how to improve one's chances of picking hits?

A: For me the trick was to be able to spot voids and other opportunities in the market and fill them with a quality product. I've been involved with wonderful and creative games like *Giants: Citizen Kabuto*, for example, that didn't have the identifiable niche and subsequently didn't sell. And then I've had titles like *Descent* (one of the first retail games that used the Internet for multiplayer gaming) that went on to sell millions.

One needs to be a student of the marketplace to pick those hit games. Developing a hit game is even harder in that you have to first identify and discover an opportunity and then do all the work to make a game happen. Every game I ever shipped had a war story behind it.

SCOTT ADAMS
Creator, *Adventureland* and Founder, Adventure International

Q: How'd you manage to hit it big off gaming?

A: As an early pioneer, I simply wanted to provide the games to play that I wished others were selling! I also tried to treat people fairly as best I could.

Q: Any key errors you made that you'd warn others hoping to follow in your foot-steps not to make?

A: Know when to cut your losses. Sometimes you must retreat before charging ahead again! I failed at that. Also, trying to totally self-finance my company was both an asset and a liability…

Q: Where does the real money lie in gaming now?

A: MMORPGs: Massively Multiplayer Online Role-Playing Games.

Q: How should someone looking to make as big a name for themselves in the business as you've done go about doing so today?

A: Become widely known and have a website that attracts a lot of visitors. Blogging and having an interesting twist to their views on the world would help.

Q: Trade secrets those hoping to make hits should keep in mind?

A: Find players who represent Joe Average and see what they like to play!

Q: Essential skills every would-be game industry player should possess?

A: Perseverance, and having a dream that you are willing to drop all else to follow.

Q: The most common fallacy about those who succeed?

A: That they are different (i.e. better) than anyone else. Many are simply in the right place at the right time; others may be cutthroat businessmen that walk all over people. And really, most important to remember, success is not always measured in dollars in the bank. In 100 years how much do you think this will all matter? Try thinking (and planning) for eternity instead. For example, the life of Mother Teresa measured against a gaming superstar? Which one do you think in the long run made the right choices?

Q: Once you break the bank, what stumbling blocks should you watch for?

A: It is still important to watch the bottom line and cash flow. Also, don't forget: The bottom line is important, but more important is your own sense of ethics. [If you don't play fair], you can win the round, but eventually, you *will* lose the game.

TED PRICE
CEO, Insomniac Games, Makers of Ratchet & Clank

Q: You've enjoyed more than your fair share of success over the last decade – surely it didn't all come down to luck?

A: Actually, I'd prefer to talk about Insomniac's success as a company, since any success I've had is directly attributable to what Insomniac has achieved. There are a lot of reasons Insomniac has been successful as an independent developer. Everyone here loves making games. Everyone here has an opportunity to contribute to what we make and where we're going as an organization. We offer a lot of creative freedom. We're independent and not under a giant corporate thumb. I could go on for several pages...

But what's been most important to me personally has been everyone's commitment to open communication and constant collaboration. This is a commitment that's stayed consistent since we began almost 14 years ago. What I mean by "open communication" is that we make huge efforts to keep everyone in the company fully informed of what's going on with all our projects and with the company. And by "collaboration," I mean that we push people to work face-to-face with others on the complex problems we encounter versus taking an insular approach. In my opinion, giving a lot of weight to these two concepts is essential when you're working in a field like videogames where so many different skill sets are involved.

We're not perfect in either area. But we try really, really hard to address communication problems and collaboration issues as soon as they crop up. And we're always experimenting with new ways to improve on both.

Q: The biggest mistakes you've made during the company's come-up?

A: Lots. But I'll focus on the biggest mistake I've made: Refusing to delegate. It took me years to figure out that I was the worst bottleneck in the company. Early on, a lot of crucial decisions were routed through me, especially design and art decisions. As the company grew and I began to manage more and more people, I couldn't effectively balance what I had to do to run the company *and* to contribute to the games. I was holding on to far too much responsibility as well as micromanaging.

A few years ago, we instituted a department head structure that forced me to let go of trying to manage every person in the company. Then we introduced our project management team, which inherited the responsibility for creating and enforcing schedules. Both moves meant that others ended up doing a much more effective job at something I had been struggling to do for years.

At first I had a lot of trouble staying out of everyone's way. I drove a lot of department heads crazy by continuing to micromanage. But over the last couple of years, I've realized that everyone in the company is far, far happier and more productive when I just let people do their jobs without interference from me. I'm still involved in design and creative direction. And I still run the company. But I feel very comfortable delegating big decisions to many others here. Fixing this issue has certainly helped make Insomniac a better place.

Q: If I were looking to cash out on gaming, these days, where would I want to turn?

A: This industry moves very fast and is constantly changing. There's a pretty good chance that what's making money for developers and publishers now won't be raking in the dough five years from now. (Unless you're Blizzard, that is...)

Anyway, there's money everywhere in the business – handhelds, consoles, PC games, casual games, hardcore games, downloadable content, etc. But there's no way to identify the best company, genre or platform to make money on. And while it's important to find a place where one can be successful and make money, I think it's even more important to find a place where a) people are passionate about what they do and b) you're passionate about whatever it is the team is doing. When people have passion and drive, great things happen and success usually follows.

Q: But let's be honest – in this era of corporate giants, it's pretty hard to stand out...

A: True. So if you want to make yourself attractive to future employers, I'd recommend a few things:

1. Demonstrate Loyalty – Don't jump from company to company. Choose where you want to apply wisely and stick things out even when times are bad. Follow through on your commitments and finish the projects you start. Even when things suck, you'll always learn something. Personally, whenever I see a resume where someone hasn't stayed more than a few years in any one place, it's a big red flag for me. The resumes that are *most* attractive are those where the applicant has been at his or her previous companies for over 5 years and has shown advancement within those organizations.

2. Know Your Craft – We get far, far too many resumes from folks who desperately want to be in games, but who don't want to make the effort to gain an education in their desired field. You need to know your stuff cold if you want to get into the best companies. Plus, the videogame business has become an industry of specialists. Many companies no longer look for a "programmer" or an "artist."   They look for engine programmers, effects artists, riggers, etc. To be successful in a more specialized world, it's important to demonstrate that you can handle these more niche roles – another good reason to seek out training and take it seriously.

3. Work On Great Games – This is a bit harder to control, especially if you want to demonstrate loyalty and are working in a place that doesn't produce amazing titles.

But having a bevy of AAA titles on one's resume speaks very, very loudly. Do whatever you can to join driven, passionate teams and you can accomplish this.

Q: Sage advice – but what about someone working in a sterile, mega-corporate environment?

A: I think the answer depends on your company culture. Here at Insomniac, those who stand out demonstrate the kind of traits that are commendable in any industry: Teamwork, creativity, problem-solving ability, efficiency, passion for the craft, reliability and drive. Yet, more importantly, they also demonstrate these traits *consistently*.

Q: Is there a formula for developing hit games?

A: Obviously, there's no formula or there would be a lot more hit titles. But I'd say the key ingredient is working with a talented and motivated team. The team is where everything starts. If you have great people, great things will happen.

Q: The most common misconception about those who succeed in the videogame industry?

A: That they did it alone. While I agree that our industry needs "rock stars" to elevate our profile with the general public, I think it's important to remember that today's most successful games are big, hairy beasts that require a team of dedicated zookeepers.

I believe that when people do well in the industry, it's because they've worked with others of like mind who contributed as much blood, sweat and tears as the ones who are given most of the credit. It's something we deal with at Insomniac all of the time. For example, I'm generally given much more credit than I deserve on our games simply because I run the company. It's up to me to make sure others receive their due in whatever way I can. If I don't, people get pissed off and rightfully so.

Q: Once you break the bank, what stumbling blocks should you watch for?

A: I'll tell you if I ever break the bank. But I imagine hubris would be the big one.

Q: Something every game industry mogul should remember?

A: Mogul, huh? I'll bet you most developers would cringe at hearing that term.

Anyway, a good industry mantra is "you're only as good as your last game." With more and more smart, creative and motivated people entering our industry each year, no one can become complacent and assume that the same old thing will continue to work for each game. The competition level has always been insane and if you falter, someone else will be there to take your place, whether we're taking about companies, franchises or individuals.

But I think this competitive atmosphere is what actually keeps a lot of us in the industry. It's stressful, fast-paced and sometimes infuriating – but it's still a lot of fun.

DANIEL BERNSTEIN

Founder and CEO, Sandlot Games, Makers of *Cake Mania* and *Tradewinds*

Q: For someone who started out with little more than a dollar and a dream, how'd you manage to eventually wind up doing so well in the business of videogames?

A: By sticking to why it was I got into the business in the first place, and not being distracted by diversions like work-for-hire projects. Instead, as a company, we focused on our main goal – the creation of original IP in the casual gaming space.

In retrospect, we probably didn't grow as fast as we could have, or enjoy the benefits of short-term cash, as a result. But it was the right decision to make from a long-term standpoint. We concentrated on being creative and focusing ourselves as a game studio first, then letting other elements of the business like marketing and distribution evolve later on when needed to support that.

Work-for-hire projects can be profitable, but the real value is in growing a business' long-term revenue potential. *Cake Mania*, as an example, no longer stops where the online downloadable game ends. Even if you don't count sequels, there's the retail, mobile, handheld versions… Basically, when you control the IP, it opens up tremendous opportunities for you. But if you don't control it, you can't capitalize on these chances.

Q: Mind explaining a little further?

A: Sure. To clarify, we made the decision to create a business that's almost like a traditional media company that controls the rights to its IP and licenses out content. Others focus on building high-traffic websites or portals where people can socialize and shop. But I truly believe that consumers simply go where the best content is. The trick is that you have to differentiate in terms of the material you're offering, and really make it stand out, to create that kind of distribution. It's like with the premium cable channels: You tune into HBO to watch certain shows because you know you can't see them anywhere else.

Q: The next great platform aspiring execs should be focused on if they're really hoping to cash in off the medium would be…?

A: In all honesty, there's no one right platform to focus on except the ones that are making money. The funny part is that there are so many competing for people's attention now that are like bright and shiny objects that there's all this noise being created. People need to learn to be smart about how they do business, and learn to sort through the confusion.

I've gone through the dot com boom and bust. And I wind up laughing a lot at some of the decisions people make. A lot of picking the right platform to roll with just goes back to business fundamentals. You have to ask yourself: How does that shiny object relate back to the consumer? I have to question the wisdom of developers who just jump on a platform because it's "the next big thing," like the iPhone. OK – now how are you going to make money off that?

There's something to be said for not being the first to market, but the best: You can learn a lot from people who got their asses handed to them by showing up unprepared for the party. That said, calculated risks are important – just don't forget to calculate properly before taking them.

Q: Speaking as a self-made man, got any handy strategies for rocketing up the corporate ranks you'd mind sharing with industry hopefuls?

A: Learn as much as you can. Coming out of school, I was a programmer and musician: I didn't know anything about business. But the president of [game maker] Monolith let me go out and license some Russian games (the *Rage of Mages* titles) I liked, and suddenly, I was working on the licensing side.

I remember asking my wife if I should do this – I was a musician, remember, and thought I should stick to the sound department. But she simply asked me: When else would you get an opportunity like this? And so I took it. So that's the best advice I can give. Do the same: When you see the opportunity, take it.
You can't be afraid of failure either – it's inevitable that you'll fail, but so what? You'll learn from it. And, many times, on someone else's dime. I've done plenty of bad deals myself, but I've learned from them, and by the time I got to Sandlot, I had a clear vision for what the business should be.

Q: Finally, is there any particular game business stereotype that you feel might need airing out?

A: Yes – a misconception that haunts any game development organization: The fear and loathing that surrounds various departments like marketing, biz dev, sales, etc.

As a game developer myself, I started out fearing the marketing department.

(Often with good reason, or so I thought, such as the time a new female marketing manager removed the sword in [pioneering online game publisher] Kesmai's logo, because she felt it was "too phallic.") But if you want to effectively lead an organization, you have to understand the value of all pieces of the business puzzle, and how they fit together.

The best insight I can share to help dispel this stigma – just try putting yourself in these people's shoes, and understanding the challenges and issues they face on a daily basis.

RAY MUZYKA
CEO and Co-Founder, BioWare

Q: Credit for your string of hits ranging from *Jade Empire* to *Neverwinter Nights*, *Mass Effect* and *Star Wars: Knights of the Old Republic* lies where?

A: BioWare's success is based entirely on the fact that we have a lot of very humble, hard-working and smart people at our company who are allowed to take creative risks. We put quality as our number one studio priority at BioWare, because we believe it leads to long-term success, and as a result we don't release a game until we've achieved and exceeded our high quality targets.

Q: How can someone make themselves a bankable commodity in the game biz?

A: In my opinion, you shouldn't be looking to make yourself a 'bankable commodity,' but rather think about what values you believe in and set high goals for yourself and your organization, then stick to those values and goals. For BioWare, the values we believe in are quality in our products, quality in our workplace and entrepreneurship – all in a context of humility and integrity. Our studio mission is to deliver powerful, emotionally-compelling experiences, and the best story-driven games in the world.

Q: Is there a way for someone working in the development or executive trenches to make themselves stand out?

A: There are a lot of ways to stand out, but in order to create enduring success as an executive you must be willing to commit yourself to what you are passionate about. And surround yourself with people who are passionate subject matter experts in their fields, always remembering that long-term successful consumer brands are not built overnight or with just one product. I've always felt fortunate to be part of an industry that I love and which is always changing, which has made it all interesting and fun, and helped make the long hours, hard work and some-times hectic pace worth it.

Q: The most common misconception about those who succeed?

A: The most common misconception in business (and it seems to keep coming back once every generation) is the myth of the superhero. As an entrepreneur, never forget how important the people you work with are to your organization's long-term success. Rather than being a solo mission, entrepreneurial success really is founded on finding the best people to embark with you on your journey, and continually focusing on taking care of the people you surround yourself with.

Q: The one single rule for succeeding in the games business that should never be forgotten?

A: Stay humble. If you truly understand what it takes to make something success-ful, you find that it is never just one person or department who makes something successful. Rather, it is the culmination of teamwork from a variety of different people that drives the success of your organization and brand, long-term. Humility is one of the core values that my co-founder Greg [Zeschuk] and I try to instill in everyone around us.

ABOUT THE AUTHOR

SCOTT STEINBERG is CMO and publisher of technology supersite **DigitalTrends.com**, which helps over 40 million readers monthly comprehend how games, gadgets and other tech-related products fit into their everyday lives. He's also managing director of Embassy Multimedia Consultants (**www.EmbassyMulti.com**), which counsels developers, publishers, retailers, distributors and financial institutions regarding the development, publishing and promotion of computer and videogames worldwide.

Steinberg's other books include *Videogame Marketing and PR* (**www.sellmorevideogames.com**) and *The Videogame Style Guide* (**www.gamestyleguide.com**). The Industry's most prolific author and radio/TV host, this former *Los Angeles Times* Game Design columnist has covered gaming/technology for 300+ media outlets from CNN to *The New York Times, Rolling Stone, USA Today* and *TV Guide*, including virtually all computer/videogame publications. He's also the founder of half a dozen companies including copywriting outfit Clandestine Media Group, PC game licensor/publisher Overload Entertainment, book publisher P3: Power Play Publishing and Games Press USA, the ultimate resource for game journalists.

Past ventures include turns as a VP of Product Acquisitions for French videogame publisher Microids, Director of Acquisitions for DreamCatcher Interactive/The Adventure Co. and game designer/PR director for Iridon Interactive. He's additionally a proven hitmaker and talent scout for several of the world's largest and most-renowned software houses, and a successful self-publisher of PC/console titles, e.g. *Heavyweight Thunder*, which was produced out of a back bedroom and sold over 75,000 units worldwide. As a decade-long career spanning every discipline from administration and development to finance, marketing and public relations illustrates, he lives and breathes interactive entertainment.

Reach out to him online at **www.scottsteinberg.com**.

"A necessary part of moving game journalism, and games, to the next level."
- Dean Takahashi, Author, *The Xbox 360 Uncloaked*

The IGJA and Games Press Present

The Videogame Style Guide

and Reference Manual

Foreword by Dan "Shoe" Hsu
Editor-in-Chief, *Electronic Gaming Monthly*

DAVID THOMAS, KYLE ORLAND
AND SCOTT STEINBERG
Author of *Videogame Marketing and PR*

WRITE LIKE A PRO

Fitting neatly between *The AP Stylebook* and *Wired Style,* and formally endorsed by Games Press, the ultimate resource for game journalists, *The Videogame Style Guide and Reference Manual* is the first volume to definitively catalogue the breathtaking multibillion-dollar game industry from A to Z.

Exploring the field from yesterday's humble origins to tomorrow's hottest trends, biggest names and brightest stars, *The Videogame Style Guide and Reference Manual* contains all the tools you need to realize a distinguished career in game journalism, or go from enthusiast to editor today!

Features:
- CLEAR RULES FOR USAGE AND STANDARDS
- HUNDREDS OF IN-DEPTH ENTRIES
- NOTABLE NAMES, GAMES AND COMPANIES
- COMPLETE GUIDE TO GAME CRITICISM
- HISTORICAL TIMELINES

OUTCAST

A JEWISH GIRL IN
WARTIME BERLIN

INGE DEUTSCHKRON

TRANSLATED BY JEAN STEINBERG

Fromm International Publishing Corporation
NEW YORK

Translation Copyright © 1989
Fromm International Publishing Corporation

Originally published as *Ich Trug den gelben Stern*
Copyright © 1978 by Verlag Wissenschaft und Politik

Designed by Jacques Chazaud

Printed in the United States of America

First U.S. Edition

Library of Congress Cataloging in Publication Data
Deutschkron, Inge.
Outcast : a Jewish girl in wartime Berlin.
Translation of: Ich trug den gelben Stern.
1. Jews—Berlin (Germany)—Persecutions. 2. Holocaust,
Jewish (1939–1945)—Berlin (Germany)—Personal
narratives. 3. Deutschkron, Inge—Childhood and youth.
4. Berlin (Germany)—Ethnic relations. I. Title.
DS135.G4B4213 1989   940.53'18'0943155   89-23337
ISBN: 0-88064-116-9

OUTCAST

1

"You're Jewish," my mother said to me. "You must let the world know that that doesn't mean you're not every bit as good as they."

What did it mean, being Jewish? I didn't ask. What interested me was what was going on outside in our corner of Berlin, on our quiet street. I liked looking out of the window of our apartment on Hufelandstrasse. It may have been nothing more than a sleepy little corner, yet for a ten-year-old there was much to see. I could watch the other children play. I was not allowed to play outside; my parents thought it wasn't safe. I, of course, didn't agree. I knew all the children by name, but

I wasn't allowed to play with them. All I could do was watch. It hurt.

My mother tried to make me understand what she meant by her remark about my Jewishness. I no longer remember what she said; all I know is that I did not understand. But even later on I refrained from touching on the subject, from asking for an explanation. I sensed that it would upset her, and me as well. At that time, in early 1933, I had other, more pressing, problems. I was about to transfer to another school.

The principal of the Königstadt Lyzeum of Berlin in which my parents had enrolled me was astonished to learn that the school I had attended for the past four years was a secular institution. Religion was not part of its curriculum, and its educational methods were far more progressive than those of most other schools. "So, your daughter attended a secular school?" he said with barely disguised sarcasm. "You must show them," my mother said to me after we left his office, "that a secular school is as good or even better than the others." This piece of motherly advice meant as little to me as the revelation that I was Jewish.

I knew that my parents were Socialists, and like most children growing up in a loving family I identified with my parents. My father held some sort of office in the Social Democratic Party, and devoted much of his free time—as a teacher he

had more than most—to party work. I took it for granted that all aspects of life were supposed to constitute a conscious, uncompromising affirmation of socialism, whether by being active in the People's Welfare Organization or shopping at the co-op.

Not only did I share my parents' belief, but it also filled me with self-confidence and pride. It may seem odd, but my fondest childhood memories are not of vacations or other childish pleasures but of sitting with adults in some smoke-filled backroom of a Berlin pub helping fold leaflets. And I was also proud to have my parents take me along on one of their "symbolic" walks, at which Social Democrats "accidentally" bumped into each other and greeted each other loudly with the slogan "Freedom." The May Day demonstrations gave me a taste of the shared feeling of commitment and unity of politically engaged people.

Of course I was not completely unaware of the gathering political storm clouds; no one involved in the political battles of the early thirties could fail to notice them. In my mind's eye I can still see all those different demonstrators: the Communists with their red flags and their bands; the men of the Social Democratic defense organization, with whom I identified; the militarily precise brown columns of the SA, which frightened me. There are indelible memories—of a Communist, mortally

wounded in a clash with Nazis, struggling to get back on his feet, of accounts of pitched street battles between political adversaries, including between Communists and Socialists.

Who the Nazis were, what they were doing and what they wanted, I learned from my father. Hitler means terror, dictatorship, war, he used to tell me. He campaigned tirelessly in the last free election before Hitler's takeover. "Berlin will stay Red," he proclaimed in meeting after meeting, indoors and out. He did not let up even when our next-door neighbor was wounded by a bullet meant for him.

Even though I was not familiar with all the details and did not quite understand everything, I sensed the general tension. When stones were thrown at an electioneering banner we had strung along our balcony, I knew intuitively that I too was involved in the battle.

On that evening, March 31, 1933, I looked out the window, but not at the children at play. I had trouble concentrating. I felt apprehensive; an indefinable sense of danger was in the air. I knew that the Nazis, as their first public anti-Jewish measure, were planning a boycott of Jewish businesses on April 1. I kept looking in the direction of the corner pub, which I couldn't see from my window. It was a known Nazi hangout. I listened for my father's footsteps; he should have been home long ago. Mother too was uneasy. She kept going to

the door to peer down the staircase. She came into my room, pushed me away from the window, and, more harshly than she probably meant to, told me to go and play dominoes with Lotte, our helper, while she herself remained at the window staring out into the dark.

I sat down with Lotte and listlessly began our game. Suddenly the bell rang. My mother appeared in the doorway. Lotte didn't move. At that moment our fear took concrete shape, filling the room. With great self-control, my mother asked Lotte to answer the door. As soon as my mother heard the familiar voice of one of our political friends she ran to the door and pulled him into one of the other rooms. All I was able to hear before they disappeared were the words: "Your husband must get out of town immediately."

Our visitor left, and my mother also got ready to go out. I was terrified, but I didn't say a word. I felt she wasn't even aware of my presence. Outwardly calm, she told me she was going out to look for Father, who probably was still tied up with exams at school, and that she'd be back soon. Without another word she was out the door. Lotte nodded silently. She wasn't much older than I, probably around eighteen, and I don't know which of us was more scared. We tried to resume our game, but it was no use. We kept listening for familiar steps that didn't come.

I don't remember how long we sat like that,

only that Mother didn't return until quite late. Again, she appeared very calm as she told us that Father would spend the night with friends. She didn't tell us why, and I knew that it was better not to ask. Without further protest I went to bed, but from my room I could hear her telling Lotte that Dr. Ostrowski had been arrested and also Mr. Weber, that no one knew what was going to happen next, that it might be a good idea for us to pack some bags and spend the next night somewhere else.

Two men who were friends of the family had been arrested, and apparently my father was also in danger. "The Nazis keep pointing at your apartment," our visitor had told Mother. Everybody in the neighborhood knew our politics.

"Arrests"—it was a word I had begun to see and hear a lot, but until that evening it had been an abstraction. Now it became frightening reality. At that time the Nazi actions still were directed primarily against their political opponents. The Jews had not yet become prime targets. The overwhelming majority of Berlin Jews was not politically involved. My father's few Jewish friends from his college days neither understood nor sympathized with his politics; some even said that Hitler was the only one who would be able to bring order into the political chaos of the Weimar Republic. As for the arrests of those days, they were simply "excesses."

The night passed without incident. The next day my father came back. There was nothing unusual about him; he appeared to be in good spirits. Apparently the father of one of his students, out of gratitude that his daughter had passed her baccalaureate, offered to put him up for the night when he heard of his predicament. His host was a nonpolitical Jewish doctor, and Father made us laugh with his story of sleeping in the doctor's office amid the medical instruments and a skeleton that cast weird shadows. It was all still strange, unreal. None of us could dream that the day would come when we'd be deeply grateful for such a shelter.

Outside they were marching with the "steady, firm steps" of the Horst Wessel song. They tore the black, red, and gold banner of the Weimar Republic in shreds and carried placards with slogans like "Germans, don't buy from Jews. World Jewry wants to destroy Germany. Germans, defend yourselves." All this I could see from the window of our apartment. We didn't go out that day. My parents had more important things on their minds. The doors of the two big bookcases in the den were open. Pamphlets, papers, books were piled up helter-skelter on the desk on which my father corrected his students' papers. My mother ruthlessly cleared out books while my father watched in helpless misery. Books were among my parents' most prized possessions; their

first joint purchase after their marriage had been a book. The political classics, Marx and Engels, were not weeded out that day, but Mother did move them to a less prominent place on the shelves. My parents still believed that one could not simply renounce these works and their teachings. The immediate problem was to get rid of the neatly bundled piles of anti-Nazi pamphlets and speeches. Every time my mother consigned another pamphlet to the scrap heap, Father would protest mildly. "Are you sure?" he'd ask, and Mother, who'd always been the more practical of the two and had developed a nose for danger, would respond almost gruffly.

Lotte dumped the books and manuscripts my parents had held so dear into an empty laundry basket, a procedure involving repeated trips to the den. While my parents were busily engaged in the radical reorganization of the bookcases and desk drawers, Lotte had to find a way of disposing of all the discarded materials. It could have been done fairly easily in the laundry room in our basement, but that might have aroused the suspicion of neighbors and the superintendent.

Overnight, distrust had entered our lives. We did not know what our neighbors were thinking. Apart from a polite exchange of greetings in the hallway, we'd had very little contact with them. Could we be certain that these neutral neighbors

had not suddenly turned into opportunistic supporters of the new order? If so, they spelled danger, for we had never made a secret of our
opposition to the Nazis. In the past we'd never
concerned ourselves with our neighbors' politics,
but now we watched for any clue, any gesture or
expression, that might signal what they were
thinking.

No, the laundry room would not do. The unavoidable act of destruction would have to take
place in the apartment, in the kitchen stove. But,
as we soon found out, the stove could not handle
that volume of paper. In no time at all our kitchen
was filled with thick smoke. That posed yet another, unanticipated, problem. We did not dare
open the kitchen window to air out the room,
because the neighbors in the back court might become suspicious and call the police or fire department. I had never been in the buildings in the rear
of the yard. All I knew was that the people who
lived in those buildings were poor, without having
any clear notion of what poverty meant. That day
the houses in the rear bustled with activity. Radios
blared forth martial music, and there was a constant coming and going.

Lotte chased me away from the kitchen window. She had opened it just a crack to let out at
least some of the smoke. Standing at the stove,
covered with soot, and desperately trying to "pro-

cess" the paper mountain, she looked like the witch in a fairy tale. I got out of the kitchen under strict orders from Lotte to close the kitchen door and not come back. It was a very trying time for a little girl who was forbidden to share in the activities of the adults and made to feel in the way, and who also was upset by their incomprehensible, mysterious doings. Who could have explained to me what was happening in Germany in 1933, why people were being persecuted, demeaned, and maltreated because of their race, their religion, or their political beliefs? Did I ever learn to understand it? I don't think so.

When the fire in the kitchen stove finally went out and all the paper had been reduced to ashes, we breathed a sigh of relief. My mother began to plan her next move. "As soon as it turns dark we're going to Spandau," she decided. I liked the idea. Spandau, a district of Berlin, was where my aunt Elsa Hannes, my father's sister, lived. She and her husband had no children, and they spoiled me shamelessly. As the prosperous owners of a men's clothing store, they lived on a far grander scale than my parents.

We left our home on the evening of April 1 as unobtrusively as possible, practically stealing away. After the noise of that day, all those drums, fifes, and marches, the quiet of the evening was almost tangible. Not many people were out on the

street. A few Jewish shops bore the traces of what had happened: a Star of David painted on one store front, broken windows in another. That was all. It is not unlikely that in view of the now peaceful atmosphere my parents were asking themselves whether they might not have been able to stay in our apartment, whether what we had been witnessing was nothing more than a bad dream that would pass as suddenly as it had come.

What we heard in Spandau also sounded reassuring. True, SA guards had posted themselves in front of Uncle Hannes' shop. One of them even excused himself: "It's just one of those measures . . ." Customers were not molested. The mood that evening was very strange. Hope resurfaced that in the end everything would turn out all right.

We stayed in Spandau for a few days, and then returned to our apartment. But it no longer seemed like our old home to me; it had lost its reassuring aura of security. I kept listening for strange footsteps presaging imminent danger. My parents did not seem quite as worried. Some of our friends who'd been arrested by the Gestapo were released. I overheard only fragments of their accounts: "I had to run along a long corridor, and when I didn't follow their commands fast enough, they beat me until I lost consciousness. . . ." Others refused to talk about their experience, and still others never came back. They were sent to concentration camps;

very few of them survived. The initials "KZ" [*Konzentrationslager*] had not yet acquired their ominous overtone. Names were whispered: "Oranienburg," "Dachau."

A week later, on April 7, 1933, my father received a letter from the regional school authorities informing him that he was subject to the new regulations concerning political enemies and Jews. Reading that portentous letter he turned pale. He studied it carefully, hoping that it might still lend itself to a different interpretation. But it was unambiguous. The Law for the Reorganization of the Civil Service stipulated the termination of employment of all those whose "political activities did not guarantee" that they would under all circumstances unreservedly defend the state, as well as all those of non-Aryan descent who had not served in World War I. My grandmother used to speak with pride of her three sons who had served their "Fatherland." Having thus served, my father did not fall under the regulations governing non-Aryan employees. His transgression concerned his political beliefs and activities. The careers of those categorized as politically suspect were effectively destroyed. Overnight they lost their jobs, became unemployed. They were kept on the payroll for three months after their dismissal, and those with more than ten years of service were granted three-quarters of their pensions. Whether and how they

could rejoin the labor force remained an open question.

Those of our Jewish friends not affected by the new regulations tried to reassure my parents, telling them that some solution was sure to be found. After all, wasn't someone like Hitler needed to put an end to unemployment and to the maltreatment of Germany by the Allies? Wasn't it obvious that things just couldn't continue the way they were? They pointed to Mussolini and his successful draining of the Pontine Marshes. Hitler would work similar miracles. They failed to mention that under Mussolini, too, people died because of their beliefs. Most Berlin Jews would smile condescendingly when they heard that people were leaving Germany because of the new laws. How silly of them to panic. Nor did my parents consider emigrating. "After all," said my father, "I'm a Prussian civil servant; I can't just run away."

Hope for a turn for the better prevailed. And Jews were beginning to get used to the fact of discrimination. They accepted it and accommodated themselves. The principle that Jews who had served in the war were not subject to the various restrictions was for the most part adhered to. As if to underscore their "privileged" position, as late as August 1935 they were still decorated for active service in the last war. My father was among the recipients of that medal. It was a grotesque situ-

ation: A man who was fired for his political opinions was being thanked by police officials for his service in the war. They shook his hand and congratulated him on the honor they were privileged to bestow in the name of the Führer and Chancellor. My father still has the citation signed by the chief of police of Berlin. Incidentally, this privileged position of the veterans was not honored in the provinces, where they were subjected to the same indignities as all other Jews.

The political parties and trade unions had been destroyed and their leaders arrested. Individual resistance seemed pointless. The mass intoxication of the victors did not abate. May Day 1933 was a particularly difficult time for us. The streets of Berlin were filled with battalions of Hitler Youth, SA, and SS and their marching bands. We closed our windows to shut out the words of their victory songs: "The rotting bones are rattling," "When Jewish blood spurts from the knives," and so on. We did not want to hear how this special day was being reshaped and violated by the new rulers.

His early involuntary retirement and inactivity weighed heavily on my father. And the two-thirds pension was inadequate. What to do? He was despondent. The fact that some of his friends who were in the same boat were not as downcast did not change matters. Moping around at home was

not the answer, and so in the summer of 1933 we moved to one of Berlin's many garden colonies where two of our friends, Kurt Hähnel, the former trade union official and metal worker, and Hans Weber, the former city councillor and printer, owned cottages and a bit of land. It became a meeting place for a small group who, like my parents, had been shut out of the new Third Reich because of their political beliefs. Among them was the carpenter Paul Garn. He too had lost his job for being a Socialist. It meant the end of his world. My memory of Hans Weber is of a gaunt, unsmiling, gray-haired man who took his time before venturing any firm opinion on the current scene. The people I liked most of all were the imposing Kurt Hähnel and his wife. They were probably the youngest members of that group, and despite their worries, they always found time for a word with me. But that was not the only reason I liked them. In contrast to the resignation of the others, my father included, they radiated energy and a readiness for combat. On weekends the circle of former Socialist party friends expanded. I remember in particular the harnessmaker Jakob Hein and the Junghans family, mostly because we stayed in touch. The men gardened or played cards. And so we spent the summer of 1933 visiting with the Webers and Hähnels.

The political situation naturally dominated their

conversations. All of them were convinced that the National Socialist nightmare could not last more than three months at most. It was an irrational hope. Hadn't it been these very people who tried to warn their fellow citizens that Hitler meant war? Now that he had come to power, what made them think that he was about to relinquish it?

My parents decided to move to another part of Berlin, one where they and their politics were not known. They found a smaller garden apartment on Uhlandstrasse. By coincidence, Walter Rieck, the dean of a secular school who had been suspended for political reasons, moved into the apartment above ours. And he was instrumental in getting Dr. Thaus, a colleague who had suffered a like fate, an apartment there as well. This arrangement had its advantages for all of us, apart from the obvious one of shared beliefs. Our three families all had financial problems; the reduced pensions were inadequate. Dr. Thaus managed to get a contract to address envelopes and cards, and we all pitched in and helped. Unlike the adults I enjoyed this tedious chore. Jenny Rieck took in sewing to help support the family. My father gave German lessons to foreigners, primarily Chinese students at Berlin University. After Father found a regular job Dr. Thaus took over his students.

The other tenants in the building were ob-

viously aware of the bond among our three families. Not a day passed without our getting together in one or the other apartment. Domestic and foreign affairs naturally were the main topic of discussion. The Röhm Putsch of June 30, 1934, raised renewed hope that the Hitler regime would collapse. Wasn't it obvious that it had begun to self-destruct?

The fact that the other tenants were aware of our closeness didn't trouble us. The new neighborhood where no one knew us made us careless about the dangers connected with political nonconformity, until we were rudely reminded of it one morning when two Gestapo officers appeared at our door with a search warrant. Mother and I were the only ones at home. I was sent to the kitchen, where I promptly buried my nose in a book, not sensing that my mother might be in danger. In retrospect I am still ashamed at not having acted with dispatch. When the Gestapo men were finally gone, Mother asked why I hadn't rushed to tell the Riecks about our visitors. Her question made me realize that I had failed her. I was only eleven at the time, yet I still thought my failure was inexcusable.

The two Gestapo men stayed for an hour, going through every shelf and closet in our apartment. They came away with very little; nothing but two pamphlets, *Marx and the Jews* and *Heinrich Heine*.

What they'd hoped to find in our house and at the Riecks's, who were next on their list, was incriminating evidence of conspiratorial activities. They made no secret of the fact that we and the Riecks had been denounced by our downstairs neighbors. The story they'd told the Gestapo was almost bizarre. According to them, Dr. Thaus, who was travelling, was transmitting news and other information for use in our antigovernment activities. Consequently they took it upon themselves to confiscate letters from Dr. Thaus to the Riecks, which, so they said, contained "puzzling" remarks that we, the alleged conspirators, incorporated into our anti-Hitler propaganda. "Their typewriter was going day and night." True enough, my father was busy at work on his typewriter. To supplement his meager pension he had taken a job as a building manager. And in the imagination of our neighbors, Mrs. Rieck's electric sewing machine had become a duplicating machine turning out leaflets that were then taken to a distribution center by Rieck's daughter Ursel. She had been seen leaving the house carrying a suitcase.

Ursel Rieck was a nurse and occasionally was on night duty. Hence the suitcase. Try as they would, the two investigating Gestapo officers could find no evidence to support the alleged conspiracy. The two house searches had yielded nothing, and nothing changed in the closeness of our

three families. As for the neighbors who had denounced us, we snubbed them ostentatiously. The
fact that this baseless denunciation had no consequences made us feel that justice in Germany
had not vanished altogether.

2

The political situation and the changes it wrought in our lives notwithstanding, my transfer to a new school was an important chapter in my life. Soon after Hitler came to power the school I had attended for four years was closed and its teachers discharged. I knew none of the girls at the Königstadt Lyzeum, my new school. I discovered that five other Jewish girls were in my grade when I went to our class in religion taught by Miss Katz. Other than that I had very little contact with my Jewish classmates, except that occasionally I came to their defense. In my old school, which was coeducational, I had been forced to learn how to defend myself. In my new surroundings I was soon given the chance to make

use of that skill even though I personally was never the target of any teasing. However, some of the girls liked to taunt two of the other Jewish girls who were smaller and weaker than the rest. They used to run away when they were made fun of. Naturally this only invited more teasing and more aggression.

At noon I would walk home with one of my classmates, Erika Seidel, a prototypical German girl with long blond braids. She wore the brown vest of the BDM, the League of German Girls. When we got to my door she would raise her arm in the Hitler salute and say, "Heil Hitler." I don't know whether she noticed that I never responded in kind. I was proud of my small gestures of political opposition, particularly of my refusal—and it was not easy—to contribute to the countless collections for various national and social causes. Even though I liked the sound of the coins as they dropped into the cans and the colorful lapel pins given to all contributors, I resisted the temptation to be one of the crowd.

Our move to our new apartment meant yet another change of school. When my mother told the principal that I would have to transfer to another school, he, who had been so skeptical about the quality of my previous one, said that he hated to see me leave. I don't know whether he was complimenting me on my performance or trying

to distance himself from the anti-Semitism of the new regime. Voiced opposition to the Nazis took many subtle forms.

The atmosphere at my new school, the Princess Bismarck School, was altogether different. About half of the students were the children of old, well-to-do Berlin Jewish families. Our teachers were obliged to greet their classes with the mandatory "Heil Hitler," but they did so with barely disguised disdain, and they treated all of us, Jews and non-Jews, equally. The only exception to this egalitarian attitude was the daughter of a high-ranking SA official, who had to be promoted regardless of her lackluster performance. Nor did the school change the name of Robula, a retreat it maintained near the city. We loved that little place, which had been named Robula in honor of Robert Burg, the former principal who had been instrumental in its acquisition. Although Robert Burg, who was half Jewish, had emigrated, both students and faculty continued to speak of him with warmth and respect. Some Jewish teachers were also still there, and I never heard anyone utter a single anti-Semitic word.

My stay at Princess Bismarck School was also comparatively brief. When the school authorities decided that Jewish children could no longer take part in outings or go to Robula or join in activities like swimming, my father decided to enroll me in

a Jewish school. He didn't want to expose me to that much discrimination. He opted for the Jewish middle school, one of the few accredited Jewish schools still in operation, which meant that I would be eligible for matriculation in a higher institution of learning "after Hitler." When my parents notified the Princess Bismarck School of their decision to take me out, my homeroom teacher called to say that although she was sorry to see me go she understood our decision.

Like all other Jewish schools in Berlin, the middle school I went to was overcrowded. That hadn't always been so. In pre-Hitler Germany only those Jewish parents, by no means a majority, who set particular store by a Jewish education and Jewish identity sent their children to Jewish schools. Moreover, by the time I came to my Jewish school, Jewish children whose fathers had not served in World War I had already been forced out of German schools. In the past, even many Orthodox Jews believed that secular schools offered a better preparation for life in Germany. The Jewish schools focused on life in a Jewish community, the kind of community favored by Jewish immigrants from eastern Europe.

When the Third Reich introduced their more restrictive measures isolating Jews, excluding them from the public sphere and barring them from mingling with other Germans, attendance at the hand-

ful of Jewish schools skyrocketed. New Jewish
schools were established, but not nearly enough
to meet the demand. The officially accredited middle school naturally had the most applicants. In
1932 it had had an enrollment of 470 students; by
1934 that number had rise to 1,025.

When I think back on my first day at that school
I can still remember how confused I felt. In my
old schools no class had more than thirty children;
here there were never fewer than fifty. Under
these circumstances orderly instruction was all but
impossible. Students and teachers kept coming
and going; some emigrated and others transferred
to us from German schools. In 1935 all Jewish civil
servants, including Jewish teachers at German
schools, were forced out of their jobs. We lived in
a constant state of uncertainty. Concentrated, co-
herent instruction was impossible. The same problems that preoccupied our families preoccupied
our teachers. The atmosphere at school reflected
the uncertainty and insecurity that dominated our
lives. Should one emigrate? Should one stay here?
Was it still possible to have any kind of decent life
in Germany? It is not surprising that our teachers,
living on the edge, were not able to raise the level
of learning to greater heights. Still, there were
some who managed to maintain admirable inner
calm and stability. Nor did we have a cohesive
student body. The difference in the social and in-

tellectual backgrounds of the students was bound to affect the teaching.

Yet despite all these drawbacks and deficiencies, we did learn something, perhaps not the same things we would have learned under normal circumstances, but nevertheless something that was useful under these extraordinary conditions. The curriculum was designed to impart skills that would also be of use in case we emigrated. Thus the study of foreign languages, Hebrew in particular, was stressed. And in the junior and senior years we were also taught shorthand and typing and an hour a week of commercial English and French. In addition, optional courses in sewing and cooking were offered. This sort of curriculum obviously short-changed traditional subjects like history, mathematics, chemistry or physics, not to mention literature and the humanities generally.

The Jewish schools made a commendable effort to come up with the best possible solution under the circumstances. Since Jewish children were barred from the athletic fields and gyms used by other schools, the Jewish schools of Berlin acquired an athletic field and sponsored their own sports meets and contests. Those were the high points in our lives. Perhaps my only really happy memories of my school years are the times on that playing field. When I was there I felt as though a weight were being lifted off me. Of course, when we got

on the underground to go back home we were rudely brought back to reality. It is surely no accident that I cannot remember our ever playing a single silly trick on any of our teachers. True, among ourselves we called some of them by their nicknames, but even those had come down to us from previous generations of students. With few exceptions my memories of those days are bleak. And the dark, forbidding building did not help. When I think back on specific incidents they invariably seem to have taken place on days when the sky was overcast. I cannot recall a single memorable event taking place on a sunny day.

We probably weren't model children, but we definitely were not as carefree and playful as other children of our age. We were restrained. Going home on the underground, we were careful not to call attention to ourselves, not to laugh too loudly or in any way attract notice. Even if we didn't talk about it, we sensed that people could tell that we were Jewish and possibly consider us fair game, although I must admit that nothing untoward ever happened to me.

In looking back at those days, I am struck by the fact that we children never discussed our situation. When one of us said good-bye because she was emigrating, we of course envied her, not because she was exchanging our insecure existence for greater security but because of the adventure

awaiting her. Neither we nor many of our parents seemed to realize that with each passing day our life was becoming more dangerous. We knew that people were being arrested, and when a girl was absent from school for a few days, we would whisper among ourselves that someone in her family had probably been arrested. Then one of us would go to that girl's house to find out what was wrong, and when she returned to school we would instinctively shun her, as though she were marked. But after a few days we'd get used to her misfortune and readmit her to our circle. Perhaps we also sensed that the same thing could happen to any of us.

That is how we found out about the first wave of mass arrests in June 1938, in which fifteen hundred Jews were swept up. They were people with "prior records," those officially designated as "asocial, parasitic elements." A cousin of mine who once had been fined for being involved in an automobile accident was among those arrested. I suppose the reference to the victims' "prior record" was supposed to still any doubt about the reasons for their arrest. Although indignant about the blatant illegality of the action, we were not directly affected by it.

Another, seemingly innocuous, incident hit me much harder. It happened at a photo studio. Like any other sixteen-year-old I was vain, and so when

the photographer told me to push my hair back behind my left ear I became angry and tearful. There was nothing extraordinary about his suggestion; he had no ulterior motive. Still I felt humiliated, as though I'd been struck. However, I prided myself on my self-control and was determined not to show how upset I was. Yet I knew even then that despite my best effort the picture would show me looking bitter, defiant, and tearful. My reaction was triggered by an absurd Nazi racial theory postulating that Jews' left ears were indicative of their Semitic descent. That is why passport photos of Jews had to show the left ear. On July 23, 1938, it was decreed that all Jews past the age of fifteen had to carry an identity card with a photograph. And lest there was any doubt about the racial classification of the passport's owner, both its cover and inner pages were stamped with a large "J."

Going home from school on the underground or bus, I would try to get close enough to other passengers to compare their left ears with mine. I couldn't see any difference. My ear, which I examined closely in the mirror hundreds of times, looked exactly like the ears of the Aryans in Berlin.

I didn't tell my parents about the incident at the photographer's; I was afraid they'd laugh at me. A story was then making the rounds among Jews about a man at a Nazi rally who was asked

to come up to the podium to show what the ear of a pure Aryan looked like. Naturally the Nazi speaker didn't know that his model Aryan was a Jew, and of course the man didn't enlighten him, and so the ear of a Jew was used to demonstrate Aryan purity. The story may or may not have been apocryphal. It didn't matter. Jews loved it because it helped them bear the humiliation of this particular indignity. To further emphasize the "criminal element" of Jews, their identity cards also bore their fingerprints. Left index finger, right index finger . . . I can still remember how the police officer in our precinct carefully, almost tenderly, wiped the black ink off my hands. Was it only my imagination or was he even more embarrassed than I by this demeaning procedure?

This identity card was the document I had to sign with the newly added middle name Sara. Henceforth my name was to be Ingeborg Sara Deutschkron. According to a regulation of August 18, 1938, all Jewish males had to add the name Israel to their given name, and all Jewish females the name Sara. After January 1, 1939, all documents and official papers had to have the new name. Failure to use it in all official dealings was punishable by up to a month's imprisonment. I admired my parents who, in my presence at least, were able to shrug off this sort of petty discrimination with a condescending smile.

The anti-Jewish regulations of 1938 seemed to indicate that the Nazis were serious about their declared intention to solve the "Jewish question." Among the most far-reaching was the denial of all assistance and tax relief to Jewish businesses, and the regulation of April 26, 1938, requiring Jews to register all their assets, both domestic and foreign, in excess of 5,000 Reichsmark. This gave the Nazis a complete overview of the total Jewish assets in Germany. As civil servants of moderate means my parents were not affected by that regulation, but I still remember the turmoil it stirred up among our relatives and friends. Uncle and Aunt Hannes came from Spandau to ask my father for advice. And those of our friends who had called Hitler a needed restorer of order now were strangely subdued.

In June Jewish businesses were ordered to make public the fact of their Jewishness. On Kurfürstendamm painters were busily inscribing the owners' names on storefronts, prominently emphasizing the newly added Israel or Sara. In July Jewish physicians lost their accreditation; some were still permitted to work in the role of "caretakers" of the sick; Jewish lawyers came next.

On October 28, 1938, between fifteen and seventeen thousand Polish Jews living in Germany, including those who had become German citizens after World War I and subsequently were dena-

turalized by the Nazis, were taken from their homes at night and shipped to the Polish border. All they were allowed to take with them was ten marks and the clothes on their backs. When they got to the German-Polish border they wandered around in no-man's-land because the Poles refused to let them in. To avoid admitting the Polish citizens being persecuted in Germany, the Polish government invalidated the passports of all those who had lived outside Poland for more than five years.

On the morning after the night raid there were numerous empty seats in my classroom. When the teacher called the roll, many names went unanswered. Wordlessly she put aside the lesson books of those who hadn't responded to their names. Rarely had our classroom been that still. We were old enough, and had already heard and seen enough, to figure out what had happened the previous night, when the Nazis raided the section in which so many Jews from Eastern Europe lived.

All these events were signs that the Jews in Germany were systematically being deprived of the very basis of their existence. Moreover, the state did everything in its power to humiliate and harass them. The handful of Jewish skilled laborers in Berlin seemed to fare best, and they were also in a favorable position in the event of emigration. With one stroke they had become the aristocracy among German Jews. Yet I remember clearly how

ridiculous it all seemed at first, how we all laughed when Uncle Hannes enrolled in a course in candymaking sponsored by the Jewish Community. My father, who had trouble hammering a nail into a wall, took a course in shoemaking and apprenticed himself to a Jewish cobbler. I suspect he did it because it made him feel that he had investigated every available possibility and had prepared for any eventuality. I don't think he actually believed that he would ever become a shoemaker. We still have a pair of practically unused leather shears as a memento of that chapter of our lives. Ultimately my father found a job at the Theodor Herzl School, a Jewish private school.

The Theodor Herzl School was licensed to teach foreign languages. There the students received a Zionist education. For my father that meant a major readjustment. As a former high-school teacher who believed in secular education, he was anything but a Zionist. However, his dedication to teaching helped him overcome whatever reservations he might have had. He decided to broaden his field and enrolled in night courses for teachers of religion. Having been brought up in an Orthodox home, he was not completely at sea. Under the pressure, hostility, and active anti-Semitism of the Third Reich, he reaffirmed his ties to Judaism. He also took up typing and bookkeeping, two subjects for which he had little aptitude, but his en-

ergy and powers of concentration helped here too.

Although never called on to teach religion, he was soon given a chance to make use of his newly acquired office skills. He had been promoted to assistant principal of the Theodor Herzl School, but after Jews were barred from teaching even in Jewish schools, he became its administrator. That position, together with a night job as housing manager, helped support the three of us. True, he worked so hard that I almost never saw him, and my mother, who had worked in an office before she was married, also helped out. Our life had changed. Money worries now dominated our everyday existence. Our political friends found themselves in a similar predicament. Mr. Rieck and Dr. Thaus also found jobs that kept them going.

In view of this preoccupation with survival, the political situation was no longer uppermost in our thoughts. And we no longer counted on an early end to National Socialism. Hitler had succeeded where the Weimar Republic had failed: He had won the respect of the outside world, he had done away with unemployment, and he had abrogated the Versailles Treaty.

3

It was evening. Sitting in the dark, we heard the door creak. Someone must be trying to open it quietly. Mother flinched, jumped up, and ran to the door.

"Martin, what are you doing here?" she called out to Father, who stood in the doorway looking exhausted, pale, helpless, and shrunken.

"Are you mad, coming here?" Mother was incredulous.

"I think I have to turn myself in," Father said very slowly and softly. "After all, I'm still a Prussian civil servant, and if the police are looking for me I can't just hide."

"That's sheer madness." Mother was in despair. In answer to her question about where he'd

34

been all day, he said at the school, of course. Mother couldn't believe her ears. "Even after you got my call?"

"Where else should I have been?" he asked. Now he said he was going to spend the night at home, and tomorrow he'd decide what to do.

On the morning of November 10 the news had spread that all hell had broken loose in Berlin during the night. SA men wielding axes and clubs had roamed through the streets, smashing windows and looting Jewish-owned businesses.

Early that morning we went out to see for ourselves. We were stunned by the scene that confronted us. Broken glass, smashed window displays, and merchandise littered the sidewalks of Berlin's shopping district. Inside the shops it was no better: mountains of broken furniture and smashed chinaware, torn dresses, squashed hats.

Thick smoke hung over the ruins of the synagogue on Fasanenstrasse. We didn't dare inspect the damage too closely. We already knew from radio reports that synagogues throughout the country had gone up in flames, victims of the "spontaneous rage" of the German people, as police and firefighters stood by and watched them burn.

While we were standing there a barber came out of his shop and, grinning from ear to ear, called out to my father, "Hey, you Jew!" My mother,

unafraid as always, wheeled around. "You damn swine," she said. Father turned pale. "For God's sake, keep quiet." But Mother, undaunted, looked up at the barber and again shouted, "You damn swine!" And then, calmly turning back to Father, she said, "After all, there's a limit to what one can take."

In the provinces this outburst of "spontaneous popular rage" reportedly had taken even more ominous forms, with Jewish private houses being attacked. These events were purportedly only the first step in "retaliation" for the "cowardly murder" of Ernst vom Rath, a diplomat at the German embassy in Paris, by Herschel Grynszpan, a seventeen-year-old Polish Jew. It was not until after the war that we learned the reason for Grynszpan's act: to avenge the deportation of his family from Hanover to the Polish border. At the time there were also rumors of a homosexual relationship between vom Rath and Grynszpan. "The mask is torn off the face of world Jewry," screamed the headlines. The papers were filled with detailed accounts of the illustrious career of Ernst vom Rath.

On November 7 Grynszpan had walked into the German Embassy in Paris and asked to speak to Ambassador von Welczek. He was received by vom Rath, and Grynszpan, apparently mistaking him for the ambassador, shot him. Vom Rath was

critically wounded. The German radio issued hourly bulletins about vom Rath's condition. He died on November 9. It is safe to say that during the two days he lay dying, his mother was not the only one praying for her son's recovery. "If only he doesn't die . . . ," so began all conversations among Jews. There was the wholly understandable fear that the Nazis were going to use vom Rath's death as a welcome pretext. And indeed, within hours, on the afternoon of November 9, we got a telephone call informing us that one of my uncles, a wealthy businessman, had been picked up in his home by the Gestapo and presumably taken to a concentration camp. That was all the caller could tell us; the arresting officers provided no further information. Minutes later we received similar news about a close friend of ours, a Berlin gynecologist.

That day the telephone, that harbinger of bad news, didn't stop ringing. My parents began to call friends who hadn't been in touch. Some didn't answer at all, while other calls were answered by frightened women whose husbands had just been picked up by the Gestapo. Most of those arrested that day were either intellectuals or well-to-do business people.

My father left the house as usual the next morning, but he ordered me to stay home. He was very depressed. My parents were going to keep in touch

by phone. Mother went about her chores as usual. At ten o'clock the doorbell rang. I could tell that Mother was as frightened as I. She opened the door. Two tall men in civilian dress with well-fed blank faces stood there. Saying they were from the Gestapo, they asked to come in. Mother asked them for their IDs. They produced them and headed for the den. One of them sat down at Father's desk.

"Where is your husband?" he demanded.

My mother stood in front of him, holding on to the desk. "I have no idea," she said calmly. "He left the house this morning as usual. I expect he went to work, though I'm a little concerned because I haven't been able to reach him."

The two men paid no attention to me. I was standing in the doorway, trembling with fear.

"Tell your husband to report to his police precinct as soon as he gets home," said the second one, who was standing, surveying the room.

"Of course," my mother answered and escorted the two callers to the door. No sooner were they gone than she flew to the telephone.

"Look and see whether they're coming back," she called to me. And while I stood with my ear pressed to the door to listen for footsteps, she dialed the school.

"You've got to disappear as quickly as possible," she told my father. "They're after you!" She

promptly hung up, flung herself down on a chair, and began to consider various options: Maybe Ostrowski should be told; he might be able to hide Father for a few days. But of course Father knew that himself. Maybe even now he was on the way there. We'd just have to wait. There was nothing more we could do for the time being. And then she went back to her housework. That, however, wasn't so easy. She couldn't concentrate, and I got underfoot. Finally she suggested that we go out and do our shopping. The best thing, she said, was to act as though nothing had happened.

Outside we found the dress shop next door in ruins. Ripped dresses and bolts of cloth were strewn about. Like all the others hurrying by, we pretended not to notice the evidence of that savagery. Apparently people were unwilling to face the depredation, or maybe they were afraid they'd be taken for looters.

At Mrs. Gesche's grocery the atmosphere was unchanged, perhaps even a little friendlier than usual. There were allusions to the previous night. "What is happening here?" Mrs. Gesche shook her head in disbelief. The Gesches had many Jewish customers. "They always bought only the best quality, even for their help," Mrs. Gesche said. "The 'others,' " she sniffed, "think the cheapest stuff is good enough for the maid."

Our shopping done, we returned home. To her

horror Mother discovered that she had locked us out. "My God, suppose the phone rings and it's Father calling." She was distraught, but she calmed down and went downstairs to ring the superintendent's bell. Smiling as though nothing out of the ordinary had happened, she asked her for help and apologized for the bother. "It's nothing," the superintendent assured her, "people lock themselves out all the time." She invited us into her kitchen to wait for her husband. There we sat on her wooden kitchen chairs, looking out through the open door into the yard. An ideal observation post: From there one could see everything that was going on outside and everyone who came into the building. Did she know about our morning visitors? If so, nothing in her behavior gave any hint of it.

"What on earth do you think you're doing?" my mother hissed at me. I had discovered a small picture of Hitler next to the wall cabinet and my mother had caught me sticking out my tongue at this guardian of the hearth. Suddenly we both began to laugh and the tension was broken. Actually we were safer here than in our own apartment. Finally the superintendent's husband arrived; he too was very reassuring and let us in with his passkey. How good it was to be back within our own four walls, even if they were no longer as safe as before.

There was no word from Father. Mother was mending some laundry, and I sat next to her. Periodically I'd get up and run to the door or look out the window. It was getting dark, but we were afraid to turn on the light. Where could he be? Mother didn't want to call the school again. Our phones might be tapped. As we were sitting there wondering what to do next, the door opened and Father walked in.

Mother went to the phone to call Dr. Ostrowski and asked him to come over. "Let him decide whether you ought to report to the police or not," she said. Father was pacing restlessly. In my parents' eyes Ostrowski, the former Socialist mayor of the village of Finsterwalde and later borough president in Berlin until his ouster by the Nazis, was still a figure of authority.

"Are you crazy, Deutschkron?" Ostrowski said when he appeared at our house with Grete Sommer, his companion. "You're going to go with Grete to her parents' house." We knew Grete's parents well. They now ran a grocery store. Her father, Bernhard Sommer, was a former trade-union official. He had left Finsterwalde because he and his politics were well known and it would not have been easy for him to make a new start there. Nobody, not necessarily out of conviction but more likely out of fear, was eager to employ somebody who'd been "disciplined" by the Nazis. So he

moved to Berlin, where nobody knew him. "And you two also shouldn't stay here," Ostrowski told my mother. "Suppose the Gestapo come back and asks questions?"

We left in two taxis, driving off in two different directions. Ostrowski took Mother and me to the house of Mrs. Giese, an elderly Socialist who had been dean of a nondenominational school. We had never met, but we knew her by name. Ostrowski had called to tell her of our plight. Despite the lateness of the hour, she told him to bring us right over. She lived in a two-room apartment she shared with her parakeets, Nikki and Pippa. They had the run of the house and did not take kindly to the two interlopers. We made up a sort of bed with the help of two chairs, while the birds fluttered about. My mother was afraid they'd get entangled in her hair. We spent a sleepless night, and not only because of the two parakeets. The next night Mrs. Giese shut the birds up in their cage. That, in their opinion, was an inexcusable violation of their freedom of movement, and they made no secret of their displeasure.

Nikki and Pippa helped make our almost two-week stay at Mrs. Giese's memorable. They would perch on a curtain rod and, having learned to imitate my mother's voice, would exclaim, "Martin, are you crazy?" My father occasionally left his "exile" at the Sommers' and came to see us to talk

over our situation and make plans. After all, we couldn't hide out forever, even though for the moment we were comparatively safe. On the rare occasions when we dared venture forth after dark, we'd see men and women who seemed to be in a similar predicament. They would meet in doorways, exchange a few hasty words and small packages, and quickly separate again.

Mrs. Rieck, who of course knew where we were, had gotten word to us that she thought the Gestapo had come back. She had seen two men at our door and asked them whether they were looking for the Deutschkrons. When they answered that they were, she pointed to all the milk bottles at our door and said, "Can't you see, the Deutschkrons have gone away?" The men left.

"Do you think I ought to report?" my father kept asking over and over again. He wouldn't get it into his head that resisting this new state and its criminal laws by "illegal" means was right and proper. These arguments always culminated in Mother's forceful exclamation, which the two parakeets mimicked to perfection. Had it not been for Ostrowski, Father probably wouldn't have listened to Mother.

My parents also sometimes discussed the possibility of emigration. I heard them say that maybe they ought to write to our relatives once they were back at the apartment. My father had a cousin in

England. In the past our contact with her had been limited to the ritualistic exchange of New Year's greetings. But now we occasionally sent her word via friends about developments here. Perhaps my father could go to England. It was a tempting idea, but after about two weeks, when we were all together again and it seemed as though the Gestapo had suspended its anti-Jewish campaign, we learned that England would admit only those who had been in concentration camps during those November days.

"So one first has to be in a KZ to be saved," my father said bitterly. Some men were in fact released from concentration camps if they could show proof that they were going to emigrate. What a sight they were, with their shaven heads, haggard, mistreated, bewildered. Very few were willing to talk about what had happened to them, and not merely because they'd had to sign a statement attesting to having been well treated. We heard that many had died in the camps, and not only the old and the frail.

New anti-Jewish decrees were promulgated. A fine of one billion marks, payable in four installments, was levied against the Jews of Germany to compensate for the death of Ernst vom Rath. Furthermore, the Jews themselves, not their insurance carriers, were responsible for the obligatory prompt repair of their business premises. Accord-

ing to the official proclamation, the damage they had suffered was the consequence of the German people's displeasure over the campaign of international Jewry against National Socialist Germany. This declaration was followed by an edict closing museums, parks, concert halls, and theaters to Jews. On November 23, 1938, the official Nazi newspaper, *Völkischer Beobachter*, editorialized that the German people had embarked on the "final, unhesitating, uncompromising solution of the Jewish problem."

Reluctantly the Jews of Germany came to realize what the future held in store. For many it was too late: The opportunities for emigration were dwindling. More and more countries were closing their doors or laying down stringent conditions—guarantees of substantial sums of money, close relatives to sponsor them. How many German Jews still had disposable funds or relatives abroad who qualified as sponsors? Not a single country eased its immigration policies even one iota after the glass-smashing spree of November 9–10. The German Jews, even the most German among them, realized that the events of that night were an omen of worse to come. Some said that indeed it was now five minutes to midnight. In fact, for most of them it was five minutes past midnight. It was already too late.

4

Very small and very pale, that's how my father looked standing at the window of his railway compartment on that memorable day of April 19, 1939. He was clutching the window handle with both hands as though seeking support. Mother was standing on the platform and saying over and over again, "You'll try, won't you, to bring us over to you as soon as possible. It doesn't matter what arrangements you make for us—whether as maids or cooks—only get us out of here."

Father kept nodding. To me he seemed more disheartened and helpless than ever. He looked at his two sisters and his brother and their families, all of whom had come to see him off. All around

us people were rushing about, but we took no notice of anything or anyone. One of my aunts was sobbing uncontrollably; the others wiped away silent tears.

My mother and I were confident that we would soon be able to join Father in England, but the rest of our family had no realistic hopes of getting out. His oldest sister was married to a disabled veteran. Her life had not been easy. Her first marriage had ended in divorce because she had led what was then genteelly referred to as an "irregular" life. Middle-class Jewish families of her time held very rigid views about morality, and a woman who was both beautiful and rumored not to take her marital vows too seriously was likely to be treated as a pariah. My aunt's second marriage to a not very well-to-do veteran was considered just punishment. Naturally it had been a traditional Jewish "arranged" marriage, and she was expected to be grateful.

The other sister was married to a much older man. That marriage was built on money and position, not affection, and she stuck to it "for appearance's sake." Her husband was not very strong and thus was not a viable candidate for emigration. Only my father's brother still had an outside chance. He was something of a black sheep, said to have been involved in shady business deals. The family lived in constant fear that

he would bring shame on their good name, and they didn't take his talk of emigration seriously. Like many others, he was hoping for a visa to one of the African or Asian countries that supposedly were willing to take in refugees.

"Perhaps we can go to this one . . ." Fingers crisscrossed maps. "Maybe Paraguay?" "Have you looked into New Zealand?" "I heard that so-and-so has gotten a visa to Panama." "They say you can get a visa to Venezuela for ten thousand marks." And on and on it went. These speculations were like endless parlor games, while country after country, some sooner than others, closed its borders to Jews from Germany.

One of the cruelest incidents in this game of dominoes was the odyssey of the S.S *St. Louis*, which sailed from Germany to Cuba on May 13, 1939, with 930 passengers aboard. All of them held what they believed to be valid documents, which they had bought for huge sums. They did not know that shortly before they boarded their ship, Cuba's president had invalidated their visas. The *St. Louis* arrived in Cuba on May 27, and the Cuban government refused to let it dock. After extensive negotiations, it was forced to turn around and head back to Europe. The Cuban navy was ordered to use force when the German captain, in a courageous stand on behalf of his Jewish passengers, refused to leave Cuban waters. Some of these hap-

less passengers eventually found refuge in Belgium and France, but no one knows how many actually survived the war.

My father was lucky. Before the events of *Kristallnacht*, he had not been completely convinced of the absolute necessity of emigration, but that day in November persuaded him that life in Germany had become impossible. But where could we go? My mother had an uncle in America who had visited us from time to time in Germany and led us to believe that he was rich. But then we heard from a cousin who had emigrated to the United States that the uncle was something of a braggart. And in the absence of relatives to guarantee that prospective immigrants would not become public charges, the American government did not grant immigration visas. But even with such guarantees, the immigration quotas were woefully inadequate. At the American Consulate at Stuttgart alone, 110,000 applicants vied for the 850 monthly visa allotment.

In their desperate quest many German Jews turned for help to people who themselves had emigrated only shortly before. After all, wouldn't they be the ones most likely to understand their plight? But here too, understanding was not always forthcoming. I can still remember the shock of our friends the Blumenthals over the response of their family in Brazil. "We're planning to open

a second store," they wrote. "Once that's done we'll apply for visas for you." In their desire to get out of Germany, people resorted to all kinds of schemes, including proxy marriages with foreigners and forged papers.

Although Britain's restrictive immigration policy did not seem very promising, Father had applied for a visa to Palestine some time earlier. On May 12, 1939, Britain set a five-year limit of 75,000 on the number of immigrants to Palestine. Still, the mere fact of having applied for immigration gave my parents a feeling of security. They had acted, even if they had never thought that they might actually have to emigrate. Moreover, they weren't Zionists. They were Jews brought to an awareness of their Jewishness by circumstances beyond their control, and Jewishness was not synonymous with Zionism. Socialist ideology had always downplayed the Jewish question. If Jewishness was a problem, it was one that would be resolved once socialism had triumphed and class differences, the real cause of anti-Semitism, disappeared. People like my parents who were committed to these ideas could hardly be expected to become Zionists overnight. Their return to Judaism had not been an easy matter. For some of my classmates life in *Eretz Israel* was the epitome of happiness, or at least so they said. I thought them a bit silly. I felt far more adult for believing, as my

parents did, that everything would pass and that we would again be able to live in Berlin in peace and harmony. We just had to figure out how to survive the Nazis.

Consequently, my parents were not particularly upset when a friend of ours returned from Palestine with horror stories about conditions there. I still have vivid memories of his accounts of the plague of insects in the dirty harbor of Haifa, of the strange people he'd seen there. Everything in Germany, even Nazi Germany, was simply so much better. Anyway, my father had chosen Palestine for purely practical reasons; by going to Palestine he would not be forfeiting his pension rights. By virtue of an agreement, the Jewish settlers in Palestine could borrow investment funds for their agricultural communes and repay them in Palestine. Out of these funds immigrants who qualified were paid their civil-service pensions. My father's pension, although quite modest, was enough to give him a start in a foreign land should it ever come to that.

Even though British policy limited the possibility of emigration to Palestine, Great Britain eased immigration into its own country after November 1938 for those who had been in concentration camps, or who had relatives in England and could prove that they had applied for admission to other countries. In other words, England

was prepared to grant temporary asylum to a select few. The name Camp Richmond, the place in which those fortunate enough to qualify were sheltered, had a magic ring. We later learned that the barracks first had to be made habitable by their future inmates. But whatever its conditions, this transition camp saved many lives. England and Sweden also opened their doors to children, even though many of them, separated from their parents, suffered psychological damage. At one point my parents suggested that I leave Germany without them. I objected violently, and that was the end of that.

I am sure that my reaction to their proposal was prompted by something I had accidentally witnessed in the summer of 1936 at a railroad station as we were about to leave on a vacation. At that time, Jews could still travel, and anyone who could possibly manage it took advantage of the opportunity to get out, if only for a few days. As we were waiting for our train we saw some cars with the lettering "Genua" being coupled to our train. They were filled with young people waving good-bye to their parents crowding the platform. The youngsters were obviously on the way to Palestine. That scene, those painful emotional farewells, remained etched in my memory. It contrasted sharply with my feeling of happy anticipation. Neither my parents nor I ever talked about what we

had just witnessed, but the memory of it stayed with us.

One day my father heard from his cousin that she was prepared to have him come, but only him, because the British government required substantial monetary guarantees. Also, the fact that he had applied for immigration to Palestine facilitated his temporary admission to England. This news came as a tremendous relief. There was reason to hope that Mother and I might eventually be able to follow Father to England, perhaps as household help. Judging by the visa policy, household help was in great demand. Compared to Shanghai and Aleppo, the only other places still admitting German Jews, England seemed the ideal choice. I remember Father looking up Aleppo in an encyclopedia and learning that among its distinctions was the fact that a communicable skin disease was named for it. The idea of going there did not hold great appeal, nor did China, about which we also knew next to nothing, except that there were constant wars and that Europeans there lived in abject poverty. England was an altogether different matter.

We had already given up our apartment more or less involuntarily. Although landlords did not yet have the legal right to evict Jewish tenants, they could do so without much difficulty. And our landlord took prompt advantage of the situation.

In view of the fact that my father was about to emigrate and we hoped to follow him very soon, it didn't make much sense to hold on to the apartment. Consequently my parents, on the assumption that we would be leaving soon, decided to crate our household goods and ship them to Hamburg for storage. I can still see them scanning every single piece, trying to decide whether it was worth taking along. They'd been told that furniture would always come in handy. We had to assume that at first we would not be able to afford very spacious quarters, which meant that items like the desk or the bedroom set had to be left behind. Here too, Mother's common sense overcame Father's indecisiveness and hesitation. Every piece of furniture held a special meaning. The books posed the greatest problem of all. Politically suspect volumes had already been weeded out in 1933, but now the rest also had to be discarded. We decided to leave the disposal of the things we couldn't take with us to a "specialist," someone who had no emotional ties to our possessions. Then the buyers and the dealers arrived. They were like vultures: "You're not going to take this Meissen vase with you, are you? That's only extra ballast." "Those are nice drapes. Are you planning to take them?" "How about adding a few more books to this pile?" Nobody stopped to think how painful it must be for us to watch the dismantling

of our home. All they could see, the well-to-do and educated and the poorer and less-educated alike, was the chance of furnishing their homes at bargain rates. Greed was the common denominator.

Once we were down to the barest necessities we began packing. Everything was crated in the presence of an official of the foreign exchange office, who checked every single item, large and small, against a list compiled by us. The crate also contained some of my old toys and games—dolls I could not bear to part with, my teddy bear, my skates and tennis racquet.

My father had his passport with the "J" prominently stamped on it. He also had paid the Reich departure tax, one of the sadistic fees levied on Jews forced to emigrate. He kept putting off the date of his departure, until one day the Nazis made the decision for him. He was summoned to report to the Gestapo one Saturday morning at nine. Since we weren't observant Jews, this particular touch of gratuitous cruelty did not especially affect us. When my father appeared a few minutes before nine, the officer in charge put down his newspaper, looked up him, and shouted, "What time were you ordered to appear, Jew?"

"At nine," answered my father.

"Then see to it that you're here at nine. Now get out!"

My father left the room and waited outside until nine on the dot. Now the officer was ready for him.

"Is your name Deutschkron?" he asked. And without waiting for an answer he shouted, "A Jew has no right to a name with the word 'Deutsch.' " Then he asked him the names of both his grandmothers.

"Russ and Besser."

"Take your choice. Either one." Since his name was Deutschkron, my father thought that "Russ" [Russian] was inappropriate, and so he decided on "Besser." He signed a document in which he "voluntarily" asked for permission to change his name from Deutschkron to Besser. This incident persuaded my father to leave as soon as possible, since his passport with the British visa was in the name of Deutschkron. A few weeks later my mother and I were also summoned to the Gestapo and asked to "voluntarily" apply for a change of name. By then, however, Germany was at war and the Gestapo, given the manpower shortage, did not pursue the matter.

After Father left, my mother and I moved into a furnished room. We didn't care very much what it looked like. After all, we were only going to be there "temporarily." The room was large and full of old furniture. Our landlady's eyesight was failing, and the bath and kitchen were not particularly

clean. It was a typical old-fashioned Berlin apartment, with a long foyer, squeaking floors, and dark rooms looking out on an inner courtyard. We decided to take the room because our friends Max and Lily Blumenthal had also rented a room there. Now that Father was gone, Mother found the presence of friends comforting.

Lily and Max had been living in furnished rooms for some time. Unlike us, they were not planning to leave. Max was a former banker. They had tried living abroad but had returned to Germany. Lily was suffering from tuberculosis. It still seemed preferable then to live in poverty at home than in a foreign country with few opportunities for a man unaccustomed to physical labor. So here they were, eating up the remnants of their former wealth, waiting for a miracle to take them out of their misery.

My father's letters were interesting. He was discovering an entirely new world. Not many work opportunities were open to him, and he did not get a labor permit. Still, we considered him one of the lucky ones, particularly since it was becoming increasingly obvious that Hitler was moving toward war, agitating about Danzig and the Polish Corridor. It didn't seem possible that the West would again accede to his demands. My mother kept writing letters to Father urging him to get us out of Germany as quickly as possible. "Don't you

read the papers?" she'd ask. Overt references to the political situation were risky. She wrung her hands in despair when she got a letter that either ignored her pleas or tried to assuage her. She was afraid that my father, like so many others who had left, was no longer able to assess the situation in Germany. The letters of emigrants often sounded as though once they crossed the border they forgot everything they had gone through. The fact that it wasn't easy to find employment for us in an English household—the only way my father could get us into England—was something Mother could not accept. I can still hear her urge Paula Fürst to impress the German situation and the likelihood of war on my father. The former principal of the Theodor Herzl School, Paula Fürst was scheduled to chaperon a group of children leaving for England on August 3, 1939. To everyone's surprise she returned to Germany because she didn't know what to do in England. In Berlin she had her pension and her friends, while abroad she had no one. Many German Jews were still talking like that.

Paula Fürst's description of the perilous situation in Germany and the likelihood of war apparently did impress my father. Shortly after her return we got the good news that Mother and I were to start work in the home of a professor in Glasgow—Mother as cook and I as her helper. Now, we thought, nothing could stand in our way

anymore. Then a few weeks later, on August 23, came the alarming news of the pact between the Soviet Union and the Third Reich. We were stunned. It was an incomprehensible betrayal of the free world by the Soviet Union, the natural ally in the fight against the Nazis. Then we began to wonder whether this agreement might avert a war, at least for the immediate future. Still, we saw young men with backpacks and cartons on the streets of Berlin—obviously a secret mobilization of reservists. At regular intervals the radio and the papers urged the people to prepare air-raid shelters and to check their gas masks.

We were not regularly in touch with our old political friends. Dr. Ostrowski had promised Father that he would look after us, and he had invited us to his house once. He was very demoralized. August 23 was a bitter disappointment for all Socialists and Communists. "The swastika flag in honor of Ribbentrop flying in Moscow, Hitler in a friendship pact with the Soviet Union. Now nothing will stop him," said Ostrowski, unable to believe the turn of events.

The anti-Nazis were faced with a paradox. On the one hand they wanted a war because they were convinced that Hitler would lose, because it was the only way Germany could get rid of the Nazis. Hitler could not win a two-front war against the Soviet Union and Poland on one flank, and Eng-

land and France with America on the other. By ruling out that possibility for the time being, the pact promised to solidify Nazi rule.

On August 27 our superintendent distributed food-ration cards. Ours bore the initial "J." The significance of that did not become clear to us until later, when we found out that it meant that we were entitled neither to extra rations nor to unrationed food. My mother was in a dreadful state; endless formalities were connected with our emigration. She slept poorly, and I was of no great help. However, the Blumenthals were. Sitting with them on the balcony of their room, we discussed every phase, every nuance of the developments. I enjoyed these sessions, for I liked Max Blumenthal. He was the first adult male to take notice of me. I was attracted to this distinguished-looking man with the dark eyes and hair and high forehead. Of course I kept my feelings secret. Sometimes he danced with me or took me out to a café. He had records of Schubert and Hugo Wolf songs and taught me to love them. Strange as it may sound, those days were a high point in my life. I was a seventeen-year-old with no opportunity to meet young men. And I didn't even know that this was not a normal state of affairs.

"Just like back in 1914," said my mother, pointing to the horses being led by soldiers down the street. Hitler most certainly was getting ready for

war. The pact with the Soviet Union gave him breathing room, time to challenge the West without fear of intervention by the East. The newspapers were full of horror stories about Polish atrocities against ethnic Germans. It was reminiscent of the pre-Munich days in 1938, when the Führer was shedding tears over Czech persecution of Sudeten Germans.

On September 1, the blow fell: The German army crossed the Polish border. "This is it," my mother said dispiritedly. Now England, as Poland's ally, would have no choice but to intervene. We tried to put a call through to my father. "Please, operator, try once more," Mother pleaded. But England did not answer. And that is how things remained for six long years.

5

September 1, 1939, looked like a rehearsal for war. In the afternoon air-raid sirens went off. Even now I still don't know whether or not the threat of an air raid was real. More likely the government wanted to impress the people with the gravity of the situation. And the people, sheeplike as ever, went down to the air-raid shelters with their emergency supplies—a bottle of water, some food, a first-aid kit, and a gas mask. It was all somewhat ludicrous. People sat quietly in their assigned places, listening and wondering what the alarm was all about. Outside, "above ground," it was eerily quiet. Our air-raid warden in his new gray uniform checked the names of those present against his list and issued pompous orders about

extinguishing possible fires and how to get to the emergency exits. We Jews were relegated to a corner of the shelter, and there we sat quietly, not daring to look at our "Aryan" neighbors until the all-clear sounded about half an hour later. Then we waited respectfully for all the Aryans to precede us before going out ourselves.

That night we experienced our first blackout. Self-appointed busybodies ran around checking blackout curtains to make sure that no light was showing through. People crowded onto the streets to see what Berlin looked like without street lights and neon signs. It was still a novelty. The moon and stars provided the only light. The Gedächtniskirche, that ugly landmark on Kurfürstendamm, looked almost beautiful etched against the moonlit sky.

The Nazis took advantage of the declaration of war to issue a number of highly restrictive edicts. They no longer had to fear criticism of the outside world. The harshest measure affecting non-Jews was the ban on listening to foreign broadcasts. Violators were subject to severe punishment and, toward the end of the war, even the death penalty. The government asked people to report anyone found listening. Since foreign broadcasts were vital sources of information about developments abroad and foreign reaction to events in Germany, such as arrests of anti-Nazis, anti-Jewish measures, and

resistance within the military, most opponents of the regime ignored the law but took precautions.

"I still have my earphones," Franz Gumz told us gleefully. Earphones were at a premium in Berlin. It was far too risky to try to buy them at a store where one wasn't known. Mr. Gumz was the owner of a laundry we'd been patronizing for years. When he came to pick up or deliver our bundle he'd sit down with us and talk politics. He was a simple, guileless man, a member of a persecuted sect, the Jehovah's Witnesses, and he hated the Nazis. For him as for so many others, the nightly BBC broadcasts were a source of information, hope, and reassurance. Listening wasn't easy because the broadcasts were jammed. Too often all that could be understood was a word here and there, out of context. And if you listened to foreign broadcasts, you had to make sure to turn the dial back to the local setting as soon as it ended, a warning the BBC announcer issued just before signing off.

The alleged reason for the proliferating anti-Jewish restrictions and regulations was to prevent Jews from engaging in "antistate activities." The radios of Jews were confiscated and their telephones disconnected. They were not allowed to leave their homes between the hours of 8 P.M. and 5 A.M. (9 P.M. in the summer). During air-raid alarms they had to stay in the shelters until the

all-clear sounded, to prevent them from signaling the enemy. They no longer were protected by rent laws. They had to hand over any furs, binoculars, cameras, and electrical appliances still in their possession. Mother and I ignored these regulations. We no longer owned a radio, but we didn't turn in any other proscribed article. Instead, we stored more and more of what we still had left with the Riecks. (Almost all Jews had some trusted non-Jewish friend who helped them out in this way. Valuable oriental rugs, musical instruments, fur coats in sealed garment bags were stowed away in their basements and attics.) Finally Jews were barred from theaters and concert halls and movies. Parks and public recreational areas were closed to them, except for special park benches marked by Jewish stars. Entire sectors of Berlin were closed to them altogether, including the district of government offices.

With the heedlessness of youth, I told my mother I had no intention of abiding by these restrictions. I wasn't ready to spend my life without occasionally going to a play or concert or for a walk in the park. I couldn't bear the thought of spending all my time in the company of Jews exclusively. All they ever talked of was Nazi persecutions and their own anxieties—a litany of fear, apprehension, and self-torture. We called this network disseminating ominous news the JBS, the

Jewish Broadcast Service. I even managed to persuade Mother to come with me to some plays and concerts. Most of these offerings were on a very high level. The Nazis did not stint in their support of the arts as morale boosters. As a final indignity, Jews were even forbidden to send their laundry out to be done or go to a hairdresser.

I am convinced that every Jew violated one or another regulation. If, for example, Jews had restricted themselves to the allotted diet, they would never have had the strength to do the hard jobs assigned to them. The overwhelming majority of Jews in Berlin had friends or neighbors who helped them get food beyond their official ration, grocers who gave their old customers a little something "extra." Once a week Mother and I paid a visit to Richard Junghans, our old Socialist friend who had opened a grocery after being ousted from his union post. He gave us fruit and vegetables. And our old butcher, Mr. Krachudel, sold us the same cuts and amounts of meat as in the past, without any ration stamps.

"What will it be today?" his wife would ask as politely as ever. "Stew meat, or maybe a roast?"

If getting enough food had become a matter of some urgency for the Jews of Berlin, it also created a problem for the non-Jewish population. Many of the decent people who risked denunciation for helping their Jewish friends and customers will

have to go unsung; those they helped are no longer here to tell of it. We heard an altogether believable story about a Jewish woman who threw lemons and apples out the window when she heard the Gestapo at her door because she didn't want to compromise the shopkeeper who had sold them to her.

We received letters from Father via the Red Cross, and we were allowed to send a twenty-five-word message once a month on a special form. We'd spend hours trying to formulate our little missive. We didn't want to upset him unnecessarily, yet at the same time we wanted to tell him, and through him the world, as much as possible about our life in Berlin. We tried to get our message across by allusion and circumspection, not realizing that people in free countries had forgotten how to decipher cryptic language. My father's eagerly awaited but irregular Red Cross letters were promptly passed around among all our friends and relatives. As the war wore on and the reciprocal bombings became increasingly severe, the mail became more and more irregular. But when a letter finally did arrive, we poured over it and analyzed those twenty-five words as though they were a learned treatise. Some "real" letters from Father came to us via neutral sources, from friends in America or Shanghai, but they took weeks, even months, to reach us. They more than anything else

made it painfully clear to us that we were prisoners with no chance of escape. True, a fortunate few still managed to emigrate after the war broke out. Via circuitous routes they got to Shanghai or the United States, and others spent a fortune for visas and transportation to Palestine on unchartered ships. Not all of them made it.

We were not surprised by the collapse of the Polish front, only by the speed of its fall. It was difficult having to listen to the gloating over the German radio after each victory. We couldn't understand what was happening in the West. Wasn't the Maginot Line supposed to have halted the German advance? That was what we were banking on until it collapsed. There were occasional air-raid alarms in Berlin, but not a single bomb was dropped. And when the first bomb finally did fall, people couldn't stop talking about it. The site of that first attack attracted hundreds of spectators.

On April 1, 1939, my schooling ended, not by my choice but because the Nazis closed all Jewish schools. Still, I had enough credits for graduation. We girls celebrated the end of school by dancing with each other. We had taught each other to dance because the dancing schools traditionally attended by middle-class girls were of course closed to Jews. Nor were we able to go out with boys our age. The fear of possibly being recognized by a Nazi in a movie or a café put a damper on any

thought of flirtation. Gert, one of my fellow students, went home with me on the underground every day even though it took him out of his way. It was our one chance of seeing each other and exchanging a few words.

The question of what to do while waiting to emigrate was not a difficult one. I didn't have all that many options; I could either work in a Jewish household or in a factory. There weren't many places where Jews could learn a trade or profession. For some reason the Jewish training school for kindergarten teachers had not yet been closed, so I decided to enroll in its one-year course. I was convinced that I would emigrate before I could finish. As far as I and most of my classmates were concerned, this was a temporary solution. Under normal circumstances most of us would have gone to college. The head of the institute, Dr. Leonore Fraenkel, the non-Jewish wife of a Jewish emigré, ran the school as though teaching us were the most important thing in the world. I was beginning to enjoy the school; the courses in psychology and education opened up new vistas. What we were taught there undoubtedly exceeded the minimum requirements. Even Hans Hinkel, the Nazi "culture czar" who sat in on our exams, had to admit that the level of instruction was very high.

A Jewish kindergarten was the scene of my first venture into early childhood education. It was a

very tense place; the teachers were almost as worried about their future as the parents of their charges. Yet in some ways this kindergarten was no different than any other. Little children, blond and dark-haired, blue- and brown-eyed, played and romped and filled the room with their laughter.

As part of my practical training, I had to work with a family in their home. I was sent to the Keils, who lived in a project for poor Jewish families next to a synagogue. (Incidentally, this same synagogue now serves the small Jewish community of West Berlin.) The people who lived in that project took their meals in its communal kitchen.

The Keils had been the well-to-do owners of a chain of shoe-repair shops. However, for reasons I no longer remember, Mr. Keil was arrested in 1933 and his business was confiscated. He returned from the concentration camp a broken man, penniless, sick, and unable to work. Since Jews were no longer eligible for government assistance, the Keils became charges of the Jewish Community. When I met them, Mrs. Keil was pregnant with their third child. Their apartment consisted of one big gloomy room furnished with iron bedsteads, a kitchen table and some wooden chairs, and another tiny room for their seven-year-old son. I was supposed to help Mrs. Keil with the cleaning and with her three-year-old daughter. I

didn't like this job. The Keils' poverty was disheartening, and Mrs. Keil made me very uneasy. She looked sad and neglected. I was glad to get out of there, away from the depressing atmosphere of the project and its poverty-stricken inhabitants. Also, I was afraid that Mrs. Keil might go into labor while I was there. But I was lucky. Before the baby was born I was sent to a similar job in another part of Berlin, this one in a working-class district. It was a neighborhood of sunless tenements without private bathrooms. Tucked away in a cold dark corner of each floor was a communal toilet.

The husband of my new family was in a concentration camp. The wife was a resolute young woman. They had a young baby whom I was supposed to tend. The poverty of these people had not been brought on by the Nazis. Until then I had not known that Berlin also had its share of poor Jews. The family's single room was airless, dark, and cold. The sofa and the rest of the furniture was broken and dirty. A friendly, chubby baby boy crawled around in this thrift-shop jumble. To his mother's dismay, he was not yet toilet trained. She hated washing diapers, and when he wet himself she hit him with a stick. There was nothing I could do about it. The baby's cries followed me all the way home. The woman obviously found her child a terrible burden.

After this stint I was assigned to the home of two elderly sisters in a good section of the city. They shared a one-room apartment and spent their days waiting for the inevitable. They had no family, and no one ever came to see them. They took care of themselves and their apartment as best they could and were grateful for whatever assistance I could give them. Pale and drawn, they never gave any hint of what they were going through or whether they had seen better days.

Soon after the war broke out the Nazis stopped my father's pension, explaining that his residence in an enemy country obviated any legitimate claim to the money. Even though there weren't many things Jews could still spend money on—food was rationed and Jews didn't get clothing coupons—still it meant that we'd have to tighten our belts. We decided to move into a cheaper furnished room. Our new landlords, the Krzcesnys, were a friendly elderly couple with a tubercular daughter who died before she could be deported. Another daughter was unsuccessfully trying to arrange for passage to Australia for the family. We enjoyed our stay with them. They were kind people who shared what they had and made us feel part of the family.

We were living in an illusory lull. We were at war, but after the fall of Poland things quieted down. Occasionally an air-raid alarm sounded, but

the British raids were so inconsequential that most people never even bothered to get out of bed. The Berliners joked that the British must be cross-eyed because their bombs either missed their mark or fell on meaningless targets. It was very different from what we had imagined war would be like, the war we had expected Hitler to lose very quickly. But instead of losing, Hitler launched an attack on England. For us Jews all this was very frightening. Suppose, contrary to all expectations, Hitler were to win the war? Mrs. Oppenheimer, the wife of an old friend of Father's, said to my mother, "We won't live to see it. We won't survive." I don't know where she found the courage to say what none of us wanted to hear or admit. She had sent her thirteen-year-old son to England before the outbreak of the war. She and her husband had vowed that the Nazis would never get them, and true to their word, they committed suicide as they were about to be deported.

By sheer accident I found out a great deal more than was generally known about the negotiations between the Jewish Community and the Gestapo. Having finished my one-year course, I took a job as a so-called house daughter at the home of Dr. Conrad Cohen. Not many other choices were open to me. Household work was still preferable to work in a factory, the only other alternative.

The Cohens lived in a five-room apartment. Dr. Conrad Cohen, his wife, Leonore, and his eleven-year-old daughter Marianne occupied the four rooms that were my responsibility. His parents lived in the fifth. In addition to cleaning, I had to wash windows, do the laundry, and look after Marianne. I worked from seven in the morning until late in the evening. The only difference between me and a maid was that I was called "house daughter" and ate with the family.

Unlike life in other Jewish households, nothing seemed to have changed at the Cohens. Everything here exuded comfort. Oriental rugs, paintings, old prints, antique furniture, silver and crystal. Nothing had had to be sold or put away for safekeeping. Life in the house of Conrad Cohen, formerly a respected lawyer from Breslau, continued in its customary style. Dr. Cohen said he couldn't live any other way. His dinner guests sat down at an elegantly set table. This dramatic contrast to the disintegration, pain, and uncertainty all around us struck me as unreal. To my dismay, Dr. Cohen did not depart from his habit of wearing a freshly laundered shirt every day, a rare luxury at that time. It was also taken for granted by the rest of the family, particularly by his parents, that he was entitled to all sorts of delicacies and special foods.

His father, the elder Dr. Cohen, was a kind,

gentle man. His mother, on the other hand, fought with everybody. Her son's welfare was paramount, and she made no secret of the fact that she did not think her daughter-in-law, wealthy though she was, worthy of the honor of being married to her Conrad. The atmosphere in the household was anything but pleasant. No wonder that Marianne was spoiled and was given anything she wanted. I worked so hard that I had no time to think about myself. Sometimes I cried out of sheer exhaustion, and the many nights I had to go to the air-raid shelter even though no bombs fell made matters worse. I was constantly hungry. Once, to my mortification, I was caught nibbling on a dish I'd prepared for Dr. Cohen.

Dr. Cohen was the head of the welfare department of the Reich Association of Jews in Germany, the coordinating body of Germany's Jewish welfare agencies. All the agencies operated under Nazi direction. Conrad Cohen, an extremely intelligent man, did not talk much about his work, but occasionally he would mention being summoned to the Gestapo. "That's always like a high-wire act," he once said. He was never sure whether or not he would come back home after such a visit. "A missing cake of soap could break my neck." We all knew what that meant.

Moritz Henschel, the chairman of the Berlin Jewish Community, lived in the same building as

the Cohens. By then, Henschel's job consisted mainly of an unceasing effort to make the life of Berlin's Jews as bearable as possible. The war had torn families apart. Many of the people ousted from their trade or profession were unable to perform the heavy labor to which they were assigned. It was a widely held belief among Jews that the officials of the Jewish Community and the Reich Association were in an enviable position, that they enjoyed various privileges, even that they wielded some power, a belief these officials initially encouraged. Not surprisingly, those who did not share in the advantages of the Cohens envied them.

Among the frequent guests in the Cohen household were the Lilienthals. As late as 1939, Mr. Lilienthal, a former judge and secretary general of the Reich Association, still refused to emigrate because he believed it was his duty to "see things through." Other active members of the Reich Association, people like Paula Fürst, Hanna Kaminski, and Franz-Eugen Fuchs, also convinced themselves that they were "still needed" in Berlin. Later I realized that they knew they were deluding themselves as they sat around the table talking about Heine and Goethe, Kant and Hegel as though nothing had changed. At the time I simply thought them bizarre. I felt more comfortable among people closer to reality, a reality most of us could not escape.

* * *

My father's prosperous sister and brother-in-law had to give up their apartment in Spandau and move to a small room they rarely left. Afraid to go out because they were so well known there, they had been forced to sell their business to one of their employees for a pittance. My father's other sister worked in a Jewish old-age home to support herself and her disabled husband. His brother and family, now poor, shared crowded quarters.

My mother took a job in one of the welfare offices of the Jewish Community. Her clientele was large. Since I was living at the Cohens', Mother left our furnished room and moved in with an old friend of hers, a seventy-year-old woman with a big apartment she would have been forced to give up had she not rented out rooms. With her pince-nez and neatly piled-up hair, Aunt Olga, which was what I called her, moved about her apartment like a queen. She loved the grand gesture and expansive locutions: "My fabulous niece! A superb woman! What a wonderful human being!" She spoke only in superlatives.

Even though she had been forced to sell many of her lovely things, she still had some pieces of old furniture. When she sold something she managed to persuade herself that she was doing it because she wanted to, not because she needed the money. She lived in her own contented little world, had her regular card game, loved company,

liked to laugh, and ignored all bad news. And even in those dark times she managed to hold fast to her love of people.

She and her neighbor Elsa Becherer were fast friends. They met "surreptitiously" on the back stairs. Every piece of cake baked in the Becherer household was shared with us. Elsa Becherer was a confirmed anti-Nazi who listened avidly to the BBC for any scrap of news to buttress her hopes and views about the Third Reich. A believer in astrology, she said that according to the stars Hitler was merely a passing phenomenon that could not last. She could be very persuasive. Her husband was in the army, and she rented out a room in her apartment to a half-Jew who was not subject to military service. Her numerous friends included not a single Nazi. When I knocked on her door she would invite me in and introduce me to her guests without a trace of embarrassment. I enjoyed those evenings, for there the conversation was not about emigration or worry over the future. One of her friends, Walter Skolny, a blond, blue-eyed Jewish businessman, couldn't understand for a long time what the Nazis had against him. Mrs. Schroeder, a typical Berlin superintendent with a big mouth and a big heart, who knew everything about the people in the building and the street, was another one of her intimates. A tall, strong, stern-looking woman, Mrs. Schroeder became

gentle, almost loving, when talking to us. She didn't know the meaning of fear. Sometimes she got carried away and become too outspoken and ironic. Only once did I see her look afraid, when a policeman rang our doorbell. She followed close on his heels.

"Your blackout curtains aren't tightly closed," he said, and then, coming nearer, he whispered to Aunt Olga, "You're Jews, aren't you?" a fact made obvious by the star on the door. "For Heaven's sake, close them right away. If my colleague should see it he'd arrest you."

He disappeared, but Mrs. Schroeder came in, muttering angrily, to check the curtains. After she left, Aunt Olga acted as though nothing had happened. "How stupid of me to forget," she said, and turning to Mother she asked, "Ella, where are the cards? Let's play."

6

"Tell me, Ali, what do you think, is Peter going to come back?"

Eva Diemenstein's eyes filled with tears. Peter, her husband, had been arrested soon after they'd gotten married. She didn't know why, and nobody knew where he was. The police officers merely shrugged their shoulders when she tried to find out, and the Gestapo wouldn't talk to her at all. Alice Licht, called Ali, stroked Eva's face reassuringly: "Of course Peter will come back." There was an uncomfortable silence. We all knew that Ali was lying; when the Gestapo arrested somebody it was usually for good.

We were talking while standing in line at the Jewish Employment Office. In April 1941 the gov-

ernment announced that Jews would no longer be allowed to employ household help. This meant I had to leave the Cohens and, like all other Jews, was subject to compulsory factory labor. The employment office processed the placement of forced labor. Dr. Cohen had offered to help me find a job in a "good place," even though Jews were not supposed to look for jobs on their own. Some jobs were more desirable than others. It was common knowledge, for example, that Siemens and AEG, unlike I. G. Farben, treated "their" Jews decently. Dr. Cohen had set up an appointment for me with a Mrs. Prokownik at the Jewish Community. Without asking many questions she sent me to see Otto Weidt, the operator of a workshop for the blind.

I climbed up the creaky wooden stairs leading to Otto Weidt's sparsely furnished office. This was my first meeting with him. A slender, tall man with light hair and clouded blue eyes, he was legally blind. And although his vision was blurred, his gaze was penetrating. He asked me to sit down and began questioning me about my family and my father's political background. As he listened to my answers, he periodically inhaled oxygen from an apparatus by his side. When I was finished, he said, "All right. Go to the employment office for Jews the day after tomorrow. There'll be others there waiting for me. We'll see what can be done."

I was already at the door when he called after me, "By the way, don't be surprised if over there I'm not as polite as I am now." I laughed and said good-bye like an old friend.

On the appointed day I found myself on line with Eva, Ali, one of Mrs. Prokownik's sisters, and some men I didn't know, all of us patiently waiting for Otto Weidt. He arrived, greeted us curtly, and before disappearing into the barrackslike building he told us to speak only when spoken to. Fifteen minutes later the door opened and a man came running out, shouting and ranting: "I'll teach you manners, you lousy Jews!"

I thought to myself that this had to be Eschhaus, the infamous head of the employment office. He had once been fired from a job in a Jewish textile company, and ever since he hated Jews with a vengeance. That qualified him for the position he presently occupied.

Now everything happened very quickly. Eschhaus walked down the line, and suddenly stopping in front of Mrs. Prokownik's sister, he shouted, "How did you get to the Weidt workshop?" "Through the Jewish Community," she answered simply. This was a fatal mistake, because finding one's own job was strictly forbidden. Now Eschhaus became even shriller: "What do you think you're doing, you Jewish crooks?" A stream of invective poured down on us. We didn't know

what was going on. Otto Weidt was nowhere to be seen. Apparently something had gone wrong; someone must have denounced him. An assistant came rushing out, and Eschhaus told him to place us in the worst, most difficult jobs. We were going to be punished for having had the audacity to look for jobs on our own.

"I'll show you," Eschhaus kept yelling. Ali and I were sent to the I. G. Farben plant that manufactured parachute silk. Subdued and downhearted, we forgot all about Eva Diemenstein and her Peter.

The atmosphere in the I. G. Farben office was curt and unfriendly. We stood silently in front of someone who checked our papers. Then someone else handed us our working papers and a Jewish star, which we had to pin on our work apron. "And don't you dare forget it . . ." Wearing the Jewish star had not yet been made mandatory, but I. G. Farben jumped the gun. And they emphasized our isolation still more by herding us into a separate canteen with only a table and no chairs. A surly Aryan supervisor acquainted us with our duties: We had to stand for ten hours in front of a rotating spindle, watching to see that the thread did not become twisted or tear or run out. The room was hot and noisy, the work exhausting and boring. Conversation was impossible. During our breakfast break we had only one topic: how to get

out of there. The older Jewish workers told us about the petty persecutions they were subjected to. Some managed to obtain medical releases for reasons like abdominal problems that made it impossible for them to stand at a machine for hours at a time. Ali remembered that she had a history of ulcers, and before long she managed to get a medical release.

Ali and I had little in common with the other Jewish girls working there. They came from very different backgrounds and spoke a different language. They thought us odd. What sheltered lives we had led! We hadn't known that Berlin also had a Jewish proletariat. I can still remember how startled I was when one of the girls—she couldn't have been more than eighteen—wanted to know whether I had a steady boyfriend.

I too was eager to get out of that place, but I didn't know how. I was young and healthy, and try as I would I couldn't think of any disease that would qualify me for release. I don't remember how I finally came up with the idea that saved me, but one morning I put on the highest heels I had ever worn, and kept them on for ten hours standing at the machine, and another three hours standing in the train to and from work. Jews were not allowed to sit. It was torture. After three days I couldn't bend my right knee. My mother was beside herself. She was afraid they'd accuse me of

sabotage. I needed medical certification that I couldn't perform work that required me to stand, and I was certain that a Jewish doctor would be reluctant to issue such a certificate. At the time Jews were still allowed to consult non-Jewish doctors. Our friends the Riecks recommended Dr. Damm, an Aryan doctor they thought trustworthy. They didn't know him very well, but they felt sure that he was not a Nazi. Dr. Damm examined me and said that of course I couldn't do any work that required me to stand. Not only that, he also certified that I needed sick leave.

At first nothing happened. I. G. Farben put me on sick leave. The amount they paid was ridiculous. The base pay of Jews was minuscule to begin with, and from this pittance they withheld the special tax levied on Jews and Gypsies. After some weeks I had to report to the factory doctor. Mother was terrified. He kept me waiting for hours, and I kept thinking of Mother while I sat waiting. Finally my turn came.

"Take off your slip," he said, pointing to an examination table. I told him politely that what bothered me was my knee. His dismissive gesture made it clear that he wasn't interested in what I had to say.

"Have you ever had sexual intercourse?" he asked. Neither the question nor the embarrassing, rather painful examination had anything to do

with my complaint. He never even looked at my knee; still he recommended that I be released because, he explained, I. G. Farben was not about to keep me on paid sick leave forever. The examination had been humiliating, but I was ecstatic. I'd won my release. I flew home. Mother had been waiting for hours and was worried sick.

The next thing I did was go to see Weidt and Ali. Weidt beamed. This was what he enjoyed. He was a gambler and risk-taker and liked a good fight. He suggested that we should try once more to get me a job in his workshop. As Ali's case proved, the incident with Eschhaus had long since been forgotten. Who knows, maybe Weidt had managed to find the right perfume for Eschhaus's wife or girlfriend. Nazi officials were not above trading their principles for bribes.

Weidt had army contracts, and that made him an "essential producer." The army, after all, needed brushes and brooms, and this entitled him to allocations of raw materials such as horsehair and synthetics and, of course, to workers. Occasionally, when pressed, he would even fill army orders. But most of the time he managed to use these materials for "other" purposes. Everything, including brooms and brushes, was in short supply, and therefore could be bartered. There wasn't a shop in Berlin that didn't do business with Weidt: horsehair brooms for perfume or clothing or um-

brellas or food. Of course he didn't have enough raw material to satisfy all the demand, but he did have supplementary sources of supply. The policemen of the nearby precinct gave him horsetails; soldiers on leave brought him horsehair from the occupied territories. Weidt paid them black-market rates. The sighted Jewish workers in his shop processed these materials, and the blind workers, about thirty men and women, then made them into brooms and brushes. Without these "black" raw materials Weidt could not have employed as many people as he did, all but three of whom were Jews. The unmarried blind Jews working there— some were deaf as well—lived in the Jewish Home for the Blind. Some had been born blind and some had been blinded in accidents or had become blind as a result of illness. And even though it was strictly forbidden, Weidt also had Jews working in the office. Both Ali, who became a very good secretary, and Werner Basch, a fine bookkeeper, had been assigned to Weidt as laborers, and that is how he carried them on the books. Ultimately I too wound up working in the office.

Weidt said that he would once again approach Eschhaus about hiring me. Off he went to the employment office, he with his white cane and I limping behind him with my heavily bandaged knee, also leaning on a cane. Eschhaus was waiting for us. Weidt turned to me and ordered me to wait

outside. Standing in the doorway to Eschhaus' office, he said to the secretary, "Give this Jew a chair. She can't stand." I sat down, leg extended, heart in throat. After a while a smug Weidt came back out, followed by Eschhaus. Shaking Weidt's hand, he said, "We're really grateful to you, Mr. Weidt, for taking all these people nobody wants off my hands." Weidt smiled magnanimously. We left, and at a safe distance from the office we stopped and started to laugh. Weidt took off his badge certifying him as legally blind and I started to play with my cane, our gesture of defiance of reality. He was almost blind, and I had a bad knee that continued to give me trouble for years. But at that moment none of it mattered.

Back at the office Weidt told me that for the time being he had no work for me, but that he had spoken to a friend who needed temporary help during the vacation season. I would be Weidt's employee on loan to somebody else.

Kniepmeyer's workshop for the blind also made brooms and brushes. Since it was vacation time I didn't meet any of the other workers. Before going on vacation, Kniepmeyer's secretary showed me around. All I had to do was answer the phone and take care of urgent correspondence. The secretary had no idea who I was; only Kniepmeyer himself knew. He treated me with polite reserve.

Because of the labor shortage, temporary help was not easy to find, so Weidt had done him a favor by lending me to him.

At first I was very bored. The mail was finished in an hour and the telephone didn't ring very often. I was completely alone in my office, which adjoined the large, deserted workshop. Mr. Kniepmeyer did not spend much time there. After a while I noticed that he was becoming friendlier. One day he called me into his office. He looked imposing sitting behind his desk. On the wall hung a portrait of the Führer, and occasionally Mr. Kniepmeyer wore a swastika pin on his lapel. He asked me to sit down, and told me that he'd been watching me for some time and had come to the conclusion that I was not like other Jews. He inquired about my parents, how long our family had lived in Germany, and where we had come from. I told him that to the best of my knowledge our family had been in Germany for generations. He listened, shaking his head slightly. The phone rang, putting an end to our first conversation. I didn't know what to make of it.

The next day he again had me come into his office and asked still more questions about my situation. He seemed upset by what I told him. Germans who closed their eyes to what was going on around them had no idea how Jews were forced to live. When I told him how small our food rations

were, he brought me a basket of fruit. They were from his garden, he said, adding that that was all he could give me without arousing his wife's suspicions. He didn't dare tell her about me. He added that he would try to bring me some coffee on the pretext that he'd like to have coffee at the office. Our talks became more and more friendly. I gingerly began to touch on politics, on the war and Hitler. I tried to make him see that Hitler couldn't win. He was skeptical.

His workshop, he said, was much more modern than Weidt's, and he asked if I wouldn't like to see it. He led the way, and somewhere among all the brooms and brushes, he moved very close to me. I was terrified. I resisted, but I was afraid of being too overtly rejecting. Besides, I was completely inexperienced in those matters. He seemed to understand, and let go of me. Almost shyly, planting a chaste kiss on my forehead, he said that I was the first Jewish woman he'd ever been close to, that I was pretty, intelligent, friendly, and desirable, very unlike his idea of a Jew. I didn't know what to do. I was supposed to work there for another two months, and I didn't dare tell anyone about what had happened, not my mother, not Weidt. He had already done so much for me, and I didn't want to bother him with my problems. I didn't know how to handle the situation, and Kniepmeyer kept after me. I managed to hold him

at arm's length, but this only seemed to encourage him.

One day his son came to the office to help out. He of course had no idea who I was. He was a nice young man about my age, and the two of us worked well together. He came back the next day. I was glad, because now I didn't have to be alone with his father. Kniepmeyer naturally noticed that his son was also showing an interest in me. "My son's got good taste," he said to me with a smile, and then for the first time he became more insistent. I managed to elude him. I decided to call Weidt, who was angry that I hadn't told him about this before. "I'll put an end to it. I'll call him and tell him that I need you back here right away." And he did. I had to go back to Kniepmeyer's only one more time, to say goodbye.

Weidt put me in charge of the shipping and the telephone, neither of which was very time-consuming. I did my best to show my gratitude and earn my keep. It wasn't easy. Ali had done a fine job organizing both the office and the boss. Weidt, who was about sixty, had never before been as prosperous as he was during those war years. With great skill he made a lot of money producing "black" goods. And Ali proved of invaluable help. Weidt's wife, Else, enjoyed this unexpected windfall in her own fashion, traveling all the time and

staying in luxury hotels, and he enjoyed indulging her.

I admired Weidt. He became a kind of substitute father. I was impressed by his forthrightness, so like that of my parents. Ali wasn't altogether pleased with my attachment to him; however, if there were any tensions, they eased after Hans Rosenthal came into my life.

Before Hitler, Hans Rosenthal had been an engineer at a large technical company. Now he was the purchasing and distributing agent of the Jewish Community. Weidt was only one of a number of suppliers with whom he was on excellent terms. Even the Gestapo knew that he was able to get them goods that were hard to come by.

Hans was in his late thirties and single; he lived with his mother. Before long he began coming to our office more and more often. I made no secret of the fact that I liked him, perhaps also to escape the unwelcome attentions of Werner Basch, our bookkeeper, a good-looking man in his early thirties. With his well-groomed, prematurely gray hair and fixed smile, Werner looked like an overanxious salesman. He was probably the first bookkeeper Weidt had ever had, and it took him months to bring order out of chaos. Weidt, who was anything but systematic, didn't particularly appreciate Basch's efforts, but he let him work away at his ledger and listen to his favorite opera broadcasts.

"Ah, Verdi," Basch would exclaim ecstatically. He had been sent to Weidt by the Jewish Community, where his wife, Ilse, an intelligent though not particularly attractive woman, had an important job. Theirs was not a happy marriage, and Basch began to take an interest in me. I won't deny that at first I wasn't averse to a little harmless flirtation; however, one day, when we were alone in the office, he became more blunt. I was indignant. I, the sheltered daughter of a proper bourgeois family, was outraged. I wasn't used to such behavior by a married man. I much preferred Hans Rosenthal's attentions. He was modest, friendly, intelligent, proper, and gentle. We took occasional walks together, which were all that was possible under the circumstances. The more difficult things became, the more I clung to him. Except for my mother, I had no one to confide in, and so I was doubly grateful for another human being to talk to. In those days many marriages between Jews grew out of just such a desire to escape loneliness.

Weidt obviously enjoyed watching his love-struck office assistant and tried to facilitate our meetings. He knew of the obstacles, and so every now and then he'd throw a little party in his office for us and Ali and Werner and Ilse Basch. He would buy meat on the black market and have the superintendent prepare a meal. Those improvised

evenings are among my rare pleasant memories of that time.

But we were never allowed to forget what was happening all around us. "Scram," Ali would call out, and quickly put on the apron with the star and disappear into the workshop. Basch and I would scramble out of the office and up the stairs. Gustav Kremmert, Weidt's non-Jewish partner, would then sit down at Basch's desk, and Erika, a non-Jewish apprentice, would sit in Ali's chair. It was a drill we'd practiced often. From our listening post on the stairs we could hear Weidt talking to Franz Prüfer, the acting chief of the Jewish section of the Berlin Gestapo. Weidt had invited Prüfer to come and see how he was running his shop with Jewish workers, and Prüfer would drop in unannounced from time to time. Weidt would take him through the workshop, show him the purportedly separate lavatories for the "Jewish swine," and yell at a blind Jewish worker. "Is this supposed to be a broom?" he'd ask angrily, and tell Prüfer in great detail how he managed to get good work out of these Jews by disciplining them. "I don't know how I could fill the army orders without these Jews," he'd sigh, and Prüfer would nod approvingly.

While this inspection was underway no one in the shop dared make a wrong move. But once Prüfer was gone Weidt would come back to the

workshop and explain why he had acted the way he had. Of course the people there knew anyway. The tension eased and they could laugh, and Weidt would give them cigarettes. We in the office got wine, but none of us ever got drunk. We were far too tense.

7

A man got up from his seat in the underground. "Please, sit down," he said to me in a loud voice, pointing to his vacant seat. Most of the other passengers pretended not to have heard. It was the morning rush hour, and I was not the only one standing. I was convinced that if it were not for my Jewish star the man would not have offered me his seat.

It was September 19, 1941, the day on which the edict compelling Jews to wear the yellow star at all times went into effect. The evening before I had sewn the yellow badge on the left side of my coat, as instructed. The Jewish welfare agencies had provided every Jew with four of these insignia.

Fearing demonstrations of "spontaneous" out-

rage, Ali and I had agreed to meet in the morning. We were not afraid of the Berliners themselves. Ali was working at Weidt's place, I at Kniepmeyer's. I had an additional minor problem. There was a young man who for some time had been taking the same morning train as me. I had no idea who he was. We had never exchanged a single word, yet I felt there was a bond between us. I didn't think he was Jewish, and I must admit that I was afraid of his reaction when he learned that I was. As it turned out, my fear was unfounded, for after that morning I never saw him again. Perhaps it was coincidence, or perhaps he was afraid. At any rate, not everyone was as brave as the man who insisted that I take his seat. I whispered to him that I was not allowed to sit, and he understood.

When I got off at my stop he followed me and offered to escort me. Surely that wasn't forbidden, he said. We walked a few steps together and then I asked him to leave, which he did. I could not tell him the reason why his company created a problem for me. At Kniepmeyer's I could not be seen with the Jewish star, so I did what I was to do so many times: duck into a doorway, take off my coat, and put on the jacket without a star that I carried with me. It was not an entirely risk-free procedure. If an informer were to see me, I would suffer the same fate as those whom the Gestapo stopped on the street to check whether their star

was sewn on tightly enough. If not, it was the concentration camp for them. I went through my coat-changing routine often, not only because Jews were barred from using public transportation except when going to and from work, but also because our grocer would not have been able to wait on us if I had come in wearing the star; nor would Mrs. Gumz have been allowed to do our laundry or give me the meat she got for us at the butcher's. And of course I continued to go to concerts and the movies and theater. With the star, none of this would have been possible. The change of clothes was not simple. To begin with, I had to find a place in which to do it. I could neither leave nor return to our house without the star; the people there knew me. And there were other problems. If I happened to run into a Jewish acquaintance who did not notice that I was without the star and wanted to stop and talk I had to be rude and rush off.

"Please," my mother would plead with me, "be careful. Don't overdo it. Go without the star only when it's absolutely necessary." I promised I would, but of course not wearing the star made life much more bearable.

Jews, I among them, at times also had some touching experiences. Occasionally a stranger would come up to me in the subway or on the street and slip something into my pocket, an apple

or meat stamps, things to which Jews were not entitled. Still, there is no denying that the Jewish star served its purpose: It set us apart. Some people looked at me with hostility, others with sympathy, and still others averted their eyes.

I remember how I hated being stared at. Once, at the station, waiting for the train, a woman kept walking past me and staring. Finally I couldn't stand it any longer. "You've probably never seen a Jew before," I said. She turned beet red. "Go ahead, you can look at me. I don't mind." She walked away without saying a word.

Another time my mother and I went shopping. It was winter and it had snowed. Suddenly somebody grabbed us by the arm, handed us a shovel, and ordered us to start cleaning the street. We had been so busy talking to each other that we'd failed to notice all the Jews busy shoveling snow. I put on my happiest face and told Mother to sing to help us pass the time. We also managed to signal to Jews who were about to turn the corner to make a detour. After a while the Nazi who had commandeered us grew impatient, grabbed the shovel, and told us to scram.

Jewish children suffered the most. From age six, they had to wear the Jewish star. Children can be cruel, and Jewish children were subjected to the same kind of nasty anti-Semitism as adults. Unless restrained by their elders other children would hit

them. When I was not wearing the star and I'd see a Jewish child being taunted, I would grab the little tormentor by the scruff of the neck. It was a foolhardy thing to do. Thus, it was as dangerous to go without the star as to wear it.

Between four and five in the afternoon, the hour specifically set aside for them, Jewish women could be seen out in the street doing their shopping. They could not possibly get all their errands done in one hour, particularly in districts that still had a relatively large Jewish population. The women ran from shop to shop, and the rushing made it more difficult for shopkeepers to give a little something extra to their regular customers. Still, they found a way; people are resilient, they learn to adjust. We did. However, it was obvious that the situation of the Jews in Berlin was becoming more and more critical. Rumors about the horrors yet to come were rampant. I asked Mother to spare me the bulletins of the "Jewish network" she brought home from her office. I didn't want to hear them.

"What if these rumors turned out to be true after all?" Mother asked.

"What's the good of all this worrying and trembling," I said. However, there came a day when one such rumor turned into grim reality.

On October 16, 1941, Mr. Hefter, an employee of the Jewish Community whose exact function I

no longer remember, rushed into the workshop. Extremely agitated, he asked to speak to Mr. Weidt immediately. He and Weidt were old friends, and I knew that Weidt often gave Hefter some little thing, a nailbrush or duster perhaps, which could be traded for something else. Hefter went into Weidt's office, and minutes later Weidt asked Ali to join them. When she came out again looking drained and pale she walked slowly over to her desk and cradled the desk lamp as though trying to warm herself.

"Ali, for Heaven's sake, say something," I implored. Something terrible must have happened. Slowly and with great effort she said, "Tonight several hundred Jews are going to be picked up at their apartments and sent to the East, to camps."

I refused to believe it. "Do you think it's true? I'm sure it's just another rumor."

"No, no. Hefter must know what he's talking about. The officials of the Jewish Community had to draw up the list for the transport."

At that moment Weidt and Hefter came out of the office.

"We were sworn to silence. But I couldn't keep it to myself any longer. I had to tell somebody." Hefter was in despair. His eyes were brimming with tears. "Please don't tell anyone else."

Werner Basch, whose wife also worked in the Community, remained skeptical, but Hefter told

him that only a very few people there were involved in the preparation of the lists, and they
were sworn to absolute secrecy.

I wanted to know more. Why? When? Who?
How? Hefter continued his restless pacing. From
his rambling account we learned that all those who
had recently filled out the form sent them by the
Community requesting them to list all their pos
sessions, including such items as bed linens and
rugs, were to be deported. The lists had to be
returned to the offices of the Community.

"Oh, my God, Mrs. Hohenstein," I said to myself. Mrs. Hohenstein, a sixty-five-year-old widow,
lived in one of Aunt Olga's rooms. When she received such a form, Mother and I couldn't understand why she had and we hadn't. We thought
we would probably also get one. That had been
three weeks ago, and since then none of us had
given the matter another thought.

Neither Weidt nor Ali nor Basch nor I was able
to work that morning. All we could do was try to
digest what Hefter had told us. It was mind-
boggling. They obviously weren't talking about labor camps. It was unlikely that they were planning
to send frail sixty-five-year-old women like Mrs.
Hohenstein to a labor camp. Perhaps she had been
sent that form in error, perhaps it was all a mistake
that would be straightened out, perhaps this entire
incomprehensible story wasn't true.

"Whatever you do, don't leave the house after eight o'clock tonight," Weidt said to me. "And wear your jacket with the star if somebody should ring your doorbell after eight." Jews had to wear the yellow star indoors and out.

I ran home with the news. Mother refused to believe it. It was, after all, quite literally unbelievable, yet we couldn't stop talking about it, about whether or not to tell Mrs. Hohenstein. What should we do? Suppose it turned out to be just another rumor? Why alarm her? But suppose it *was* true? Could she prepare herself? Obviously not. We continued to discuss it even after she was taken away. Perhaps she could have fled. But a woman her age, not in the best of health—what could she have done?

Shortly after eight our doorbell rang loudly and insistently. My mother just sat there, stunned. "Oh my God," she whispered. There was no doubt about who was at the door. I put on my jacket with the star and opened the door. Two tall men in leather coats asked whether a Klara Sara Hohenstein lived there. I pointed to her door and went back to our room.

"We must tell Aunt Olga," Mother said.

"But that's not possible. It's incomprehensible," Aunt Olga exclaimed. Sitting around our table we tried to hear what was happening in Mrs. Hohenstein's room. I don't know how long we sat

there like that, not daring to speak. We couldn't hear much except footsteps. Then Mrs. Hohenstein called for Aunt Olga. Aunt Olga, trembling, got up from her chair and asked whether there was something she could do. Mrs. Hohenstein calmly informed her that she was being taken away, and that she would get in touch with us as soon as possible. Anxious to put a stop to any speculations, one of the men said that the room would be sealed and that nothing could be removed from it. Then the old lady was taken away. The door closed behind them. The last sounds we heard were the footsteps of the two men and the old lady. Then all was silence.

Mother and I went out into the foyer, where we found Aunt Olga frozen in horror, arms at her side, mouth half-open as though she was about to scream, staring at Mother. "Ella," she cried out and threw her arms about her. "What's happening here?" My mother repeated what she had told her before. But Aunt Olga obviously could not or did not want to believe it.

I couldn't stand it. "We've got to do something. We've got to tell the others, do something," I repeated over and over again.

Our doorbell rang twice. Mrs. Schroeder was standing outside. She had seen Mrs. Hohenstein leave. "What do they want with Mrs. Hohenstein? What's going on here?" We told her what we

knew. She held on to the table and bowed her head, her shoulders shaking. "Criminals! Murderers!" she cried out. We had a hard time calming her down.

I felt it was up to us to let Mrs. Hohenstein's children know what had happened. But how? Jews had no phones. Would Mrs. Schroeder go to them and tell them about their mother? She protested violently. "No, I can't go to those people and tell them that their mother has been carted off. That's too terrible." Finally she agreed to go with me. I didn't think I'd be running any risk being out after eight that evening; the Gestapo had more important things to do.

I no longer remember how and what we told Mrs. Hohenstein's daughter and son-in-law. They listened without saying a word, and we left as quickly as we could on the pretext that I ought not to be out that late. We ran home. The moon was not shining that night. Everything was dark.

The next day we heard that the people who had been taken away were at the Levetzowstrasse synagogue waiting for their transport, and that it was possible to bring them things. But then the rumors grew wilder. Everything was being taken from them, they were being beaten, they weren't given any food. Mrs. Hohenstein's son-in-law came to see us. He knew he was not allowed to go into her room, but something compelled him

to stand in front of her door one last time, in front of the room in which she had spent the last days of her life. He stood there and with pinched lips told us how he'd gone to the synagogue and tried to give his mother-in-law a food package to take along on her trip. But like all the others who had come to see their relatives off, he was turned away. "They are being taken care of," an employee of the Jewish Community told them. "Don't worry. Everything possible is being done for them."

Under cover of darkness my mother and I went to the synagogue on October 17. We didn't dare go too close. From across the street we tried to see what was going on inside, but all we saw was that the lights were on. That in itself was unusual for an ordinary weekday. We could not imagine what the past twenty-four hours must have been like in there. Rumor had it that more than a thousand people were herded together waiting to be taken away, the majority over sixty-five and unable to work. We breathed a sigh of relief that we were still able to work, and we felt ashamed. The walls of the synagogue and the guards in front of it were not the only things that separated us from the people inside. We had been separated from them by arbitrary procedures.

On October 18 this first transport left Berlin for Lodz. A few weeks later we received a form letter that said, "I am well. I am in Lodz. Send me some

packages." And it had a number printed on it, probably the same number already tattooed on her arm.

Yes, we sent packages, and continued to do so for a long time. We put in bread, dried vegetables, and whatever else we were able to scrape together. We never heard from Mrs. Hohenstein again.

8

Mr. Levy, blind, trembling, terrified, stood in front of Weidt.

"I've gotten the list, Mr. Weidt."

In his hand he was clutching one of those notorious forms that were the prelude to deportation. After the first Jew in Berlin had been deported, we all knew the real purpose of the forms on which Jews had to list all their worldly goods. Otto Weidt's hands shook as violently as Levy's. He tore the paper from him.

"Give it to me," he demanded. The little man stepped back. Weidt put on his coat, asked Ali for his white cane, and stormed out of the office without telling anyone where he was going or what he had in mind. We stayed in the office. Gustav Krem-

mert and Erika, his apprentice, didn't know what to say. Kremmert put his hand on Levy's shoulder and clumsily, almost emotionally, tried to reassure him. "You'll see. Everything's going to be all right."

Hampel, our salesman, came in, and in his customary hearty fashion wished us a good day. Kremmert propelled him out of the office, probably to tell him what had happened. Levy went back to the workshop. Today there was none of the usual animated chatter. The blind workers sat wordlessly at their places doing their jobs as skillfully as always.

Behind the workshop was the room where sighted workers under the direction of Mr. Horn prepared the materials for the blind workers. Horn, who came from Poland, spoke a Yiddish-accented German and seemed to live in a state of perpetual fear. The closest he ever came to laughter was a slight change in the set of his lips. Horn's seventeen-year-old son, one of the handful of helpers employed by Weitz, was learning his father's trade. Competent people like Horn were hard to find. Weidt needed him, and he worshipped Weidt.

Ali hinted that Weidt might possibly have gone to the Gestapo with Levy's list, and the rumor spread quickly throughout the shop. I no longer remember exactly when Weidt returned, only that

when he did, he headed straight for the workshop without even taking off his coat.

"Well, that's taken care of," he told the trembling Levy.

"Taken care of?" Levy asked, puzzled.

"Yes," said Weidt. "After all, how am I supposed to fill my army orders if they take my workers away?"

People began to laugh, at first just to themselves and then more and more openly. They understood. Levy tried to kiss Weidt's hand; Weidt warded him off. He strode into the office like a proud victor. But he said, "It worked this time, but who knows what'll happen the next time?"

The machinery of deportation had been set in motion. It became a terrifyingly well-oiled operation. The Gestapo established the ground rules. They notified the leaders of the Jewish Community that a thousand people were to be rounded up for a transport that was to leave Berlin on such and such a day. According to Dr. Cohen, this order was followed by the request for the Jewish Community to assemble the candidates. The first such transport was composed of those over the age of sixty-five. Then came those unable to work, people on public assistance, single mothers with children. The categories changed constantly. Being blind and over sixty, Levy fell into one of the categories of eligibles. When those not employed in essential

industries also became subject to deportation I too received one of the dreaded forms. My mother was devastated.

"I'll register voluntarily. I won't let you go by yourself," she declared. For days we argued about it. She was working in a factory manufacturing radio batteries and therefore was considered essential. Of course I was afraid of what lay in store for me. We didn't yet know precisely what fate awaited the deportees, but instinct told us that it was sure to be worse than what had gone before. I was also curious. What had happened to those who'd already left? What could I expect?

I went to see Dr. Cohen, my old employer; I still occasionally helped out in his house.

"Give that thing to me immediately," he said, and that was the last I ever saw of the list. Apparently there had been a mix-up in the Jewish Community; it was intended for someone else. Mother was completely exhausted by the tension of the past few days, and for a while I was haunted by the thought that someone else was going to take my place.

Subsequently, workers in essential industries also received the forms if their jobs were not considered sufficiently important—unskilled laborers or messengers. The AEG, a public utility, and Siemens protested the depletion of their labor force. They told the Gestapo—probably with greater jus-

tification than Otto Weidt—that in view of the labor shortage, production would be hampered if they were to lose their hard-working Jews. Still the trainloads of deportees kept rolling. Families were torn apart; old people were separated from their children.

The first transports of people over sixty-five left for Theresienstadt in June 1942. Among them was my eighty-five-year-old uncle Paul Litten, at one time one of the most distinguished citizens of the city of Köslin in Pomerania. A man of means and cherished by his five children, he had been taken care of by the two daughters who were still in Germany. His three other children had emigrated and had promised to get him out. But it was never to be. By the time he was deported he could scarcely walk without assistance. "Don't worry about me, my children," he tried to reassure his daughters when the Gestapo came for him. He knew that he was leaving forever.

Later his unmarried sister, Aunt Gustel, was also scheduled for deportation. We went to see her; Mother brought her a warm jacket. She was living at the Jewish old-age home. When we got there we found the old people packing. Yes, of course they'd take care of themselves, of course they'd write, they kept repeating to the relatives who had come to help them pack and see them off. Nobody believed a word they were saying. We

all knew we would never see any of them again.

"I'll look after Paul," my gentle, helpless maiden aunt reassured us. Her wealthy brother had supported her all her life, and now she was going to look after him at Theresienstadt.

"After all, Theresienstadt can't be so big that I won't be able to find him," she said. My mother helped her pack her meager belongings into a big carryall. Looking embarrassed, she put the tin bowl, the dish given to the old people, into the bag: "Like a pet bowl, no?"

Inside the building there was the kind of confusion that accompanies a move and packing; outside stood the weeping families who had already said their farewells. Slowly, haltingly, they left the place from which their relatives were starting on their journey into death.

The building was already filling up with new victims—"temporary residents" brought there to wait for their transport. Aunt Olga was one of them. On the day specified by the Gestapo the Jewish orderlies had shown up.

"Olga Sara Rosenberg, you've been given the list. We hope you are ready for your transport. Come with us."

The Gestapo personally escorted the first "shipment," either because the action was supposed to be kept secret or perhaps to see how the victims would react. They need not have worried. Not

only did the Jews obey unresistingly, they were scrupulous to a fault in carrying out the orders. Along with the lists, the Jewish Community sent a letter of instruction to the victims:

"Your departure has been officially ordered for (date). On (date) you can drop off your baggage between 9 A.M. and 1 P.M. at the hostel on Pestalozzistrasse. On Monday (date) at 6 A.M. your apartment will be officially sealed. You must be ready at that time. Your apartment and room keys must be handed to the officer."

This order was accompanied by a memorandum of instruction from the Jewish Community: "We ask you to follow these instructions and to prepare for the move calmly and sensibly. The designated persons should keep in mind that their demeanor and their orderly compliance with the regulations will contribute substantially to the smooth processing of the transport. We naturally will do everything within our powers to stand by the members of our Community and help them in any way we can."

The orderlies appointed by the Community, mostly younger men, included teachers and lawyers and clerical workers who had lost their jobs. They followed orders. True, at times they could be cruel, prodding the victims along: "Quick, get moving, aren't you ready yet?" But perhaps delaying the inevitable would have been even more

heartless. They overpowered Aunt Olga. Fighting desperately against being taken away, she had to be carried out on her chair to the waiting truck. The orderlies had to fill their quotas. They never spoke a kind word, except that occasionally they were heard to say they didn't enjoy what they had to do. Perhaps they were hiding their feelings behind their gruffness.

Mother and I had had to move into one of the so-called Jewish houses. Eleven of us shared a five and a half room flat, in keeping with a directive that allowed one room for every two Jews. The apartment had one bathroom and of course only one kitchen. Mornings in this shared apartment were frantic, with everyone intent on getting to work on time. Lateness could result in deportation. Doing more than one's duty seemed to ensure safety, or relative safety. Anyone who dared to spend more than a few minutes getting ready was forcefully reminded to hurry up. The attempt to set up some kind of schedule was doomed from the outset. Clashes and hostility were unavoidable. And when people returned in the evening, exhausted by the hard labor reserved for Jews, and found the kitchen crowded, they took out their frustration on the lucky ones who had gotten there first. Anyone who dared leave the kitchen even for a moment had to be prepared to find his or her pot removed from the stove and replaced. It

was not unusual to hear somebody tiptoeing into the kitchen late at night surreptitiously to prepare something received from a non-Jewish friend or merchant. We lived in an atmosphere of fear, envy, thievery, even denunciation. Most of the people in this shared apartment were middle-aged and unaccustomed to manual work. They were not very strong, and the meager rations—Jews received neither meat nor sugar nor vegetables nor fruit—were not meant for people doing heavy labor. And the fear of the unknown, of what the future held in store, did the rest. Sundays they slept or spent idly in their ugly, poorly furnished rooms. And their fear never left them.

The deportations continued relentlessly. It was at this time that Dr. Cohen was arrested, as he had anticipated. As often before, he was ordered to report to the Gestapo, where they accused him of some minor violation of his supervisory duties. Apparently a piece of soap was missing from one of the institutions under his aegis—a complete fiction. Some days later his wife learned that he was being detained at Gestapo headquarters on Alexanderplatz. She tried to bring him food, but was turned away. They didn't know where he was, they told her.

Subsequently she was allowed to bring him some fresh laundry, and he smuggled out a note in the dirty laundry he gave her: "I would never have believed that I could bear this," he wrote.

He was kept in jail for a relatively long time, without trial, without a hearing, without assistance. Then his wife no longer heard from him. When she tried to deliver his laundry she was turned away. Nobody knew where he was, whether in a concentration camp or even whether he was alive. His wife ran from office to office, begging former colleagues to help her, but nobody, even those who dared to inquire, got any answer. "You'll find out in good time," was the cynical reply.

Leonore Cohen was almost glad when she and her young daughter were picked up one morning. She asked whether she would be taken to her husband. The answer was yes, she would. His aged parents were left behind in the apartment. One day a Gestapo officer and his wife came knocking at the door demanding to be let in. The officer told the elder Mrs. Cohen that they had come to pick up her son's personal effects. She asked him where her son was, but he said he couldn't tell her. Mrs. Cohen showed the officer the dresser drawer in which her son kept his warm underwear. The Gestapo man doubted that her son would have any need for most of those things. Then he and his wife conferred about the quality of the down quilts and oriental rugs, and packed up whatever caught their fancy. After they left Mrs. Cohen went to work cleaning up the mess they had made.

The Gestapo picked up Leonore Cohen the

same day on which a number of her husband's colleagues of the Reich Association of Jews in Germany were deported. At 8 A.M. on June 22, 1942, the Gestapo came to the association's headquarters and arrested the staff as they arrived at their offices. Conrad Cohen had meanwhile been sent to the Mauthausen concentration camp. There he committed suicide by walking into the electrified barbed-wire fence. He knew that he could not survive the camp.

On May 29, 1942, the Gestapo conducted a mass raid, picking up five hundred men in their homes. Nobody knew why. Only later did we learn that it was in retaliation for the assassination of Heydrich. My friend Max Blumenthal was among the five hundred.

The arresting officer told Max's wife, Lily, that her husband would be back home by nightfall. Evening came, but he didn't return. She waited a few more days, and then was told to get ready for deportation. Almost elated, she came to see us to say good-bye: "I'll be with Max again." What she didn't know was that Max and the others were already dead. Having heard a rumor to that effect, I cried uncontrollably. Mother told me to calm down lest Lily get the idea that Max had been more to me than just a dear friend. She didn't realize that Max, the first man to pay attention to me, had given me a sense of what it meant to be young.

More and more people we knew disappeared; the only thing that stayed with us was our fear. I cried a lot and clung to Hans Rosenthal. Whenever we parted I cried, afraid that we'd never see each other again. My mother didn't much care for this friendship. She thought it senseless to embark on a relationship in times like these, and she knew that Hans, almost twenty years my senior, was something of a father figure to me. I thought I was in love with him, and I might have been, or perhaps it was only a desire for somebody to be close to. Mother was afraid that I might marry him and leave her.

"And then you'll go to Theresienstadt with him and I'll have to go to Riga by myself." She stubbornly clung to this notion, and finally she forbade me to sleep over at the Rosenthals' on Saturdays, as I had occasionally done. It was the only chance Hans and I had to spend a quiet evening together. There had been nothing more than an occasional kiss, but Mother didn't believe me.

The apartment Hans shared with his mother was his father's old medical office. Nothing had changed there, and I felt at home. Mrs. Rosenthal tried to intercede with my mother, telling her that Hans and I were never alone, but it was no use. A mutual friend who heard of my mother's injunction offered us the use of his room during the day to give us a chance for some quiet hours alone.

Yet although I looked forward to those moments, I felt uneasy. Hans, self-confident and open, brought up the topic of a physical relationship. "Under ordinary circumstances," he said, "we'd have been married long ago. What do you want me to do?" But I cried and pleaded with him not to press me. All I could think of were the dangerous times we were living in. My nerves were frazzled, and I was afraid of the unknown. Yet whenever we said good-bye I feared that we'd never see each other again. Then I cried even more, but I could never let Mother see my tears.

One day they came for Hans and his mother. I only learned about it after he returned to his apartment. On that same day the Gestapo also drove up to the Jewish Community offices and locked all the exits. They said that the shrunken Community did not need such a large staff and that they had come to pick up excess personnel. Ilse Basch, the wife of our bookkeeper, was present, but she was not among those they took away. She later told us how Alfred Berliner, an actor with the now defunct Jewish cultural organization, suddenly got up, put on his hat, politely said good-bye, and left the room. Just as politely he tipped his hat to the Gestapo man guarding the door, who returned his courteous greeting. Berliner then calmly walked down the stairs, saluted the Gestapo man posted at the main gate, and disap-

peared in the crowd. At that point the Gestapo realized that one of their intended victims had gotten away.

Hans Rosenthal and his mother were sent to the former Jewish Home for the Aged, now a collection point for deportees. It was an eighteenth-century building next to Berlin's oldest Jewish cemetery, the one in which Moses Mendelssohn lies buried. When Hans' name was called out, one of the Gestapo officers who was familiar with Hans' excellent contacts among Berlin's wholesalers wondered aloud whether it wouldn't be wiser to make use of his connections than to deport him. And so the Rosenthal apartment was unsealed and Mrs. Rosenthal unpacked their belongings. "For how long?" she asked her son.

My father's sister Elsa informed us that she and her husband were going to be deported and asked us to come and see her. Since she lived in Spandau we had not seen much of her. Jews not only had no telephones, they were not allowed to use public transportation except for going to and from work or under extraordinary circumstances. And Mother's job at the factory was extremely taxing; she had little energy left for excursions. But now of course we went to see them.

It was the day of their deportation. Two overstuffed backpacks were propped against the doorway of their small room, which was filled to the

rafters with the heavy furniture from their old apartment. The only items not there were their expensive rugs, which they'd given to trusted "Aryan" friends for safekeeping "until we return."

Aunt Elsa and her husband sat huddled together, waiting and crying. My uncle's dark eyes were red-rimmed from lack of sleep as he sat stroking my aunt's arm. In their almost thirty years of marriage he had never publicly displayed so much affection for her. And all the while he murmured, "Mommy, my Mommy." My aunt, thin and small, her eyes swollen from crying, sat with bent head, trying to hide her pain. "Greet Martin for me," she said over and over again. My father was her favorite brother. And she kept kissing me. My mother was extraordinarily controlled, and although utterly convinced that it would never happen, she kept assuring them that we'd all be seeing each other again. But my aunt only shook her head and said, "You must go. Who knows when they'll be coming for us."

We left. To this day I can hear the squeaking of the stairs. As we stepped out from the dark hallway into the wintry street we saw a police car approach. We stopped to watch. Two Jewish orderlies wearing the yellow star went into the house. They reappeared minutes later behind my aunt, who was lugging the heavy backpacks. She walked quickly, as though eager to get it over with.

My uncle followed haltingly. They didn't look back as they stepped into the car, not a single backward look at the city that had been their home for almost thirty years. I cried. My mother, although just as moved, warned me to control myself. "Suppose somebody were to see us?" We had gone out without our stars. We were the only ones on the street. Strange how the Berliners knew when to make themselves scarce so as not to have to see what was happening on their streets. It is anybody's guess how many watched from behind their curtained windows.

The trains carrying the deportees left from the Grunewald station. Initially they had left from a more centrally located station, but that was changed after witnesses to those early deportations were overheard making remarks that did not necessarily connote approval. And perhaps this new, more remote terminal also made it easier for the Gestapo to go through the meager belongings of their victims one more time and steal some hidden treasure.

Aunt Elsa and her husband were the last of our family to be deported. My father's other sister had been deported from the old-age home where she had worked after her husband's death. My father's brother and family disappeared without our ever learning about it. All we heard was that the Gestapo had not been persuaded by a medical cer-

tificate stating that he was not fit for transport. My cousin, her husband, and Bela, their adorable three-year-old daughter, were among the first to set out on this terrible journey. We never heard from any of them again.

In November 1942 we learned about the gassings and executions for the first time via the BBC. We could not and did not want to believe it. And our ranks were thinning.

One day we heard that Vienna's Gestapo was coming to Berlin. Vienna was already cleansed of Jews; Berlin had been derelict. Our local Gestapo apparently wasn't efficient enough, and so the Gestapo of Vienna was brought in to take care of Berlin's Jews. The lists were done away with; the Viennese Gestapo had a better way. They sent big moving vans to houses that still harbored Jews and simply shoved the people in. And if they cried out for their wives or children they were told that they were sure to meet them again. After that everything was silence.

Käthe Rosenthal, Hans' mother, was among those picked up in one of these raids. She wanted to tell them about her son, but they cut her short: "Your son doesn't interest us." She went into the van and the apartment was sealed. At the collection point she asked a Jewish orderly to get word to her son. Hans immediately got in touch with the Gestapo. They still needed him, and so for the

second time he and his mother were allowed to return to their home.

Together with the Gestapo came three Viennese Jews who had worked with the Gestapo in Vienna. When Ali told me that she had met one of them when she worked with the Relief Committee of Jews in Germany, I thought this was a stroke of luck. Shortly after that she brought him to the office. I don't have any clear memory of Robert Gerö. All I remember is that he wore glasses, had a mustache, and spoke with a Viennese accent. We called him Schmidt. Weidt treated him with respect, as did all of us, in the hope that he might help keep us safe a little while longer. The anti-Nazi Weidt, determined to protect his Ali and the rest of his Jewish charges, had no problem in winning Gerö over, and Gerö must have been touched by Weidt's determination. At any rate, he took us under his wing and began to come to our get-togethers.

Those moving vans became the scourge of Berlin's Jews. One day they drew up in front of Weidt's workshop and took away the blind and deaf workers. I will never forget it. Without saying a word they put down their tools, gathered their belongings, took each other by the hand, and quietly made their way down the stairs. Some of the workers were married to sighted women on whom they depended. But the Gestapo weren't interested.

They were shoved into the vans like all the rest. Weidt, powerless, was seething. The Gestapo officers refused to discuss the matter with him. They said they were doing their duty, and that meant bringing the blind and the deaf to the collection point near our workshop. Shortly after the van left Weidt also went out. He had not said a word, and none of us dared to speak to him. And once again he took his white cane to go to the Gestapo.

In the late afternoon his workers returned. There were no witnesses to how Weidt had managed to persuade the Gestapo that these workers were essential. Possibly he underscored his argument with some presents. All we know is that he made sure that the workers were released then and there. He wouldn't listen to any promises that they would return later. Otto Weidt stood in front of the collection point and waited for them and walked back to the workshop at the head of this procession of people with the yellow stars on their aprons. But Weidt knew that this was the last time he would be able to pull it off; he told us so.

9

"There's something you've got to promise me," Mrs. Gumz beseeched my mother, holding her hands in a viselike grip. "You must promise me," she repeated over and over again. It was a cold, dark day in November 1942, and the transports of Jewish people had been rolling for a year. They were going toward the east, though nobody knew their exact destination.

"What is it you want me to promise you?" asked my mother, puzzled. "I can't promise you something without knowing exactly what."

"You must," Mrs. Gumz demanded. Somewhat embarrassed, she added softly, "If I tell you what it is you might hesitate."

"All right," my mother acquiesced. "I promise."

Mrs. Gumz laughed, pleased with herself. "You just promised me that you and Inge won't let yourself be deported like the others."

"But Mrs. Gumz," Mother cried out, freeing her hands. "I don't understand any of this. Did anything happen to make you say this, and how do you think we can do it?"

"Fritz, that young soldier next door, just came back from the East, and he told us what they're doing with the Jews there. And Fritz had to sign a paper that he wouldn't talk about what he'd seen. But who can keep such a promise?" she whispered tearfully.

"So what we've heard on the BBC is true," my mother murmured to herself. There'd been vague allusions to gassings and executions that none of us had believed or, rather, wanted to believe. It was literally unbelievable.

Mrs. Gumz seemed to have anticipated my mother's question. "We'll help you, I promise. My husband and I have already decided. You're coming to us." It was that simple. And as we were leaving the shop, she called after us, "Don't forget, you promised."

"We have to discuss this with Ostrowski," Mother said to me. "It's not all that simple."

We went to see Ostrowski. "The Gumzes are such innocents, they're not aware of the possible consequences of their offer," she explained. But Ostrowski demurred. "It's a great idea. Of course, that's what we'll do. Grete and I will help them."

After Ostrowski's dismissal from his civil service post, Grete had opened a stationery shop and rental library. Former Socialist functionaries were under constant surveillance, and a respectable business of this sort served the dual purpose of providing a source of income and allaying suspicion. Since Ostrowski and Grete lived in a tiny apartment, they obviously could not have taken us in.

"Don't worry," they said. "There's the shop, there's our boat house, and then there are others in Berlin who think the way we do."

Reassured, and loaded down with delicacies we hadn't seen for a long time, we left them. Mother was convinced that we should take the risk and "go underground."

"Hitler can't last much longer, three months at the most," Ostrowski assured us. Hungry for hope and optimism, we welcomed his soothing words. I don't know how he managed to make his analysis of the situation so convincing. Considering that he got his news from the BBC, it is hard to understand how he could have predicted the imminent end of

the Nazis in 1942, when Hitler was still at the height of his power.

But the decision had been made. The only thing not yet decided on was the date of our "submersion." We wanted to put it off as long as possible. We tracked the Gestapo's moves very closely. Slowly but systematically the Jews of Berlin were being deported. One evening when I returned from work I found a note from Mother, who was working the night shift. It read: "I can't go on; we must hide as soon as possible." What had happened?

She told me that while I was at work the doorbell had rung. She opened the door Two Gestapo men stood there, an officer and his driver. They had come, they explained, to pick up something from the room of one of the tenants who had been deported the week before. The officer asked my mother what she was doing at home. She explained that she was on the night shift. Well, he said, in that case she might just as well come along with them, and he tapped her on her behind. He then asked her to show him her room.

"Good. Get ready, pack some of your things, you won't need too much. We'll wait," he said to her, and he and his driver sat down.

Mother didn't know what to do. She pretended not to understand what he meant, picked up some

sewing, and sat down too. The Gestapo man then asked her whether she lived alone. She told him no, she had a daughter.

"Let's get going," he said. My mother said that if she was going to be deported she'd like to be with her daughter, and that her daughter was still at work.

"What do you think?" the Gestapo man asked his driver. "What should we do, take her along or let her stay?"

The driver, who had buried his head in a newspaper, shrugged. The Gestapo man got up, came close to my mother, and reached out to touch her. She tried to dodge him. When he turned away for a moment the driver gestured that the officer was just playing a game. She returned to her sewing, but the Gestapo man planted himself in front of her and yelled at her to get ready, that she was coming with him. She again pleaded with him not to take her without me. Finally the officer turned to his driver and laughingly asked him again what he thought they should do, take her or let her stay. When the driver said let her stay, the officer said okay, but next time she wouldn't be getting off so easily. Mother said she had no idea how long this cat-and-mouse game lasted. To her it had seemed an infinity.

It must have been around that time that Robert Gerö came to the workshop and said that if I was

planning to go underground I should do so soon, that he wouldn't be able to protect me much longer. Not many Jews were still left. The Viennese Gestapo was sure to accomplish its mission of completely ridding Berlin of Jews, and Gerö thought it couldn't take much longer. I told him that we were planning to go underground soon. We went to see the Gumz family. "Do you really think," my mother began, but before she could finish the sentence Mrs. Gumz, eyes shining, said, "Yes."

Of course I told Weidt about our plans. He promised to help in any way he could. When I mentioned that we still had a few things we would like to keep out of the hands of the Gestapo, he offered to store them for us.

My mother began to make preparations. Every afternoon when I returned from work I found a packed suitcase, which I took with me to the workshop the next morning. According to a new regulation, Jews could no longer dispose of their personal property; we Jews were merely the beneficiaries of official largesse, the temporary proprietors of goods on loan from the state.

Mother and I still had two couches we thought might come in handy at some future time. Weidt was a practical man, so I asked him for advice. "I'll have them picked up by my van," he said, though he knew as well as I that he was taking a

risk. But he wasn't afraid. "It'll be done so quickly nobody will see it." He was going to have them picked up in the morning, at a time when most people were at work and my mother would be at home. A few days before we went underground, we asked our landlady to put the beds she had originally wanted to give us back into our room. As for the few things we had to leave behind, I destroyed them, making sure that nobody was going to get any use out of them. Once our preparations were completed, we set the date for our disappearance.

"You say your friends will take you in. That's all well and good, but what are you going to do all day long? Sit around and twiddle your thumbs?" Weidt asked. He was right. We hadn't thought of that. He, however, had. "You can keep on working here. We have to see what we can do about legalizing it." I didn't understand a word he was saying. He told me to go home and not to worry; he was sure to come up with an answer.

A few days later a Mrs. P. showed up at his office. I knew that she lived in the vicinity of Alexanderplatz and that she was involved both in the black market and with young women engaged in prostitution. I had never paid much attention to her; all I knew was that she was on good terms with Weidt. Shortly after she left Weidt called me

into his office and asked whether I had fifty marks with me. I looked at him in astonishment and nodded.

"Here," he said. "Mrs. P. has gotten you a labor book." He held it out toward me. Speechless, I stared at the Nazi emblem on the cover. "From now on you're Gertrud Dereszewski," Weidt said. "Just be sure to remember your new birthday." He smiled gleefully. Apparently Gertrud Dereszewski was one of Mrs. P.'s girls who had no intention of letting herself be inducted into the labor service. Preferring her present line of work, she had decided to sell her labor registration in exchange for an ID with her picture certifying that she was employed in Otto Weidt's workshop for the blind. I got an identical ID, except mine had my own picture on it. Gertrud Dereszewski was registered with the health insurance and labor offices.

Then came the day of our move, January 15, 1943. The door of our apartment building had closed behind us when Mother noticed that she had forgotten her watch. She was shaken. Should she go back for it? It was almost like a bad omen. Afraid of being seen, we cautiously made our way back. We had already removed the stars from our coats. Leaving like this in broad daylight with heavy shopping bags could easily arouse suspicion. We tiptoed back into our stripped, cold room,

and there was Mother's wristwatch on the table. She took it, and off we went to the Gumz household. They welcomed us warmly.

"I'm so proud that I was able to persuade you," said this lovely, simple woman as she led us to a little room behind the shop.

"So many people come and go here. Nobody'll pay you much attention," said Mr. Gumz. He was as convinced as Ostrowski that Hitler's days were numbered.

I no longer remember the first night we spent there. I was so exhausted that I fell asleep as soon as my head hit the pillow in the big bed that I was to share with Mother for the next few weeks. The following morning I went to work as usual. Gertrud Dereszewski's papers had made me legal. To explain my new name to customers and salesmen, I said that I'd gotten married. Ali and Weidt were vastly amused, and Ali bought me a wedding ring. As the new Mrs. Dereszewski, I had to listen to many a joke about my wedding night, but nothing could faze me.

For the time being, my daily routine didn't change. My mother had a harder time with her enforced idleness. She tried to help in the house, but that was not easy because the Gumz family was rather disorganized. Meals were irregular; they ate when they were hungry. And Mother couldn't even help with the cooking because

the stove stood under the laundry drying rack, near the ironing board and the mangle, and Mrs. Gumz waited on her customers while preparing the meals. Mother was glad to see me come home and keep her company. When she complained to Mrs. Gumz about feeling useless, Mrs. Gumz would give her some socks to mend and tell her to be glad to have a chance to rest. She couldn't understand that my mother's new situation, her "illegality," made her restless. Still, in the first days of that illegality we slept much better than before. We no longer feared the new torments the next day might bring.

In the evening Mr. Gumz tried to listen to foreign newscasts on his radio. Sitting there in his shirtsleeves, he'd almost crawl into his set. If the German jamming was successful he'd be in a bad mood the rest of the evening, twirling the dial until he finally got something, some bulletin contradicting Hitler's official version of the events of the day. Then he would grin from ear to ear. While all this was going on, his twelve-year-old son seemed to be engrossed in one of his games, but it was obvious that he knew exactly what his father was up to. He did not belong to the Hitler Youth. "We managed to keep him out," Mr. Gumz told us proudly. "I told them he had flat feet, and the doctor certified it. That means he can't march."

Mrs. Gumz was afraid for her "daddy." "He talks too much, don't you think?" she said. Gumz didn't know the meaning of caution. When customers came in and said "Heil Hitler," he would come out from the back of the shop to see who it was, then strike up a conversation and try to shake their confidence by letting them know how he thought it would all end. "How many do you think are going to survive? No more than there's room for under a big tree," he'd say. Some people listened to him skeptically, others were afraid. He may not have changed any minds, but people were beginning to fear that Germany might have to pay dearly, even if events did not yet bear this out. "We're going to die of our victories," a customer once said to Mrs. Gumz, who was not as outspoken as her husband. She just observed people and made an occasional sarcastic comment. "Oh, our Führer will manage," she'd say. "Don't you worry."

The Gumz family laughed a lot. To please me, they'd invite Hans Rosenthal to dinner, which was usually rabbit stew. Rabbits were being raised in backyards and basements and on balconies all over Berlin, and people foraged in the parks for fodder for their next Sunday dinner. The Gumz Sunday dinners also featured vegetables from their little garden on the outskirts of Berlin, and homemade fruit wine. No wonder we laughed a lot.

I remember one evening when Hans was our guest and a fairly heavy bombing raid put a sudden stop to our gaiety. The Gumz apartment was on the ground floor, which meant we didn't have to go to the air-raid shelter. Hans was very worried that the air-raid warden of his building would report him missing. It was way past 8 P.M., the curfew for Jews. The fear we had been able to put aside for a few happy hours was with us again. The bombs that were falling seemed insignificant by comparison.

One day, soon after going into hiding, I was sitting in my little corner at Weidt's when I heard a woman's voice. It was familiar, but I couldn't place it right away. She asked for me.

"Deutschkron," said Weidt. "She hasn't shown up at work for days. Is there a problem?"

The unexpected visitor was Mrs. Wachsmann, the Aryan wife of one of the roomers at our last address. I hid under my desk. Ali, who had gotten up to see who it was, spotted me and immediately sat down in front of the desk. Mrs. Wachsmann told Weidt that we, the Deutschkrons, had vanished without paying our electric and gas bills or leaving the keys.

"Why come here?" asked Weidt.

"I saw your van pick up their couches, so I thought . . ."

Weidt interrupted her. "I just remembered,

Deutschkron didn't collect her wages. I'll deduct what she owes you from her pay. How much is it?" And Weidt instructed the bookkeeper to settle my debt out of those "uncollected" wages.

"Does that take care of it?"

"But what about the key?" Mrs. Wachsmann persisted.

"I'm afraid there's nothing I can do about that. If Deutschkron shows up here I'll tell her to return it."

Thus pacified, Mrs. Wachsmann left the office. I crawled out of my hiding place, embarrassed that I had forgotten about the bills. "Don't worry," Weidt reassured me. "Those things happen." We then tried to figure out how I could return the keys without arousing suspicion that Weidt and I were in touch.

Some time after that visit I went to Grünau, a suburb of Berlin, and mailed a letter with the key and money for the unpaid bills. I wrote Mrs. Wachsmann a brief note explaining that I hadn't realized I had taken the key with me until I found it in my purse, and I also apologized for my failure to leave the money. We never heard from her again, and I soon put the whole business out of my mind.

It was obvious that Ali would also have to disappear. She and Weidt kept discussing how best

to go about it. She said that of course she wouldn't budge without her parents. Weidt thought and thought, and finally came up with the idea of renting additional storage space for his finished goods, and in the room behind all those brooms and brushes he set up living quarters for three people. One evening the three members of the Licht family moved in. Ali continued to work in the office as Weidt's secretary, except that now her wages were largely in the form of food. Her father also was given a job in the workshop. Only her mother spent the day in hiding. None of the other workers knew about this arrangement, although many suspected it.

One day Mr. Horn came and begged Weidt for help for himself and his family—his wife, son, and daughter. Weidt came up with another plan. The area at the end of the long, narrow workshop was used as a closet for the employees. It had no wall in the back, and that opening became the entrance to the Horns' hiding place. Weidt was also going to supply them with food.

Next came the eighteen-year-old Bernstein twins, Marianne and Anneliese. Marianne, who was blind, was doing work at home for Weidt. They too pleaded with him to help them. Once again he called on Mrs. P., who took the two girls in. She still had a spare room, a hole in the wall,

she called it. Everything seemed so uncomplicated; Weidt was developing unsuspected organizational talents. He was as delighted as we were. We thought of little beyond our next hiding place.

10

J ust as we were about to sit down to eat, Mrs. Gumz turned to us with an embarrassed smile. "Our neighbor has been asking whether we had company. I told her yes, that a cousin of mine from Pomerania was staying with us." Nobody said a word. My mother bent her head. She understood.

"We must leave here," my mother said to me when we were alone. "After all, how long can a visit last?"

It certainly was not comforting to learn that a neighbor had been nosing about, even if she had no ulterior motive. And then perhaps she did. And what would happen if she were to mention the visitor to other people, such as the building su-

perintendent or block warden or air-raid warden? We could tell that Mrs. Gumz was worried, even though she didn't come right out and say so.

Mrs. Gumz suggested that perhaps we could go for the weekend to Drewitz, where the Gumzes had a little garden cottage. We said that sounded fine. We had very little choice. "We'll follow you on Sunday," said Mrs. Gumz.

When we got to Drewitz we found a primitive, weather-beaten cabin without either running water or indoor plumbing, surrounded by a vegetable garden, fruit trees, and shrubs. But a fire in the iron stove helped make the room cheerful. It was furnished with cast-off family treasures. And there was also a well-populated rabbit hutch.

The cabin was an ideal hiding place for an extended weekend, but if we were to stay longer we would be certain to attract attention. On the way there Mother and I discussed our options. We shied away from articulating what we knew to be true, that our stay with the Gumz family was drawing to a close, and we did not look forward to another talk with Dr. Ostrowski. We were afraid that we were rapidly becoming an intolerable burden to all our friends.

"Perhaps you can speak to some of your other friends," Mrs. Gumz suddenly said while busy preparing the Sunday roast, "and see what can be done." She never once said that she could no

longer keep us. "Yes, of course, tomorrow," said Mother. The food stuck in my throat. And then Mrs. Gumz added, "We'll of course continue to help, with food and so on." Her eyes were moist; she was obviously suffering. Her husband got up from the table and went out to putter in the garden.

"We'll have to give up," said Mother, her eyes filling with tears as she fingered the tablecloth. She too got up and left the room. Mrs. Gumz was silent. Finally she turned to me and said, "You must understand. We don't like having to do it."

"Of course," I answered. "We'll find a way." I only said it to console her, because I certainly had no idea what we were going to do.

As far as Ostrowski was concerned, I had my doubts about how much he could help us. The small apartment he shared with Grete Sommer was in her name. His Jewish wife and son lived in a larger apartment. Even though his marriage was in name only, he did not get a divorce; he was not about to deliver his wife into the hands of the Nazis.

Ostrowski listened to us. "Of course we'll help you." But how? To begin with, he said, we could spend the night at their place, sleeping on the floor.

"That's no problem," said Grete. Then she came up with a better idea. "I can put down a

mattress in the cubbyhole behind my shop. There's a toilet and a sink in the cellar." After dinner each day they could take us to the shop and lock us in. In the morning I could leave the shop through the front door, pretending to be an early customer, and go to work. And Mother could help out in the shop or in the apartment. We were as happy as we could be under the circumstances.

"Won't we be in the way in that small apartment?" asked Mother.

"After all, how much longer can Hitler last?" Ostrowski was still convinced that it was only a matter of months.

We took tearful leave of the Gumz family. "Oh, I'm so sorry," Mrs. Gumz said over and over again. "You'll come and visit, won't you?" She was almost pleading with us. We promised that we would. My mother was not unhappy to get out of the dark room in that disorganized household.

Weidt's delivery van brought our couches to Grete Sommer's shop, our new asylum. At night we put the couch cushions on the floor of the tiny room and turned out the light so as not to attract attention to our unusual arrangement. As for our other belongings, rather than keep them in Weidt's shipping room, we gave them to Mrs. P. for safe-keeping.

There were three things Mrs. Mausch, the

building superintendent, hated with equal fervor: her husband, Hitler, and Nazis generally. She was a thin blonde, strong and determined, and she made no effort to control her violent temper. When she got going she didn't care who was listening. "One day she's going to talk herself into prison," Grete prophesied. "It's too bad, but that's why we can't take her into our confidence. She would certainly look after you, but in one of her fits of temper she might give you away." And so we had to tiptoe around the shop, hardly daring to move, listening for any unusual sound, fully aware that this arrangement could not last forever either.

"What will we do on weekends?" asked Ostrowski. Of course we couldn't stay in the shop. That was bound to attract attention. As always, Grete came up with an answer. "How about going to Schildhorn?" She really took pride in outwitting the Nazis.

The weekend of February 13 the four of us set out for Schildhorn, where our hosts owned a boathouse. It was a cold, gray, rainy day. By the time we got there it was turning dark. The darkness made us feel secure, and Mother and I took advantage of this rare opportunity to talk to each other. We wondered how Father was, what he might be doing and thinking. Suddenly Ostrowski loomed up in front of us. "What do you think

you're doing, talking so openly? Suppose somebody heard you?"

Thus reprimanded, we fell silent. Ostrowski of
course was right.

"And let me tell you," he continued, "if something were to go wrong, you'd have to find another
place. I have to survive. I have plans for the future." A self-confident man, he was convinced that
he was destined to play a role in a democratic post-
Hitler Germany. I knew that Mother was near
tears. My feelings for Ostrowski, whom I had always admired, were beginning to change. I kept
quiet.

The boathouse was miserably cold. "Before you
know it, it'll get too hot," Grete said cheerfully as
she made a fire in the little stove. At first there
was just a lot of smoke, but soon it became warm
and cozy. "This is the first time we've inaugurated
the summer season on February 13," Grete
laughed.

The boathouse consisted of two cubicles with
space for only two wooden bunks, some chairs,
and a kitchen corner. It was a summer weekend
retreat. Ostrowski kept a boat in which he and his
cronies went sailing on the Havel, where they
could discuss politics without fear of being seen
or overheard.

Except for the crackling fire, there was no
sound. Throughout the weekend the weather was

cold and unfriendly. On Sunday Grete's parents paid us a visit and brought us things we hadn't seen for a long time: cold meats and bread and butter. We talked about the political situation.

"According to the BBC," Bernhard Sommer told us, "the situation in Stalingrad is really bad." Ostrowski jumped up. His face was radiant. "This is the first clear indication that Hitler is on the ropes. And once things begin to go downhill . . ."

"We're not there yet," warned Mr. Sommer, "we've still got a long row to hoe."

"No, everything's collapsing like a house of cards," Ostrowski insisted. He predicted that the officer corps would not accept a defeat, since they were not responsible for the orders of "that lunatic." Sommer knew that there was no point in arguing with Ostrowski, the incurable optimist.

I kept in touch with Hans Rosenthal. He called me at Grete's or we met in the workshop. Once, as we were standing close together in the corridor, the representative of a film rental agency suddenly appeared.

"Oh, how nice," she called out. "Mr. Dereszewski, isn't it?"

Hans nodded and pressed his briefcase to his chest to hide the yellow star.

"Congratulations on your marriage. You and your bride must come and visit me. By the way,

how would you like to come to a private screening of one of our pictures?"

"We'd love to," I answered promptly.

"In that case, come the day after tomorrow. I'll leave the tickets for you at the box office." She said good-bye and assured us again how happy she was for us. After all, nowadays there wasn't all that much to celebrate.

"What will we do?" Hans asked after she left.

"We'll go," I said. "Without the star, of course."

It felt strange, walking into the big theater. Our hostess greeted us with a smile, and we took our seats among people chatting about this and that. We breathed a sigh of relief when the lights went out. The film was a light, popular entertainment.

Champagne was poured amid chatter of film projects, vacations in Italy and France and skiing holidays. These people didn't seem to know that there was a war on. I envied them their carefree life. The women were well-dressed. Soldiers brought back silk stockings and dresses, furs and shoes from the occupied countries. The dress I was wearing was one I'd had as a teenager before the war. I felt out of place, and Hans and I left as soon as possible. We'd had a glimpse of a world that existed side by side with ours. The people who lived in it spoke German just as we did, and while they may not have been Nazis, they knew nothing,

or perhaps did not want to know, of the misery and suffering of the people who, although their next-door neighbors, had been excluded from their society. Hans returned to his apartment where he might be picked up any day, and I to my hiding place behind the shop.

One morning I was sitting at my desk as usual when the phone rang. I answered.

"This is the criminal police."

"Yes?" I replied, frightened.

"Do you have a Gertrud Dereszewski working for you?"

"Yes. I'll connect you with our personnel office." I put him on hold. "Ali," I said turning to her for help, "the criminal police are asking about Gertrud Dereszewski."

"Quick, switch the call to Weidt," and she rushed off to his office, while I stood petrified, listening at the door.

"Dereszewski," said Weidt. "Yes, she works here. What, she's been picked up in Hungary?" He continued to listen. "In that case I don't want her back here. I'll send you her work book. Thanks for letting me know." Turning to me he said, "That's not good."

"Does this mean I've got to leave here?"

"No, no, but you no longer have legal status. We have to remove your name wherever you're registered—the health insurance office, the labor

office." I kept the ID. In an emergency the Dere-szewski dates still might be useful, but my situation obviously had taken a turn for the worse. I was depressed. Ali tried to console me, although her situation was not much better.

It was around February 25 when Hans called me at Grete's.

"Whatever happens, don't go to the workshop tomorrow." I wanted to know why, but he refused to give me any reason. I promised to stay put.

The next morning police cars raced through the streets. They stopped at house after house; uniformed and plainclothes officers went inside and came out with yet more victims. They were rounding up the last Jews still in Berlin. They took them out of homes and factories, just as they found them—in nightdress, in work clothes, with coats or without. Looking out of the window, I saw them, and can still see today how, paralyzed with fear, they were pushed into the waiting cars by policemen, SS, and civilian officials.

The police cars took them away, deposited them somewhere, and came back for new cargo. They blanketed the city. People stopped in the street, whispered to each other, and then quickly went on their way, back to the safety of their homes, peering out from behind curtained windows to watch what was happening. Mother and

I were terrified. Where was Hans, and where were all my other friends from the workshop? A Berlin without any Jews was inconceivable.

"For Heaven's sake, don't leave the house," Grete implored us. We were sitting in her apartment. I was crying; Mother, Grete, and Ostrowski were brooding. What was there to say? Grete suddenly cried out, "Those swine," got up, and left the room.

The "action" was completed in a few days. And then the Jews were gone. Nobody screamed, nobody protested. (We learned after the war that between October 1941 and the end of the war sixty-three transports carrying thirty-five thousand Jews had left Berlin.)

On Monday I went back to the workshop. It was eerily silent. Nobody was there, neither the Jewish blind workers nor the Jewish sighted finishers nor Werner Basch, our bookkeeper. They were all gone. Only the handful of non-Jewish workers still sat at their benches. Charlotte, one of the blind workers, was crying; she missed her Jewish friends with whom she had worked for so long. Fritz, who'd operated a "hat store" (Berlin slang for begging) before coming to Weidt, kept repeating, "God, oh God, what are they going to do with them?"

And then there still were the underground people—Horn and his family, blind Dr. Frey, who was

hidden somewhere or other, and Ali and her parents.

"I'm ruined," Weidt exclaimed. "I don't know what's going to happen."

"Try to get something else," Ali advised me. "Who knows when, if ever, Weidt will find other workers? But come to us whenever you want, perhaps things will soon change." But it was clear that nothing would ever be the same again.

Where could Hans be? I kept asking myself over and over. I did not dare to go to his house. All I could do was wait. Mother kept telling me that he knew how to get in touch with me. Finally, the Monday after the roundup, he called me from a public telephone. He and his mother had been picked up for the third time, but once again he had escaped deportation. He was allowed to remain in Berlin, at least for the time being. I was indescribably happy. But what did it mean? He would probably be living at the Jewish Hospital. The Gestapo still needed him as a source of scarce goods like floodlight frames and luxury bathroom fixtures not available through ordinary channels. Hans was able to get them from wholesalers who knew that the life of the Jew Hans Rosenthal depended on them. Hans must have been the only Jew in Berlin still wearing the star, except for some partners of mixed marriages.

Grete tried to cheer me up. "Don't worry. I've

meant to ask you anyway whether you don't want to work with me in the shop." I was stunned. I, the underground Jew without papers, work in a shop and talk to Germans as though nothing had happened?

"Why not? Nobody knows who you are. You're Inge, my friend. That's all there is to it." As simple as that.

At first the two of us worked together. I had to learn the prices and acquaint myself with the books in the rental library, as well as learning the fine distinctions among the regular customers. First came the "colleagues," the local shopkeepers entitled to the precious stationery, a commodity as rare as butter or meat. In exchange, Grete got milk and vegetables without ration stamps, and the butcher's wife gave her twice the amount of meat she asked for. I soon learned the ins and outs.

Then came the category of anti-Nazis, people Grete had known since she first opened her business in 1933, long enough to feel sure about their politics. They often dropped in for a chat, mostly about the previous BBC newscast. They were allowed to take out books from the so-called poison cabinet, the works of banned Jewish, foreign, and politically suspect writers. Instead of being listed by author and title in our card file these books had a code. These old customers of course also got such

precious items as stationery, pens, and toilet paper. If Grete sold these things to Nazis or people she didn't know, the items were of inferior quality.

Grete had very few Nazi customers. They said, "Heil Hitler," when they came in, and I answered them with "Heil Hitler." Not Grete. She said, "Good day," except when officers of the nearby police station were present. Then she would make a point of saying "Heil Hitler" very distinctly, and if old customers were present they would smile knowingly. I asked Grete not to leave me alone in the shop if possible. I was not altogether free of fear.

"But no one even suspects that you're Jewish." Grete laughed. And indeed who would have believed that a "secret" Jew would have the nerve to work openly in a shop? Gradually I got used to the situation and was able to be a real help to Grete.

On the Sunday before Easter, as I was getting ready to close up and take the unsold greeting cards out of the display window, I found a purse. The poor woman, I thought to myself. I opened it and in it I found a three-months' supply of ration stamps for household goods and notions as well as food ration stamps. What a treasure—but I couldn't possibly keep it. According to the identity card this gold mine belonged to one Amanda Heubaum, a woman about my mother's age. What

should I do? I put the purse down and continued with my work. And then I opened it again, and in a separate compartment I found a postcard-sized picture of Adolf Hitler. That did it! However, I wanted to leave the final decision up to Grete. She knew her customers better than I. It didn't take us long to decide. The Führer's picture made our decision for us. "Whoever carries that picture around," said Ostrowski, "is showing sympathy for that criminal." And anyway, he assured us, her stamps will be replaced when she reports the loss.

"And if not," said Grete, "I won't mind either." We were ecstatic. All the things we could get for those stamps! For once, Mother and I would be able to contribute to the communal household instead of being on the receiving end.

For a while everything seemed to be going smoothly. I got used to working in the bookstore, and the customers accepted Miss Inge, Grete Sommer's friend. Some even preferred dealing with me; Grete tended to be moody. It was hard, running both a business and the household. Ostrowski was not the easiest man. He wanted his meals served on time. He liked the good life and felt it was his due. Grete somehow always managed to get hold of delicacies for him. To begin with, there was her parents' grocery; they gave her as much butter as she wanted. Then there was

Mrs. Mausch. She worked as a cleaning woman for a dairy wholesaler and for a butcher. Out of these two enterprises, Mrs. Mausch smuggled merchandise, hidden in her work clothes, which she either sold or bartered. Butter for coffee, coffee for meat, for soap, for whatever. Grete became so caught up in her black market activities that she scarcely had time for anything else. And finally, there was the janitor of her apartment house, Mrs. Sell. Her husband was stationed in an occupied country, and he brought things that hadn't been seen in Germany for ages. All of them helped supply Grete.

One day Paul Garn and his wife came to visit. They were having a hard time. Paul had lost his trade-union post in 1933. He was no youngster, and he was troubled that through his work—he was now a common laborer—he was contributing to Hitler's war effort. A dyed-in-the-wool anti-Nazi, he felt he was involved in a criminal enterprise and was helpless to do anything about it. His wife was sickly. They were childless and devoted to each other. The one subject that was sure to get them all stirred up was the Nazis. When they came into the room Mother Garn, as she was called, greeted us with these words: "Deutschkrons, you're coming to stay with us for a while. We just decided on it." Paul Garn nodded in agreement.

"It's not good to stay in the same place too long," said Grete. "Inge, of course, will continue to come to work as usual."

We didn't object. How could we? Mother responded with the customary polite formulas. "Are you sure we won't be in the way?"

"Well," said Mrs. Garn, smiling, "it won't be a vacation for you. As you know, we have only two rooms. You can sleep in the kitchen."

We left most of our belongings at Grete's and moved in with the Garns. They lived in a workers' settlement in north Berlin that had been built in the twenties, before Hitler. The houses were light and clean; the rooms were small, and the apartments had private baths. These houses with their indoor plumbing were innovative examples of decent housing for working-class families.

The kitchen had a coal range and was warm; winter the Garns spent most of their time in the kitchen. The living room and balcony were reserved for the summer and for guests. A comfortable sofa stood in the kitchen under the storage shelf for pots and pans. I had long since gotten used to sharing a bed with Mother. She never left the Garns' house. She spent her days sitting in the kitchen with them, knitting or sewing or helping with the housework. It wasn't easy for her, especially since nobody knew how much longer we would have to live that way. She was very de-

pressed. It was easy for me to talk, she said, I was going out to work while she was shut up in that little room day after day like a prisoner. Grete saw to it that the Garns would not go hungry because of us, but Mother grew more and more restless. One evening when she and I went out for a walk, she told me that a neighbor had dropped in. Mrs. Garn couldn't stop her.

"Oh, you have company?" Always that damned question.

"Who knows what she's thinking," said Mrs. Garn after the neighbor left. "She looked so funny."

"We'll have to leave again." Mother was worried. But where could we go? "We can't go back to Grete."

I was looking for an excuse to visit Weidt again. Maybe he'd come up with something. But when I got there I found everyone very gloomy. Ali and her parents were still safely ensconced in the storage shed. With its brushes and brooms, it seemed the perfect hiding place. However, Mr. Licht was very ill, and no doctor could be brought there. Even Weidt did not know anyone he could trust.

"What will happen if he doesn't survive?" Ali asked. Weidt was very worried. His self-assurance seemed to have deserted him. In addition, he had serious financial problems. Although he had found a few blind workers, he did not have nearly as

many as he needed. He risked losing his army orders, and was threatened with cancellations unless he could deliver by a given date. In the past he would have filled the orders at least partially, but now he could not even do that much. I felt I could not possibly burden him with my problems, and left. At Grete's I was usually able to forget my worries. I was kept busy keeping our records in order, which Grete had been neglecting for some time.

"Why bother? Once the war is over I'll dump it all and devote myself to politics," she used to say. "It can't take much longer now."

For me the work was more than just a pastime. More and more Grete left me to myself in the shop. She even gave me the keys. At first I had picked them up from her in the morning and returned them at night. No longer. Now Grete only stopped by from time to time, like a guest, and she was pleased with the way I was running things.

On the way home from seeing Weidt I was overcome by the fear of what would happen if we had to leave the Garns. One night there was an air-raid alarm. "You've got to stay up here," Garn said. We were afraid, not so much of the bombs, but what if the house were hit and we were found? And then one day the bell rang, and again the nosy neighbor pushed her way into the kitchen before Mrs. Garn could stop her.

"Well, this is a long visit." And it was true, we'd been at the Garns' for weeks. No sooner had Mrs. Garn closed the door behind her uninvited guest than she told us with barely disguised fear, "You must leave. It can't go on. I'm afraid. I'm not well, you know . . ." Her eyes filled with tears. Paul Garn turned away. He said nothing and started to fuss with the stove.

"But of course, I understand," said Mother. And, barely audibly, she asked, "What are we to do now?"

Nobody had an answer. That night we slept very little. The next morning we packed our few possessions.

"Don't cry, Mrs. Deutschkron, we'll find a way," Grete consoled her when we told her what had happened. She planted herself in front of Mother, arms akimbo. Ostrowski tried to soothe us. "I'll go talk to Rieck. Until then you stay here."

Grete made coffee, and when we sat down together not knowing what to say, she banged her fist on the table. "You don't think that we'll just send you away, do you?"

"I know, Grete, but where should we go?" It was a question that remained unanswered for some time, because Ostrowski was not able to find Rieck right away.

11

"My husband was murdered by the Nazis." Lisa Holländer's voice was harsh and resolute. After they arrested him, Lisa tried for months to find out what had happened to him. Everywhere she went she was turned away without an answer, until one day she received a package from the concentration camp with her husband's blood-stained trousers and a note informing her that he had died of heart failure. Lisa's unambiguous statement about her husband's fate underscored her readiness to take us under her wing. Not only did she not hesitate even for a moment, she seemed to welcome the opportunity to help us. "I *want* to do it," she said. Lisa was the sister of our old trusted friend Jenny Rieck,

and it was Jenny's husband who took us to her.

When Lisa married Paul Holländer she was the young mother of an illegitimate child, at a time when illegitimacy was still a terrible stigma. Paul, a prosperous Jewish businessman, adored and spoiled her. When she expressed a desire to study French, he hired a tutor, who happened to be my father. She in turn was devoted to her husband. And then one day the Nazis came for him, accusing him of having violated one of their financial regulations.

"You can stay as long as you wish. I've got plenty of room," Aunt Lisa, as I soon began to call her, said to us. It was like an invitation to tea.

We could hardly believe our good fortune. Lisa paid no attention to the danger we posed. We didn't know how to thank her. I even got my own little room, something I'd never had before. Mother slept on the couch in the living room. Aunt Lisa lived in the so-called Rosenhof, a housing complex built around a rose garden. The superintendent of the complex lived in one of the other houses, which suited us very well indeed. It meant there was nobody to spy on us.

Aunt Lisa not only looked determined, she was. Nothing and nobody could faze her. The fact that neighbors or the block warden might ask pointed questions did not bother her one bit.

"There's nothing more I can lose—they've al-

ready taken what was dearest to me," she said. When the Nazis came around with their collection boxes she slammed the door on them. My mother once ventured that in view of our presence it might perhaps be wiser to make a small contribution, but Lisa wouldn't budge. "They're not going to get a single penny from me, and that's that."

We lived well during our stay with her. We pooled whatever money we had for our household expenses. I ate my lunch at Grete's, who had begun to pay me in the form of butter and other precious foods, the wage scale being based on current black-market prices. And of course Grete had also introduced me to all the various food shops in the neighorhood.

"I can't leave the shop at the moment," I'd tell the girl from the neighborhood grocer when she came to our shop. "Do you think you could bring me some milk?" And minutes later she'd be back with milk. Mrs. Mausch, who liked to drop in for a chat, would occasionally bring me some blood pudding. "Would you like some?" she'd ask. Blood pudding was to be had for half the stamps required for other meat products. Mrs. Mausch got so much meat illegally from the butcher shop where she worked that she could afford to turn up her nose at blood pudding. The girls from the vegetable store also gave me whatever I needed, without ration stamps. But even though we were

comparatively well off during that period, our cash reserves were dwindling rapidly. We were paying rent to Aunt Lisa, and occasionally we had to shop on the black market. It was essential that Mother find some work. Hans Rosenthal came to the rescue. He took her to see Theodor Görner, a printer with whom he had some dealings. Görner had no use for Hitler and the Nazis. He told Mother he didn't want to know her real name, that he would call her by whatever name she chose. Mother decided on Richter. Görner offered to give her the ration stamps she needed for the canteen.

Mother was paid the standard wages, and that was a great help. She told her co-workers that she was a widow, that her late husband had been a teacher. Her marital status encouraged one of her fellow workers, a widower by the name of Kruse, to pay court to her.

The Görner plant, which made printed textiles, was classified as an essential enterprise. The other workers confided to Mother that Görner was an old Communist, but that didn't bother them. Most of them made no secret of how they felt about Hitler. Only Mr. Kruse warned her to be careful. He said that even though he did not particularly like the Nazis, the others weren't all that desirable either. He'd been in the merchant marine, he told her, and he knew all about the British and the Americans.

Our life was almost normal. We had jobs and a place to live, and we ate as well—or as poorly—as most other Germans. We hoped for an early end to the war and listened to the radio, pretending to understand enough Dutch to know what was being said. We idolized some of the BBC announcers and cursed when their broadcasts were jammed; their intimate knowledge of the situation in the Third Reich impressed us. They even made reference to Auschwitz, although we didn't discuss it. It was too frightening.

Aunt Lisa didn't object to Hans' visits. Of course he didn't wear the star when he came to see us. He was living with his mother in the old Jewish Hospital, where there were still a few Jewish doctors. The Gestapo was using the hospital as a prison for Jews not fit for transport, keeping them there until they recovered. If "illegals" like Mother and me were picked up, they were also kept there until their deportation. Hans was forever warning me of the danger of being picked up. The Gestapo had a list of people who had eluded them, and they had Jewish informers to help find them. They too lived in the former hospital. Hans told me of a Jewish girl who'd made a date with a friend to meet at an underground station. She had confided in him that she was illegal. Arriving at their meeting place, she saw her "friend" in the company of two Gestapo men.

Acting with lightning speed, she jumped down to
the tracks just as a train was pulling in. She lost
part of a foot in the accident. Hans was called to
bring her to the hospital by ambulance. He told
me that the girl—I later found out that she was a
former classmate of mine—had had enough presence of mind to destroy the ration cards given her
by non-Jewish friends in order to protect them.

Hans also told me the story of two young boys,
one nine and the other seven, who hadn't been
deported because their mother wasn't Jewish and
they had not been brought up as Jews. Their
mother and grandparents were dead, and their
father and all their Jewish relatives were in camps.
The boys, alone and hungry, scrounged and
begged for food. I asked Hans whether he happened to know their name. Yes, he said, it was
Phillipsborn. Mother and I almost jumped out of
our skins. The two boys were the sons of my cousin Willy, who had been arrested in 1938. His wife
had divorced him in order to be able to keep the
children. After her death they were taken to a
Jewish home. We tried to think of how we could
help them, but in view of our own situation our
hands were tied.

One day an utterly dejected Hans arrived at
our house. "They're all gone," he said. The Gestapo had "cleaned out" the workshop for the
blind. Apparently old Mr. Horn, Weidt's brush-

maker, had run across an old Jewish acquaintance and told him that he was living illegally, and about Weidt's workshop. A few days later the Gestapo came to the workshop and, ignoring Weidt's protests, went to the back, opened the door to the closet, shoved the clothes aside, and pulled the entire Horn family out of their hiding place. While this was going on, other officers arrested Alice Licht's parents. Ali might possibly have saved herself, but she chose to stay with her parents. Weidt carried on like a madman. Ignoring all danger to himself, he went to the Gestapo and persuaded them—nobody knew how—to have Ali and her parents sent to Theresienstadt, a privilege the Gestapo accorded only to "special" Jews. We didn't know that Theresienstadt was only a way station on the road to Auschwitz. We found that out only later, when we received a card from Ali written on the train taking her to Auschwitz. She had somehow managed to smuggle it out and have someone mail it.

When I went to see Weidt in his workshop a few days after the Gestapo raid, I found a lonely, broken old man. There was no trace of the old fervor. He just sat staring into space.

"You're the only one left," he said, putting his hand on my shoulder. He got up from his chair, took a brand-new coat off a hanger, and urged me to put it on.

"Take it, take it!" He'd had the coat made for Ali, but it hadn't been ready in time. I was extremely grateful. My coat was beginning to look threadbare.

"You can return it to Ali when she comes back," and when he noticed my hesitation he added, "I'll go to Auschwitz. I'll do something. I can't just let her die there." I thought it was a cry in the dark rather than a positive assertion but I was to find out that I was wrong.

All these developments weighed us down. We kept talking about all the people who'd been picked up by the Gestapo, and we were frightened.

Aunt Lisa's apartment was ideal. The neighbors knew one another, but there was little contact among them. Air raids had not yet become a major problem. Since we lived on the first floor we weren't as much at risk as those living higher up. The likelihood of a police raid on Grete's shop or Görner's plant was remote. Still, we were extremely tense.

On August 23, 1943, we celebrated my birthday with a bottle of wine Aunt Lisa had somehow managed to find. We went to bed feeling happy when suddenly I was awakened by an ear-splitting noise. The window frame and splinters of glass landed on my bed. All hell had broken loose. We hadn't heard the siren. This time the British at-

tacked Berlin with all their might. I jumped out of bed and began to dress in the dark. The house was shaking like a ship in a storm. We tried to steady ourselves, holding on to whatever was still standing. Aunt Lisa thought we should try to make it down to the shelter, but that was impossible. Doors, windows, and walls came tumbling down amid indescribable noise. The dark, windowless hallway seemed a safer shelter.

Aunt Lisa was convinced that this attack was aimed at the nearby headquarters of the army high command and the SS. How was she to know that this was merely the first of many mass raids? After about twenty minutes it was all over. We'd been lucky to escape with only broken windows and torn blackout curtains. Through the empty window frames we could see the reddish sky. It was like a gigantic fireworks display, with flames rising up and bursting into millions of sparks before dissolving into black smoke. The acrid smell of smoldering fires blanketed the city. People were screaming, fire engines raced through the streets. And there we were, happy despite the scare we'd had, because the British had finally begun to unleash their power. Then began the hard work of making our apartment habitable again. We swept and cleaned and hammered, smiling all the time.

"For Heaven's sake," warned Mother, "don't be so obvious." We never got back to sleep. We

heard the distant sounds of buildings collapsing. Next morning we were able to see the full extent of the damage. It was considerable. Large portions of the transportation system had been knocked out. Bent tracks rose up from deep craters; the overhead wires of the trolleys hung down in tatters. Still, air raid or no, the people of Berlin had to go to work.

For us things had changed. We knew that in future attacks we could not stay in the apartment. Aunt Lisa came up with a solution. She didn't like going to the cellar anyway. The idea of burrowing under a building troubled her; she preferred the nearby public shelter. No one there was asked for an ID, which meant that we could go there without fear of detection. The only problem was that we'd have to run out of the building as soon as the air-raid siren went off if we were to make it to the shelter in time.

We packed a small suitcase with a few essentials. I must admit that I began to feel nervous as soon as it grew dark. I hadn't gotten over the shock of that hellish night, the racket of the falling bombs. Mother teased me. She felt sure, she said, that no bombs would ever hit us. Good for her, I thought, but I was afraid. Each night I listened for the raids, and they arrived punctually night after night. As soon as I heard the siren go off I began to prod Aunt Lisa and Mother to get moving. They

were so slow. I ran ahead of them to the public shelter, which did not offer any real protection against the kind of bombs the British were now dropping. We found the same people there night after night. They didn't talk about the war or the general situation; they just sat there and waited. "Well, we've been lucky once again." That was the standard phrase when the all-clear sounded and we could go back to our homes.

The raids after that first massive attack of August 23, 1943, were not as heavy; they merely made people uneasy. By the end of November, however, the British resumed the massive attacks.

"I've lost everything," said Käte Schwarz, one of my customers, as she came into the shop on the morning of November 23. "The apartment is gone. Nothing is left. I couldn't save a thing. A direct hit."

Käte Schwarz was married to a professor of Roman law at Berlin University. She liked to drop in for a chat with "sane people." Even if she hadn't said this I would have known that she listened to the BBC. She used the same formulations I'd heard over the air.

"How much longer?" asked Mrs. Steinhausen and Mrs. Wiese and Mrs. Schwarz. Their husbands had been drafted, and they all hoped that Germany would be defeated and rid of the Nazis.

On the day on which she was bombed out,

Käte Schwarz stayed longer than usual. She obviously wanted to be alone with me.

"I'm going to move to Ingolstadt," she told me. "There is nothing to keep me in Berlin now. I have relatives in Ingolstadt." Then she hesitated a bit before beginning again: "Miss Inge, I feel I've gotten to know you. I know how you feel . . ." At that moment another customer came in, and again she waited before continuing. "You've got to help me!" I was astonished. "When I leave Berlin somebody else might get into trouble." She paused, as though gathering courage. "Inge, I've hidden a Jewish woman. Could you now take over for me?"

She looked at me searchingly, her face tense and perhaps also a bit frightened. After a moment I began to laugh out loud. Käte was bewildered.

"Well," I said, "now that you've been so frank with me I have to tell you the truth—I too am a hidden Jew." Käte stared at me in astonishment.

"But Miss Inge, why didn't you tell me? Why? I would have helped you." The words poured from her. "From now on of course I'll also help you. What do you need?"

I told her how we were living, that Mother and I were both working and making enough money to pay our rent and the little food we were able to buy—red beets and other root vegetables.

"Can I help you with bread and butter stamps?

173

From now on I'll give you some stamps every month."

"But you don't have all that much yourself," I remonstrated.

"Don't be ridiculous, Inge. And anyway, that's not your problem." Again she looked at me with deep concern. "Why didn't you tell me before? I see it almost as a lack of trust."

I told her that we and our protectors thought that the fewer the people who knew our secret the better.

"You're probably right. But Inge, promise me, from now on no more secrets. You tell me if you need something, and if at all possible I'll help." And then, almost pleadingly, she added, "You'll look after Lotte, won't you?"

Lotte Eifert was tall and dark-haired. I am ashamed to admit that I did not like to be seen with her. I thought she looked Jewish, or what was then taken for Jewish. She was a casual acquaintance of Käte Schwarz's. Lotte had been brought to Käte by mutual friends when she, Lotte, was in danger of arrest. When Käte was bombed out she managed to find a place for Lotte with friends. Subsequently Lotte answered an ad for a governess in Potsdam and got the job. She felt safe there. She had her own room, bombs weren't falling on Potsdam yet, and the father of her charges was in the SS.

12

"Calm down! It's all over," shouted one of the men. Our bomb shelter reverberated. The noise was deafening. There must have been a direct hit in our immediate vicinity. The wooden door of the shelter flapped helplessly. Dazzling rays lit up the sky; orange and red flashes of light outlined the buildings; columns of thick black smoke rose up. I sat huddled against my mother and thought I could tell where the bombs were falling. But the one we did not hear had fallen practically next door.

"It's the ones you don't hear that hit," a soldier volunteered. He was on home leave from the front, and he said that a night raid over Berlin was far worse than a day in battle.

When it looked as though the planes had dropped their entire cargo, some people cautiously peered out of the shelter. It was a devastating sight. Fires were burning everywhere. Once the all-clear sounded we set out for home. For some reason we were sure that our house had been spared. Although we were happy to see the army headquarters and the SS complex in flames, we were outraged that those fires were being put out while all around people's homes were burning to the ground. We knew that there wasn't enough fire-fighting equipment to extinguish all the fires after a raid, but it was infuriating to see the files of the SS taking precedence over people, who made no secret of their feelings. Harsh words were heard. In situations like this the Berliners did not hold back.

When we came to our house, we were appalled to see that the top floor was on fire.

"It's an incendiary bomb," our neighbors told us. "We could put it out if we had water." To try extinguishing it with the bit of water in the pail beside the sandbag in front of each apartment was absurd.

"We'll just have to stand here and watch the whole house burn down." People were bitter.

"Well, in that case let's save whatever we can."

I ran over to the headquarters building where the soldiers of the Waffen SS were lugging files out.

"Don't you think it's more important to help us save our belongings?" I asked sharply.

"Go with her," one of them ordered. He was a young man, an ethnic German from Hungary. I asked him to come with me to Aunt Lisa's apartment and help us salvage the most important things. Our neighbors advised that we try to save some of the smaller pieces of furniture. We put everything out on the street. It was raining, but we hardly noticed. We simply carried out everything we could. Every now and then the soldier took my hand. He asked me to meet him the next day. I told him I would, but that first we had to get the furniture out. The fire spread slowly; smoldering beams came crashing down. It was no longer safe to go back into the building. The young soldier went back one last time and managed to bring out Aunt Lisa's easy chair. Then we stood by helplessly watching the fire work its way down from the roof. The date was January 30, 1944, the time 3 A.M., and it was cold. When my mother tried to unroll a mattress to sit down on, a flame shot out from it. Apparently phosphorus and air were a combustible mixture. We stood there on the street lit by the flames, not knowing what to do.

"What am I to do with all this furniture?" asked Aunt Lisa. Suddenly, salvaging the furniture seemed insane. Who was going to help us cart it away? And if it was left out in the open it was

sure to disappear. The neighbors said that we should all go to the NSV (the National Socialist welfare agency) and ask them for help, that that was what they were there for. Lisa went with them while we stood watch over the furniture. It was slowly beginning to dawn on us that we were homeless, but we couldn't quite take it in yet.

"You've got to go there too," Aunt Lisa told us when she came back from the NSV. "It's a complete madhouse. You must take advantage of it." She smiled slyly. "They're feeding everybody who claims to have been bombed out, and they're distributing food stamps for the coming week."

We went there promptly. It was exactly as Lisa had described it. We, Ella and Inge Richter, were registered in their files as bombing victims and given precious food stamps. They urged us to eat a hearty breakfast. In a hastily set-up canteen we found pots of coffee and meat sandwiches. They told us to come back at lunchtime, and we did. We hadn't eaten that well for some time. As bombing victims we were given things we hadn't known still existed.

"They're afraid of us," someone whispered to us. "In Hamburg people who'd been bombed out rioted."

However, even the NSV couldn't tell us what to do about our furniture. "We're sure no one will steal it," they reassured us.

The next morning Walter Rieck showed up. He had heard about the attack on our neighborhood. His wife and daughter were in Bavaria, but business had kept him in Berlin. He was staying with a Mr. Hentze in Potsdam, in a former workers' colony of mostly small one-family houses with garden plots. Hentze was a civil servant in the finance ministry. Because he had refused to join the Nazi Party in 1933, even though he had no history of political involvement, he had never been promoted. "Better that than making a deal with criminals," he said. After the Riecks were bombed out in Berlin, Hentze made a small apartment next door to his own available to them. It belonged to his daughter, whose husband was missing in action, and she didn't need all that room. Charlotte, a young film actress who had been staying with the Riecks, went to Potsdam with them.

"The three of you are going to come to Potsdam with me," Rieck declared after he saw the mess. "You've got to get some sleep. After that we'll see what can be done."

"What about the furniture?"

He made a gesture of dismissal. Aunt Lisa just nodded and said, "Let's go."

We were so exhausted that we fell asleep on the train. Our hair was black with soot, our faces covered with dust, our clothes wet and singed. Everything reeked of smoke. For the time being,

Rieck put us up in his small apartment while he went back to the small attic room where Charlotte was staying. We were so tired that the significance of this didn't register with us.

We needed a few days to gather our thoughts. It was clear to us that we couldn't remain in the apartment. Rieck suggested that we try to find a place in the settlement. It wouldn't arouse any suspicion there if we failed to register with the police. No Berliners did, because they would then lose the special rations to which people living in bombed cities were entitled.

With Hentze's help we, the Richters, as we now called ourselves, found a little shed on a piece of land belonging to a Mrs. Fabig. It was a former combination goat shed and laundry room.

"Well, if you think it's livable," said the white-haired lady with the work-worn hands and a friendly smile.

"Better a less comfortable place than Berlin."

"I can believe that. Sometimes we can even see the flames from here."

We struck a bargain. The little hut was a solid stone structure with a concrete floor and a sound roof, a screened window and wood doors. It was unheated. We could cook on the brick stove that originally held the copper washtub, and we hoped that this would also give off some heat. The old stable became our bedroom. At the urging of Mrs.

Fabig, kind neighbors brought some cast-off furniture for the bombed-out Berliners. We discovered that we had hit upon an absolutely ideal hideout; the shed was not considered habitable, and thus was not registered at the housing office.

Of course Mrs. Fabig, the widow of a construction worker, had no idea whom she was sheltering. In addition to paying her a nominal rent, we spent a great deal of time with her playing cards and gossiping.

My mother claimed to be the widow of a teacher. We were accepted in the settlement as decent, hard-working people. In the morning we took the train to Berlin to work. Everything appeared to be in order. The fact that we brought back food and even coal, which I managed to steal from the cellars of bombed-out houses, didn't arouse suspicion, since as supposedly legal residents of Berlin we were entitled to rations. We collected firewood in the woods near the house, but it was green and didn't burn well. More important were the mushrooms we found there; they made many a meal for us. We soon became expert in preparing them, and invented some delicious dishes. Unfortunately, the mushroom season was brief. Would we ever again take a walk in the woods for the sheer joy of walking, without having to search for food or fuel? It seemed like a pipe dream.

Sometimes we'd get up in the middle of the night to watch Berlin burning. The increasingly frequent British raids inflicted enormous damage, reducing whole sections of the city to rubble. The people were afraid of what the night would bring, but their morale didn't break. The bombings only made them angrier, because the destruction seemed so pointless. "Why don't they attack really essential targets instead of our houses?"

Grete and Ostrowski had left Berlin. They too had been bombed out and were now living in Calau, a few hours distance from Berlin. They came to Berlin once a week, "visited" the shop, inspected the ledgers, and were happy to see that everything was under control.

"It can't last much longer," they'd say. I was getting so tired of that empty phrase. I was now completely on my own in the shop. I had slowly built up a good relationship with the other shop keepers in the neighborhood, and I had also begun to do the buying. Grete had lost interest in the business. And even though the paper goods I managed to get were of inferior quality, I was able to satisfy our regular customers.

One day Hans stopped by. We hadn't been seeing much of each other because he was not allowed to go out except on Gestapo business.

"Regards from Walter Skolny," he said to me.

I understood immediately. Like me, Skolny was

"illegal." He had apparently been denounced by a Jewish informer and been arrested. Hans didn't leave me much time to brood over this monstrous deed.

"Here, take these," he said to me. "They're the keys to the apartment where Walter had a room. Try to get the black market stuff out of there before the Gestapo gets it."

Walter Skolny had no friends who might have hidden him; he had tried to compensate for his lack of friends by scattering money made on the black market. For a while this worked. The people who rented rooms to this handsome young man didn't ask too many questions if the money was good enough. Apparently Walter had gotten involved in some deal with a man he didn't know, and had trusted him. The next day the man showed up at their meeting place with the Gestapo in tow. Walter tried to flee, but they shot him in the leg. Now he was afraid that the Gestapo would find all his black market goods and make matters even worse for him.

Hans told me how to get into Walter's room without arousing the suspicion of his landlady. "Please, go there soon, before it's too late." He told me to put what I found into one of Walter's suitcases and take it to Mrs. Grüger's bakery.

I couldn't do it that same day; I had to hurry to get to Potsdam before dark, before "the English"

came. Next morning I left earlier than usual, and with my heart in my mouth went to Walter's room. Suppose it was the wrong door? It wasn't. I looked around and opened his closet—bacon, silk stockings, liquor, coffee—a dizzying array. I had not seen anything like this for I don't know how long. I stuffed everything into the suitcase, which I could hardly lift. With sweat pouring down my face, I got out of the apartment without being seen. Once outside, I took a deep breath. Fortunately I didn't have far to go.

When I arrived at the bakery the woman behind the counter looked at me suspiciously. "Mrs. Grüger," I said, "I'm bringing you regards from Walter."

She seemed surprised. "I haven't seen him for ages," she said cautiously. I told her what had happened, and her eyes filled with tears.

"I don't know how many times I've told him to be more careful. What a catastrophe." She couldn't stop crying. Suddenly she turned to me and asked, "Who are you anyway?"

I told her. She heard me out, and when I finished she said, "From now on I'll help you. You'll take Walter's place." And reaching down she took a bag, threw in rolls and cakes without counting, and said, "Please come whenever you need something. Promise?" And she again broke into tears. She asked one of her helpers to take over and pulled me into the room behind the shop.

"Everything is so terrible," she sobbed, and confided in me that she was hiding a Jewish friend, a lawyer named Hans Münzer, in her bakery. He was so frightened of being asked for his identity papers by the watchdogs, the Berliners' name for the military police, that he didn't dare leave the house. There were many deserters, she said, and the MPs were all over the place. Mrs. Grüger alternately cursed and cried: "Those beasts, just look at what they've done." She gave vent to her hatred of the Nazis without fear or caution. "Every morning I put bread and rolls in front of the door for the POWs who march past here. You should see them pounce on it, the poor devils."

Her husband was altogether different, quiet and shy, but he shared her feelings. "Yes, indeed, they're criminals," he said slowly but firmly.

Hans came back to Grete's shop to tell me that the Gestapo hadn't found anything in Walter's apartment except a very surprised landlady who had had no idea who her tenant was. Apparently the Gestapo had arrived shortly after I left. Walter was grateful, sent his regards, and hoped to see me again soon.

The way the war was going now made such hopes credible. Unlike the fall of Stalingrad, which was celebrated with ceremonies honoring the fallen heroes, the retreat in the East was not announced. The official propaganda machine did its level best to convince the populace that victory was

near, that Germany had to win and would win. "If we don't, what's to become of us?" asked some of my customers who, although they were not Nazis, nonetheless feared, and understandably so, that if Germany were to lose the war they would all be treated as Nazis.

We knew from the BBC of the magnitude of Germany's losses and the damage inflicted by the air attacks. And now the Americans had begun to launch daytime raids over Berlin, which possibly were even more damaging because they directly affected production. The smoking fires of those attacks turned day into night. In their desperation people stopped the few private cars that were still allowed in the city and pleaded for lifts. Even horse-drawn carts were a rarity. Once, while riding on such a cart pulled by a worn-out nag, I spotted a man sitting on the sidewalk. He was covered with debris; blood was running down his head. He had obviously been buried under the rubble. He begged for help. Nobody paid the slightest attention. I jumped off the cart, and the driver reluctantly helped me pull the man up.

"Now I suppose we'll have to go by way of the hospital," he muttered angrily as he urged his horse on. On the way we saw many more people wandering around in a daze.

During the daytime raids I tried to get to a bunker made of concrete. It seemed to offer greater

protection. The noise of the attacks did not penetrate those bunkers, although even those mammoth structures shook under the force of the detonations. And when the all-clear sounded and we emerged from our shelters, we looked around and saw the destruction inflicted while we were huddled together underground.

My greatest concern during those daylight raids was my mother, who worked in another part of the city. I had no way of finding out whether she was safe; telephone service was haphazard. Rumors about which sections had been hardest hit, about fires burning out of control, swept the city. At the end of a day like that, I'd rush back to Potsdam filled with dread. But there was one day when I couldn't wait to shut the shop and rush home, and it had nothing to do with any raid. Hans had called me up in the afternoon and asked where my mother was. I told him at Görner's, as usual.

"Something seems to have happened there," he told me. "I don't exactly know what, but something happened."

I was sick with fear. I don't know how I managed to get through the day. I arrived home out of breath, having run all the way from the station. When I saw Mother standing at the garden gate, I broke into tears.

"Why didn't you call me?" I asked her.

"How was I to know you'd heard about it?" she said, somewhat miffed at Hans' calling me. But he had meant well.

What had happened? That morning Mr. Görner had called Mother into his office and told her that the Gestapo were going to be there any minute. He told her to behave normally so as not to arouse any suspicion, that their visit had nothing to do with her. He had barely finished speaking when the Gestapo arrived and ordered all the employees to line up. They did as they were told. For a moment, Mother contemplated going down the back stairs, but luckily she decided to follow Görner's advice. The Gestapo had sealed off the rear door. When all the workers were assembled, a Gestapo officer told them that the plant was being closed because Görner had behaved like an enemy of the people.

Apparently years earlier he had adopted a half-Jewish child, and now he was trying to enroll the child in a higher school. Such behavior, the Gestapo said, was tantamount to treason. At any rate it was a violation of the German racial laws. If Görner was willing to tolerate this bastard child in his home that was his affair, but he could not burden a German school with it, nor expect German children to sit next to a Jewish child.

Nothing happened to Görner himself, but the plant was closed. It was a fatal blow to us; it meant

that Mother was now unemployed. What were we to tell the neighbors? All women under the age of fifty-five had to work. We decided to say to them that the plant she worked in was closed for a month because of a shortage of raw materials. It was an altogether plausible explanation. Now that she wasn't working, Mother occasionally came to Berlin with me to help me carry the coal I collected.

One day in the underground a soldier sat down next to us. He kept staring at me; finally he leaned over and asked, "Aren't you Inge Deutschkron?"

I looked at him in astonishment and answered no, I wasn't. Suddenly I remembered who he was. His name was Helmut Wende, Jenny Rieck's ex–son-in-law. Mother quickly intervened, saying that the gentleman was obviously mistaking me for someone else. He looked startled and excused himself. We took our bags and got off at the next stop. Helmut Wende may not have been a Nazi—for all we knew, he may even have been an anti-Nazi—but we could not risk admitting who we were.

Another time in the underground we were even luckier. At one of the stops two men came into our car and announced that they were making an identity check. Fortunately we were at the front of the car and they were at the other end. Before they got to us the train pulled into the station. We jumped off without waiting for the train to come to a full stop and ran down the stairs.

What now? We couldn't just turn around and go back up and wait for the next train, even though this was the direction we were going in. We decided to walk to the next station. It was of course entirely possible that we would run into another identity check there. When a train finally came we decided to stand, in case we had to get off in a hurry. Luck, however, was with us that time.

13

One morning Dr. Ostrowski and Grete walked into the shop with a woman they introduced as the sister of a friend of Ostrowski's. It was highly unusual for them to come to Berlin unannounced in the middle of the week, and I began to feel uneasy. When Ostrowski went into the little room behind the shop I followed him. Grete was showing their friend around the shop, explaining things. Ostrowski turned to me and rather curtly informed me that they couldn't keep me there any longer, that it was becoming too dangerous.

I froze. As far as I knew we hadn't encountered any problems. For almost eighteen months I had been working there as though it were the most

natural thing in the world, had sold stationery, lent books, greeted customers with "Heil Hitler" or "Good day." The shop was important to me; I felt secure there. It meant that I didn't have to be out on the streets running the danger of identity checks or informers. I had made friends with the neighborhood grocers, contacts that were of invaluable help. I could not believe that all this was now to come to an end.

"What happened?" I asked.

"Thank God, nothing yet, but for all we know something might. Controls are being set up all over the place."

Ostrowski explained that these controls were supposed to ferret out women under fifty-five who had somehow managed to evade compulsory labor service in war-related enterprises. I was much too confused to understand any of this, nor did I care what his reasons were. The fact that I was about to lose my job overshadowed everything else.

"What am I supposed to do now?" I asked.

Obviously I couldn't spend too much time in our goat shed without arousing suspicion among our neighbors. Here was a man I had relied on; now I began to feel that he didn't care what might happen to me. All he said was that the war would soon be over and he couldn't afford to take any risks, that he wanted to survive. "It's only a matter of weeks," he added. It was now the fall of 1944.

"How often I've heard this," I said to him. "By the time the war ends we'll probably be dead."

"How ungrateful of you." Ostrowski was annoyed. "I don't understand why you're carrying on like this." And again he explained to me that he was likely to play an important role in Germany's political future and that he could not afford to let concern about my fate cast a shadow over it. On the verge of tears, I assured him that I fully appreciated everything he had done for us, but that I was now at my wits' end. Mother had already lost her job and was reduced to spending her days taking long walks in Sanssouci, the gardens of the old Imperial Palace, and with winter coming even that would have to stop.

"Well, in that case you'll just have to take your walks along the river." He laughed callously. I felt that something inside of me was breaking apart. Here was a man who had helped us. He must have done so because of his opposition to Hitler. But apparently now that Hitler's defeat seemed imminent, he could think only of what was going to happen "afterward." From time to time he had asked us whether once the war ended we would remember all he had done for us. Mother assured him that of course we would. Now that the war was nearing its end the only thing that seemed to matter to him was he himself.

I calmed down, gathered up my things, and

took the train back to Potsdam. I couldn't get out of there fast enough. When I got home Mother asked me how come I was back so early. "Dinner isn't ready yet. We're having mushrooms." Her unsuspecting question showed how secure we were beginning to feel, more secure than we had ever thought possible. I broke down and told her what had happened.

"Ostrowski must know what he's doing," Mother said. She had boundless confidence in him. "You mustn't be ungrateful," she added when I told her how I felt about him. I simply could not understand how he could have sent me away without concern over what was to happen to me.

"I was nothing more than cheap help grateful for her monthly pay, for that pound of butter he was able to get for next to nothing in the country."

Mother did not share my indignation. "Now you'll be able to go walking with me in Sanssouci," she said, trying to cheer me up. "Maybe Ostrowski is right after all, and it will all be over in a matter of weeks."

So now every morning, instead of going to work, we set out for a walk in the palace grounds. At first I enjoyed these outings. It was another world. The lovely gardens with their floral borders were as carefully tended as ever. The palace and the outbuildings were untouched—a peaceful

world of trees and birds amid all the chaos. When it rained we went sightseeing in the palace. There was an occasional air-raid alarm, but that didn't frighten us. We would keep close to the air-raid shelter—the former wine cellar of Frederick the Great—without actually going in. We were still confident that Potsdam would be spared. The alarm was usually a warning of a raid over Berlin. Once, near the shelter, a group of men wearing strange-looking uniforms walked by, escorted by two armed German guards. Curious about who they were, I moved closer to them. They were speaking English.

"Inge, please be careful," Mother warned. The men were British officers, prisoners of war. Throwing caution to the winds, I addressed one of them in English. Less foolhardy than I, he turned to see whether the guards were looking before he answered me. He told me that they were housed in a nearby prisoner-of-war camp. As he spoke, one of the German soldiers looked over at us without intervening. I paid no attention to him. I showered the officer with questions about what he thought would happen when the war was over. The other prisoners watched in amusement. Mother, appalled at my imprudence, hung back, motioning to me to join her. The English officer, conscious of the possible danger we were in, said that he would answer my questions via a mock conversation with

one of his fellow prisoners. Everyone agreed that now it could only be a matter of months. They were well informed about how the war was going. The officer I was talking to also thought that the mistakes of Versailles would not be repeated. Another said that Versailles was responsible for Hitler's rise to power and that it was too bad that Germany hadn't gotten rid of Hitler on its own.

Unable to stand it any longer, I confided that I was Jewish and hiding out. I mentioned that my father was in England, but as I was speaking I realized that mine was an incredible story. There was no time for an exchange of names. The all-clear sounded and the prisoners were led away. For days I could speak of nothing else but this encounter in the midst of the war, and how much it had meant to us. It gave us confidence. The end was in sight.

One evening there came a knock at our door. When we opened it, there stood Walter Rieck. He looked terrible, his face ashen, his eyes bloodshot. He threw himself down, took off his hat, and after a brief pause said hoarsely, "Listen, I was called to the Gestapo at Potsdam today. They asked whether it was true that I was harboring two Jewish women."

"Oh my God," said my mother, jumping up and burying her face in her hands. "Where could it have come from?" Who in Potsdam could have suspected us?

"It's got to be a denunciation," said Rieck slowly as he turned away from us. "I had the feeling that the Gestapo also didn't quite believe the story, or they wouldn't have bothered to ask me about it." We were far too frightened to feel reassured by this.

"We've got to get out of here immediately," said Mother, "but where to?" We were obviously in danger here; despite Rieck's conviction that the Gestapo hadn't laid much store by the denunciation, we had to assume that they would follow it up. Rieck agreed that it would be better if we were to disappear, at least temporarily. He sat down with us to figure out what to do.

"There is Linke's apartment," he said slowly. "Why not?" Karl Linke, an old Social Democrat and former school principal, owned a house managed by Rieck. When the bombing of Berlin began, Linke had left and came back only rarely to attend to his affairs. Most of his furniture was still in the apartment. Wouldn't he object, we asked? How could we get in touch with him to ask? Rieck didn't know. He thought and thought, and finally said, "I've got the keys; I'll take all responsibility. I know Linke." We acquiesced; we had very little choice. Most of our friends had been bombed out, so there was nobody else we could turn to. We left our goat shed, which we had thought such a safe haven.

"You'll have to invent some excuse for leaving so that you can come back here if the Gestapo

doesn't find this place," Rieck said; Mrs. Fabig obviously could not be told the truth. Rieck advised us to take only the barest necessities with us. Then he left, promising to send his wife and Aunt Lisa over with the keys to Linke's house.

By now we had been living illegally for almost two years. The war was drawing to a close, the Allies were winning, yet we were still in constant danger. The trains carrying deportees continued to roll eastward. (In 1944 Berlin was still sending monthly transports to Auschwitz. The number of deportees rarely exceeded thirty, mostly people who could no longer endure hiding out or who were found by the Gestapo. Thus, on January 5, 1945, only days before Auschwitz was liberated, seven men and seven women were deported to Auschwitz from Berlin. And in March and April 1945 Jewish men were still being shipped to Bergen-Belsen and Sachsenhausen, and women to Ravensbrück.)

We got out our suitcases, hastily threw in some things—food, clothing, whatever we needed to survive—but we still did not know what to tell Mrs. Fabig. While we were packing and fretting, Aunt Lisa and Mrs. Rieck walked in. Mother made no secret of how desperate she felt, and I too could think of nothing else. "If the Gestapo should still show up tonight, it's all over for us," said Mother. The last train to Berlin had left, and in this small

community we were sure to be found immediately. Mother was absolutely frantic. How could we get away without Mrs. Fabig noticing? And suppose Linke didn't want us in his apartment? Up to then our two visitors had listened without saying anything. Suddenly Jenny Rieck buried her face in her hands and began to cry uncontrollably. Then she put her arms around Mother. She too was on the verge of tears. Only Lisa Holländer remained calm.

"You've got to leave here before sunrise," she said firmly. "Even if the Gestapo should come they won't be here before five." That made sense. Aunt Lisa offered to borrow a garden cart from the Hentzes and help us take our things to the station. But in Berlin we would be on our own. The only question still remaining was what to tell dear old Mrs. Fabig. She was so trusting and kind. She and her late husband had scrimped and saved to buy their little house. Her sole means of support was her meager pension and what she grew in her little garden. She obviously was not a Nazi, but still we dared not confide in her. She was a timid soul, and she had children and grandchildren to think about. Finally we decided to leave her a note saying that I had made an "incautious" remark in the shop in Berlin and feared that I'd been overheard. We therefore thought it best to leave for a while to spare her any possible unpleasantness in case someone denounced me. As soon as we thought

it safe, we would return. We promised to get in touch, and told her we were leaving our rent money and belongings.

Aunt Lisa also promised to explain it all to Mrs. Fabig in person. Mother couldn't stop crying. Neither of us slept that night, and we got up before dawn. Mother kept prodding me to hurry up. Shortly before five o'clock Aunt Lisa appeared outside our door with the cart. In stockinged feet, so as not to wake anybody, we dragged our things out and put the letter to Mrs. Fabig in her mailbox. I pulled the cart, with Lisa and Mother pushing from the rear. It took us about twenty minutes to get to the station. On the way we met some people, mostly foreign workers. At the station we unloaded our things and bade Aunt Lisa a tearful good-bye. She promised to visit us soon at Linke's.

Apprehensively we lugged our things to the platform. Once in Berlin, we checked some of the things at the station and went to Linke's house. We tiptoed up the stairs and rang the bell. When nothing and nobody stirred inside, we unlocked the door. We found ourselves in a dusty, stuffy, three-room apartment that obviously had not been lived in for some time. We decided to use just the bedroom. It was furnished with twin beds, and since its windows faced the inner courtyard, we felt it offered greater protection against spying eyes. Also, there was no common wall with the

adjacent apartment. We walked softly and spoke in whispers. When we finally lay down, we fell asleep immediately and did not wake up until Walter Rieck let himself in. It was past noon.

"Don't worry," he said, "they haven't come yet, and if they don't come right away there's probably no danger." But of course, he said, caution was advisable. Mother was not so easily reassured, but Rieck was optimistic. "I told you I had the impression when I was at the Gestapo that they weren't taking the matter all that seriously," he kept repeating. And over and over again he told us not to worry, that he was taking full responsibility as far as Linke was concerned. He still had not been able to reach him. He was being exceptionally kind and considerate.

Later Aunt Lisa and Jenny Rieck also came by, and they too seemed relieved that everything had gone so smoothly. Lisa had spoken to Mrs. Fabig, who was very understanding and grateful for our considerateness. She sent us her warmest regards.

We were getting used to our apartment; there was no denying that in every respect it was more pleasant than the goat shed. The next few days passed uneventfully until one afternoon when we returned to the apartment and found a piece of yellow cardboard, the same color as that infamous star, under the door. And pasted on it, in letters cut out of a newspaper, were the words "Rieck—

Deutschkron—Jews." We were thunderstruck. Except for the Riecks and Aunt Lisa nobody knew where we were. Nobody could have followed us. It was eerie, inexplicable. Mother began to cry. "Where do we go now?" she repeated over and over. Fortunately, Aunt Lisa came to see us that same day and told Mother to calm down. Then she told us the entire story.

"When Walter went to the Gestapo," she said, "they told him that somebody had reported that he was hiding two Jewish women. He denied it, and the Gestapo said that they too had their doubts. He asked to see the anonymous denunciation. They showed him the letter and asked whether he recognized the handwriting. He had to admit he did. It was his wife's, Jenny's."

Mother jumped up. That couldn't be! Jenny Rieck, who'd always been so wonderful to us, was going to hand us over to the Gestapo? It was absolutely absurd.

"No, and that wasn't her intention," said Lisa. "Apparently she was doing it because she was afraid of losing her husband." In our preoccupation with our own problems, we had failed to notice that Walter Rieck and the young actress, Charlotte, had been having an affair while Jenny was in Bavaria with her daughter. Lisa also told us that Jenny had made an unsuccessful suicide attempt and apparently had become irrational.

"And yesterday I saw a piece of yellow cardboard just like this in her purse."

Lisa tried to reassure Mother, saying she was confident that even though Jenny seemed to have lost her mind, she did not mean to harm us. That was why the information to the Gestapo was so vague; she probably just wanted to scare her husband. Both Lisa and Walter tried to make us understand Jenny's behavior and told us to ignore this latest incident, saying that Jenny would never go so far as to actually hand us over to the Gestapo. And they pleaded with us to behave as though nothing had happened. Fortunately we had no chance to find out whether we could or not; we never saw Jenny again until the end of the war.

Although Linke's apartment was very pleasant, we knew that we could not stay there too long; sooner or later we were bound to attract attention. Rieck had told us that he had heard from Linke, who was planning to come back, but he did not know exactly when. In those days there was no telling which trains were running and when. One day, when Mother had gone out, I heard the door open and went out into the hall. Linke came in with a young woman whom he introduced as his secretary. I introduced myself and told him that Rieck had given us temporary use of the apartment, that I regretted that we'd been unable to contact him and get his permission, but that Rieck

had assured us that he was taking all responsibility. We were going to stay only for a few days until we could find another place. Linke was somewhat taken aback, but he assured me that it was quite all right, not to worry. And he and his secretary went into one of the other rooms. I felt very uncomfortable.

"We must get out of here," I said to Mother when she came back and I told her about Linke's surprise visit. Rieck also came to see us that day and reaffirmed that Linke did not object to our temporary stay at the apartment, but I would have liked nothing better than to leave right away. There was no way of telling whether Linke actually meant it or whether he only pretended to because he had been caught red-handed. But for the time being there was no place else we could go. We had long conferences with Mrs. Grüger, Aunt Lisa, and Walter Rieck, and we finally came up with a solution.

14

"Well, I guess by now Councillor Lewy is probably also rotting in a mass grave." König and the blond woman leaning against him laughed. I managed to keep my composure with difficulty. Of course I had known König was a Nazi before I began working for him.

After losing my job at Grete Sommer's, I began to look for another one. I couldn't possibly spend all of next winter taking walks in the gardens of Sanssouci, nor could I stay in the goat shed all day long. Once again Mrs. Gumz came to the rescue.

"Come to us. You can help with the ironing." The woman who did her ironing had left and help was not easy to find. And so for a while I became

an ironer, struggling with the heavy iron and the stiff men's shirts. "It takes fifteen minutes to iron a shirt properly," Mrs. Gumz said to me, and showed me how to do it with the help of a damp cloth. The ironing board faced the door to her shop, which allowed me to see everyone who came in; in turn everyone could see me, but I got used to it. When old customers asked questions, Mrs. Gumz explained that I was just helping her out. Obviously this arrangement could not last forever. Once again Walter Rieck came up with an answer. "Would you be willing to work for a Nazi?" he asked. I laughed. "Why not? That's safer than anyone else, isn't it?"

Walter Rieck was the agent of the building in which König had his shop. König had told Rieck that yet another of his salesclerks had been drafted into the labor service and he didn't know what to do. König's stationery shop and rental library were far bigger than Grete's, and he also dealt in rare books. Rieck told König that his old friend Inge Richter, in other words me, was working only part-time in her defense job because of a leg injury. Rieck also told him that I had to help support my widowed mother, and that he felt certain that I would be willing to help out temporarily. König was delighted, if only because my supposed employment meant he would not have to register me with the labor office and risk losing me.

I went to see him, and he apparently liked me. The blond saleswoman was still there to show me the ropes, and until she left he treated me with reserve. Once she was gone, he began to engage me in conversation. I liked this shop with the lovely old books, some of which he had acquired at auctions. He appreciated my interest in books and showed me some of his treasures, which, he said, he was not going to sell "unless absolutely necessary." When the war was obviously nearing its end, he became more outspoken. "Perhaps one day to an American," he volunteered with a knowing smile. I said nothing and acted completely neutrally, even when he said that the war could not possibly be won. He confided that he was a member of the Nazi party, and showed me his party badge, which he wore under his lapel. But if the situation called for it, he was ready to display it. We greeted each other conventionally with "Heil Hitler." Once he invited me out to dinner. When I said regretfully that I didn't have any food stamps with me he waved it off. "My friends serve me without stamps." And in fact at the restaurant he was treated with deference, the kind of deference shown a man one would rather see leave than enter. I asked him how it was that he was not in the army or the Waffen SS.

"One has one's connections." And, laughing, he added, "Through the party, of course." He

liked me, and I was very careful not to do or say anything that might be construed as encouragement. "Do you speak English?" he once asked me. I said I did.

"Well, that's wonderful. Then you can carry on here when the Americans come. As a party member I probably won't be able to." And again he laughed. I said nothing. It would have been pointless. Having heard his comment about Councillor Lewy I had no illusions about him; still, I smiled and was friendly. When he was not in the shop I felt much more at ease there than at Grete's; I felt safer at a known Nazi's. He of course had no "poison cabinet" of banned books; they had long since been disposed of.

Walter Rieck told me how pleased König was with me, with my industry and intelligence. In the closing days of the war, when the use of public transportation was restricted to essential personnel, König was able to get me a pass, which I claimed I needed to take me to my other job, that imaginary essential job of mine, at the opposite end of town.

"Which of these two do you want?" he asked, holding out two different passes, one green and the other yellow. Naturally I took both and gave one to Mother. The green one was issued to workers in various essential industries; the yellow one was more restrictive, and yet another color-coded

pass, a red one, was for workers in such vital industries as water supply and energy. My relationship with König made Mother uneasy. "Suppose he finds out who your are?" She worried, and she had every reason to. Dedicated Nazi that he was, there is no telling what König might do if he were to find out the truth. I refused to let it bother me, however. The advantages of my situation far outweighed all other considerations.

Mother too had found work. Because of the mounting frequency and severity of the bombings, Berlin had closed its schools and evacuated the children to safer regions, areas like Silesia, the Sudetenland, and the Bavarian Alps. However, not all parents were willing to send their children away, yet they wanted them to keep up with their studies. They posted notices on billboards and trees asking for tutors. Mother decided to answer one such ad. She claimed to be the widow of a teacher, and also that she had done some tutoring in the past, which was true. The parents of her first pupil were pleased with her and told their friends, and soon she found herself presiding over a group of children and making good money. As fate would have it, the fathers of her charges were all members of the SS. Both the children and their parents greeted my mother with "Heil Hitler." Unlike König, these people up to the very last refused to believe that the Red Army could vanquish the

Third Reich. Mother, who never allowed herself to become involved in discussions with her employers, occasionally overheard them talk among themselves.

"When do you think the Führer is finally going to use his miracle weapon?" the children would ask her. Mother pretended that they were just trying to distract her, and instead of answering their questions told them to pay attention to what she was trying to teach them. She and I used to vie with each other over which of us was working for the worse Nazis.

The most important thing as far as we were concerned was the fact that we were now "off the street" and making enough money to look after ourselves. But getting food was becoming increasingly difficult. Occasionally I would go back to one of my old sources and get something off the books, but I no longer had anything to offer in exchange. On one such visit Mrs. Reschke, the owner of the grocery near Grete's, came up to me. Her helper, Agnes, had also been drafted into the labor service, she told me. She simply couldn't understand it. Wasn't supplying the people of Berlin with milk an important enough job? She didn't know what she was going to do. I cautiously broached the subject of my helping her out occasionally, perhaps on Saturdays, a very busy time for her.

"That would be just wonderful," she said with

obvious relief. "After all, people here know you. You wouldn't have any problems with the customers." And she added that this would finally give her some free time to visit her husband, who was stationed near Berlin. We agreed that I would help her out two afternoons a week. When I arrived home I was elated. "Just think," I said to Mother, "now we'll have cold meats and cheese and butter and milk!"

Mother was worried. "You mustn't steal so much. That's bound to attract attention. Take a little less, and whatever you do, don't forget to put money in the cash drawer for what you take." I just laughed.

So I began to work for Mrs. Reschke. It was much harder than I had anticipated. The weighing and figuring was a problem—so and so many grams for so and so many stamps. All those fractions, and slicing the cold meats and ladling out the milk and collecting the ration coupons and taking the money—much more complicated than checking out books. Most of the customers, pleased to see me again, were patient with me. One Sunday Mrs. Reschke decided to pay her husband a visit. I promised to take care of the milk customers for her.

"You already know your way around," she said, and taking a basket of things with her, she left. I was ready at nine, but the milk hadn't come

yet, and soon there was a long line of women waiting patiently. When the milk finally did arrive, they rushed into the shop, all wanting to be served at once. I was glad; all those waiting people made me very uneasy. Suppose they took out their frustration on me and reported me. They'd had too much time to look me over.

The driver of the delivery wagon poured the milk into the huge cans. I took the first bottle to fill it, but however hard I tried, I came up with an empty ladle. There was only foam, no milk. Nobody bothered to tell me that I had to wait for the skimmed milk, the bluish liquid that was what was then being sold, to settle before trying to ladle it out. Sensing the impatience of the waiting women, I became nervous. In my desperation I dropped the ladle into the can. Trying to fish it out, I thought they were all looking at me, some with disdain, some with impatience. I was sweating, and by the time I had finished and the line dwindled, I was completely exhausted.

Mrs. Reschke's black cat came over to me, meowing piteously. She made me feel uneasy; neither cajolery nor petting had any effect on her. She eyed me ominously. After the customers were taken care of, I sat down at the table in the little room behind the shop and began to paste the ration stamps on the sheets, just as Mrs. Reschke had shown me. On the table in front of me were

the big sheets of paper and the piles of colorful stamps—blue for meat products, yellow for dairy goods, brown for bread—and a glue pot. I spread the glue on the paper and pasted the stamps on it. When customers came in I stopped what I was doing to take care of them. After one such interruption I came back to the shop just as the cat was jumping off the table. Pasted to her fur and paws were those sheets with the precious stamps. Try as we would, both the cat and I, we couldn't get the stamps off. The cat could neither shake them off nor would she let me help her. When I finally managed to hold her down, she scratched my hands and arms. I salvaged whatever I could. Stamps were scattered all over the place—on the furniture, on the floor, wherever the cat had run to. The table looked like a war zone. The cat had obviously sat down right smack in the middle of the sheets and glue. I worked like mad trying to straighten out the mess.

The last thing I wanted was to create problems for Mrs. Reschke. She always gave me something to take home, but since she did not know that we had no ration cards, I always helped myself to a little extra. When I was alone in the shop I weighed everything I was "stealing" and put the money into the cash register. Sometimes Hans Rosenthal came, holding his briefcase to cover the Jewish star, to do some "shopping." If there were cus-

tomers present, I'd slip him some food stamps, which he then "redeemed" with me. In front of customers we also pretended not to know each other. Other than that, we saw each other only rarely.

One Saturday afternoon when I arrived at the shop I found that it had been burglarized. The window was broken and covered with cardboard. In those days toward the end of the war that was not an unusual sight. The foreign workers hadn't been getting enough food for some time now, and they broke into food stores at night. I hesitated about going in, but before I could turn back Mrs. Reschke saw me and called out, "Good for you to have come. The criminal police will be here at any moment to make out their report. That means I won't have time to look after the customers."

What should I do? It was entirely possible that the police would want to question me as a suspect and ask for my papers. On the other hand, I would really make myself suspect if I were to leave then. I decided it was wiser to stay. Two police officers arrived before long and greeted me with a friendly "Heil Hitler." I escorted them to Mrs. Reschke in the back room. Coffee was on the table. While they sat down with her I went back to the store, waited on customers and tried unsuccessfully to listen to the conversation in the back room. They were gone a long time, and I grew more and more appre-

hensive. After about an hour Mrs. Reschke came out, took a sausage and some packages of butter, and went back to the two men. After another hour the two officers, clutching their stuffed briefcases, left with a smile and a friendly "Thank you." I felt vastly relieved.

"They didn't make any sort of inquiry?" I asked.

"No," Mrs. Reschke answered with a laugh, "They only showed me how to report the loss to get back as much as I can."

15

"It was terrible, absolutely terrible," said Mother brokenly, seemingly overcome by the horror she had witnessed. Shaking her head and staring into space, she removed her headscarf and sat down at the long wooden table. She kept moving her hands restlessly over the tabletop and repeating, "Awful, too awful."

The fair, baby-faced Hitler Youth stood in front of her helplessly, not knowing what to say. I was flabbergasted by my mother's convincing performance. And, turning to me, the Hitler Youth said, "Maybe you better eat a little something first. The formalities can wait."

Yes, we said, that would be fine. We hadn't actually eaten anything since early that morning.

The boy hurried off and made his way through the mass of refugees at the railroad station being looked after by the NSV. Those people looked even worse than us. Their clothes were in tatters, they were unkempt and utterly exhausted. Crying children clung to their mothers' skirts; cartons and bundles were piled up all around them. They didn't touch the food offered them. The women of the NSV urged them to eat. "How about a plate of soup or a cup of coffee?" The refugees were much too dispirited to eat. Nor did they realize that they were being offered food "ordinary" people hadn't seen for ages.

Most of them had been on the move for days. They had set out on their journey when the Soviet troops were at the gates of their city. They had not been permitted to leave sooner. Every inch of German soil had to be defended to the very last. Apparently the greater the number of refugees, the greater the government's fear that the population would turn on them. When people finally were permitted to flee, they no longer had enough time to make an orderly retreat. With the guns at their doorsteps, they were able to salvage only a few paltry possessions, the barest necessities.

Mother and I had left Berlin that morning for Lübbenau. To look like refugees we dressed shabbily and carried a small suitcase tied with a rope. In Lübbenau we boarded a train back to Berlin.

Mother and I had been discussing and discarding the idea of "arriving" in Berlin as refugees from the East. Finally we decided to risk it. On the one hand, we wanted to get as close as possible to the actual fighting, to the chaos, but on the other hand we didn't want to spend too much time on a train because of occasional identity checks.

Lübbenau, two hours from Berlin, seemed just the right place. As soon as we got there—there were no checks and no air raids—I bought return tickets to Berlin. We didn't have to wait long for the refugee train. We got on a car overflowing with women and children, cats and dogs, cartons and crates. Even standing room was hard to come by. The refugees exchanged stories about their experiences. Some came from the town of Guben, others from the countryside. All of them had stories of the depredations of the Soviet army—rapes, looting, and shooting. We listened, every now and then saying just enough to keep them talking. We wanted to get a detailed picture of the situation in the war zones. We learned that there was hand-to-hand fighting in Guben itself, and that every city had streets named for Adolf Hitler and for Berlin. By the time we got to Berlin, we thought we had a pretty accurate picture of what it had been like when the Russians came to Guben.

As we neared Berlin, both Mother and I felt a sense of relief. It was evening, and by now the

tension and the crowded train were beginning to take their toll. The other passengers were becoming increasingly worried. Berlin—only a very few of them had ever been there, or in any other big city for that matter. They had heard about the saturation bombings, but they could not visualize them. It was February, and in the darkness of that early evening they could not see the devastation. Mother was becoming restless. She knew only too well that at about seven o'clock the British could be expected, and that railroads were prime targets. Finally we pulled into the station, but before we even came to a full stop the few feeble lights still burning went out. It was pitch black. Voices over loudspeakers urged us to hurry; British bombers were on the way. Women were shouting and children crying. Somebody had missed a step in the dark and fallen down.

"Where is my suitcase? Somebody stole it! Thieves!" It was utter chaos. I whispered to Mother that all that confusion had given me an idea: We should say that we had lost our suitcases with all our belongings, including our papers. Mother laughed, and shaking her head, said that I must be mad. She was beginning to lose her voice, and this made our supposed plight even more convincing. Red Cross workers and Hitler Youth came over to us and offered assistance. With the help of flashlights we found our way to the

air-raid shelter. The alarm had sounded. I was uneasy; I didn't like the idea of a shelter in a railroad station. But we were lucky. After half an hour the all-clear sounded. Not a bomb had fallen. This time Berlin was not the target.

We were taken to an NSV canteen. Two Hitler Youths took us under their wing. Apparently they had taken a liking to me; there weren't many young girls among the refugees. I let them fuss over me.

"Where are you from?"

"From Guben," I answered, very self-confident.

"Where do you want to go?"

"We'd like to stay in Berlin. We have relatives here who promised to take us in."

"Fine. Where do your relatives live?"

"In Charlottenburg," I said. That's where Aunt Lisa lived.

They offered to escort us, but I primly rejected their kind offer, saying that I was familiar with Berlin and would find my way. But one of the boys persisted, saying that I had no idea how much Berlin had changed, an allusion to the bombings. He said that some streets were practically impassable. The idea of having him escort us did not appeal to me. What would Aunt Lisa say if we arrived under Hitler Youth escort? But first we sat down to our meal. I wolfed it down. Mother

warned me to take it easy; I might attract attention by eating so avidly. She was right. Most of the refugees ate hardly anything, partly because they were in shock and partly because liverwurst sandwiches weren't as much of a novelty for them as they were for me. But I didn't care. I lost all self-control.

"What do we do now?" Mother asked. She worried about the proffered escort.

"Oh," I said, "we still have to report the loss of our bags."

"Of course," said one of the boys who had rejoined us at our table. "You've got to do it right away." He showed me the way to the railroad office. Mother stayed behind at the canteen. An ill-tempered official asked me what I wanted and I told him that I wished to report the loss of our bags. He gave me a form to fill out. I described the suitcase and its contents, and signed it with the name I had decided to adopt: Inge Elisabeth Marie Richter. I knew that non-Jews generally had more than one given name. The railroad would notify us, he told me, and closed shop. I returned to the canteen to report to Mother.

"We must get out of here. This terrible scene, this whole atmosphere, makes me very nervous," she said, pointing to the larger-than-life portrait of Hitler in his brown uniform staring down at us. At that moment one of the Hitler Youth reap-

peared and whispered that British planes were again on the way and that we could not leave just yet. We became restless. Aunt Lisa would be waiting. It was very quiet in the shelter. Everyone was listening for the sounds of bombs. The refugees sat on their belongings. Many of the children were asleep, some whimpering softly. The stench in the shelter, full of unwashed people and assorted pets, was intolerable. Mother kept saying that we had to get out of there. Her hands were shaking. When the all-clear finally sounded and we returned to the canteen, one of the Hitler Youth informed me that we would have to spend the night there. It was past ten o'clock and there was no public transportation.

What now? He offered to have us put up in an emergency shelter at a nearby school. Having no choice, we followed the others along the cold, silent, blacked-out streets. A Red Cross worker took us to the school.

The auditorium and gymnasium were lined with two-tiered bunks covered with army blankets. The dogs shared the sleeping quarters of their owners. Mother and I chose the top tier so as to be able to talk without being overheard. There was a constant coming and going—somebody had to go to the toilet, somebody else had a nightmare, a child cried, a dog barked. We lay on our cots fully clothed. At the first ray of light, at about five o'clock, we got up, washed as best we could, and

told the NSV attendant that our relatives had to go to work, and that unless we could reach their house early in the morning we would not be able to get in until the end of the day. She was very understanding and said that all she had left to do was register us as refugees. She asked for our names.

"Ella Paula Richter and Inge Elisabeth Marie Richter from Guben," I answered.

"That's all I need for now. Please report soon to the nearest NSV office. They'll give you whatever further help you need."

I thanked her for her concern and carefully stashed away the papers she handed me. Mother indicated her thanks by pointing to her throat and whispering "My voice . . ."

"Of course, I understand, all that excitement," she said, and then, full of genuine compassion, she asked, "Are you sure you want to stay in Berlin?" I repeated my story about our relatives. She wished us luck and we left, or, rather, practically ran out to the nearest underground for a train to Charlottenburg. As was to be expected, the car was crowded with ill-tempered, exhausted people on their way to work. More passengers, especially people with bundles or suitcases, were not particularly welcome. When we finally got off at our stop we still had a fifteen-minute walk ahead of us. We arrived completely out of breath.

When she heard our key in the door, Aunt Lisa

came out to greet us. "My God, I didn't sleep all night. I couldn't forgive myself for letting you do this."

"But everything's all right," we assured her and told her about our adventure. By then we were able to laugh about it, about our warm reception by the NSV, and all the other events of the previous night. We showed Aunt Lisa our papers; she was as pleased as we.

"What now?" she asked.

"We have to report to the NSV for a residence permit." But in order to get one we needed an address, a furnished room somewhere. Rather than try find a room on our own, we thought it wiser to enlist the help of one of our friends.

"Of course I'll do it," said Mrs. Grüger with a hearty laugh. This was just her cup of tea. "That's just great," she kept repeating when we told her about our adventure as refugees. We showed her the papers we'd been issued. Not a single item on them was true, not even the date of my birth. I had made myself older to meet the minimum-age requirement for purchasing cigarettes and liquor, important barter items. The minimum age was twenty-five. My mother claimed to be a widow. As her maiden name she chose the name of an old school friend, and she gave Meseritz as her place of birth. I picked Guben. We were careful to rule out any possible background checks by nam-

ing towns already in Russian hands. I remembered once having seen an etching of a street in Guben named "Am Markt," and so "Am Markt 4" became our last address before we were forced to flee. Mrs. Grüger signed our registration and declared her willingness to sublet a room to us. She forged the signature of the janitor, because she thought that safer than having to answer many more questions. We told her we would use the registration only long enough to get whatever other permits we needed. We took the signed forms to the Charlottenburg NSV office to apply for a residence permit.

"You're from Guben?" The woman behind the counter looked at us searchingly. "This is not the reception center for your area. You belong in Osthavelland."

"I know," answered Mother, "but we've got relatives here."

The woman looked at us once more and asked, "But why did you come to Berlin of all places? Suppose something were to happen here . . ."

Mother looked puzzled and said, "What could happen here?"

"Well," she answered, "Berlin might fall under siege."

Mother looked at her in utter bewilderment. "But that's not possible! Our Führer would never let that happen." Once again I was amazed at my mother's dramatic talents. She was utterly con-

vincing. The NSV worker lowered her head and blushed. For all I knew, she might have been afraid that we would denounce her for defeatist talk, a transgression punishable by death.

"Of course, you're absolutely right," she said eagerly, and quickly stamping our papers, she told us to register at the nearest police station and ration board. We thanked her and left.

"Please wait until we're outside before you start laughing," Mother said to me. But once out of sight, we couldn't control ourselves.

With our precious papers in hand we went to the police and without any further difficulties became legal residents of the district. At the ration board I was astounded as they handed us all those stamps and cards and certificates.

"Is there anything else we can do for you? Do you need clothing?"

"Of course," said Mother. "When we had to flee we couldn't take much with us, and once we got here our suitcase was stolen." The women commiserated with us and gave us coupons for everything we could think of. Unfortunately we weren't able to redeem all of those coupons because Berlin's shelves were pretty bare by then.

I went to see Weidt to tell him about us. When I arrived at the workshop I found the old Weidt laughing slyly. "Ali is in Berlin!"

I practically jumped out of my skin. "How did you do it? Tell me!"

Warning me to keep my voice down, he told me how he had gone to Auschwitz shortly after receiving Ali's card about having been transferred there from Theresienstadt. He rented a room in the village of Auschwitz, paid a few months' rent in advance, and left some clothing and money there for Ali. He stayed in Auschwitz for a while, and every evening went to the camp gate to watch the civilian workers going in and out of the camp, until he decided to approach one of the Polish workers, a foreman in the I. G. Farben plant at Monowitz, who found Ali among the mass of Jewish workers there. Weidt bribed him and gave him a letter for Ali. She answered via the same route. Weidt then used the Pole as a conduit for bringing Ali medicines, bandages, and food. Ali now knew that there was a room waiting for her in the town. In January, when the Soviet troops were at the gates of Auschwitz and the Germans were beginning to evacuate the camp, she managed to steal away. Wearing the clothes Weidt had left for her, she made her way to Berlin, where Weidt was hiding her. Now it really would be only a matter of weeks before it was all over.

My next concern was the progress of the war itself. The Russians were advancing in the East, the Americans and British in the West. "We have to get back to Potsdam," I told Mother. I was not keen on witnessing the siege of Berlin. Mother did not care one way or the other. She was confident

that nothing bad could happen to us now. Remembering the bombings, I was convinced that a siege would be far worse. Potsdam, with its little houses and garden plots, seemed so peaceful.

We thought we might just as well go back to Mrs. Fabig and our goat shed, and so one day we returned to Potsdam and told Mrs. Fabig that everything was all right again, and that we wanted to sit out the war with her. Mrs. Fabig was happy to have us back. Without us she had been lonely and frightened. We suggested that she register us with the police. In their files we were now officially entered as refugees from Guben. We felt safe. In the morning we continued to go to Berlin to work, returning to Potsdam in the evening. Even though we now were legal residents of Berlin, we felt safe in Potsdam.

When we decided to rent a room in Berlin we scanned the ads posted on billboards and trees. I told Mother the location didn't matter; we weren't going to spend much time there anyway.

"Ludwigkirchstrasse 6, furnished room for two, fourth floor, name Hellwig." The location was good, near the underground, the rent was reasonable, and it was far enough from where we had last lived that we didn't have to be afraid somebody might recognize us. Mr. Hellwig, the owner of the apartment, was a man in his forties. Why, I wondered, wasn't he in the army? We liked the

room, and he told us we could move right in. We picked up our few belongings still at Linke's, planning to spend at least a few days at our new address.

"You'll have to register," Mr. Hellwig said to us. I asked him when he'd be at home to sign the form. In the evening I knocked on his door and handed him the filled-out form. At that very moment the lights went out, as happened so often.

"Damn," he exclaimed as he lit a candle, "now I can't see what I'm signing." I offered to come back the next day.

"Never mind, after all, you're not Poles or Jews." When he handed me the form I thanked him curtly and left. I was seething. Mother thought we should have searched longer rather than taking the first place we looked at. Suppose he decided to check on us? I tried to calm her by pointing out that after all, it really couldn't last much longer now. As we were sitting there debating whether we had done the right thing, the sirens went off. I jumped up. The fourth floor was no place to be in a bombing. I urged Mother to hurry. And no sooner had the alarm sounded than the antiaircraft guns went into action. We made it down to the cellar in the nick of time. The air-raid warden welcomed us as new tenants and told us we were already registered with him. I smiled politely. As we sat down I was horrified to see a man with a

Jewish star cowering in the corner. He didn't dare look up. His Aryan wife was sitting next to him. I felt sick. I would have liked to go over and stroke him.

"Don't keep staring at him," Mother warned. I tried not to, but I was overcome by an indescribable feeling of guilt.

16

We left Berlin on April 20. It was the first time that the sound of artillery fire could be heard in the heart of the city. The radio announced that henceforth only the holders of red passes would be allowed to use public transportation. My two permits, the green and the yellow, were now useless. If we wanted to get out of Berlin before the war ended, this was our last chance.

Berlin was in transition from city to rubble heap. Ruins and bent steel girders marked the places where houses had once stood. It was a surrealist landscape. Every now and then a building loomed up, a lonely landmark amid the devastation. Wood and cardboard panels replaced win-

dowpanes. The bomb-scarred facades looked like the ruins of besieged fortresses. Craters and pitted streets were mute testimony to the hail of bombs that had been raining down since 1943 with ever-increasing fury.

The American and British bombers operated almost at will; for some time the city had had no effective antiaircraft defense, but somehow people managed to survive. They lived like moles, digging in at night and coming out into the open only in daylight when it seemed safe. Then they'd begin to scurry around for food. Survival at any cost was the order of the day.

"Stay alive!" was the way people greeted each other. Only once, on April 19, 1945, at the news of President Roosevelt's death, did a vague hope resurface that things might still take a turn to the better, without anyone being able to say exactly how. But this ray of hope soon dimmed.

I was afraid. The American and British raids had taken their toll on me. The tanks blocking every crossing and the defensive barriers of discarded baby carriages, out-of-commission trolley cars, and other junk were not reassuring. I therefore thought it best to wait for the end of the war in our shed, amid the orchards and little cottages. Thanks to our new identity papers we could live anywhere we chose.

Mother finally gave in about leaving Berlin, so

one day we packed up our meager possessions, mostly food—cereals, a little flour, some potatoes, some coal—and in backpacks and handbags lugged them to the station. Every train was packed with people, all of them carrying their belongings, all of them nervous, ill-tempered, silent. What was there to say? Was there anyone left who still believed in the myth of final victory? "Defeatists will be shot on sight," it was proclaimed. People overheard making "treasonable remarks" were strung up on lamp posts with placards around their necks reading "I was a traitor."

The walk from the station to our shed took a good twenty minutes. Streetcars had stopped running long ago. Our packages were heavy, so we overcame our reluctance and asked one of the many slave laborers around the station—Russians, Poles, Frenchmen—to help us. They were worse off than most; many of their primitive camps had been destroyed by bombs, and nobody bothered to look after them. Their guards had long since been drafted into the people's militia, but because of the war they could not make their way back home.

A Russian eagerly picked up our packages even though he was just as weak as us. I thought I would encourage him by saying that the war would soon be over and he could hope to return home. He looked at me in dismay and said that

was a terrible prospect. He hoped Hitler would still win, that General Wenck was on his way to Berlin to defend the city. He was a Ukrainian and hated the Russians. I fell silent. After that we spoke only about the weather. When we said good-bye he kissed our hands.

Of course, Potsdam was no longer quite as peaceful as before. A few days earlier it had been bombed for the first time. Because no bomb had ever fallen there, people did not bother to take shelter, so there were some unnecessary deaths. Our little settlement had sustained substantial damage. Apparently the target of the attack was a nearby railway junction, but the wind must have wafted the "Christmas trees," as the flares dropped to illuminate the targets were called, over to us. Sitting in our little split trench we felt like people clinging to a raft in a storm.

"Is that what it was like in Berlin?" a horrified Mrs. Fabig asked us after that first raid. The bombs lit up the sky and fell all around us on the small houses, exploding in the gardens. There were some casualties in our little enclave too. Fortunately, the only damage to our goat shed was the loss of some bricks from the roof. I spent the next day repairing the roof with tar and bricks somebody was kind enough to give us, the poor, bombed-out Richters from Berlin. Now people here in Potsdam began to have an inkling of what

all those years of bombing in Berlin must have been like.

"We're not going to leave again. We're going to stay here until the war is over," we had told Mrs. Fabig when we got back.

"Do you really think it will end soon?" She sighed. "If only the Russians wouldn't come." This was a recurrent theme, a refrain punctuating every sentence. Atrocity stories preceded the Russians, as if to prove that Hitler had been right when he said they were subhumans who must be exterminated. Unsuspecting and full of hope, I dismissed all the stories of Russian outrages as Nazi propaganda.

"Mr. Huth ought to know," said Mrs. Fabig. Huth, her neighbor, had been a Communist "before Hitler," and most likely now was one again. I tentatively began a conversation with him across the garden fence. He beamed, and proudly pointed to the successes of the Red Army. There was no cause for alarm, he said, particularly not here in our little colony built by workers out of their savings. While we were talking, we saw another of our neighbors, Mr. Ludwig, go out to his garden. He was our air-raid warden and block warden, and he and his wife held various other party posts. Now he was prowling around, peering left and right. He couldn't see us. Opening his tool shed, he took out a spade and began to dig. He

then threw something into the hole he had dug, covered it up, and went back into his house.

Polish slave laborers from the nearby work camp later dug up what he had hidden there— Nazi membership cards and other evidence of his and his wife's political past. The Poles came to us after their German guards had left, a few days before the battle around Potsdam began. They were well informed about the people in our colony.

"We can't trace you," they said. "Who are you?" I told them. "Tell me about the Nazis here." I did, and passed their test. A little later they burned down the house of the grocer who still refused to give them food. "Just look at what that man had stashed away in his cellar," the neighbors said. They didn't feel sorry for him; he had refused them as well. In the following days women ran from store to store to buy the rations coming to them and anything else they could lay their hands on. A group of them got together and went to the abandoned camp of Organisation Todt, the labor battalion. They returned with sacks of flour and sugar, and even with bolts of uniform cloth.

The dull sound of artillery fire kept coming closer. On the evening of April 22 I walked over to the highway leading to Potsdam. Stretches had been torn up and makeshift barriers erected. Ten sixteen-year-old Hitler Youth who had been drafted into the people's militia were piling up

debris. They were convinced that these roadblocks were sure to slow the approaching Russian armies until the vaunted forces under General Wenck arrived and stopped them for good. Nobody knew where Wenck's army was, or even whether it existed at all, but everyone now spoke of it as the potential savior of the beleaguered capital. "And we also have two bazookas each," one of the youngsters told me with pride.

The next morning I listened to the artillery barrage. I heard twenty rounds fired, and then, after a silence, something that made my heart jump with joy. I strained my ears to make sure I had heard right—it was the rumble of approaching Russian tanks. I can still hear them today. I climbed out of the little split trench in our garden. For me the war was over, even though the neighbors warned me that the SS were hiding out in the surrounding woods and when the time was ripe would come out of their hiding place and take care of the Russians. I was so excited that day, trying to visualize what a normal life would be like, I could no longer imagine it.

With a happy smile I went out to welcome the first Russian soldier who ventured into our settlement. He approached us slowly. He was short and bow-legged and had a typical Mongol face, with almond-shaped eyes and high cheekbones and a crooked smile. His uniform was not clean and his

cap was perched on his head at an angle. When I spoke to him, he just stood and stared at me without opening his mouth. Something was wrong. Finally he looked into our goat shed. I offered him something to drink. He refused. He just kept standing there and staring. I was not apprehensive; I was simply filled with joy.

That afternoon some more Russian soldiers came. They walked around carefully, suspicious, searching, weapons in hand. I beamed at them. I was looking for someone to share my happiness. Suddenly one of them came up to me, grabbed my coat, and said, "Woman, come." At first I didn't understand. Then I heard women screaming for help.

I managed to free myself and ran back to Mother. "So it's true," she said. "We must show them our Jewish identity cards. They'll understand." They understood nothing. They couldn't even read them.

That day I jumped over many a hedge and ditch in search of a hiding place. In the evening we decided to go into our landlady's house. Perhaps this white-haired old woman would be able to keep them away from us. But before long we heard them banging on the door with their gun barrels. Women were crying; shots rang out. They broke into our house. Guns in hand, they pushed me ahead of them. Mother tried to intervene. I

screamed, and somehow got away in the dark. It was a bad night.

Clearly I would have to hide—once again hide. I spent the next few days and nights in the attic of a house next to the Hentzes, together with some other young women and a man and his wife; she had been raped. We went down to have our meals while Aunt Lisa or Mother stood guard and warned us when they saw Soviet soldiers approach. Then we would run up the ladder, pull it up after us, close the attic door, and put a pail of water on the door to greet anyone who tried to open it. Once one of us wasn't fast enough, and the door wasn't quite closed when two Russians forced their way into the house. They went up to the door and accused us of hiding a German soldier. Then they fired at the door. Aunt Lisa called out to us to come down. Quickly we opened the door and lowered the ladder, and before the soldiers could take in what was happening we climbed down and ran out of the house. They took the man, the alleged German soldier, with them, but he returned later. He had been able to prove that he had never been in the army.

Mother believed that our past entitled us to protection. With Aunt Lisa, she went to see the Russian commandant. She came back beaming. The commandant had received her promptly and said he was happy finally to meet some real live

antifascists. He apologized for the "excesses," but said he did not know how to help us. We would have to look after ourselves, because he could not assign a military policeman to stand watch over every soldier. Their hatred of the Germans was so great, he said, that they could not control their feelings.

That same afternoon two Russian soldiers showed up at our house. They knocked on the door and told us that they'd been sent by the commandant. They were Jews, they said. Mother called to me to come down from the attic. We sat down at the table with them and started a conversation consisting mainly of gestures and some broken Yiddish phrases. They laughed a lot. Then one of them turned to me and said that he'd like to make *chassene* (marriage) with me. We pretended not to understand him. Suddenly they both jumped up. All friendliness had vanished. They looked menacing.

"You're not Jews," one of them shouted, and fired his gun into the air. While Mother and Aunt Lisa tried to calm them, I ran away looking for a hiding place.

On May 1 the commandant showed up in person. I heard Mother call out to Aunt Lisa that the commandant was here. He was so drunk he was barely able to say the word "girl." They managed to get rid of him fairly easily. He took a bicycle

and rode off happily, his arm covered with wrist-watches, the Russians' most sought-after trophy. After that visit I did not dare leave my attic. Once I had to listen helplessly while a Soviet soldier shot his way into the house and tried to rape my mother. Somehow she managed to get him out of the house and to run away.

I spent most of my time listening to the artillery fire, the so-called Stalin organ, and from the direction of the sound I tried to figure out how the war was progressing. The fire seemed to pass over our house toward Berlin. We were enveloped in the crackling, crashing noises of war. We had lost all contact with the outside world. We knew neither what day it was nor what was going on even in our immediate vicinity. To turn on the radio would have been as pointless as trying to get water by turning on the tap.

And then suddenly everything fell still, eerily, inexplicably still. It was as though nothing was moving, as though even the animals dared not stir, as though nobody was alive and the Earth itself was no longer the same. I lay on my straw pallet in the attic and tried to make out sounds in this vast silence. Through the window I could see that day was breaking. In the distance, toward Berlin, the sky was red. Was it the dawn or the city burning? I could not tell. It was more important to find out what that stillness meant. The young woman

next to me also woke up. We whispered to each other as though afraid of breaking the silence. Until that moment the rumble of the Stalin organ had dominated our days, but now everything was still. This was the reality we had been anticipating for such a long time: The war was over! But I could no longer feel elated.

17

The war was over. But what did that really mean? Like everybody else in Germany we were hungry. And, like them, we did not know what the future held in store. Moreover, our name was still Richter because we didn't know how to go about regaining our identity. I fell seriously ill. My resistance, which had stood me in such good stead through all those years, was now overcome. The feeling of hopelessness undoubtedly contributed to my illness. Without electricity we couldn't listen to the radio. Yet even without newspapers we learned what the British soldiers had found when they liberated Bergen-Belsen, and we also heard about Auschwitz. True, the BBC had reported the monstrosities of the Nazis; still, the

actual discoveries were far more horrifying than anything we could have imagined. Yet it had indeed happened: relatives, friends, acquaintances had all become the victims of a horror without precedent. More and more names came to mind, the faces of people I would never see again, men and women who had committed no crime other than that of being Jews. I cried helplessly. I could not shake off my overwhelming sadness.

Mother did her best to cheer me up. Perhaps the reports were exaggerations, she said. But at night I could hear her crying. No word came from Father. Mail service had not yet been restored. Mother bartered her few remaining possessions for food, and Mrs. Fabig cleared a little corner of her plot for us for Mother's vegetable garden. When I became strong enough I sat in the garden watching Mother dig and tend her vegetables, and I became even more upset because I could not help. It took me two months to learn how to walk again. The day I was able to take my first steps leaning on a cane was like a holiday. By then we had no food at all, either rationed or unrationed. We were starving. I don't know how we managed to survive—certainly not by being law-abiding citizens. Once I went along with my mother on one of her forays into a cabbage patch. I watched her as with astonishing speed she threw twenty-three cabbages into the sack I was holding. When I asked

why she was taking so many, she said, "Do you expect me to count while I'm stealing?"

When the Soviet occupation authorities authorized the formation of German administrative units with limited jurisdiction, they found no dearth of volunteers eager to help restore order. The old Social Democrat Walter Rieck went to Berlin. I too hoped for a chance to play a part, though I didn't know exactly what it would be. Through all those terrible years I had never given a thought to what would happen "afterward." All our energies had focused on surviving the next hour, the next day. And before I could do anything at all I had to regain my strength, for the only way to get to Berlin was on foot.

One of our friends, Dr. Thaus, had once mentioned that "afterward" I might perhaps become his secretary. He had hopes of resuming his career in the educational system. I thought of getting in touch with him, but for the time being I could do nothing about it.

In July 1945 the first Western troops came to Potsdam, in preparation for the conference that was to decide Germany's future. The American and British soldiers were warmly welcomed, particularly by the female population. The French were not quite as popular; they couldn't compete with what the British and Americans had to offer. The Hentze's daughter befriended a British soldier

named Eddie Matthews. Since she knew no English and he no German, I occasionally acted as interpreter. One day I told him my story, mentioning that my father was living in England. I hadn't really expected a British enlisted man to understand what I was saying, but he did. He told me that he had been in the unit that liberated Bergen-Belsen. He offered to write to my father. We waited for an answer, but none came.

One day Eddie came to say good-bye. The Potsdam Conference had ended on August 2, and Potsdam now was part of the Soviet Zone. The Western Allies began to withdraw their troops. Eddie told us that he could no longer serve as a contact because once in the British Zone, he would be cut off from the other zones of occupation. So this attempt to get in touch with my father had also failed. We thanked Eddie for his efforts and wished him well.

The next morning a motorcycle with two British soldiers pulled up at Mrs. Fabig's door. There was Eddie, waving a piece of paper: a letter from my father. It had arrived that morning, Eddie told us, just as his unit was getting ready to leave. Before we could thank him properly, he and his comrade had turned around, racing to catch up with the troop transport to the British Zone.

The news that Father was alive and waiting for us reached us on August 13, 1945. Life suddenly

took on new meaning. Of course our immediate reaction to the letter was that we would try to join Father. Mother and I set out on foot for the British Military Mission in Berlin to apply for an entry permit to England. It took us six hours to get there.

"Why do you want to go to England?" the British officer in charge inquired of Mother.

She stared at him uncomprehendingly. "Because I've been separated from my husband for six years."

"And I from my wife," he answered coolly. "There's been a war." He was not inclined to listen to anything further. All he said was that for the time being no entry permits to England were being issued, not even for members of the immediate family.

One thing was now crystal-clear: Berlin offered us the only chance to find jobs and support ourselves. We wondered whether we ought to try to get an apartment in Potsdam for the interim. Officially designated victims of fascism were supposed to receive preferential treatment. Up to now the only preference shown us had been a bigger carrot ration. We talked things over with Walter Rieck, who suggested we rent a house together since he too qualified as a victim of fascism, having been fired from his teaching job as an enemy of the state. We went to the housing office, where we were told: "Of course we have an apartment

for you. The Nazis are making tracks in the middle of the night and leaving everything behind."

Soon after I again walked to Berlin to investigate the housing and job situation. I looked up Dr. Thaus, who was now a department head in the newly formed Central Administration for Popular Education, and reminded him of his earlier promise. But I needn't have done so. He had not forgotten. "Of course you can work with me," he said. I could begin in September.

I spent the night with the Thaus family, and early the next day I set out to look for a furnished room. Mother and I were still hoping to be able to join Father in England soon, and so I didn't think there was much point in hunting for an apartment. As luck would have it, I found a satisfactory room in the apartment of an acquaintance, and rented it on the spot. Flushed with success, I set off for Potsdam. When I arrived at our shed I found the door wide open and the house empty. Our next-door neighbor opened her window and in a none too friendly voice informed me that Mother had moved into Mrs. M.'s apartment.

I ran over to Mrs. M.'s. "What are you doing here?" I asked. "Mrs. M. was a Nazi official," Mother answered. "They confiscated her apartment and gave it to us."

"I don't understand how you could accept it.

I wouldn't feel comfortable living with other people's things. They may even have been stolen from Jews."

Mother calmly informed me that she could no longer endure living in the shed, which had become even more uncomfortable after it was bombed. Winter was coming. I didn't have to see her frostbitten hands to know that she had a point. And, as she said, Mrs. M. would have had to give up her apartment whether we took it or not. When the housing office offered it to her, Mother had to decide to take it there and then.

As soon as possible, I walked back to Berlin to see about our move. I no longer felt comfortable in our little settlement where nothing could be kept secret for very long. After filing some papers and being interviewed, we became officially designated "victims of fascism." Our old Nazi identity cards with the "J," the forged papers in the name of Richter, and the testimony of Walter Rieck and Lisa Holländer were all the proof we needed. Being recognized victims of fascism entitled us to the food ration category of heavy laborers, the right to an apartment, assistance in finding a job, and all sorts of other help.

In the meantime Jewish organizations from abroad had opened offices in Berlin, and they also distributed food and clothing to Jews. At the end of the war about twelve thousand Jews were still

living in Berlin. About twelve hundred had survived the Third Reich by living underground; a
few thousand more had not been deported because
they were married to non-Jews. (The Jewish partners of childless mixed marriages were not deported. The male Jewish partner of such a marriage
had to wear the yellow star, but not the female.
Jews in so-called privileged marriages, that is, parents of children who were not raised as Jews, also
were not deported.) In addition thousands of dis-
placed persons were housed in camps in and
around Berlin. The Jewish organizations also acted
as conduits for letters and packages from my father. He wrote that he had applied for permission
for us to join him in England.

In mid-September I started to work as Dr.
Thaus' secretary in the Central Office for Popular
Education, which was in the building of the former
Ministry of Culture. Only one wing was habitable,
and even that was badly damaged, but they had
somehow patched it up. The rooms were dark;
wooden boards replaced the broken window
panes. The furniture bore traces of water and fire
damage. Small iron stoves were our only source
of heat. Keeping the fire going was one of my
secretarial duties. We stored our coal allotment in
our desks and file cabinets; the files were on top
of the desks. Since we received no personal coal

rations, my boss and I took home some of the precious coal in our briefcases.

The Central Administration had jurisdiction over the five Länder of the Soviet Zone. It was headed by Paul Wandel, a Communist who had returned from the Soviet Union with Wilhelm Pieck. He had been Pieck's secretary. Almost all the top officials of our agency were Communists who had survived the Nazi years in concentration camps or exile. They made no secret of their party affiliation, nor was there any reason why they should have. Antifascists were obviously the most logical candidates for leading positions in the new government and administration. Not many were left. I overheard some of them say that they thought the Communist Party had made a mistake in 1933 when it refused to join with the Social Democrats against Hitler. Even though the Social Democrats in our office were few, I did not feel either isolated or excluded. Many of my Communist colleagues were very friendly and idealistic. They too had suffered a great deal, and that of course created a bond between us.

Before long the Communist Party launched a membership drive. In June the Soviet Military Government had authorized the formation of three political parties—the Communist Party (KPD), the Christian Democratic Union (CDU), and the Social Democrats (SPD). The Communists tried to recruit

the largely unaffiliated technical workers with
promises of better working conditions, especially
more food, the most sought-after privilege.

Supplying the top Communist officials of our
office with food was the sole, if unofficial, duty of
a fellow worker. Despite all efforts to keep it a
secret, everybody knew what was going on. When
a food shipment arrived after working hours, the
night porter or the cleaning women told us about
it. We had no shop committee, so I took it upon
myself to put an end to this secrecy. In my opinion
this special treatment was patently unfair. One day
I confronted the employee in charge of this operation head on: "I understand that a truckload of
meat came in last night. When are you going to
distribute it?" I asked, ignoring his embarrassment
over my directness. He mumbled something un-
intelligible, but my question brought results.
Thereafter food was distributed among all of us,
because I made it my business to keep track of
deliveries.

This intervention, together with my membership in the SPD, brought me into disfavor with
my Communist superiors. Like the members of the
KPD, I also had made no secret of my political
affiliation and sympathies. One of the things I had
done was organize a youth group. We hiked, went
to the theater, and held political discussions. My
active involvement with our politically unaffiliated

employees was a thorn in the side of the Communist functionaries, even though many of my friends in the KPD supported and understood me. I was told that Paul Wandel had passed the word that I was to be treated well because I was a victim of fascism. Later I realized that during this period I was still given some leeway.

The situation became more complicated when the KPD, assisted by the Soviet occupation power, began its active campaign for the merger of the KPD and SPD into a single party, the Socialist Unity Party (SED). When the SPD first advanced that idea, saying that their common suffering, their persecution and imprisonment had forged a bond between them, the KPD turned it down, because, they said, ideological clarification within their own ranks was a more urgent matter. They undoubtedly overestimated their popular appeal. When they failed to create a mass base and it became obvious that the SPD was a more potent force, they took up the cry for a unity party. With the help of the Soviet occupiers, they had no trouble forming such a party in the Soviet Zone itself, but in Berlin, which was divided into four sectors and administered by the four victorious powers, things were not that easy.

In our office, which was located in the Soviet sector of the city, the Communists concentrated their efforts on the Social Democrats. Some of the

older men who had survived Nazi persecution capitulated, afraid of yet another cycle of political pressure.

Our SPD unit had only fifteen members, mostly women, as compared to the more than one hundred fifty Communists. The shop meetings organized by the Communists featured much flowery oratory about our good fortune at being in a position to make the age-old dream of a unified workers' movement a reality. These meetings usually ended with an affirmative show of hands. At one such session I asked whether those opposed to the unity party might also be heard. That put an end to the aura of unanimity, and from then on the Communist bureaucrats made no secret of their distrust and dislike of me. At the time I did not realize what the consequences might be. Having survived the Nazis, I felt that these officials were comparatively harmless. I refused to accept the possibility that we might be deprived of our newly won freedom and the democratic order, and so I fought every such move by the KPD. Being naive and politically inexperienced, I felt confident that my political adversaries would respect my freedom of speech.

On March 1, 1946, the Central Committee of the SPD met in plenary session. As one of the delegates, I listened as the chairman, Otto Grotewohl, vainly tried to convince the meeting of the

political wisdom of joining the unity party. (Grote-wohl subsequently joined the SED; in 1949 he became the first president of the German Democratic Republic.) The majority of the delegates voted for a secret plebiscite by the SPD membership. It was held in the three West sectors of Berlin on March 31; 82 percent of the membership rejected a merger with the KPD. I was proud of having been present at that historic meeting and of my small contribution to the preservation of freedom and democracy in Berlin.

The number of my friends in the KPD shrank perceptibly. Many whispered to me that they were afraid to be seen with me. I did not understand, and told them so.

One day I was summoned to Room 36. I must admit that this made me rather uneasy. I knew Room 36 to be the office of the Soviet military officer in charge of our agency. I also knew that Dr. Thaus had occasionally been summoned there and that he returned from these meetings depressed and taciturn. If I asked him what had happened, he would not answer.

The man sitting opposite me in Room 36 wore a Soviet uniform. He spoke fluent German and asked me politely, almost paternally, about my past.

"I hear that you are politically involved. How come you haven't joined the SED?"

I told him that I couldn't be a member of two parties, that I belonged to the SPD. He naturally did not consider that a satisfactory explanation. When he repeated his question and I pointed out that the SED was not legal in the British Sector, where I lived, he said that there was nothing to prevent me from joining the SED cell at the office. I told him curtly that I did not care to. He then asked me, if I had the opportunity to go either to the Soviet Union or the United States, which would I choose.

"I would like to go to the Soviet Union," I answered. "I am a Socialist, and of course I'd like to see how this Socialist state works. I would also like to see America, because without first-hand knowledge and experience, it is difficult to form an opinion about the evils of capitalism." And then I added happily, "But soon I'll be going to England."

He sat up and asked me about it. I told him that Mother and I were planning to join my father in England.

"You're in touch with your father?" he asked sternly. He knew that there was no civilian mail service, and that Germans were not allowed to ask Allied personnel to act as intermediaries. But of course that was exactly what we were doing.

"Of course we get mail from my father, via the Jewish organizations," I answered quietly. He dis-

missed me. It was obvious that he did not want word of our conversation to get out.

A few days after this talk, a Communist friend in the personnel office told me that my papers had been forwarded to Karlshorst, the headquarters of the Soviet military government. That might mean trouble, and he advised me to get out of our office as soon as possible. I thought his fears were exaggerated, so I checked at SPD headquarters. They gave me the same advice. I immediately applied for my annual leave, which I planned to extend until I was able to go to England. Since I lived in the British Sector, I was beyond the reach of the Soviet secret service.

The decision to leave Berlin was not an easy one. In those early days after the war, Berlin was undergoing a cultural renaissance. Theaters, concerts, cabarets, art galleries blossomed. Creative forces that had been dammed up for years burst forth. We met writers and painters and actors who had been banned and persecuted by the Nazis. We devoured the hitherto forbidden books; we went to parties and danced and celebrated our new-found freedom.

My relationship with Hans Rosenthal, who with his mother had survived the Third Reich at the Jewish Hospital, gradually came to an end. All his efforts were being directed at joining his brother in the United States. I, on the other hand,

was involved in the youth organization of the SPD and in the political scene generally. In the recent past I had had to devote all my energies to survival; now I was free to pursue other interests. I could wake up in the morning without having to fear what the day would bring.

I began to toy with the idea of staying in Berlin rather than going to England. The thought of helping to build something out of nothing was extremely seductive. Yet I was also curious about England, about that altogether different world. And I wanted to see my father, after all those years. I promised my friends in Berlin that I would stay in England at most six months.

When all our papers were at last in order and we could begin to plan our trip to England, the Jewish organization that had helped arrange everything informed us that we would have to pay for the trip ourselves. Of course we had no money; it had not even occurred to us that we would have to pay. In those days money meant very little. My salary covered our basic expenses, and there was nothing else to spend money on.

By a miracle we were able to overcome this last hurdle as well. We received a package from America which, in addition to many useful items, also contained a carton of cigarettes. On the black market one cigarette sold for ten Reichsmark. That carton of cigarettes paid for our passage to England.

We arrived in England on August 2, 1946. The English immigration officers received us coolly and impersonally. As the wife of a resident alien, my mother was issued an identification card for aliens, but I was classified as an enemy alien, which meant that I was not allowed to stay in England more than six months, that I was not allowed to work, and that I had to report periodically to the police. I had a midnight curfew, and if I planned to leave Birmingham, where my father was living now, I had to apply for permission to the police. Sweets and clothing were still rationed, and I did not receive a ration card.

This reception was a bitter disappointment. I had not expected to be welcomed with open arms, but neither did I think that in England too I would be discriminated against. I was deeply hurt. Finally, with the help of an influential Birmingham politician, we got the Home Office to lift all these restrictions, but the bitterness stayed with me.

Once everything was straightened out, I was able to resume my interrupted schooling. I decided to study languages at London University, but when I realized that getting a degree would take years, during which my father would have to support me, I left school and took a job as secretary in the office of the Socialist International. I continued to play with the idea of returning to Berlin to work with the people who had saved my life in the building of a democratic society; I felt that the

solidarity shown me during those terrible war years had become a covenant.

But before acting on this, I accepted the invitation of the Asian Socialist parties to visit India, Burma, Nepal, and Israel. After spending an entire year in a different world with different customs, I came to Bonn in 1955 and began to write about my impressions and experiences. In early 1958 the Israeli evening paper *Maariv* was looking for a reporter in Bonn. I took the job, and in 1960 I became *Maariv*'s accredited German correspondent. In 1966 I became an Israeli citizen, and since 1972 I have been working in *Maariv*'s editorial office in Tel Aviv.

My memories of my childhood and youth in Berlin are still so powerful that even now I cannot look back without strong emotion. That is why it took me thirty years before I was able to write about them here in Israel, which has become my home. Israel has given me something that I had never known: security and protection, feelings that can flourish only if one can look at the world without inhibition and without fear.

When I returned to Germany, I found what I had expected. Some old Nazis and some who had shared in the responsibility for Hitler's rise to power were sitting in key jobs, even if under democratic symbols. Had there really been so few anti-Nazis? I was puzzled. For me the Hitler era was

not merely a tragic chapter in German history, to be glossed over in silence. Hitler had enveloped the entire world in a terrible war. Under his rule millions of people were killed simply because they were Jews, and thousands of Germans had had a hand in those murders up to the very end. The few who had risked their lives and resisted or helped Jews in hiding were accorded a mixed reception. The fact that they personified the survival of decency in a time of inhumanity was scarcely acknowledged. Once back in Germany, I began to feel that many of the Germans I met did not understand me or my attitude. Perhaps some saw me as a living indictment, and I may have made them uncomfortable. Others were so involved in mastering the present and the future that they had no time to waste on the past.

I asked myself whether I was not perhaps asking too much of the Germans in expecting them to understand and be horrified by the enormities of the past. The answer was frightening. I received threatening letters with SS symbols, anonymous insulting phone calls. When I mentioned this to Germans, they shrugged their shoulders and said that there were always some who remain incorrigible. And they suggested that I should not let the past dominate my feelings and thoughts, and not expect that others be dominated by it either. I found this hard to accept, because to this day I

cannot understand how it was possible for people to be capable of such bestiality. This terrible question ought to torment everyone. I felt alienated in Germany, insecure and alone. And even friends who understood me and shared my feelings were unable to help me.

I have found my home among people who either have shared my experience or who have found here opportunities for growth not open to them in the Diaspora, and who, like me, have at last found a safe haven.

"No." Rolled her eyes at me. *As if,* her eyes said in eye sign language. "Like the metal. Set my mom off. I mean OFF. She went crazy on the Internet and found that braces have nickel in them."

Never thought much about what braces were made of. Metal was metal except in science. Braces rhymed with traces. Better not mention it.

"She picked up the phone and had my orthodontist, Dr. Born, take them off today. He tried to tell her that the odds of me getting poisoned from braces were like a million to one and my teeth weren't completely done yet." Her hands rotated on her wrists like chopper blades. "And that it'd be so expensive to put them back on again. My mom was all intense, saying she didn't care about all that. She just wanted them off now. She was, like, screaming. For real. In the office." Roe was standing now, on my bed, her feet pawing my pillows. "He started cutting wires, man."

"But your teeth look really nice," I said instead of "Okay, man" in a stoner's voice, like we did anytime one of us caught the other saying "dude" or "man." It was true anyways. About her teeth looking nice, I mean, but something didn't seem right.

"They're not done. I can totally feel where they still overlap. Maybe you can't really see it, but I can totally tell." She stuck her finger in her mouth and ran the tip up the wall of her teeth until she got close to her ear. There were holes where her dice earrings used to be. I had a feeling those had been removed the same time as the braces. "And what if, what if they start to shift again?"

We were on two different tracks now, me and Monroe, and even though I had different worries, I switched back to her track. "Could you wear, like, a retainer or something?"

"My mom won't let any plastic or metal get near my mouth until we get this thing sorted."

Was it (a) worse than we thought or (b) her mom totally overreacting?

"Wouldn't it be horrible if they went back the way they were before?" She tried to catch a glimpse of her teeth in the reflection of the glass covering my Foreigner poster. I know this sounds weird, but there were moments where Monroe's face lined up with lead singer Lou Gramm's, and her rash was superimposed onto Gramm's mouth. Maybe I'm the twisted one in all this, but it was like Gramm and Monroe merged to become the Joker. And maybe you didn't know, but Lou Gramm is really really sick. He has been for a long time. I got really scared for Monroe right then.

"Say something," she said, still bouncing on my bed and staring into the eyes of thirty-years-ago Lou Gramm.

But I couldn't think of anything funny. Nothing (which is rare for me).

"Coy! Say something." Then she turned, saw my face, and hers dropped. We stood there, her face and mine, face to face. I should have said something. But, as I said, I had nada. And surprisingly, neither did Monroe for a few minutes, until this: "I thought you knew the moment I walked in the door and you were just being cool."

"I was," I said, which wasn't the absolute truth. Do you want the absolute truth? Here it is: I had been afraid to see what she was hiding under her hand.

I was right to bc afraid.

6

Research Note: Even ancient people wanted straight teeth! According to the AAO (American Association of Orthodontists), archaeologists have discovered mummified ancients with crude metal bands wrapped around individual teeth. To close gaps, it has been surmised that catgut did the work now done by today's orthodontic wire! Later, in 400-500 BC, Hippocrates and Aristotle both ruminated about ways to straighten teeth and fix various dental conditions. Straight teeth have been on our minds a very long time! I know this has nothing to do with the platypus! Look at all these exclamation points!!!!!

Monroe's face didn't seem to get any better even without zipper lips. She actually got worse. It had to be really bad, since she surrendered so easily to a total wardrobe change. Her mom forced her to wear all white organic cotton clothes, kinda like a guru, if you can imagine that. A plain white cotton bag with no logo. And the worst: slippers, as in "hospital." Worst because Monroe has the sickest collection of Doc Martens of anyone at our school (eight-eye, ten-eye, fourteen and twenty, roses, skulls, patent leather). I'm not supposed to notice this stuff, but she didn't have a bra on either. Just about started crying seeing her slugging around like an escapee from the worst part of El Dorado, or what I imagine it to be like anyway.

My mom never lets me past the place with the fish tank, so I don't really know for sure.

Monroe was waiting for me by the metal detectors, the black framing her extreme whiteness like the windows at the broke-down development. But then I got closer and saw: her rash had flamed out from around her mouth all over her cheeks and onto her forehead and eyes. Almost like a burn victim straight back from Iraq. "Monroe," I whispered. There was so much I wanted to say, and it shot across my brain like the bottom of the news channel, but she cut me off with white gloves like a traffic cop from the Bahamas or somewhere.

"Don't even say it. Docs are eighty-sixed until they make some with no metal or metallic dyes, which will be like never. I dunno. I am slain by my own treachery, hoisted on my own petard." We both knew there'd be hell to pay dressed like that even as a ninth-grader at RRJH.

"Sorry."

"Sorry is for suckers. Sorry, as John Wayne said, doesn't get the job done."

"John Wayne?" I was shocked. "Now John Wayne is your guy?"

"That's right. John freakboy Wayne. God Bless Americana. Flambéed, deep-fried, and fry-boiled."

She'd been watching so much cable it was making her crazy.

The guards fisted our bags, and we walked through and then by the office, where Principal Pornstache was sitting on the edge of the receptionist's desk like he was in some cop show. The fatty had his huge polyester crotch shot on display so we could see the white strings straining to keep his junk from falling out like a load of intestines from some sort of roadkill. I woulda done myself in before showing all that pooch to a bunch of kids. He looked shocked to see Monroe without any black—blackless—and whispered to his secretary behind the back of his hand. Typical.

Once we entered the mess, it didn't take long for the calls to start. "Why so serious?" shooting past us because her face looked more and more like Ledger's each day.

"Can I tell you a story?" I asked, trying to distract her from all the kids staring, rubbernecking, even stopping dead in their tracks and pointing. Hole-asses.

"Either tell it or don't. Asking is just so fem," she said through gritted teeth, pretending not to notice her climbing celeb status in the crowded hallways.

"Okay."

"Okay."

"Stop, Monroe. I can't think." Kids rushed by us, saying terrible things I will never repeat. "It's about when I was a kid."

"Pre or post?" That means before or after my dad died.

"Post. I used to wake up in the morning with bumps," I said, kinda quiet.

"Bumps? Do tell." She sang that last bit.

"Shut. Here's the thing, I never told anyone this: they were mostly on my ass."

Hanging her head, she started to laugh and laugh and I could see the skin crack, tiny fissures webbing from her mouth and eyes. White like dried onion skin. "Ouch. Shite. Ouch," she said, wincing and then laughing.

She reached into her cotton bag and pulled out a small tube of cream with no label on it. She dabbed the goo on the new cracks with the pad of her index finger. Most of the kids veered off into their homerooms, but some still whispered before ducking into their classes. A bunch of guys in trucker caps and fake farm gear that I know cost tons of dough pretended to get drinks from a fountain that had been broken for months. Just so they could turn their heads toward Monroe, who looked ancient, older than my mom or the fish-tank falcon dude, smearing cream on her mouth.

"Finish the story."

"Don't know if I want to now." I dug my nails into my arm behind my back because it was all so awks.

"C'mon. You gonna tell a girl with a face like this not to laugh?" She turned to me head-on, and I realized what it was like, her face I mean. Man, it was bad.

We started walking again. "Okay. So I'd wake up with these, my mom called them hives."

"All over your itty-bitty back door."

"So I'd go get my mom out of bed, and she'd talk me down."

"Down from where?"

"Where I was. Hard to explain. That's what we called it anyway." I took my best shot at a cleansing breath. "Her theory was that I was worried about something, so I'd tell her everything on my mind, everything I might be concerned about—our cat running away, to—"

"Wait." She shot her arm across my chest and stopped me near the cafetorium. I could smell the mix of ammonia and

some sort of monkey meat the ladling ladies were cooking.
"I didn't know you had a cat."
"I never told you?"
"Nope."
"Seemed I would have. Anyway, her name was Harry."
"That's a boy's name."
"Sure is, Sherlock." We'd guessed wrong when we got her
from the Strawdog family with the cardboard box in front of
the grocery store. She had fleas.
"I can't believe you never told me you had a cat."
"That's not what this is about." My messenger bag started
to feel heavy.
"Thought I knew everything about you."
"It's just a cat, Roe."
She threw her head in the sky, all dramatic, all pretend
exasperated (vocab word), all silent movie status. "Let it be
heard: everybody knows how I feel about cats."
"Check, but that's not the point of the story."
"Okay, go ahead."
"So my mom would sit me down—"
"You go ahead, really."
"Roe, not now." She'd started this game we play where
you try to stop the other person from finishing his story by
pretending to be a total idiot really interested in it. This game
(which had no name other than "the game") usually included a
lot of head nodding and shooing with your hands. Sometimes
winking. If the other person loses their shiz, you win. If you
do it without the other person noticing, you win more. If

you can get away with doing it to an adult without the adult noticing, you win the world.

"Sorry. Go ahead. Your mom would sit you down on the toilet and wipe—"

"No, on the bed or a chair, not the toilet. And there was no wiping." She did wipe my hair from my forehead where it stuck. Rubbed my back. Did this pulsing thing with my forearm. It felt awesome. That part wouldn't enter the story though.

"Not the toilet. I got it. Unwiped. It sounds messy, but you go ahead." I ignored that one. Ignoring taunts is the key to the game, even though technically I wasn't playing. "You probably had plastic or rubber sheets after all that bedwetting. What's the moral of this story, anyway?"

"That maybe you want to talk about it or whatever." I didn't tell her how much I missed it. Not the getting-the-hives times, the time afterward, talking me down. My mom.

"Talk about what?"

"What's going on with your, um, thingy." I knew better than to say "face," but I did point.

She rocked her shoulders a little. It seemed like she was trying real hard not to touch her face. That moment lasted longer than I ever would have expected. Something was happening but I couldn't break the code.

"What's there to say," Monroe said more than asked, and turned away.

7

Research Note: Nickel is a stable element and cannot be broken down or otherwise destroyed. Elemental nickel is only moderately toxic but nickel carbonyl is highly poisonous and the most likely source of nickel poisoning. Common sources of nickel carbonyl are nickel mining, refining and plating, and workers in these industries have a high risk of exposure. Wow. Ugh. Suckage.

We have homeroom in the health and life skills classroom, and Mrs. Gross was already taking attendance. Her notes on hygiene still remained on the whiteboard from the day before, and all these posters surrounded us, a few on the human body and others giving us warnings and positive messages at the same time. Monroe always stared at the guy with only half a jaw: *Terrible Car Accident? No. Terrible Addiction. Tobacco.* Gross called her name and I answered for her, which made Gross's helmet hair jerk up, but she saw Monroe and went back down for the rest of the count. You could hear her pencil biting into the grade book: check slash check check check. She was one of those teachers who was all business. You were there or not there, tardy or on time. She didn't want to listen. Said she'd heard it all in her twenty-three years of teaching so we might as well save our breath, we'd need it later in life. Her attitude made it easy not to talk. That was cool by me.

Next to the half-jawed guy was a poster in hippie colors
that reminded us to BREATHE! No one seemed to notice how
crazy it was to have those two side by side.

I patted Monroe on the shoulder. "Hey."

"What's that?"

"You missed the call. Gross." I shot my elbow toward the
front of the room. "I answered, though."

"What does that guy do?"

"Which guy?" I asked, but it was always half-jaw McJones
with her. Imagine that your face ended right below your cheekbones, just fell off like a cliff and became your wobbly brown
turkey neck. I think it's called a wattle. According to the
poster, the guy lost a third of his tongue, half his jaw, and
all the flesh connecting his neck to his body. It didn't matter
that me and Monroe didn't chew tobacco or smoke even. It
wasn't about that. "It's only an ad. They probably photoshop
the hell out of it to scare kids," I said.

"I don't think so," she said, not moving her gaze. "Like,
how does he shave?" She squinted to see the poster closer.
"How does he eat? Kiss?"

"What?" Something was up: When did Monroe care about
putting her lips on someone else's?

"Nothing," she said, almost in a whisper.

The bell rang and kids started to get their stuff together:
iPods, iPads, iPhones, iPlanners, iAsses, Kindles, makeup
bags, hats, plastic water bottles, metal water bottles, Sharpie
collections, sketchbooks, laptops, laptop bags, to-go cups,

lunch bags, Chapstick, lunchboxes. Then: shuffle shuffle feet shuffle feet shuffle.

"Hold on, everyone," Gross said, holding a yellow sheet of paper. No one listened at first, even though the bell rang a few more times, which was unush. She actually had this football player, a hulking caveboy named Gallagher, stand in front of the closed door. "Sit back down, please."

"Someone's busted," Monroe joked. "I bet the cops'll explode in here in a minute. All riot gear status."

"Drug-sniffing dogs?"

"Obvs. Butt-sniffing ones too." She smiled. "For you." I smiled back. We were safe: no stink on us.

"Lockdown, for sure. Heard about it yesterday," Newer Thomas said next to me. We had about a thousand Thomases in our grade, and most of them had some sort of description in front of their names so kids could keep them straight. Parents too. Newer Thomas had come this year from Cleveland, I think, somewhere over that way. New Thomas had transferred from another school in Arizona. I don't know if the name made the kids weird or parents saw they were weird after they were born and gave them all the same name. Whatever the reason, all the Thomases were oddballs. New Thomas said totally inappropriate things, mostly about masturbation and spleens. Newer Thomas was kind of nerdy and tried way too hard. He would probably have worn a tie if it didn't mean social suicide. You shoulda seen his shirts. Pressed. Every single day.

"Today, we need to take a few minutes to review our lock-down procedure," Gross said.

Newer Thomas nodded, all happy with himself at guessing right.

"Now, as most of you know, a lockdown . . ." Gross explained something everyone had already heard a million times before. About "incidents" in Yuma, Sandy Point, the nursing school at U of A, and that freak that shot Gabrielle Giffords. In case of an unsafe campus, there would be a series of bells that was different than a fire drill, and we'd need to lock the door and basically just hide.

"I think it's five bells," Newer Thomas said, like his inside intel was vital to our survival.

This girl in front of us got all ruffled and said to no one in particular: "My dad says schools can't protect shit and that I should try to get the hell out of here any way I can. Even out the freaking window." She was one of those fashion kids who dressed like she was thirty or something and living in L.A., not in our shite show of a town. From her lost look, I guessed she expected someone to say "Hells yeah!" or "Fight the man!" but no one said a word. To her anyway. All of her fashionista friends must have been sequestered in a different homeroom that had its own catwalk. "My dad said he'd cover for me later. Write me notes. Come down if he had to and kick some ass."

Monroe gave me a giant *whatevs* sideways glance that you could have probably seen from outer space.

Gross handed her ball of keys to Gallagher, who locked the door. You could tell that he ate up all this meaningless power crap and thought he was a badass standing there like some big dumb bouncer for a boring club everyone wanted to get the hell out of, not into.

"I hate that guy," Roe said, like he was a life-size fart.

"Okay, everyone crouch against that wall over there." Gross raised a bony finger. "Bring all your personal items."

No one moved. A few people groaned. Most just stared or "talked with their neighbor," as they say in teacherland. Newer Thomas was dying to be at the head of the line, but even he knew better by now.

"Do we really have to do this? Can't we just sorta, you know, fake it?" Lizzie Buchanan asked Gross. She was our student council president, and some teachers loved her stuff. The long-timers like Gross, though, didn't give a rat's anus about anything like that. She'd probably seen twenty-three or more Lizzies in her time and knew there were more to come. No one was that special.

Newer Thomas said, "They wanna make it so when the shooter comes, he thinks the classroom is empty. So then he'll pass us by."

"Thanks for the explanation." Monroe couldn't believe how boring this all was. Her slipper kept tapping and her fingers doing little dances on the edge of her desk. She wanted to get the hell out of there. Clear as the rash on her face. Is that mean of me to say?

"I won't have to do any of it," Fashion Girl said. "Not even." She had this rock-in-her-seat thing going, all attitude. "My dad says I could totally run out before that guy locked the door."

"That guy wouldn't lock it in a real scenario. Gross is just too lazy to get up," Newer Thomas explained. "She'd have to do it. Procedure and all."

"Doesn't matter. My dad—"

"Enough about your dad, all right?" Monroe said to the girl, pushing back from her desk. "Just jump out the window now, please. Do us all a favor."

"Those windows don't really open all the way," Newer Thomas added.

"And take him with you." Monroe pointed at our play-by-play man.

"Frickin' Jedi Star Wars nerdass freakazoid," Fashion Girl said, referring to Roe's outfit.

"Someone has Daddy issues," Monroe sang to the tune of *nah-nah-nah-nah-nah*.

I stifled a snort, and Gross said this was no laughing matter and that we'd all have to march right on over there or get sent to the office. We all moved like our bodies were made of lead. Slowly, we grabbed our stuff and zombie-walked (slow zombies, not fast ones) over to the wall underneath the posters Monroe was obsessed with. We stood there like we were all waiting for the same bus—backpacks dangling from our paws, iPods turned way up, all of us totally bored or pretending to be that way.

"Please crouch or sit."

"Mrs. Gross." Fashion Girl pointed to her new white jeans.

"Jesus. Just sit on your backpack, Tina." You could tell Gross only had a few nerves left, and this Tina was chewing on them.

During a real lockdown we couldn't use any electronic devices, but now everyone was texting complaints to kids in other classes about having to sit there. Nothing about any of this struck us as a true threat. This drill would only last fifteen minutes, when real lockdowns could last four or five hours. Food and water would be pooled, Gross said, and we had to be silent the whole time. No one was really listening. I hadn't eaten or gone to the bathroom that morning. I don't always go at home if I wake up late, and having to go made me think of something. Newer Thomas would have probably known the answer, but I couldn't talk to him now. I had to ask. I hardly ever raised my hand in class, never ever in homeroom.

"What if we have to, you know, go to the bathroom?" I didn't look at Monroe.

"All right. Might as well get to that now." Gross looked down at her yellow sheet. "As I said, during a lockdown procedure, no one is allowed to leave. So if you absolutely have to use the restroom, we will separate the class: boys on one side, girls on the other. Toilet paper will be provided." The next part got pretty sick. The girls would all surround the one who had to go so the boys couldn't see and the girl would go in the garbage can. Boys would do the same.

"No frigging way! I'd be so gone by then!" Tina mumbled, all upset. A lot of the other girls had the same reaction. They did not like this circle-pee-in-a-can concept one bit. A few scanned the room for other options, like a closet or something I couldn't see. Some looked scared. The boys mostly laughed, grabbing their junk like they were fire hoses they were spraying around the room, mostly at the girls and

Mrs. Gross, who hadn't moved from her chair all period. Gallagher still guarded the door, but he seemed lost, since the door no longer needed guarding. This new detail I'd brought out by my expert hand-raising involved everyone more than any worksheet or lab I'd ever seen. I was gonna joke to Monroe about the kids' book *Everybody Pees* and then point out Gallagher, who'd started to mope, but when I turned to her, something was up. Her eyes flashed all big and her mouth held a lot of air, like the kids in band when they play trumpet or trombone.

"Roe."

Shook her head no.

"What's up?"

"I can't handle it."

"Handle what?"

"That." She nodded toward all the girls, who had slowly drifted to the front of the class. Tina held court, throwing her hands in the air and wagging her head like those tall wavy air-tube dolls they put in front of car dealerships to get your attention. Everyone around her nodded along when they weren't checking their phones. The boys drifted to the back, still laughing and grabbing body parts. Monroe and I sat in the middle. Gross must have felt as if she'd done enough because she'd gone back to grading the pile of papers on her desk. "There is no way I could have them all looking at me."

"Not gonna happen." I almost patted her hand but stopped myself. I tried to slip my hand into my pocket, but it's hard when you're sitting. Angle's all wrong. I left it in my lap, which felt very very weird. "At least while we're here."

"I'm really worried." She shook her head no again like I didn't get it, like what she was referring to was much bigger than just peeing in a trash can in front of a bunch of girls who would never be your friends, not even under extreme conditions. My mom told me on one of my trips to Dorado that a lot of people who enter that kind of place go mute for a while. Something about having so much trouble in your life that you just shut down and some later say that they didn't have the words to express all the things they felt. Words all dried up. "You'll never have to worry about me going silent," my mom joked to Dan, but I didn't think it was funny. Dan did, or maybe he was just being nice.

"Say something," I said. We were sitting on the floor and everyone else was standing. Boy and girl voices mixed and echoed off the walls and ceiling, and the noise got crazy loud. Gross just tuned us out under her hair helmet of silence while Gallagher found his way back to the outer ring of his circle of buddies at the rear of the class. Monroe looked terrible. "Say anything."

"I love that movie," she whispered. Pause. Pause. Pause. She coughed and almost touched her face but instead just ran her hands about an inch over her skin. "John Cusack so rules."

My response was automatic: "*She's gone. She gave me a pen. I gave her my heart, she gave me a pen.*"

Hers was too: "*I don't want to sell anything, buy anything, or process anything as a career. I don't want to sell anything bought or processed, or buy anything sold or processed, or process anything sold, bought, or processed, or repair anything sold, bought, or processed. You know, as a career, I don't want to do that.*"

"*I got a question,*" I said, quoting Lloyd Dobler. "*If you guys know so much about women, how come you're here at like the Gas 'n' Sip on a Saturday night completely alone drinking beers with no women anywhere?*"

"*You used to be fun. You used to be warped and twisted and hilarious . . . and I mean that in the best way—I mean it as a compliment!*"

I'm sure if you had been in that room in one of the packs—boys or girls—and you overheard two kids repeating movie lines back and forth during a fake lockdown, you would have thought, What nerds! or What freaks!, but it was so much more than that to us. Inside those words written by someone we didn't know (but could look up) and said by a guy acting like someone else, deep inside those words were hours of watching that movie over and over with microwave popcorn in our laps and liters of Cherry Coke, afternoons listening to *Head Games*, trying to decode the lyrics and then apply them to our own lives (past, present, and future), hours watching the lights turn colors at our favorite car wash, walks in arroyos trying to find chupacabra tracks, staging little scenes with old toys to shoot with a used Polaroid camera Dan picked up at a yard sale that only had seven pictures left. When you only have seven, you choose carefully. All those moments were in me and Monroe swapping *Say Anything* quotes back and forth, face to face, in the middle of that stupid thing called lockdown practice.

Then, after we both inhaled, ready to start quoting again, the bell rang and we were released.

8

Everyone had been talking about the lockdown all morning, what might really happen, how they'd escape like ninjas or go all stealth like Navy Seals (in the desert?), who the likely candidates were to come shoot up the school one day, which teachers would get blasted first. I didn't really pay any attention to all the chatter until I went to the bathroom after first period. Ever since the budget cuts when they fired this janitor, the boys' bathroom had been a nasty assland. A lot more kids tried to hold it after that. One kid in my English class, Trevor, said he hadn't gone during school all year. Not once. He was so proud that he wrote an essay about it. Next thing you know, he'll want it on his report card. He waited or snuck off campus and went home to bust a mission. He didn't live far, so it was easier. I didn't blame him, but bragging about it was so Fifty Shades of Ghey.

I opened the bathroom door by backing into it with my messenger bag and tried not to touch anything. It was like Hurricane Katrina, with gallons of smelly water every-where—on the floor, by the sink, in the stalls. Some jackoff had stuffed up the first toilet I "visited" with paper towels, and I won't mention what another smeared on the second. A kid I didn't know wearing a white Adidas jacket was leaning on the windowsill, the only dry place, talking on his cell. Once I stepped into a stall that was halfway decent, he started talking louder.

"It's always the quiet ones," he said. "And the weird ones."

Something about the way he was speaking made me listen in. It was like he was in a play or something, with all the *one*s and the way he overpronounced. He kept it up, his voice loud and echoey in the empty piss room. Trying to hold my breath somehow made it louder. "When the quiet ones and the weird ones are friends," he said, "those are the freaks you have to keep an eye on. Deadly combo fer sure."

I had a sinking feeling that he was talking about me and Monroe. And that we were on the possible school shooters list, since Monroe came back with a mysterious rash around what kids were calling her "death eater's mouth" and weird Jedi clothes, and I never said much to anyone other than the kid with the mouth rash and weird Jedi clothes. There was a crazy amount of graffiti in my stall, years and yards of black marks and evidence of decades of janitors trying to scrub or scratch or paint it off. It made me want to go home.

"You never can tell," the douche on the cell said. "Some kids just have a death wish." Then something that sounded like "Monroe." It could have been "gotta go" or "I don't know" or "and so," but it also could have been "Monroe." Maybe I should have said something to him, but I just marched out of there like I'd heard someone calling my name in the hall, but no one was there when I emerged, so that may have made his suspicions seem even truer if he had followed me. Is truer a word? I think it is.

The halls are dead quiet during lunchtime. I poked my head into Beaker's class. The lights were off. The plastic instructional skeleton stood in the corner by the broken JAG emergency shower and the blue bucket next to it that Beaker said replaced the emergency shower.

"Mr. Beakman?" I called, kinda quiet, half hoping he wasn't around. All the metal gas hookups caught what little light there was coming in the long windows running just below the ceiling. Teachers must love classrooms when there are no kids there to stink them up, leave trash, carve their names in the desks. One time there was an all-school cleanup day to replace the fired janitor, and Monroe and I were assigned to furniture duty. You should have seen the amount of gum and (hurl) boogers underneath the desks and chairs. We had to use paint scrapers and steak knives to get all that crap off. It was so disgusting. Later, some kids complained to their parents about having to clean instead of learn (as if), so they canceled all-school cleanup day. The only thing is that now I can't look at a school desk or chair without thinking of all that shite lurking underneath.

A cough came from the closet in the back, and I saw the thin string of light under the door. Walking past the board, I ran my hand along the coolness of the chalk tray. Not thinking, I rubbed my fingers on my shirt, and they left a four-fingered white stain that I then tried desperately to wipe off. Idiot.

As I wiped, Beaker called, "Someone there?"

"Um, hello," I said, all awkward status in the dark. "It's Coy. I mean, me?" I then stepped into what I thought was a closet but turned out to be a crazy crowded combo of an

office and a closet. Beaker sat crammed at a tiny black desk
that could barely hold his ancient computer. His area was
swallowed up by shelves jammed full of textbooks, glass jars,
plastic bins, metal scales, and that kind of stuff. Whatever
space had been on the floor back in the Stone Age was now
taken up by cardboard boxes marked with codes of numbers
and letters I didn't understand. It smelled funny in there too—
dust, coffee, tobacco, and the grease my mom used to put on
my chest when I got congested.

Above Beaker's computer was a bulletin board with so
many pieces of paper pinned to it that it looked like it might
topple over any minute. Notecards were stacked so thick that
the pins strained to keep them stuck there. On the top were
the words **OF THE YEA** in bold letters, but the beginning
and ending were eclipsed by the mess.

Beaker held a half-chewed sandwich in his hairy knuckles
and looked surprised that I'd found him. He stared at my
face, then the chalk flower on my shirt. He didn't need to say
anything. He just kept chewing his floppy sandwich. I knew
what he was thinking anyway: How can I help you?

"You know I was doing my report on the platypus?"

He nodded.

"Right. Well, I want to change it."

He nodded again, the sandwich still in his hand.

"You see, my friend, Monroe?" She had a different science
teacher, Mr. Dawson, who was really young and cool, and had
tattoos and stuff. He lifted Russian barbells called kettleballs.
Everyone called him Dawg or Dawg the Bounty Hunter. We
hate that show but Monroe says Dawson is okay by her. "She

has this thing now. Metal poisoning. Her mom thinks she got it from her braces."

He raised an eyebrow like he wanted to hear more.

I rambled on about Monroe's rash and her mom making her take her braces off and what her ortho, Dr. Born, said and I got all excited and probably a little bit emotional because my voice started to crack and it was kinda hard to breathe. I think I may have told him some other stuff like how long we'd been friends and my weird encounter in the bathroom. I don't know. When he was done with his half sandwich, he did that octopus thing with his glasses just like clockwork. Then he picked up the other half. Ham and cheese, I think. Lettuce curling out of it like a green tongue.

"So now I want to do my report on nickel poisoning."

He wiped his mouth with a crumpled-up napkin and did this nod-and-shrug combo, so I just kept babbling: "I don't think that I'm gonna cure her or anything, I just want to find out what's going on, do research on that, and since it's got something to do with science, I just thought, you know . . ." I waited for him to say something. Maybe tell me that it was against district rules to spend time researching your best friend's illness, something about liability or metal poisoning not being on any standardized test, but he just chewed. It was so claustrophobic in there—all those colors that you know came from decades earlier stacked side by side or one on top of the other. **OF THE YEA** floated above his head like a cartoon bubble. I tried to imagine how the rest of my year would go with Monroe, my mom, Dan, school, but I couldn't see it. Not clearly enough to make me calm. The future was still unwritten.

Maybe I couldn't get a clear picture because of all the distractions in Beaker's cloffice. He nodded once like I had his approval, and then toward the door. I left him with his ham and cheese sticking its tongue out at me, passed through the dark classroom, took a breath, and then reentered the stream of kids swimming upstream. Lunchtime was over.

I sorta went crazy after that, with the research I mean. I started spending more time in the library during my free periods and lunch, staying up late at night online. Pretty soon, I had a whole notebook with those folder dividers filled with notes and printouts and drawings I made.

Research Note: Nickel is a metallic element used in many of the "high-tech" ultra-flexible wires, auxiliaries, and stainless steel appliances used in orthodontic practice today, including the braces themselves. Nickel is known to cause more cases of *allergic contact dermatitis* than all other metals combined. Most cases of nickel contact dermatitis are the result of direct contact from jewelry, clothes, watches, and glasses. Nickel is present in a large number of commonly used objects and can therefore cause contact dermatitis.

And that according to like the Danish Ministry or the Academy of Health, there are boatloads of foods that have high amounts of nickel in them like asparagus (which I'd be happy to give up, you know why), beans/lentils (ditto except for refry), broccoli, corn, carrots, lettuce, mushrooms, kale (hippie food), alfalfa sprouts (ditto), leeks, pineapple (yum!), raspberries (ditto), dates (ew), figs (ditto), herring/oyster/mussels (hurl), shrimp/crawfish (yum/ew), whole wheat flour/bran/buckwheat/millet/multigrain bread/muesli/oatmeal (pass on all), unpolished brown rice (who polishes their rice?), rye, bran, tea, soy protein powder (hippie cocaine), chocolate/cocoa (bummer for Roe), baking powder, marzipan (WTF?), nuts, sunflower seeds, sesame seeds, licorice, vitamins.

Poison was everywhere for Monroe.

9

I went online in the school library and ended up in a nickel-allergy support-group site where all these people told their stories of suffering. Some problems were no big deal, like how this one girl had to put tape over her jean buttons, to more serious stuff like people getting crusty welts all over their faces, to some even sicker business about how often they had to go to the bathroom and what their "evacuations" looked like (was a lot sicker on the site, but I try to be polite when I'm in my research mode). There were even color pictures on one web page that led me to do an image search, which was a very bad idea. Very, very bad. I don't know if I'd call it a collage or checkerboard or what, but I wanna say like sixty pictures of different body parts on different bodies, mostly red and bumpy like these people got attacked by a swarm of killer bees or the worst jellyfish stings or somehow poison ivy found a way to wrap around them. Horrible. Nasty. Pus and crust, pus and crust, pus and crust. Hospital beds.

"I gotta get the hell out of here," Monroe said, standing over me. All of a sudden, as in I almost crapped my pants.

"What do you mean?" I quickly crashed the desktop by jamming my finger hard into the power button. I had to try to remember where all those sites were. I coulda used my own laptop right about then. Dan said he'd think about it. "Wanna go see the Nurselor? Walk you over."

"Nope. Out of here totally. I thought I could do school today, but no way, not today." She smoothed the side of her bag, a mini-sail. My mom would have killed to dye that back in the day. Roe's face had gotten very swollen, which is probably why she wasn't in Gross's homeroom. After gawking at those photos, I had a hard time looking at her straight on. It was going to get bad for her. "Oh," she said like it was nothing, "and I'll need you to come with."

"I can't. I have—" I pointed at the dead computer screen in front of me.

"I know what you have. You can make it up easy-peasy."

Hardly anybody uses the library except for a few mathletes prepping for the nerd olympics and some kids trying to get some sleep in beat-up chairs by the broken copy machine. They'd opened old issues of *Rolling Stone* and *Sports Illustrated* on their faces to block out the light. "We'll get busted," I said.

"Right. Look at us. Me with this face and these claws." She pushed her hands out of the open cuffs to show me the places her rash had invaded. Her bumpy fingers looked like she had the Elephant Man's disease.

"Oh." I cut off the *my god!* part. "They're not claws," I lied. "Don't say that." I wanted to add: *Please put those away.*

"And you with your mom in a loony bin and—"

"Don't."

"Sorry, but it's true, and the sooner we face it, the better. We're both—" I lost the word as one of the magazine-faced zombies coughed really loud. "Let's go. I really gotta get out of here."

What was I going to do? Monroe's my best friend.

"Please?" she said. She hardly ever says please.

I agreed but regretted it immediately. I gathered up my stuff, and we walked without speaking down the hallways until we came to this nowhere land everyone called the Cage just before the double doors to the gym. Monroe opened a side emergency exit with a whoosh (but no alarm) and then a blast of nuclear light. We could hear Wapshot making kids trip over the same obstacle course he always used, with hula hoops and thick scratchy ropes, so we cut across the back of the football field and into the place where kids go to make out and smoke American Spirits, the healthy cigarettes made by Indians using Indian magic that causes less cancer. I'd seen this place when we had to run cross-country in the fall. Trail dips down into this little dirt pocket ghetto/grotto deal. From far away it looks like a shrine almost, three trees clumped together with confetti and flowers, but as you grow closer you see it's all just trash— cigarette butts and foil from the packs, broken glass and cans, shoelaces, sometimes condoms, but I don't think that's from our school. Probably hobos or high-schoolers.

I didn't say anything to Monroe because my heart was racing. I'd promised my mom that I wouldn't become a cliché, as she put it, a troubled kid with a tricky family situ acting out like, well, like what we were doing. Actually, I liked school. Most of the classes were pretty boring, but I knew what to expect, what time to switch, what would be shoved in front of my face, what teachers would be wearing or saying. What

jokes they'd tell. Seven forty-five, homeroom; first class, 8:05.
Even lunch had a predictable outcome and a menu you could
view online ahead of time, so I could plan on sloppy joes on
Wednesday, pizza on Fri. It was almost like TV, only less
colorful. There were no surprises. Even the weather was predictable: hot and hotter. That's what Dan was resisting, this
superscheduled redundant kind of life, but I liked it. Ditching
school with Monroe wasn't exactly all *Superbad* for me.

"How do you know where to go?" I called to her white
canvas of a back. I tried not to think about how she was getting
sicker every time I saw her.

Raising a finger in the air, she said, "Let it be known that
I've done this before."

"I thought I knew everything about you," I said sarcas-
tically, referring to her saying the same thing about my cat
Harry, but she didn't get it. "Are we headed to the car wash?"

"Not today."

"Comic-book store?"

"Nope."

We emerged out of the woods behind a strip mall off
Rabbit Road. Five or six stores and brown Dumpsters like
gargoyles all in a row outside blue steel doors. Nothing was
open—it was too early—but the sun wouldn't dim at all. That's
what it's like living here. You can feel like you're on a movie
set, with this bright white light in the morning, but it's still
too early for banks or stores to be awake.

"This way," Monroe said, and as she turned I caught a
glimpse of her face in the spotlight of the sun. She had a few
layers of dead skin like the peeling trunk of a birch tree and

then these deep red blotches on her cheekbones. I realized (or maybe wanted to) that I needed to be there for her, even though this little trip of hers would throw my life into a huge hassle.

We crossed this gully that was lined with river rocks and chicken wire. Wasn't easy on my feet trying not to catch the toe of my Sambas, but Monroe was in slippers so I couldn't say anything. By my watch, Language Arts was now beginning, and maybe Ms. J would take her own sweet time in getting her attendance in, but Wapshot would not. So in another fifty minutes the automated calling system would leave a message on my machine at home, but Dan wouldn't hear it until after I did. The machine would get the machine. No one could call my mom. Hell, no one could call my dad, either.

I told Monroe to wait. We were behind another set of stores, like backstage on a movie set. No stagehands, only more Dumpster gargoyles and big bundles of cardboard boxes strapped together like bales of hay. People started to pull up in their Toyotas and Hondas and Subarus to park in spaces divided by yellow lines. It was getting close to nine, I guessed.

I saw a lady with hair Dan would call the color of French vanilla ice cream. It was down to her shoulders but curled at the end. Her earrings hung from her head like gold rabbit droppings. My heart raced again, and I felt I needed to be somewhere, not home alone or at school but somewhere. "What happened?" I asked her. "Why the freakout? You won't get in trouble, but I will as sure as shitakes."

She called from over her shoulder, "What kind of trouble will we get into that would be worse than what we've already been through?"

"Poetic. Almost filmsy."

"Bite me."

"If you slow down, I will. Serious." I stopped to, well, just stop. "Why are we doing this?"

"We need to get out into the light, breathe air. Oh, I don't know. Just not there."

"You're not really supposed to be in the sun, are you?"

"Shut up," she said like she really meant it, so I did.

We walked along the backstage of drugstores, card shops, a place that sold shoes with crazy big springs on them, and something called a Vitamin Cottage. It'd been a longer walk than I thought. Everything where we live is really spread out, and we were hot and thirsty. At least I was, and I'd skipped breakfast again. Monroe started to breathe Darth Vader heavy, almost like through her braces even though her braces had been ripped off her teeth. Her face was shiny like it had Vaseline smeared all over it, and I knew that (a) sweat and sun were really bad for her and (b) she'd be itching like a licey that night.

"We should really get out of the sun. It could really make your edema worse."

She stopped and about-faced. She looked weird facing me out in the open like that. A showdown of sorts. It was like we were in a movie, but not a very good one. "What did you say?"

I knew I shouldn't have used the term from my research, but it kinda just slipped out. I pick up details and trivia like a magnet. "Um, edema. Just swollen tissues. Learned it in science. Figured that's the right term. Hey." I reached into my pocket. "Got some money. Let's get a drink."

She wanted to finish her mission of getting home, but her slippers were almost black by now and the cuffs of her sweats were the color of ashes. I scanned the area as if someone in a SUV was just gonna pull over and drive us home. "No one knows where we are," I said.

We entered the vitamin shop through the back, startling the clerk. "Who's there?" the guy called when the bell chimed.

I was still so nervous from Monroe calling me on my research that I yelled, "Just some customers!" It sounded so ghey I wanted to die.

Monroe let out a half-laugh. "Justhst somth cuthomerth," she lisped back at me.

"We're hardly opened," the guy said, like he was pissed at us for coming in and wanting to spend money. He had a neck beard and eyeballed us as we tried to figure out how the weirdo store worked. Half of it seemed like a big chemistry set, brown and gold bottles with white labels, glass rods sticking up out of jars, and little blue vials of stuff. Roots and herbs in packets. The place smelled a little like fertilizer and perfume. The other half of the store had all sorts of candles and books with purple covers and glittery bindings. Incense sticks and cones and cubes. It reeked. Dan used to light that crap until I told him it gave me the worst headache. Now he just sprays something like Lysol, but the can he uses is better for the environment, or so he says. I could see the guy behind the counter switch from watching us to a little TV he had next to a rack selling powders in packets. He looked kind of like Ringo Starr, only fatter, with skin the color of liver.

Monroe lingered in front of rows and rows of drinks—Odwalla, VitaminWater, and yogurt drinks, some sort of brown stuff that helped you "evacuate." I started to get a headache from all the crazy colors and the mix of candles, incense, and sprays. I remembered again that I skipped breakfast and planned on eating after I left the library. I couldn't remember what I had for dinner either. I've always had this thing with eating and anxiety. It had gotten worse lately, thinking about Monroe.

The pain came on like a spike through my brain. My eyes moved back and forth, and then I was dreaming we were back in Connecticut on the rocky coast. It was a sunny day and something was trapped in the rocks, an octopus maybe or a crab. Whatever it was couldn't get free. I tried to dig it out with my fingers, but there was no way to get to the creature.

"You kids have to leave." Greasy Ringo stood over me with a smudgy cordless phone in his hand. I had no idea how long I'd been out. I'd fainted a few times before, but never in a store. I could tell that he couldn't decide whether to pay more attention to me, the kid passed out on the floor, or Monroe, with her flaming swollen face and flowing robes of white.

"Jesus," she said, shaking her head.

Jesus, kid, was the look on Ringo's face when he eyeballed Monroe.

"Sorry, my bad," I said, but when I stood up I got a wicked head rush and my knees buckled so I reached out to steady myself and got a handful of Ringo's hairy stomach fat under some velour. It felt scratchy, like leaves in a Hefty bag. I kept my hands out like a blind dude as I wobbled through the store.

Outside, Monroe handed me a VitaminWater. It was blood-red but tasted like berries out of a Cap'n Crunch box. "How'd you get this?" I asked.

"Figure if he's gonna kick us out just for you chucking a dummy, then, well, we deserve it." She looked pleased with her own bad self. "These sleeves are good for something." She shot her burning hands out and then pulled them back in.

"I wasn't faking." I gulped the water just so I wouldn't do it again. It tasted awful, like ground-up baby aspirin.

"Well." She shrugged. "Now you know what it's like."

Monroe's yard was like all the others on her block, with two squares of lava rock divided in half by a concrete path, all encased in hip-high chain link. In each bed stood a cactus, and even though it seemed too hot for flowers to live, red blooms erupted on each like boils. I stopped to look at them, careful not to move my head too much from side to side. I was still a bit woozy. Monroe marched straight inside without stopping.

"You coming in or what?" she called from inside the screen.

"What?" I said in a grandpa's voice, trying to be funny, but it sounded stale.

Her living room was crammed with soft blue furniture that reminded me of huge pillows, and all over the glass tabletops and inside glass cases were British souvenirs—platters with pictures of Lady Di and that prince on their wedding day, some of those guards with big bushy hats. She had bar towels with the names of beer on them, and British flags as large as a suitcase and as small as postage stamps. In the corners were gray plastic boxes, either putting air out or sucking it in, from what I could tell. None of this stuff had been here the last time I visited a month or so before, when Roe still had braces. "I keep forgetting your mom is so British."

"You've heard her talk, dude."

"I know, but now your house looks really, really British. Sex Pistols status."

"Ma!" Monroe called and walked into the kitchen.

"Where are your dogs? That cat?" Monroe had this cat that talked. Sorta. Creepy long meows and yowls that I swear sounded like words.

"Kennel," she said, like she didn't even miss 'em. "Pepper's at a farm." Pepper was a big black Great Dane who was called Pepper because all the other names they came up with sounded racist.

"Hullo? What are you doing here? Are you well?" Her mom rushed out, face all pink, in a soft blue jumpsuit that matched the furniture. I should tell you that Monroe's mom is pretty big. Bigger than Oprah, bigger than Jack Black, big enough to be on *The Biggest Loser*. It was hard for me not to stare, especially since her face has sort of swallowed up her eyes, which are dark and thin like splinters. But if I look away or at my Sambas, Monroe busts me and says, "She's not a freak, you know. She's just heavy." And two things happen at once: (a) I think of fat jokes (she's so fat, she wakes up in sections) and (b) I know Monroe is saying, *At least my mom's not away in a loony bin. At least my mom cooks me breakfast.*

"Coy, and how are you?" Monroe's mom said really loud (she's a megaphone talker), and pulled me into her folds. Her accent, I guess, has changed, because now it sounds a lot like baby talk. "It has been too long." She turned away almost immediately, but I was stuck in there for more than a few seconds. "I would rather you be in the living room," she said to Monroe.

"I'm starved."

"Fine. Please be brief. Out of there lickety-split, yes? Hold your breath."

"I want to show you what we've been doing." Mrs. Alpert took me by the hand into the back hallway, which was blocked off by sheets of thick plastic. She drew aside one with her free hand and then another strip and another until we stepped into a room that had four or five machines humming and a man on his hands and knees on a cement floor. I could see by the boards where the real floor once stood. The man's face was covered in a gas-mask thing—a round mouth and two gray lungs on either side. Some gray hair poked out of a painter's cap in wings, and his eyes were shaded by dark goggles. He looked like a big bug wrapped in a white shiny bag.

"This is Rael, our mold specialist."

"Mold specialist?"

"That's right." She nodded. "Monroe didn't tell you?"

"Not really." Mold wasn't our favorite subject.

"Goodness, well then." Her hands went to where her hips had once been. "Our latest doctor believes that mold has compromised Monroe's immune system, which made her susceptible to the metal poisoning. Can you fathom it? She's been sleeping on a bed of mold for years."

"It was in her bed?" I shuddered. Didn't they do laundry in England?

"No, dear. It lurked under the floors. I feel simply awful. So we've ripped out all the boards and the tile in her bathroom and wet vacuumed and scraped, and well . . ." She pushed up her big dark hair, which started drooping. Exhaled big time. "Many things. We're thinking of putting in mold-resistant drywall and subflooring. Maybe pour concrete." She listed all the things they'd done and wanted to do, and I kept thinking about the development Dan and I passed, and I knew those homes had none of this expensive stuff and some of it would never even be finished anyway. Monroe's mom went on and on about organic drapes and natural fibers, but all I could see were pipes and skeleton walls, little torn dresses of fiberglass peeking out behind PVC.

"And here we will put in shelving for her anime and manga collection, but they will have sliding doors because of all the dust. You know books collect dust, right?" The way she said it, it sounded as if there might be a test in my future.

"Books collect dust. Right," I echoed. When I moved a little to the left, I caught sight of Red Rock, so I stepped over some boards to the window. Red Rock was a big bloody heart against the blue sky, and from where Monroe's bed would be positioned, she could just sit and watch as the sun dipped down and died. If it was west. I wasn't exactly sure.

"Is that facing west?" I asked Bug Man, who switched off a little silvery space-age vacuum that sucked up more invisible mold, I guess.

"You really shouldn't have that kid in here," Bug Man said, standing up. His knees were behind gray plastic ovals like little gladiator shields. "That kid" turned around, but Mrs. Alpert had already exited the room.

Being left there alone reminded me of the day after Dan and I took Mom to Dorado, six months before. I got up from my bed that morning, and the sun was glaring right into my room. Summer can last until October here, sometimes November, and it felt like a Saturday even though it was a Tuesday. The sun made it feel like someone was shooting searchlights into our house, revealing a thin layer of dust all over everything—cabinets, tables, CD cases, fruit in a bowl on the kitchen table. Even the water spots on the glasses popped like measles. Everything was bright and magnified and still. Dan was letting me have a "mental health day," which sounds like a cruel joke but wasn't.

"Do what you want all day, bro," he said, squeezing my shoulder. "Play video games, watch movies, eat crap. Your choice, bro." Sounded like every kid's fantasy (except for all the bros), but I couldn't imagine going to school, and I couldn't imagine staying home. I felt like the last kid on earth, so I wandered around my house, and into my mom and Dan's room—staring at the photos of their honeymoon in Cancun: Dan in a bone-white shirt and pants, Mom in a creamy sundress. Both barefoot. And then this framed piece of window glass with a lot of pictures pressed inside it: me in Halloween costumes; Mom and me in the back of a pickup full of musicians; me, Mom, and Dan at the farmers market. I sat on the edge of the bed, photos filling my eyes with the layer of dust across the black enamel dresser, trying to sit so still that if

someone came to rob our house, they'd pass me by, thinking I was a store dummy or dead even. I imagined someone
breaking in and yelling, "Hey kid!" but I wouldn't move or
speak or divert my eyes from the pictures—I'd just sit there
even if the robbers held a gun to my cheek or punched me
in the jaw. I would be as still as the skeleton in the bio lab,
as the kids holding water guns in the bronze fountain near
the library, as me in the photographs themselves. I would not
move. Ever. Never.

Research Note: Mold spores move into, accumulate, and settle into the lower lungs. Since most gas exchange takes
place in the lower lungs, toxins produced by the spores
travel through the bloodstream with the oxygen. The
body's reaction to the toxins causes permanent scarring
of the lung tissue, which affects the lungs' ability
to transfer oxygen into the bloodstream. Each exposure
to mold spores increases the damage. The body's last
defense against these spores is to develop an allergic
reaction that causes cold or pneumonia-like symptoms.
Or everything that Roe has.

10

The cakes Monroe's mom served me were dry—scones, I think—but the tea was pretty badass. My mom and Dan make tea too, but theirs comes in little bags, nothing like the dank stuff Monroe's mom made with a buttload of cream and sugar. Pretty soon I had two cups in me and I was hella jittery in the light blue chair, which was kinda slippery. When I say slippery I mean shiny, and even though I was really hyper, I knew better than to spill tea on a chair like that.

"How are your parents?" Monroe's mom asked, and again I didn't correct her.

"Fine," I said, knowing she wanted more. She knew where my mom was.

"Your mother? Do you still visit her weekly?"

Maybe I was pissed off by her questions, or maybe it was the tea, but I asked, "Did Lady Diana really have loads of affairs?"

Monroe half opened her mouth to say something, but then she shut it and watched us in a way that seemed almost creepy. She had that tube out and was rubbing cream up past where her bracelets once hung on one arm and where her watch used to be on the other.

"Goodness, I loved Di, I really did. Those damn-ned paparazzi." Mrs. Alpert pronounced *paparazzi* so that *pap* rhymed with *cap*, not *pop*. "They killed her. I know this sounds bizarre, but I think I could have rescued her." Her face looked more sincere than fat. "If she had come over for one cooked meal, a nice leg of lamb, say, scalloped potatoes, pudding, and lived a normal life with us, you know, doing her charity work by day, I think I could have saved her."

"What a load of crap." Monroe spoke without looking up.

"Jesus," I said. I started it, but it was her mother, not mine.

Monroe held the tube out like a laser pointer. "Do you believe in Jesus?" she asked, nodding at me. "Do you believe in God?"

"Um, awkward," I said.

"How about fate?"

"Not really sure."

If Mrs. Alpert wasn't looking like she was about to cry, I would have called her daughter out. My class had talked about fate in English when we read *A Midsummer Night's Dream*, how your life can be predetermined. I'd even heard my mother say at Dorado that all things happen for a reason, which didn't make sense to me unless the reason was that our family really sucked the hairy balls of doom. Now Monroe was on the wrong end of fate. I said the line anyway, just to say something: "My mom says all things happen for a reason."

"See! See!" Mrs. Alpert leaned in and put her beefy hands on her knees. She wears hose, even under her tracksuit. The flesh-colored waistband bunched up just above her blue velour Filas.

"You've told me that what doesn't kill us makes us stronger," Monroe said. "Which is it?"

"That was your father." Mrs. Alpert shot her eyes toward the door like she heard him coming. "I think what's happened to us is a sort of test, and if we get through it"—her eyes quivered—"I mean when we get through it, we will all come out even better."

I must have been nodding along because Monroe turned to me and said, "What are you bobble-heading about, *lambe?*" *Lambe* means kiss-ass in Spanish.

Then she pulled off the cream in sheets, the stuff she had just applied, by forming a circle with her thumb and forefinger and stripping her skin. Almost like scraping, but with her fingers, not her nails. The stuff splattered on the floor, but no one made a move to wipe it up. "We? Us? That's good. Us." What I saw in Monroe's eyes as she looked out the front window was all the shite she'd swallowed so far—hospital windows, doctor's tables, Principal Pornstache's phony smiles, *Why so serious?*, demolitioned bedrooms—and how her mother really hadn't swallowed any of it. Tasted it maybe, but not swallowed.

That was an awkward moment. The kind that makes you sweat.

Bug Man came in and stood with his legs apart in front of the curio cabinet. "*Mumble mumble mumble,*" he said under his Vader visor.

"If we must," Mrs. Alpert said with extra megaphone. "I'll just need to speak to my husband about the budget."

Bug Man turned to Monroe, who had her nails poised over her skin like a cartoon cat, her face cracking along the sides of her mouth, new fissures, deep red, different from the old, which had grown white and flaky. Bug Man focused his mask on her as if to say to Monroe's mom, *How can you stop when your daughter looks like that?* Mrs. Alpert chewed on her bottom lip like it was rubber, as if she knew they couldn't spend more money, but she needed whatever had to be done to be done. To be done. I'd seen that look on my mom a lot when I was little, before she met Dan, before Dorado, before we had health insurance, when she tried to cure my ear infections with vinegar and tube socks filled with warm rice. When we vacated places in the middle of the night so we wouldn't have to pay the last bit of rent. Always left the house spotless, though. Believe it.

Mexican standoff, Dan would say at times like these, so I said it out loud: "Mexican standoff." Everyone faced me. It probably sounded racist. I couldn't tell through his mask if Bug Man was from Mexico.

"What'd you say?" Monroe had lotion dripping down the front of her shirt like candle wax or worse. Porno worse.

"Nothing." I took a sip of bitter air from my empty cup. "Will Monroe be able to go to school?" I asked Mrs. Alpert.

"It didn't sound like nothing," Monroe spat.

Mrs. Alpert turned to me. "What, honey?"

"Harumph harumpph harumpg," Bug Man interrupted.

"Have at it then." Monroe's mom waved her hands toward the back of the house like she was shooing away a flock of pigeons. Then she turned back to me. "The doctor says Monroe should try to go to school if she is able." It felt weird talking about Monroe like she wasn't even there. It wouldn't be the last time.

"I'm not wearing a mask like Michael Jackson. No way. This is as far as I go." She pointed to the feet her Docs once covered.

What would it be like if Monroe wasn't at school? Or worse? What would *I* be like?

Bug Man turned to me, or I thought he did. I couldn't see his face with those goggles and mask, his white hazmat suit covering him from cuffs to ankles. It was like a scene from an old sci-fi movie or the astronaut from old-skool MTV.

"I need to call John to let him know," Mrs. Alpert said, to no one really, and retreated into the kitchen.

"I'm tired." Monroe stood up like she'd heard a phone ring somewhere and went into her parents' bedroom.

Bug Man left too, so there I was: alone, sitting on my shiny chair, with a cup and saucer balanced on my knee. The tea leaves told me: time to motor.

11

Research Note: All action or physiology happens at the cellular level. Each cell in the body is surrounded by a two-layer wall or fence that the cell uses to protect itself from and communicate with the world outside. The two form a dynamic fluid matrix possessing all the characteristics necessary to perform all the necessary functions of cell life. Metals and other poisons like chemicals, mold toxins, and the toxic waste from bacteria and other parasites are fat-soluble. They dissolve in and move through fat. If they gain entrance to the body, they end up in the cell walls. Residing in the fat, they cause some of the fat to change shape. The new fats are too long, have the wrong connections between elements, have a funny shape, or all of the above. The new shapes change the ability of the fats to fit into the anatomy of the cell, which alters their ability to function in the action steps or physiology necessary to sustain cell life. So the action or physiology of the body is slowed down, and illness results. What is inside Monroe's cells, and how will it ever get out? I know my mom is inside Dorado, but I don't know how or when she will get out. I'm sure Dan wants out sometimes. Sometimes it feels like I'm the one moving through fat, you know?

Two brown columns, all cracked up and broken, stood at the end of the street like sentinels. Some dude had tagged the word *Broke* on one column and *Down* on the other. If I got to Agua Fria Street I could follow it back to school, so

I busted out of those two turd piles and walked east toward
the mountains. People in Monroe's neighborhood park their
cars on their gravel yards sideways, like mechanical back-
slashes. The sidewalks were crap, with cracks and bumps
and slabs that collided like plate tectonics exploding into
white sand. Goatheads and tree roots squirmed their way
through the rocks and sidewalks, dying for water. I walked
by a low brown, low-down house with wooden shutters, a
dented mailbox, and a garden full of coffee grounds with
filters bleaching white in the never-ending sun. Did I say
it was hot? My shirt was slick with sweat from lugging my
messenger bag. I couldn't ask Mrs. Alpert for a ride. Did I
say how mixed-up I felt? I passed a house with midget pine
trees in front, like a forest for little people, then an old lady
in a satellite dish of a hat spraying Roundup in the cracks of
her bone-white parking lot she mos def called her garden. I
thought of my own mom downward-dogging it in a stress-
free yoga class or sitting in one about how to superboost
your self-esteem. What words would they use to describe
the world outside El Dorado? *Home* would probably make
her cry. *Real world* would make her think she wasn't alive
or maybe crazy, and I know she never watched the reality
show on MTV. There's this graphic novel that Monroe has
that's a total rip off of *The Matrix* where these stupid people
think they're in a nuthouse, but then—aha!—they realize
they're working for a megaglobal corporation doing market
research on what they call "base human behavior."

   I wonder how often my mom thinks of me. Of us together
before Dan? I guess after Dan too, but before Dan, it was just

me and her on our own. Fending. And now it's me. Sometimes it's me and Monroe.

. A series of painted blocks the size of computer boxes were spread in a yard like art, or so I guessed. When I looked closer at one, I saw that it was constructed completely out of kids' toys—Buzz Lightyear, General Grievous, the freaky scarecrow Spud from *Bob the Builder*—all frozen and spray-painted silver. Another toy cube covered in only gold spray paint was made mostly from the prizes you get in Happy Meals: Emperor's New Groove, Madame whatsherface, Finding Nemo, Shrek, Rescuers Down Under (your mom's pants), some random cars and generic figures. In the middle of this second block was Pikachu, my favorite Pokémon as a kid. Most kids thought obscure Pokémon like Exeggutor were the best, but a true trainer knows that Pikachu is the shiz. I used to have a badass collection of cards and did battle with this kid called Rise on the stoop when we lived in that lady's closet in NYC. This plastic Pikachu in front of my face had been caught between Tigger and some *Clone Wars* figure and turned gold by spray.

"Don't touch that," an ancient dude in a wheelchair barked from the shade of his porch. He was cloaked in shadows, so I didn't see him at first.

"I wasn't gonna," I said, leaning back a bit. He was closer than I thought. Prob spying on me the whole time. Creepy.

" 'Preciate that you weren't *gonna*."

I stepped off the rocks and caught my heel on the edge of a slab of concrete. I waved my hands in the air to catch myself, which I did, but not before looking like a sweaty humpbacked fairy flailing to fly.

"Watch it there, now," he called to me in a finger-wagging voice.

"Got it." *Old man.* One arm got away from me, and I raised my hand like I was in class.

"Got a name?" he called out from the porch.

"Huh? What?" I had to steady myself. My bag weighed more than a Thanksgiving turkey.

"Name," he said. "Were you ever given one?"

Why do all adults need your name whether you're sticking around or not? Are they ALL taking freaking attendance? "Monroe," I lied.

"Like the doctrine?"

"Sure." Brushed off the front of my pants and raked my fingers through my lid.

"Well, Monroe, I'm Mack," his shadow face called. "Want to see the rest of 'em?"

I turned in his direction. Maybe he had three arms or something. "Rest of what?"

"The sculptures you were about to touch."

"Whatever." Wasn't gonna touch shite.

"*Whatever* can mean a lot of things, including some I don't take very kindly to." He rolled himself out into the sun, leading with his bald head. He had gray hair on the sides like sorry homemade earmuffs. The freckles on the dome could have been smashed raisins.

"Don't know anything about that," I said. Rule number one: Admit nothing.

"Don't know anything about what?" he asked and stared at me for a long moment. "Look," he said, pointing to his dead legs. Crumbs lay scattered in his lap like broken glass. "You can always run. I'm not *gonna* chase you. Leave the door open, and I'll give you a clear path." He squinted and cocked his head like a dusty dog.

I knew what the real Monroe would say: *In for a penny, in for a pound.* So I followed him inside.

The dude's house smelled like caveman—dust and something sweet left too long on the stove. Bananas maybe. It was dark in there too. As soon as I entered the premises, I saw that he was full-on obsessed with the toy deal: canvases covered in plastic dogs, Barbies, Chewbaccas, then painted only one shiny color: black, silver, gold, white. There was nothing else in the living room. Not even furniture; hell, the dude lived in his own rolling furniture. His wood floors had bigass dust bunnies so huge they stood more like dust bears. Something from *Star Wars* kept entering my brainage: Han Solo sealed in carbonite by Jabba the Hutt, Han's face frozen in pain while his hands did this pushup kind of thing. I hated that part of the movie. It gave me nightmares. Funny thing was, Old Dead Legs never kept all the *Star Wars* figures in a row or even on the same cube or canvas. He spread them around, which weakened their power, I thought. A whole collection would be worth some bank.

"Where do you get this sh—um, stuff?" I asked, rubbing my chin like I was some professor in a museum.

"Kids give me 'this stuff.' I go to yard sales. You know."

I couldn't help but stare at the chair.

"I can go to yard sales, Mr. Mon-roe. I've got a motor." Pushing a joystick, he rolled forward and then jerked back with a whining noise. "People in the neighborhood leave me bags if they don't sell. On my porch." Sorta shouted that last bit.

"Are these all, um . . . Are all the toys random?"

"What do you mean, 'um random'?" He did a half impersonation on my voice, which people say is monotone, almost robotic. Kids used to tease: Take me to your lead-er.

"You know, where you put 'em? Like this." I pointed at the heart of the silver canvas. "Barbie next to a Bionicle? Really?"

"No, they're not 'um random.' Each one has to fit for the confluence of the piece. You think I just slap on some adhesive and throw them all up there? Do they look *random* to you?"

Yes, I said inside. "No," I said outside.

"Well, then." He motored out of the room we were in, and before we hit what my mom calls a sunroom we passed through an area that wasn't a hallway exactly but too small to be an office. He had a desk and behind it a small shelf with a mess of old books and other crap. Leather covers on the books. Red and black hides, dusty as shite. I thought of Mrs. Alpert saying that dusty books could make Monroe sicker. I had no idea what would happen to Monroe, and the more I tried to guess the future, the worse I felt.

He pulled a one-eighty. "What's holding you up?"

Your mom. "Um, what's that?" I pointed to a bunch of name tags clipped to a string like the tail of Ben Franklin's kite.

"Those? All this art," he said, sweeping his saggy arm across the house, "and you're focusing on those?"

I shrugged stupidly. "I like name tags." So dumb.

"Figures." Shook his head and sighed. "These are all the places I stayed."

"Like hotels?" I drew closer. I love hotels. Towels on the floor.

"Get out of here. Hotels." He waved his head and made that *pfft* sound people use when you say something idiotic. "Do you even know what comes out of your mouth? Not hotels. Funny farms, nuthouses, mental hospitals. Places you know nothing about."

"Right." Admit nothing.

"Now, come on."

Everything pointed to this guy being a creeper, but I knew he wouldn't try to hurt me or grab my McNuggets. I couldn't tell if he'd never hurt someone in his past or took out his own legs, but I wasn't worried about my safety or whatever. Not today anyway. So I shuffled behind him and his wailing wheelchair into the back, where big blocks of frozen memories waited in the white sunlight. Was this happy or sad? Would the real Monroe (*please stand up*) say these were cool and badass and ghetto? Or would these frozen blocks creep her out like thumbnails and bags of hair clipped from dead people? Dead kids = dead memories. I wasn't sure what this all meant, and as I thought of all the humans connected to all these bits of plastic, it got more intense. I saw all these kids and their stuff like the movie *Toy Story*, only scarier. All these kids and all their stuff separated, and then the toys filling some other space and then paralyzed by a cripple. Then someday, when this guy kicked, all the action figures and dolls would be swallowed up in lettuce and coffee grounds and banana peels in the county dump.

"Well, what do you think?" Wheelchair Man asked.

"Huh?"

"What do you think?" He sounded mad.

I think you are a crazy old coot was what I wanted to say. What I really said: "Out of this world." And before I could filter, I asked, "What happened to your legs?" I nodded toward the bunched-up shiny fabric sprinkled with bread dust.

"Really?" His voice sounded rough and hurt at the same time.

"Huh?"

"That's what you want to know." He moved his chair a little to try to look me in the eye, but I kept my bulbs on the joystick. I shrugged. What was I gonna say? Of course I wanted to know. Duh. "After all this, you want to know about how I lost my legs." It sounded more like a statement to me than a question.

My eyebrows rose without my permission. "I guess."

"You guess?"

"I guess."

"You guess, well. Another in a list of topics you know nothing about. I was using. Drugs, you know." He swiveled around to face me again, but I didn't lock eyes.

"Okay."

"Okay? No, not okay." He jiggled the stick so the chair trembled. "This was back in Portland seventeen years ago. Oregon, not Maine. Big difference. I was using with a bunch of folks in the attic of this house that had a slate roof. Know what that is?"

Thought of the unfinished site. "Maybe. Not sure."

"Like shingles, only made of stone. Gray in color."

"Okay."

"Okay?"

"Okay."

"Okay. So we were having a party, and I needed to get outside, get some air, and the folks downstairs weren't exactly in our party, if you can get that. So I opened the window and sat on the sill, looking out over the neighborhood." He ran his fingers down his cheek, and I thought of the real Monroe and her real face. "I wanted to see more, all the way around, three hundred and sixty degrees, so I stepped out and walked the edge of the roof." His face acted like it heard something in the other room, but there was nothing there. I waited. Awk-ward.

Then I couldn't wait: "So what happened?"

"What do you mean, what happened? Aren't you listening? I fell, dammit. Crushed my goddamn spine."

"Sorry."

" 'Whatever'?"

"I guess."

"You guess?"

All those toys on the walls started getting to me. It was like they were music, and someone had turned the volume way louder. I needed to say something. Anything. "Aren't you supposed to tell me to be careful or something like that? Stay off drugs?"

"That's not how people learn, Mr. Monroe." He crossed his arms like a pouty little kid.

Milky, that's how his eyes were, like blue milk. As soon as he pivoted, I was out that door, running back toward school.

12

I finally made it back to school on Agua Fria with crazy cars
honking at me and tagged signs, Stop (*It*), Stop (*War*), Yield (*To
My Power*), Speed Hump (*Me*). Stupid crap like that. When I
reached campus, end of last lunch had just begun. The cafetorium waited empty except for a few kids sitting around trays
piled high with milk containers, burrito wrappers, napkins,
to-go cups, and a few plastic silverware sculptures. Near the
long-ago-bailed-upon concession stand, a student band was
playing "Message in a Bottle." Believe that? I had forgotten
that this was the week Pornstache was "trying out" having
student entertainment during lunch. He'd made this huge deal
at assemblage about how this was just a test (everything at
school's always a test), and if any of the groups used profanity
or crude gestures or incited inappropriate conduct, he'd shut
it all down. Nothing the school did was ever out of fun or
niceness or, as the teachers always say, "The right thing to do."
Everything from the principal or vice came with a warning,
strings attached, assessments, surveys, or a series of things that
had to occur to make this happen or that happen. Stipulations,
I think he called them. Nothing was free or easy or, um, I hate
to say it (makes me think of *The Outsiders*), pure. And what

Pornstache never realized was that the more complicated it got, the less people gave a tit.

But "Message in a Bottle?" Bitch, puh-lease. I was drenched with sweat from all that walking, and that's what greeted me? I bought a microwave burger from the vending machine, nuked it in the nasty hot box. My burger: wet. Me: wet. And these four retro hippie dudes were playing the Worst. Police. Song. Ever. The bass player was a dead ringer for John Lennon, with his greasy curtains of hair and round glasses. The drummer was Hispanic, with lip pubes, and the singer thought he was Billy Idol or something, with bleached hair and sawed-off driving gloves, hopping around like there was an adoring crowd. He didn't look baked, but the act wasn't a goof either. Idol scrunched his face up like a balled dishtowel while Lennon looked blankly at the bulletin board with the monthly menu stained with dots of gravy. The drummer pounded his kit, and I thought how out of hundreds of kids, from the wall huggers to the pale-skinned cutters to these retro hippies to the AP ulcer kids, Monroe was my only friend at this entire school, and how if she got really sick, I'd be on my own, and as she would say, I didn't even know karate.

I met Monroe on the first day of seventh grade. We had about an hour of orientation, and I'd just moved to the district with my mom and Dan. We were on the football field, broken up by elementary-school mascots—Wranglers, Criminals, Sand Devils, Sultans. I was in the "other" category: homeschoolers, transfers, kids from special ed, Montessori, Waldorf, little hippie communes, and last-ditch learning centers. I can't say we would've won any beauty pageants. Have you ever talked to someone who's been homeschooled for seven years? They're like the Amish, only even less deodorant. All the other elementaries had developed their own fashion and style. You could spot the handshakes, chest bumping, jump hugs, air kisses, haircuts, sunglasses, cell phones, movie clips, theme songs. Each group had its own microcosm except for us: Zah zah loozahs! I'd been through this kind of shite before, and I knew you just wait it out, wait until classes start. Then everyone funnels through the same maze, rats follow rats into different compartments. I tried to walk away from the field toward Red Rock so I wouldn't feel so pathetic, and no one from any of the other groups would remember that I was in the tard one. These types of labels stick if you don't watch out—forever. And with a name like Coy, the meatheads don't need any more fuel.

So. "Dig the shoes," someone said behind me. I was wearing this pair of checkered Vans that Dan had given me. I turned. Pre-Monroe, before she was sick. She could have been in a magazine, with her blond hair that flipped up at the ends. Mom said she looked like a punk-rock Mary Tyler Moore or Bettie Page, whoever that is or was. Her black dress had all these white pockets crawling on it, and her black Docs were so polished they gave off mad glare.

Her eyes shot to the ground. "So *Breakfast Club* cool."

"Okay." I wasn't sure it wasn't an insult. "You like eighties stuff?"

"Best decade ever," she said, tapping a finger to her temple. She had drawn elaborate rings on her digits with a

Sharpie. She shot my Vans the eye again. "Maybe *Fast Times at Ridgemont High*."

"Thanks very little," I mumbled to be funny.

"You a Waldork?"

"Nope. Too much knitting."

She scanned me up and down. "Montesorry for you?"

I shoved my hands in my pockets. "Strike two."

"Homo-schooled?"

"Do I look that way?"

She turned to eyeball a bunch of girls in prairie dresses with wheat-colored hair tied back in thick ponytails, playing patty-cake.

"Just moved here too," I said, trying to keep the talk going.

"Son," she said, spitting a bit, "I've lived in this asstown my entire life."

"Why are you over here, then?"

"I was stuck over in that wasteland for seven years, including kindergarten." She jerked her thumb back to a pack of kids across the field, girls with fake tans, oversize glasses, and JUICY written across their buttocks, bobbing their heads and flipping cell phones with one hand. Once every few minutes one would toss her head back and laugh, mouth open like she was trying to catch invisible rain from the sky.

"I finally escaped. Monroe," she said, nodding.

"Coy."

13

"**Is it raining outside?**" Beakman asked me. He was all weird happy 'cause it was research day, so he didn't have to teach. The front of my shirt had a pattern of sweat shaped like a V for *vendetta*. Back was twice as bad, and my hair must have been sticking landing-strip flat to my head.

"Nice one," I said, not wanting to draw any more attention, I grabbed one of the last laptops from the media services cart. It was pretty beat-up. The letter *m* was missing, and the school's name was scratched into every square of inessential metal. As if. Like someone would steal these outdated pieces of fecal. A few kids who were even later got stuck with duct-tape jobbers.

"Please put your laptops on the desks, not your laps, even if you're a lap dawg, yo!" Beakman tried a Weezy growl. Total fail. He seemed stale and sad, obviously trying to be cool like Monroe's science teacher, Mr. Dawson. My laptop had "Lap Dance" written in silver Sharpie on the edge above the screen. This whole school needed a comedy class.

While the laptop booted up, I scanned the other kids, all waiting too. Some were texting inside the pockets of their hoodies; they didn't even have to look, they were so good. This girl named Avree had her iPhone right on top of the keyboard, playing a video with her earbuds on. Little diamond Hello

Kitty earrings under the earbuds, only these pussies flashed sunglasses and a gold tooth.

I wondered what the hell Monroe was doing. We both had cell phones, but didn't use them much. We figured we were some sort of rebels, not bugging in the addictions of our generation. Unplugged. Dan and my mom were pissed for a while when I never answered, and I figured after today's stunt, I'd be forced to turn my phone on again. But I liked having the mobile sleep at the bottom of my messenger bag, especially after seeing Avree watch an episode of what I guessed to be *Gossip Girl* in science class.

Hello Kitty made me think of that old wheelchair dude back at the *Toy Story* graveyard, and my mom at Dorado, sitting by the window, staring off into the rhino-cage gardens with the falcon guy. Once, when we were moving from Connecticut, I asked my mom, "How will they move the windows?" I was stupid young. I understood that a truck would come and my mom would drive and we'd take our stuff, but I didn't get how the windows I saw the world through would get moved. It seemed to be the sanest question to ask at the time.

"Booted up, soldier. Get moving." Beakman's fish hand flopped on my shoulder. Avree's iPhone was gone, but her headphones were not plugged into the laptop, where they were supposed to be. Her rock-star smile washed all over Beakman, like he was front row. She was good.

Research note: Mold spores are hardened containers, which possess all the DNA instructions needed to create new mold creatures or aerial eggs. If they bump into dry walls they just rebound and go back to floating, but

```
when they bump into wet walls, they stick. Out of the
broken open shell a single creature's body appears,
then a groping arm grows from that body, a leathery
hypha, albino and clear, and then from that hypha
grows another, and another, and then many more. These
hyphae are used by molds to obtain nourishment. For
some species it is the sulfur grains in concrete that
are sought, in others it's the metals in paint, or the
glue in wallpaper. All over your house these freshly
appearing mold creatures will plug into the walls via
their hyphae. Sci-fi status in a terrible way.
```

"Coy."

"What the—?" I asked, deeply lost in the hyphae madness.

The Nurselor, in a crazy bright blouse, was standing over my left shoulder. She had serious long hair that ended in what my mom calls feathering. Maybe I always spot ears first, but she had peacock plumes as earrings, the kind with the blue eye-like thingy in the middle.

"Huh?" Did someone die?

"Can you come with me?"

"I'm, uh . . ." I pointed at the computer screen.

"Just save your work."

"You can't save a website, lady," I said, which sounded all smartass but wasn't meant to be.

Avree laughed but then stifled it.

Nurselor reached down and grabbed my bag.

"I'm cool," I said, and stole it back from her. The whole class was staring at me, Avree smiling like this was some big joke and I was taking the fall for her or something. Beakman just raised his eyebrows and pushed his lips together, filling them with air like he was about to play the trumpet. When someone shows up to pull you out of class, it's never good news like you won the lottery or a trip to Cabo with Megan Fox. It has happened to me before. I was in English class last fall, and we were reading *A Midsummer Night's Dream* out loud, or "aloud," as my teacher called it. I was told to go to the office and bring all my stuff. When I asked Ms. J why, she did as Beaker did—just shrugged. She never asked about it or me again, neither. At the office, Dan was standing with his hands all balled up.

"Car accident?"

"Let's go."

It was then he started with all the patting and shoulder squeezing. Mom had had an episode at home. She called Dan, and he raced there, and the place was all torn up like there'd been a robbery during a hurricane. He called 911, an ambulance, and the ER, who got her a place at Dorado.

But here I was, being escorted down the hall by a woman with hippie clothes, light perfume, a whisper voice, and bad shoes.

"How did you know?" I asked the Nurselor, because they don't call home until they process the info. That takes a day. Two, if you get lucky. Everyone knew that.

"Mrs. Alpert phoned."

"She called you?" Shockage, but tried my best to hide it. "Why?"

"She was worried about you, Coy. Said you just disap-peared." Fartknockers. Already had my name. "I know the family very well."

Monroe had gone to a counselor for a while. I never did. After my mom went to Dorado, Dan asked if I wanted to see anyone, and I said "No way," and he said "Cool," and that was pretty much it. I had to act pretty kiss-ass cheery for a while—but that's all it took to keep me away from the f-ing therapist's office.

"I've looked in your file, and I'm surprised you've never come to see me," she said, closing the door behind us. No windows. No air. "To talk."

"My grades are fine." Report cards be truth.

"Not about academics, per se. Do you want some chocolate?" She pointed to a bowl of Peppermint Patties, fetal Snickers, and something called Bliss in a sexytime red wrapper.

"No thanks."

She grabbed the bowl and held it under my chin like a spit bowl. There was weirdness all over my life. "Always makes me feel better."

It seems like it always makes you feel fat, is what I felt like saying. But she wasn't that fat actually, so even in my mind the joke didn't really work.

Looked around, which took like two seconds. The nurse room next door was a lot bigger. "This is really a small office. Are you in trouble with the district or something?"

"You're right, Coy." She had that annoying habit of speaking slowly and sticking in my name whenever possible, like she'd known me forever. "It is small, but it's private, and better than having meetings near bandages and such. I worked at a school where we were forced to hold meetings in the gym or cafeteria. Not much privacy there, right?"

"I bet," I said. Totally unnecessary, and pretty lame.

I swore she looked over at the box of tissues and then at me, trying to connect us. Her cinder-block walls were painted gray, and there were posters made by the same company on each one. Famous people—MLK, Ghandi, someone called Maya Angelou, and one on the door of Albert Einstein. There was one big chair for her, a smaller one for me, a computer, and a big exercise ball. A table stood between us, with those annoying puzzles where you had to wind a nail around another bent nail, or put a 3D pyramid together. That kind of crap. There was even a bowl of condoms right next to the chocolate. So fucoid funny, but I couldn't laugh because I was under investigation.

"So." She squeaked out a smile and placed her hands palm down on her lap.

"So."

Deep yoga breath for her. "Why don't we start with what happened today?"

"Monroe felt sick, so I walked her home." I rubbed my hands on my jeans.

"Why didn't she just call her mother, or come see me?"

I sat up straight. "You'd have to ask her that yourself."

Scooching her chair up, she said, "Coy, this isn't a police interrogation. I'm just trying to help."

"But I'm fine, really." I heard this interview one time with a guy who faked crazy to get out of jail, and he got stuck like forever in a mental hospital. It was in England, and he said it's harder to convince someone you're normal than it is to prove you're a nut job. His advice was not to overdo it. Play it subtle-like. He pronounced the *b* in subtle. It sounded badass the way he said it.

"Don't you think it was somewhat irresponsible of you to leave campus and then Monroe's house without telling anyone?"

"Not really."

"Why not?"

I thought about watching all three of those people going off in three different directions—Monroe, her mom, and Bug Man—and me sitting there with scone crumbs in my lap like some old man in a wheelchair trapping toys in cubes and hanging depressing name tags like tombstones. I made it, didn't I? No one was hurt, and no one was bothered. "I just don't." There was nothing to do but shrug.

We sat there, and I knew she wanted me to tell her about my mom and how I felt and then back to the beginning, start at the beginning with your dad, Coy, and I could see there were actually four boxes of tissues blooming around the cell like dried white flowers and she wanted me to cry but I wouldn't. I held back all that shitake and concentrated on the Maya Angelou poster because it was the one I was facing. *I've learned that people will forget what you said, people will forget what you did, but people will never forget how you made them feel.*

"Well, Mrs. . . . ." I realized I never got her name. Figured.

"Sunday," she said, sitting up straight like me.

"Are you kidding?"

"Not in the least."

I nodded. "Day of the week or ice cream?"

"Day after Saturday."

"That's funny."

"It is?"

"Dan, my um stepdad, has this joke when we like see rude people who litter or spit hairy clams on the sidewalk in front of you, you know. 'Like school on Sunday: no class,' he says. No disrespect. To you, I mean."

"None taken."

Standard awkward time followed, since no one was speaking. Awk-to-the-ward. I turned my head toward the exercise ball, and she said, "Bad back," like she could read my mind. I nodded like I cared. Then there was more silence. I could hear the hum of the computer fan. I couldn't take it anymore.

"Mrs. Sunday, I don't really want to have a heart-to-heart with you."

She blinked her eyes a few times. Very blue. Had those eyes like the cat in *Shrek*—all wet, like she could cry after taking a dump. "If you change your mind, I'm right here. In the meantime, can I loan you a book?"

"Huh?"

"To read. Maybe we could talk about it sometime?"

"Sure," I said, just to get the Einstein Angelou King Jr. out of there.

She reached around and plucked a book from the low shelf and handed it to me. The cover had a big mouth on it, but the lips were all sewed shut. "You know, Coy, everything we discuss here is confidential."

I stood up. "Does that mean you can excuse me from missing class this morning?"

"Sorry. That's admin's deal. Already in the system. Nothing to do with me."

"Thanks very little," I mumbled.

"You are very welcome." She opened the door.

14

This trip to Dorado I kept my eyes open because I had that book Nurselor Sunday gave me, and I told myself I'd power through it because she'd probably bet that I wouldn't. Besides, it would keep her off my case and out of Pornstache's office if I told him I was reading a meaningful book the nice counselor lady loaned me. Thank you baby Jesus.

"Doesn't that make you sick?" Dan still drove like he had his learner's.

"What?" I didn't look up.

"Reading in the car."

"Negative."

"It would make me boot."

"Huh?"

"You know"—he turned quickly to me then back to the road—"hurl, launch, yack, pray to the porcelain god."

"You can just say 'throw up,' you know. It's totally fine."

Dan was already mad at me, though he called it "disappointed," because of my "severe lack of judgment." He said I should have called him at work (as if), but mostly I think he was mad because my mom was so upset, and he had to take the morning off to drive me to see her. Wasn't any picnic for me spending my first day of spring break going to Dorado to get lectured. But the good news was that Dan was already over it by the time we were in the car, and he was more like me—ready to duck and dodge when we faced the music.

The book was about a boy named William who refused to talk at school because he went to a lame-ass place where kids gave him "atomic" wedgies and put rotten fruit in his locker. I knew after the opening pages that she gave this book to all the lost souls who weren't crying in her office after the first fifteen minutes. I could just smell it.

Dan and I passed by the stages-of-decay construction site, the crane still frozen, paused in midair over the middle section like a claw. I guessed no one needed the crane, or maybe it cost more to move than just leave. Or maybe the whole town was broke. Dan says that kind of shiz all the time. William decided to make a fort in these prickers behind school to hide in at lunch or anytime during his free periods, which they call "flexes" in the novel. He steals over there and writes stories in a notebook about a boy named Mailliw (so cheesy, or should I say os yseehc) who has tons of friends and scores winning goals in soccer games. Weird for me to read a book about a kid writing a book about a kid. Next I'll write a book about a kid writing a book about another kid. It'll be in 3D and make you boot if you read it in the car.

My mom was polishing the edge of the registration desk with her palm when we got there. We could see her through the glass doors, wrapping her arms around herself when she spotted us. Dan was a dog and held the door for me so I had to walk in first. Mom chewed the inside of her cheek, and some guy with a cookie duster on his lip, dressed in matching Dorado yellow sweats, was standing a few feet behind her.

"Hi." I was going to ask her how she got around the rules. Inmates weren't supposed to linger in the reception area.

"I've been waiting." Her smile could have squeezed juice from meat.

"We got here as quick as we could," Dan said, jingling the keys in his hand, all nervous like.

"Isn't it against—," I started, but she cut me off.

"What the hell is going on at home?" she asked. We both took it like she was nailing us individually. We should have hatched a plan and got our stories straight. Idiots. All that time in the car: wasted.

"Listen—," Dan said.

"It's not—," I said.

We looked at each other almost—I hate to admit this—like brothers. Both in deep trouble.

Mom patted her lid and spoke quickly. "Did you notice my hair?"

Dan scrunched his face. "What?"

"Look." She shook it like some shampoo commercial, and I could see what she meant. She hadn't gotten it cut. Thin strands of color, fine as thread, shone, but you really couldn't tell unless you looked closely and the light was right up on them.

"Martha did it. You should see. She has this magnifying glass she clips over her eyes and takes these surgical tools and ties each piece of silk."

The guy with the 'stache stepped toward us, which got my mom back on track.

"Oh shit." She led us into the usual room. I saw the girl with the pencil pigtails by the fish tank. "Why did you do it, Coy? I told you I didn't want this to happen."

"Nothing is happening, Joan." Dan sat down slow and easy. "He cut a few classes. Not a war crime here."

"I want to hear from him. Please."

He held his hands out. "Just saying—trying to calm us all down before—"

"I think I have a right to know what my son—"

Dan leaned back. "Our son."

"You know what I mean. You're not the one sitting here almost fifty miles away, stressors going off, when you're supposed to be getting well, resting."

"I hear what you're saying, but—"

"If you heard me, then you'd just. Stop. Talking."

While they fought, I flashed back to that crane, climbed it, crawled up the metal crosshatches, got to the top, and saw a grid of the construction site and then zoomed out and saw the whole city: greenbelt near the river, Red Rock range, brown stretches of development, and all those unfinished homes. The blocks of houses morphed into Wheelchair Man's blocks of gold and silver and black. I searched for Monroe's house, but I couldn't find it. She's buried somewhere, I thought, she's stuck and I can't—

Dan swiped his jumble of keys from the table. "I'm out of here. I'll be back when I can breathe freely." I understood he was pissed, but the breathe comment was a little nancy.

He marched by reception and shot out the doors. The woman behind the desk barely glanced up from her screen.

"Who's that guy?" I pointed to Mustache Man standing near the column.

"Quinn is one of the counselors here. He's been worried since I found out about you running away. It's nice to have people who care."

"I didn't run away. I'm right here. Hello." I waved like a true spaz.

"Leave school, then. How's that? Since I heard about you leaving school unattended, I've been a little upset." She turned on her pinched face.

"That why you got your hair done?"

"What?" She ran her shaky hand through her silky strands. "I thought you liked it."

"I do."

"Did I tell you they're silk? Don't they look like silk?"

I tried not to cross my eyes. "I don't really know what silk looks like."

Mustache guy coughed, and we both looked at him. He waved us off. Real cough, not a secret Dorado signal.

"I need to tell you something," she said.

"No, you don't."

"I really do."

"No Ringo Starr. Please?"

"No Ringo Starr, though there's nothing wrong with a little—"

"Help from my friends? Jesus." I turned away and saw Pigtail Girl tap on the tank's glass two times.

"I was going to say, inspiration from an otherwise banal source." She glanced up to the ceiling and clicked her tongue. "When your father died, it took all I had to prop myself up, hold you straight, find a place to live, get jobs, register you at schools, and then find Dan. A decent guy, right?"

Nodded. Sure.

"Once I did all that, all that propping, I finally exhaled, and it felt like all the air flew out of me until I was paper-thin, two-dimensional, empty. Is any of this making sense?"

Paper dolls. "Sure. No. Whatever."

"And I'm not angry. I was, about your dad, about what I, we, had to deal with. But I'm not angry anymore." She shot an over-the-shoulder eyeball at Quinn. "But when I found out that you'd wandered those streets all alone and not one person on earth knew where you were and you never took that personal safety course, I—"

"That was for girls. The brochure was pink."

"Well—" When she breathed in like she was empty, I knew she would cry. And hard. I reached my hand over to hers, but it was too late. Hers were already jammed up under her neck like she was trying to keep her jaw from falling off, and I think I said I was sorry but the sun was shining off her wet cheeks and caught the colored silks in her hair, and for a second I thought we were back in Connecticut at the little carriage house on a day right before I started kindergarten. A picnic with a blanket and honey ham sandwiches and lemon-ade and fruit all on a big flat gray rock near the Long Island Sound. The tablecloth had a strawberry pattern and Mom's lips were full in the middle, but when she smiled, they got thin on the ends. I threw crumbs of bread to one ADHD seagull who dipped down to catch 'em. The sun was warm, and so was the rock. The air was cool.

"I need to call Dan. Is that all right, sweetie?" She patted *my* hand now. "Really need to connect."

"Sure. Whatever." What was one more freakfest?

Wrapped around her right ring finger was one of the silk strands, a red one, like a super-thin licorice ring. She'd yanked it out.

Quinn the bodyguard led her into the door behind reception, and I looked over to the fish tank. A few inmates sat on the low couches, talking, leaning in. A man was crying and blowing his nose like a horn, another was ripping tissues out of the box like he was shucking corn. The pigtailed girl had moved to the sliding door by the rhino cage, but she didn't step outside. I so wished Monroe was with me, cracking jokes or playing four-way speed—a card game we used to rock before her hands got all messed and cracking. I was pretty good at it. I could see a few hands at a time in my mind. Sunday's book was in Dan's car, and he was probably on some side road listening to Hank Williams cranked way up. That was the mad/sad music he played, songs about lonesome whippoorwills, howling trains, and ex-wives and girlfriends.

Monroe said country music was a contradiction in terms, but I liked it. Old Hank sounded like he knew what he was talking about, hard times and pain. Hungover, too, prob. Dan caught me singing along one day when I thought he was in his man cave and recommended I check out more of Hank, only one or two by his son Hank Jr., and his grandson

Hank 3, who Dan said played both classic country and death
metal, which sounded megaweird to me. Told him will do,
even though listening to Hank the First was close enough to
social suicide for me.

The thing with my mom is that if she's not back in five minutes, she'll be at least an hour. Always been that way: shopping,
errands, phone calls. Bathroom even. I was stuck there for a
while with no book or PSP or TV. I shrugged even though
no one was there to see me do it, my nerdy habit. I got up and
walked over toward the fish tank but swung wide, so I could get
into Pigtail Girl's line of sight. I made a deal with myself: if she
looks over, I go over. I walked slowly, trying to curve out as much
as I could while seeming to be headed for the tank. At first, I
moved my arms back and forth like I was moving faster than I
was, but that seemed super ghey and robotic, so I dropped them
to my sides. Just as I was about to hit the roadblock of couches
where I'd be forced to make a choice to go left to the tank or
right to the cage door, she turned and saw me. I stopped. She
didn't look away. What she did was come right over.

Up close, her glasses made her eyes look smaller. "Noob?"
she asked.

"Huh?".

She rolled her eyes. "New patient?"

It was then I realized that I'd been covering my name tag
with my arm. "No, no. Visitor." I stupidly tilted the square of
plastic up toward her face.

"Oh," she said, slightly disappointed, and looked outside
toward the rock garden. The one with the waterfall. Her hair

was a slightly darker shade of blond at her scalp than it was
sliding down her pigtails. "Nice rides."

"What?"

"Your shoes. How old?"

"I don't know. I got them a year ago. Maybe two?"

She wore slip-on sandals the color of toast. Her hands
moved from her sides up to her waist, then to the ends of
the pigtails, where she gave a few tugs. Almost in a repeating pattern.

"I meant you, not your rides. I'm sweet." She paused.
"Sixteen, can't you tell?" She smiled in a forced jokey way.
Her teeth were very straight and very white. So was her skin.
White, I mean. No zits or freckles. Small ears. "Careful,"
she said. "POS approaching." She moved her eyes toward a
counselor who was about to walk past.

When he was safely down the corridor, I asked,
"Piece of Shit?"

"Parent Over Shoulder. Where do you go?"

I guessed she meant school. "Red Rock Junior."

"That place is an epic fail, right?" Her hands hooked on
the waistband of her sweatpants.

I had no idea how to answer that. "Sure. I guess."

"Anyways, my BF went there and pretty much got busted
every day. He bailed. Yolo, right?"

"Right." I started feeling sick to my stomach talking to this
girl. I had no idea where she was coming from. She looked
totally normal, but obviously something was wrong, and it
felt like whatever she had was infecting me. So much that I

couldn't understand anything she was saying. Almost like she was speaking in code.

"He p-owned that school. People said he was creepin' around, you know, but they were all a bunch of tards." The same counselor came out of the hall, and she tracked him as he headed toward reception. "You're not a tard, are you?"

"What?"

"JK. I need to have some fun around here, K?"

I made a noise that sounded like those clicks African tribe members make.

"What do you do for fun?"

I thought about it for a second before I told her the truth: "I have absolutely no idea."

"Wouldn't it be fierce if we could photobomb all the security cameras? Straight and tight, right?"

Over her shoulder, the counselor moved to approach us, but I didn't want to tell her. I felt exhausted and something else. As I watched him get closer, I could see that the holes where her earrings once were had started to crust over, little flecks of red and brown closing in the circles.

"Ready to go?" the counselor asked her.

"I'm five by five," she said, and left me standing there, wondering what the hell had just happened.

In a daze, I wandered back to reception. The receptionist hadn't really moved since we'd arrived. I think she was Chinese. Not a hair was out of place, and her skin was as chalky as powder. Maybe it was powder. Or porcelain.

"There's a guy here, I can't remember his name," I said, leaning on the desk, feeling sucky. "Lindbergh. Lindy. I don't know his last. Guy's got a falcon. A hawk, I mean. There can't be many of those, right?" I threw her a weak smile, but her face didn't budge. She wore black hipster glasses. I think they call them cat's-eye. "Can you call down to him or something?"

Still stared.

"My mom is—"

"I know who your mother is," she said, stone cold.

"My mom's in a meeting, so she'll be a while. He told me to call him."

"I'll see if he's available." Inmates don't have phones in their rooms, so I knew she was pinging whoever was in charge of his cell or block or whatever. They don't even pump Muzak at Dorado. So quiet. Time drips by in globules.

"He'll be up in a minute."

"That's awesome, thanks a lot." I stepped away, but remembered. "Oh, and can you tell my mom I'm with him and I'll be back? If you don't mind, I mean."

Matrix nod.

I started heading back to the table where I was before, but Chinese Trinity said "You can wait right here" like she meant it.

"I was just over there, like a minute ago." I pointed. "I know the rules, I won't go—"

"He will just be a minute. Please have a seat." She smiled like she was squeezing enamel juice from her teeth.

That's the thing about adults behind desks. Pornstache, recepticons at school, data processfools, even some teachers like Mr. Lord last year—adults behind desks get fat (though this one was thin as a mechanical pencil) and hardened. It's like they've all become cops. I'm a harmless-looking guy. Some mean kids would say I'm weak looking. I'd been to Dorado a lot, and she knew me, she knew Dan and my mom, had probably read her file, and she had to be all hardass like that. I wanted to say something smart or mean. At least she could get up from behind the desk and talk to people. I was mad enough to break something, but instead my eyes started pissing a little like a total puss. That only made me madder. I called her some nasty things under my breath. She didn't even look at me, and my knees were shaking. Fool, I thought. Baby. Orphan.

"Hey, Buster Brown. How's it going?" Lindy man said.

"Okay."

He had his hand on my neck (in a nice way) and called to Trinity, "I'm gonna take this roughneck out back, okay?"

"Sure thing, Mr. . . ."

"I got him, won't let him out of my sight." He shook my neck a little. "Thanks, Daisy."

"Daisy? Her name is Daisy?" I asked when we were out of Matrix range.

"Yessir. Why? Have a thing against flowers?"

"No, um, I mean, she doesn't really act like a Daisy." He was a fast walker. I wondered if he'd practiced in malls.

"What name would you give her?"

"Death Star."

He laughed a little. "Come on. She's not that bad. She's just doing her job. You got to get to know folks sometimes before they warm up."

He waved at the people still sobbing by the fish tank and another counselor watching the door. Lindy was the kind of guy everyone seemed to like seeing. No sight of the code-talking girl.

"They added a parrot fish, you know." Then: "Everything okay with your mom?"

"Yup."

"So why are you all riled up?"

"Nothing."

"Doesn't look like nothing to me, but if you don't feel like gabbing, that's fine."

"Gabbing?"

"Chewing the fat. Kibbutzing. Spilling the beans. Talking. You know."

"Oh."

"Did you tell your mom you were visiting me?"

"I left word with Death Star."

He coughed out a laugh. "Daisy."

"Whatev. She's, my mom's, you know, on the phone with my stepdad. It's a long story."

"Family stories usually are."

We walked into a white hall with rows of wood doors with simple black numbers painted on them. I'd only been back this far when my mom first got to Dorado. I needed to see where she'd be sleeping, since we'd slept together most of my life. The rooms were pretty boring—you were only allowed one "personal item" or something, not a lot of stuff from home. My mom had wanted to pimp her crib with pillows and posters of Chet Baker and glass jars with smelly crap that gives me dain bramage. Dorado said no, all distractions to why they were here. So my mom chose a picture of me and her and Dan at a pumpkin festival north of town. The photo's pretty orange—pumpkins and hay and afternoon light, and I have an orange shirt on to be a smartass, but no one took it that way and you can't explain irony to sticky little kids and hicks and toothless hoboes running the tilt-a-whirl.

"Just heading out here." In front of us was a metal door leading outside.

I stopped, which made a squeaky stepped-on-a-mouse sound on the linoleum. "Can I see your room?"

"Why? Nothing much there."

"Just to see where you live."

"We're not really supposed to." I could tell by his face he wasn't saying no.

"I'll be quick."

He spun on his heels. "I've had both knees replaced," he said, grinning. I followed him down a side hall, which was exactly like the main hall, bulletin boards and bathrooms in exactly the same places. His room was in the middle, 1704, even though I knew there weren't 1700 rooms there. Sometimes they do that, hotels and apartments, maybe trying to make it feel bigger or they like to confuse you, or maybe they have cameras watching you get lost like an idiot and guys like Quinn with Chinese Trinity on his lap sit up there eating takeout burgers, crumbs on their pants, laughing at the fools getting turned around like rats.

"Here it is," he said, opening the door. No locks. "It's nothing special."

His bed was made perfectly like it was just born—tight yellow blanket (no wrinkles), a pillow like a baby cloud. Monroe
would have sang: *so an-al it's pain-ful.* The linoleum floors
were almost shining. His one personal item wasn't hard to
see: large model airplane—not plastic though: wood painted
silver, "Spirit of St. Louis" in script on the side.

"Badass."

"I hope that means you like it."

"So badass. Can I hold it?"

"Sure."

I wove the model plane through the air, but I didn't make
any engine sounds, thank god. "It's so light."

"Sure it is, it's made from balsa wood. I had to hand sand
the whole thing from the fuselage here to the wings and
the tail." He ran his fingers over it like he was blind. "No
decals, no kits."

"Don't you wish it could fly?"

I could tell by his breath and then his face that he was
really thinking about my question. "A lot I could say about
that. I owned a Cessna once—a 1962 one eighty-two, red and
white. Beautiful thing. I flew a radio-controlled plane for my
classes back when I taught fifth grade. I've lost all that. So
the honest truth is, yes, I wish it could fly, sure."

Something cracked when he closed his eyes, so he took off
his specs, which I noticed looked like the glasses pilots wore
in movies. He rubbed the lenses with a tissue plucked from a
perfectly arranged box.

"We should make like a tree."

"And leave," I said. I had to.

He tilted his head, pleased. "Know that one?"

"Corny science teacher."

"I feel your pain."

He put his plane back at exactly the same angle and brushed the dust from the table with the side of his palm. Then he pulled at the next tissue so it looked like it was blooming out of the box.

"I never used to live like this. There were piles of papers all over my desk, projects, lots of electronics, a regular Messy Marvin you could've called me, but here you have so much time, and I guess having a neat room is nice to come back to, right?"

"Ever worry about someone taking it?"

"The *Spirit*?" He looked at me like I belonged at Dorado. "Now, how many people would want an old man's model airplane? Especially here."

"Lots of people." I felt a smile rise on my face. He thought I was being nice, but that was only the half of it. A quarter maybe.

15

This heavy metal door opened up on a back patio that had some chairs and loungey things and a mesh cover for shade. Vines grew up wooden posts. A field led to a row of trees.

"Greenbelt. Big Sandy River's just over there." He pointed away from Dorado.

I had no idea. "My mom never told me about all this."

"A lot of folks don't like coming out here. Too much space. Some aren't allowed. I should say 'not encouraged.' My mistake." He wiped his brow with the back of his hand. "Some overheat." He laughed.

He led me to the end of the portal to this cage-like thingy. Even though we were in some shade, it was still hot as frap. Hanging next to the cage was a glove, long and thick as Hellboy's stone arm, and Lindy slipped it on. "You need to step back a bit and be still. He's still—"

"Young?"

"Getting used to humans." He reached into the cage, and the hawk climbed out onto his arm. It flapped its wings a bit and then settled. I couldn't really hear what Lindy was saying as he slipped a leather hood over the bird's head. He whispered into the thing's ear. Do birds have ears? They must, right?

We walked out into the field about halfway to the green-belt. I could hear the tiny bells attached to the bird. Inmates could easily escape across the grassy field to the cover of the trees. They didn't wear bells.

"Be still," he said to either one of us. I froze. He slipped off the little crown of leather, and the bird bristled. It looked around all back and forth, like it was being followed. Then Lindy held his arm high in the air, and the bird flew off, circling the bosque.

I have to admit even now it was all pretty awesome. The hawk circled and circled and then swooped down like it was falling, hurt maybe, but it wasn't. Then it grabbed something off the ground. The object was small, so I figured: mouse. Digging in with its talons, the hawk took a pointed bite and pulled the meat out in short red strings.

"Any of this rubbing off on you?" Lindy asked. His leather arm was in the air, and he was slapping it. He kept moving his gaze from me to the hawk, which was now back in the air, trying to catch the breeze coming off the river.

I asked him what he meant. The bird was super fast once it got high enough to soar.

"Are you interested in any of this?"

"Sure, why not?" I shrugged. The outstretched wings tried to catch all that air. "Pretty cool."

"Because you seem distracted." He let out a low, sharp whistle.

I dug my hands in my pockets. "I'm always like this, I guess."

"And how's that working for you?" He whistled again.

"What do you mean?"

"The way you are—like you just said."

"I guess I never thought about it." I turned a dirt clod over with my foot. Nothing underneath.

The bird then opened its wings in flight to slow down and landed on Lindy's arm with a whoosh. He slipped something small into its beak.

"I never really thought you had a choice," I said, wanting desperately to pet the bird lightly on its head. I also wanted to keep my finger, so that's why I didn't do it. "Who you were."

"Me too. Forever I thought that." He slipped the hood back on. "But now I see different."

I rolled my eyes. "We're proud of you." Another adult being weird.

"Look at me. I never thought I'd be standing outside with you—a good kid—hawk on my arm, outside in a bosque in Arizona." He slipped something into his pocket, then checked the area for who knows what. "Once I was a manager of a regional airport, had a plane, quart-a-night guy, flew to Reno just to gamble for the night. Then I'd fly back broke and loaded. I drove a Corvair and had a wife. Almost had two. I still have a son, officially anyway." The bird started getting pissed, ruffling its feathers, flapping its wings, moving its legs. "Hold on. Easy now. So what I'm saying is, you're old enough to see that even though your mom's in here and your dad is—"

"Dead."

"He is? Okay, okay. Sorry. I wasn't aware." He looked at the ground, all guilty, but then had to look back up because the bird was really freaking out. "Easy now. Okay. Your dad has passed. Hold on. Settle down now. He doesn't usually.

Jesus." His face lost all calm. "His eyes might be dried out. Does it feel dry to you today?"

I had no idea.

He slipped the ropy tether thing onto the bird, and right after he did, the falcon flapped and took off, flying right at me. Wings, crazy big and dark, passed right before my eyes like a veil or a cloud. I ducked, but its talon caught me on the side of the face, slashing me next to my right eye. I touched the wound, and my hand came away bloody.

"Wait a sec." Lindy didn't know what to do: a bleeding boy and a spastic bird. "Okay, hold on."

Research Note: A bird and falconer, both properly trained, can enjoy a hunting relationship for many years.

"Hey!" he yelled.

I left him there in the middle of the field struggling with the hawk, walked over the patio, and passed through the hallway with the wood doors and plain black numbers. In order not to cry, I pretended I was a wounded spy, slinking around corners not being seen by the cameras the pigtailed girl wanted to photobomb, and then I heard a *whap whap whap* like the hawk's wings and I acted like a falcon was after me, ready to tear the hair from my scalp, rip the flesh from my face in strips, feast on my brains. I actually ducked. More than once. I do that sometimes. Used to pretend that some serial killer like Gary Ridgway was breaking into my house, and I had to lie perfectly still and he'd go away. That's how I got to sleep—pretending to be dead in my bed. It was weird but it worked. Almost cozy. I still do it sometimes if I can't sleep. The trick doesn't work as well now as it did when I was little.

Dan and my mom were at their table, hands in hands. I just let the blood run.

"Did you have fun with Mr. Lindbergh?" my mom asked. "Oh my god."

Dan stood up. I could actually see him processing the sight of me on the whiteboard of his brain. Then he ran off in the direction of Daisy Death Star.

"What happened?"

"Hawk."

"God." She stood up and then pulled me close to her. "A hawk did this?" I could hear the panic and confusion in her voice.

I pushed her away. "Don't. You'll get blood on your—"

"It's okay." She grabbed my hands in hers and pulled me back. "I'm your mother."

As she was hugging me, I felt the heat fire up in my brain. "How well do you know Lindy?"

"Mr. Lindbergh?" She turned in the direction of reception. Easy to tell that she was trying to be calm. "A little. We've become casual friends. Could you sit down?"

I didn't sit. "But you don't *know* know him."

"I don't understand what you mean." Behind her, Dan was fast walking with a young guy with a shaved head dressed in a white shirt and red tie. In his hands the man carried a blue box with a handle, a red cross painted on the side.

"I mean, you don't know why he's here, right? He could have killed his wife drunk driving or accidentally—"

"Coy, your face. Please."

"—and left her dangling on the wheel while he crawled out on the median and puked. I mean booted," I said, turning to Dan, who looked very confused by my insult. The guy slipped on white plastic gloves and tried talking to me, but I ignored him.

"Did he say that to you?" my mom asked.

"It doesn't matter. You still don't know him." I felt something cold on my temple, and then, all of a sudden, I started crying. The fact that they couldn't see how goddamn hypocritical they were being made it worse.

"Sit, please."

"You sit," I said, which was stupid, but I didn't care. "I've got the most messed-up parents in the whole world." Lindy burst through the door by the fish tank and did this stiff-legged run right up to us.

"I love you," my mom said.

"I am so sorry," Lindy said, rubbing my head. I pulled away. "He's still new," he said. He meant the bird, but it sounded like he meant me.

"Every mother loves her son." I knew saying that would hurt her bad, and while my mom and Lindy were talking and Dan was conferring with the guy, I thought about running away but I was in the middle of nowhere—the bastard bosque—no bus nearby, hailing a cab from Chinese Trinity Matrix would be impossible. I had no money, and honestly the only place I could think to go was back in time, and there are no buses for that. And it was stupid to be that sci-fi nerdass.

So I just stood there as Tie Guy Gorilla-Glued my wound and then spread a bandage over it.

"Isn't that great, no stitches?" Dan asked, far too excited. "Wow. Amazing technology. When did they invent that again?" he asked Tie Guy.

"Take me home," I interrupted.

"Don't you . . . ," my mom said, she and Lindy standing there like the concerned parents, and Dan the older brother who had the car for the night asking his buddy about a new type of carburetor.

"Can we go, please?"

"He's probably had enough excitement for one day," Lindy said, crossing his arms.

"Coy." For a woman who cared so much about stains at home, she was remarkably chill about the blood splatter on her shirt.

"Do you need to keep saying my name?"

"I guess I do."

"Well, it's embarrassing." She pulled me to her again. I stood stiff as a post.

"Let go," I said to her. "Let's go," I said to Dan. Then I walked out.

Research Note: In the first few weeks, the falconer remains with the falcon all the time to establish as close a relationship as possible with the bird. The bird is restrained by tethers around its ankles. During the day the bird perches on the falconer's leather sleeve while the falconer holds the tethers, and is always kept near the lure—a bundle of feathers. By night, the tethers

are attached by a shorter cord to a swivel on a small
mushroom-shaped wooden perch on a stake in the sand.
This allows the falcon a certain freedom of movement,
while ensuring that it cannot escape. The falconer names
the bird and constantly calls to it so that it comes to
recognize his voice from great distances.

16

I could see her before I even passed through the metal detectors, a single line of bleach against the dirt-brown wall: Monroe, away from others, her white hood up, sleeves swallowing her hands, shoes made from some type of canvas. *She should have had a bowl in her hand begging* was a dick thing to think, but I did, so I pushed it out of my mind. I almost fell on some noob's backpack because I couldn't take my eyes off her. I hadn't seen her at all during the week we had break. I'd almost forgotten what she looked like now.

"All made of hemp. We can smoke it when I'm done," she said, like she'd rehearsed too much, but I could hear the exhaustion in her breath. She was weak.

"I'll have Dan build us a really big pipe." I made a point to grin. I felt so happy/sad to see her. It was hard for me not to get pissed at all the faux bangers, minivan gangsters, sluts and nerds and anime animals for staring like it was Halloween, but imagine you're in junior high or middle school and someone is draped in bone white with her hood up like she's a junior KKK member. If I didn't know Monroe, or if it wasn't Monroe, I'm sure I would have made jokes with Monroe—*Who's the ghost? Where's the lynching?* Prob. Thinking all these mean things doesn't make me feel like a hero in Choose Your Own Adventure, I'll tell you that.

The hall was thick with rolling backpacks and kids heavy with bags like turtles grown in an REI store, kids slipping cell phones into tight pockets and tucking earbuds into hoodies before entering noisy classrooms. Monroe was telling me that her parents were now building her a guesthouse.

"A bubble?" I asked.

"No, buttlick, a guesthouse made from all organic materials and health-oriented products and stuff. Central HEPA air filter system, mildew-resistant shower curtains, soy-based paints. JFGI."

"It sounds like your own El Dorado," I said, bracing for a dead-arm, but Monroe was already down the hall, and maybe it was the shitty fluorescent lights on all those bodies dressed in blacks and browns, but she seemed to be floating away, a flickering light about to go out or one of those lines at the eye doctor's that gets fuzzy and then disappears. I could feel my heart beatboxing my chest, so I ran through the crowd getting raked by water bottles in mesh pockets, pointy elbows, and sharp binder edges, but with her hood up, Monroe hadn't noticed me missing. She was still at it: "big-screen TV, anti-dust of course . . ."

"Lucky stiffy," I said, even though there was nothing fortunate about it.

We talked our way right through homeroom about my meeting with the Nurselor—"emo"; book she gave me—"yawn"; Wheelchair Man—"creepy cool"; and Lindy—"awks." I didn't mention Pigtail Girl or the way she made me feel.

"See, told you we wouldn't get in trouble. *We outlaws,*" she half-sang and then finished the lyric about busting out of I-don't-know-what. I recognized the song.

"Tupac? Thought you were done with him like forever ago." We were each allowed a few digressions outside the eighties. Hers had been Tupac for a while; mine was secretly Hank Williams, but I told her it was the Beatles.

"I started listening again, cracker. Not so bad for our white asses."

"Okay, guess I forgot you were an OG." After our brief stints as runaways and the shite-storm aftermath, I was happy to be back with Monroe in a place that had a schedule to it. As much as we said we're rebels and stuff, I got kinda freaked out when the future was so unwritten. Even in the cheesy book Sunday gave me, I knew what was gonna happen. William had just met this hip new teacher named Davis who would pull him out of his thorn bush and help him become captain of the debate team or something equally nerdy. The plot was not hard to spot but also didn't ring true, an adult doing so much to save a wimpy kid. Everyone knows teachers (and most adults) are too busy and tired for liquidy crap like that.

17

Monroe and I had only one class together, our elective: Colonial Studies. It pretty much sucked. While other kids got digital photo, creative writing, hip-hop history, or the art of the graphic novel, we got the closest thing to a real class with real work. Monroe said it was a conspiracy, but I think electives have to do with your other classes. Schedules and all. Or something. Ms. Liebner was all mascary, with ash-colored eye shadow under her painted-on brows. She never learned anyone's names—we were "people" collectively and "sir" or "miss" individually. She loved the overhead projector, drawings of Jamestown, bulwarks, and where some guy with a broom beard found a seventeenth-century pistol. Colonial Studies. As an elective. Every day I went into that old Home Ick classroom, I felt like dying. Monroe did too. And we had to present our "findings" at the end of the year at a presentation where you dressed up like colonial settlers, you know, like those old-timey photos idiot families and tard love couples sign up for at the Red Rock mall.

"People," Ms. Leapyear started, "today we're going to approach this unit on clothing and textiles in a more hands-on learning style, okay?" That's the other thing she did: ask if things were okay with us even though we had no say in anything. Ever. Jimmy MacConnell said "No, Mrs. Leapyear" in the beginning of the semester and Leapyear leaped all over his pimply case. All that phony veneer cracked, and out came a spitting succubus from hell's anus—actually grabbed him and pulled him into the hallway and marshaled his sorry self to the Pornstache bunker, all for sowing discord. Monroe said Jimmy could probably sue, but damn, that class was silent as church when she returned.

"Before we get to that, I want to go over the objectives and outcomes of this unit." Everything Leapyear did could be found in our workbook—some handouts still in that blue from when they ran it off on a machine with a drum or something, type as smeared as her lips and brows at the end of the day. Believe it.

"Outcome on your face," Monroe whispered from inside her fabric cave. She was trying really hard not to act sick, but I knew better.

I laughed. I had to. "You're lucky you have joke insurance."

"True," she said. "Told that one maybe twelve times this year already, and I'm not done yet."

"Agreed."

"To investigate the . . . ," Leapyear continued.

"To instigate the . . . ," I said, which was lame.

"To inseminate the . . ." Monroe beat me.

"Will you please be quiet? I'm trying to learn over here," Elizabeth Buchanan said. She had long blond hair like she'd just left a salon, always with a plaid bow of some color—her trademark—pinned in it. She carried a wicker lunchbox with a plaid handle. Her résumé: student council president, Model

UN, Speech and Debate. She always made announcements at assemblage for Pornstache or other teachers: *Keep the cafetorium clean! Bake sale for Darfur! Clothes drive for Liberia! Halloween carnival will be awesomely awesome!* She was easy on the eyes, as Dan would say, but Monroe hated every cell of her original settler organism. Roe leaned across me, her hood covering my face like a veil. I could smell some kind of grassy lotion. She asked, "What exactly are you learning, lezbo?"

Elizabeth flipped her hair but looked in the opposite direction. That takes coordination. "It's pretty obvious, isn't it?"

"That's the thing, Lezzie, it's too obvious. All in the book." Monroe tapped the text with her finger. "Besides, why do you need to know how to repair a Monmouth cap?"

"Because it's interesting."

"Interesting how?"

"How our forefathers—"

"Foreskins," I said, but no one laughed.

"Look outside," Monroe said, all drama and trauma, but the shades were drawn. "Do you see any settlements out there? Any forts? Monuments? We don't live anywhere near all the thirteen colonies. Our state was a part of freaking Spain then. *Puta, por favor.*"

"Well, I believe it's an interesting aspect of our education." Elizabeth's face did this little jerk thing, like a bad dance move.

"It's trivia, like the biggest erect penis on record measures thirteen inches. The smallest is one and three-quarter inches." Monroe looked right at me.

"Don't," I said, pretty embarrassed being the only member there with a member.

"Don't be a lesbro," she snapped at me.

"Lesbro?" Elizabeth asked.

"It's a dude who is a close friend with lesbians," I told her.

"I'm going to tell Ms. Liebner."

"You go ahead, Tree." Monroe was getting pissed. The term came from the evolution of *popular* to *poplar* to *Tree*. It was our way of insulting the in-crowd without them knowing. "Alert the mother ship. All I need to say is the student council prez is making fun of the leper and the orphan."

"Stop doing that," I said. Hated that. So hated that.

"Silence, lesbro."

I remember what I was thinking at that exact moment: how Monroe was my best friend and all, and she had the worst deal in the school, hands down. But I couldn't help wondering if all the anger she kept inside was making her even sicker. All that stress was flaring her illness, speeding up whatever was doing all that harm.

Elizabeth stuck her chin in the air like she was saying *Hmmph!* or *Well!* But she knew better than to go there. Leapyear got started on a presentation about the material and how colonial settlers grew flax to turn into linen. It was pretty funny stuff if you look at it that way. You have a choice in school: laugh or be bored to death. She had an ancient overhead sheet that looked like it'd been soaked in monkey piss. On it was a drawing of an old hag behind a flax wheel with these hand-drawn arrows pointing out different parts of the wheel. Everyone in class was either half asleep or antsy, moving around or messing with someone. At home, half these guys were either playing or making video games with sick 3D graphics, some connected to other players all over the country, and here we were watching a teacher who looked like a man in bad makeup slapping sheets of plastic on a big lightbulb. I felt bad for Leapyear, thinking she's doing something and not knowing that no one is paying attention. Even Elizabeth looked strained to stay awake. It's like my mom saying she's growing or becoming clear, but I know everyone—Dan's poser posse, Monroe's parents, Sunday, and the teachers who know me—thinks she's as crazy as a pack of feral cats. Even though she's in those saffron-colored clothes at Dorado, everyone thinks she's yanking out her hair in a padded cell or something. It makes you wonder why anyone really gives a colonial rat's ass.

". . . and manipulation." Leapyear brought out these square wood boxes, laid them on the front table, and asked us all to come up. "Feel the weight. You can see how our forefathers and foremothers . . ."

"And foreskins," Monroe whispered from her hood.

"Called that one first."

"You always call foreskins. You love foreskins. Want yours back?"

I might've blushed. I'm not sure. I try not to do that.

". . . how they toiled to create garments that lasted. Have you ever held anything like this? Feel the weave, the strength. I have an idea, people! Take your two fingers . . ."

". . . and insert them into your rectal cavity," Monroe continued.

". . . and rub your neighbor's shirt to feel the modern-day cloth," Leapyear continued.

Everyone around Monroe looked at her in all that clean whiteness, but she shook her head as if to say, *Don't even.* A lot of kids pinched other kid's butts, but Leapyear didn't notice. Elizabeth rubbed the bottom of my shirt, and I can't say I hated it.

"Now pass around this." Leapyear handed the clump of scratchy raw flax to Elizabeth, who was hovering next to her like she was ready to chimp-groom Leapyear's hair.

"It's so coarse!" she exclaimed, like she was in a production of *HSM* on Broadway, not in the lamest elective in the school's history. The remnant worked its way toward Monroe, who kept her hands inside her sleeves in front of her, Chinese-like. Some people nodded or smiled in Leapyear's direction, while others rolled their eyes to their friends. One guy made a pig noise, which wasn't very funny, since none of this diseased pelt came from anything close to resembling pork. After it was passed, each student wiped his hands on his pants or grabbed a squirt of sanitizer from the side of the class. The TB remnant was coming closer and closer to Monroe. I couldn't see her face, since she'd bowed her head, and her hood obstructed my view. Her hands were still sheathed in her sleeves, long tubes of white fabric. I nailed Leapyear with my eyebulbs, then Monroe then Leap then Roe, and then Jimmy handed it to the area in front of where Monroe's hands should have been. She shook her head. Leapyear faux-coughed, so I reached out to grab the thing and nodded my head like a spaz to try to throw her off, but I could tell from her pointed brows that she was PO'd.

She handed each table a box full of the different stages of the flax-to-linen process, and asked us to go back to our tables and assemble a time line, using the overhead as a guide, by the time class was over. She said we all needed to participate equally, so it was me, Monroe, Elizabeth, and Flip, a kid who always had these big headphones around his neck and a wool Volcom hat, even though it was a hundred degrees outside. Elizabeth elected herself captain and started sorting the stuff, putting it on different areas of the table. Leapyear had slapped on the step-by-steps on the overhead, and my group just watched Elizabeth do what she did best, take over like a pretty little dictator. Flip's forehead raised like a curtain, and his eyes shot sideways as if someone was watching. Finally he sat down and flipped a pen in his fingers like a helicopter blade going forward and reverse, over and over. Monroe was stuck inside her bleached tent while Elizabeth flicked her head side to side to make sure (a) all the pieces were there, (b) the clockwise order matched the overhead, and (c) we could each have a part. I just wanted to get done with this lame thing as quickly as I could. A lot of school is just getting on to the next thing, and I figured this artsy-craftsy crap would be easy to motor through.

"I'll do the rippling," Elizabeth said. "Flip, you can do the retting, Coy braking, then Monroe will finish up by hackling." A dead man could see that she was giving Monroe the easiest part, but it didn't help.

"I'm not touching any of it," Monroe said, retreating into her hood.

"Ms. Liebner said we all have to participate." Elizabeth sounded pretty nice about it, actually.

"Nope."

"We won't get credit if we all don't do something."

"Come on, you hardly have to do anything," I said softly.

Monroe turned, leaning out of her hood, and shot me her mean look that told me to back off. No more joking about lesbros. We were past that into new fiery-furnace territory.

"I gotta bust a mission," Flip said, and got a pass from Leapyear, which just made her pay closer attention to our happy little group of love.

"I'm not failing because of you." Elizabeth fiddled with the crap in front of us.

"It's a goddamn elective, Lezzie."

"You still get a letter grade."

"You'd have to unload in her mouth not to get an A." Monroe slapped the emphasis on *you*.

"Come on," I pleaded. Leapyear was turning sideways now to walk between tables, obviously noticing the severe suckage in our group. I had the urge to flee, get out, screw school, but of all the places I'd been lately—Wheelchair Man, Sunday, Dorado—nowhere seemed any better than the next. I was tired.

"What's happening here?" Leapyear asked. We all went numb.

"Flip is in the bathroom," I said.

"Who?" When she was confused, her clown makeup got all crooked.

"Gerald."

"I know. I gave him the pass," she said, covering up her spot of weakness. "Why aren't we making progress, people? Time management is part of the assignment." No one said anything. Even Elizabeth, with her GPA and academic profile that would lead to the presidency of some fascist corporation, didn't want to rat. Not right away, anyway. A long pause filled our little area, like locker-room steam.

"Well?"

"Monroe won't do anything," Elizabeth said finally.

"It didn't take much to break you," I said.

"Coy, come on." Her eyes welled up, and she dragged her fingernail across her palm in a way that made me think she wasn't so happy-go-lucky after all. Maybe she had some sleepless nights.

"Ms. Monroe, you need to participate." Leapyear got Monroe's name from Elizabeth saying it. "Look at me when I'm talking to you, Ms. Mon-roe."

The class sniffed out the drama and all pretended to work, going through the motions of removing flax seeds with this big metal comby thing. I could hardly take it, all that posing. Ms. Leapyear wasn't the kind of teacher who kicked you out right away, nor was she the "not my paycheck" kind of pencil-pusher either. She was OLD school, been teaching since that Little House was on that goddamn Prairie.

"Ms. Monroe!" Leapyear grabbed the mess of rough hay and shook it at her. "Do this, young lady."

"No!" Monroe said, as sharp as broken glass, and yanked her sleeves back. Those arms. Red scabs and streaks of crimson, some new bumps, some still in the process of scabbing over.

Kids don't usually gasp outside the snuff films they show in driver's ed, but here they did. For reals.

"Monroe!" I realized my cracked voice had my mother in it, like a track on a recording. The way she used to say "Coy!" when I'd balance on the edge of a boulder overlooking Long Island Sound, or when I'd climb the thick trunk of a cotton-wood tree and couldn't get down, so she had to find some husky man to come let me step on his shoulders or fall into his arms. My mom says I don't sound like my father, but I look like him. It's the eyes, she says. All in the big eyes and a little mouth.

But Monroe wasn't on the edge, she was over it now, crying, her ragged arms in the air like rhubarb stalks with bloody red flowers as big as fists.

"Peo, I, uh, peo," Leapyear started saying, but it was like something was caught in her throat. Elizabeth's face was all someone-let-a-fart-pinched, and I spotted Flip walk in the room, assess the situation, and walk right back out. No one knew what to do—all these supposedly tough football meat-heads who smashed stuff in locker rooms and asked Monroe, "Why so serious?"; Elizabeths who attended coalition meetings with teachers and youth summits with the mayor; Trees who could make you feel invisible; stoners in their Volcom hoodies and Timberlands—all of them frozen like toys in blocks, the biggest block we call school, and Monroe crying, exposed like her insides were all turned outside.

"I'll take her to the counselor," I said. Leapyear had the scream grimace plastered across her mug. "It's okay. We can make up the lab later." Leapyear still frozen. "No really, it's okay," I said in my best soothing voice. I grabbed my bag and then Monroe's bag and slung them over my shoulders while I steered Monroe between the desks and out the door. Flip was leaning against the wall, trying to hide the fact that he was on his cell. "Yes, I am not shitting you," he said, but then cut off his speech when he saw us. The halls were pretty empty, a few kids hitting the flu fountains and then turning and staring at us doing our Driving Miss Crazy routine. This one mainte- nance dude who always says the same thing at the end of the day—*You don't have to go home but you can't stay here, don't fall in love,* which makes no sense at all, since tons of kids have after-school activities at school, and I'm sure plenty fall in love too; maybe he's baked—he stopped spraying this toxic stuff on some tagging, put his hand to his mouth, and hummed, *Mmm mmm mmm,* like it was a goddamn soup commercial.

Monroe's crying hadn't stopped, but it was lighter now, I guess, and she walked stiff like a zombie, letting me lead her past the computer lab, something she'd never in a million years let me do except in seventh grade when we used to play Ray Charles, where I'd put my hand on her shoulder and close my eyes. Her job was to try to lead me all over the school, and I had to guess where we were based on the stench (cafetorium), lousy tuba playing (band room), or sickly sweet smell (girl's bathroom). "Office!" I'd yell because I smelled burned paper and stale coffee, heard the phones ring, the copier running, and the recepticon saying "Red-Rock-Junior-High-how-may- I-help-you" like help was the last thing she actually wanted to do. Our final destination was the auditorium, where she'd seat me at the piano and I'd bang on the keys and yell the words to "What'd I Say," one of Dan's must-listen-tos. Then it was always her turn.

"Monroe, it'll be okay," I said, but it didn't sound like me. I knew that kind of talk would never clear her if she were healthy.

18

I found my way back to the Nurselor's door. On the front was a bulletin board I hadn't noticed when I was hauled in last time. Framed with purple ribbons, the board had more quotes pinned to it, all neatly written on piss-yellow index cards (p.s. I hate index cards). I knocked, and Sunday opened it, all dopey-faced. She was sitting on the exorcise ball and had a mouth full of powdered doughnut. Pretty sick. I hate seeing teachers eat. It seems unnatural somehow. And this specimen was in a black skirt straddling a rubber orb with powdered sugar all over her mouth like Scarface with his mug in all that nose candy. Some sugar dust had gotten on her skirt too. She should know not to eat a powdered doughnut with a freaking black skirt. Or to not wear a black skirt when she craved doughnuts. Jesus. And she was in charge of helping people?

"Oh! Sorry," she said, and started spastically wiping her mouth and lap. "I thought you were someone else." The wiping lasted longer than a few seconds, and then she grabbed some tissues from her many boxes and did her cheeks, the ball, the arm of the chair. It was almost like we were a couple wanting to buy her windowless prison cell (solitary confinement really), not a guy feeling totally awkward with his crying and freaked-out friend.

"Monroe, are you okay? Thank you, um . . ." She stumbled, and her hand twitched.

"Coy."

"Right, Coy. I'm sorry. Caught me by surprise. Come in. Monroe, you sit here," she said, leading her to the chair I had sat in last time.

"Well." I reached for the doorknob and shuffled my feet, in case she didn't get the signal. "I guess—"

"I'd like you to stay. Fill me in. Okay?" she asked with a weepy earnest face.

"I guess," I said. She had already taken the bigger counselor chair. I stood, leaning up against Einstein, which was kinda weird and uncomfortable— looking down on Monroe and Sunday like they were rehearsing some scene from a play. This was the kind of weird that shows up in your dreams. The Nurselor's face was all liquidy, like she wanted to give me a hug, but I was wrong.

"Do you mind?" Nurselor asked me and nudged her nose toward the exercise ball. FML. If it was any other reason, I would have said "No freaking way" or pulled some sort of James Bond move and said "I prefer to stand," but Monroe seemed really messed up, so I dropped my messenger bag in the corner under old Maya and slid between them and plopped down on the ball, which was bouncier than I'd guessed, and I launched forward and—get this—ended up with a face full of Sunday's skirt, my hand grazing her boob as I was trying to grab on to something. F to the M to the L. And this was how messed up Monroe was: she didn't even laugh. It was that bad.

"It takes some getting used to," the Nurselor said as I pushed myself up on the arm of her chair. "Okay, then. Let's all breathe for a moment here." She put her hands on her lap and took a loud pull through her nose and then shot it out her mouth like she was blowing out candles on a cake. My mom pulled that crappage, Dan too when she dragged him to yoga class, Pilates class, something called Egoscue.

"Who'd like to tell me what brought you both to my door?" she asked, like it wasn't clear that mute Monroe was bugging out, and I was idiot messenger who had no idea what to do. Monroe peered down from under her white hood, face all chapped and wet like she'd been stuck in a blizzard somewhere after receiving f-ing really bad news, only it was a hundred outside and she *was* the bad news. I couldn't decide what to say. It wasn't Leapyear's fault or even that *lambe* Elizabeth's, but I didn't want to make things worse by telling the truth and upsetting Monroe even more. And I couldn't sit back and do nothing because the ball kept me shifting and reshifting my weight like a rocking boat. So I said, "We were in Colonial Studies, and Monroe had a hard time." End of story.

Monroe shot me a look. I held my hands up: *What do you want me to do?*

"Okay," Nurselor said. "That's a starting place. Can anyone build on that?"

Did I say enough how much it sucked being there?

Sunday turned back to me. "Coy, can you give me a little more?"

"Not really." I burned my eyes at Monroe, but she wasn't looking.

"It would help."

None of us were going anywhere until someone said something. I'd be stuck on that ball forever, and my butt was sweating profusely (vocab word).

Sunday horse-breathed again. "Surely there is somewhere we can start."

"I have no idea, and don't call me Shirley," I blurted out automatically, which is the stalest joke on the whole crippled planet, but I couldn't help myself and then felt sick afterward and clamped my Aspy mouth shut.

"Monroe, I don't know if you know this, but Coy came to see me while you were out." Sunday had nice nails, but they were short like a man's. No color but shiny, healthy. "He said you were going through a rough patch. That's okay. We care about you, don't we, Coy?"

I kept my eyes on her hands. I didn't want to look at her or at Monroe. I didn't really want to look at anything.

"He cares about you and was worried about you and didn't know where to turn. Is that how you feel, Monroe?"

Out of the corner of my eye, I could see her nod. Sunday's lies were so easy to spot, even for me. I'd never say "rough patch," especially to a school counselor. Monroe dropped her hood, and her hair stayed matted against her head. She pulled her sleeves back a bit too so I could see what was left of her nails and all those red streaks.

"Monroe, I need to ask you some questions," the Nurselor asked. "Did you eat breakfast today?"

"Yes."

"What did you eat?"

"Toast and tea." She paused. "A tangerine."

"Good, that's great."

I could hear Nurselor's voice loosen. She was happy Monroe was answering. I was too. It seemed better than silence.

"Have your periods been regular?"

"No."

"That's okay. When was your last period?"

"Don't remember."

"That's okay. Are you evacuating your bowels?"

"Yes, sir. Thank you, sir."

"When was the last time you saw your doctor?"

"Which one?"

"The one you've had the longest. General doctor."

"Last week."

"What did he say?"

"She."

"What did she say?"

Monroe took her own cleansing breath, and after, her jaw went all stiff. Then it shot out: "That's it. The doctor doesn't know. Can't say why all this is still happening to me." She lightly placed her fingertips on her eyes. "I've changed my diet, changed my sheets, my clothes, put all my stuff into plastic bags, my house is being rebuilt, and she can't say for sure what is causing all this."

Even though I was trying my hardest to sit still on the ball, I felt like I couldn't breathe. I wanted to rip that door open,

punch through Einstein's ragged homeless face. I remembered
Ms. J in Language Arts at the beginning of the year and how
we did this writing thing. We were supposed to describe a
conversation between two people, like we were a fly on the
wall. That's how she put it. She said some other things like
what you call fly on the wall in English smart talk. Something
something point of view. But not fly. When we were finished,
people "shared," but I didn't because I wrote about my mom at
Dorado, and I knew I couldn't be forced to read it. Ms. J almost
took off her clothes, she was so excited about everyone's pieces.
Then she said, "Don't we all wish we could be flies on the wall?"
She was all giddy like a huffer or a fairy in Shakespeare's wet
dream. Sitting there, nothing to do with my hands, listening
to Monroe talk about hating her face in the bathroom mirror
and visits to the hospital in the middle of the night, made me
want to find Ms. J and cold-cock her fat face. I didn't want to
be a fly or anything else and hear all this shite.

"No one wants to see a face like this," Monroe said
cold stonely.

"Do your parents know how you feel?"

She shook her head no, running her fingertips across the
scabs the way you would over carved initials in a tree. "They're
not stupid."

"You should tell them."

"That's the thing. I almost did. Then they were at the
dining room table surrounded by paper, bills, and my dad
had his hair in his hands trying to figure out how they could
afford to build me a goddamn guesthouse. I knew being in

my own place would be cool, except I couldn't really have anyone come inside with me. Ever. And I didn't want to be in a bubble, even though it isn't really a bubble."

"What do you want?"

"My old life back, however much it sucked."

"It didn't suck," I mumbled.

"I think that's totally fair," Nurselor said, but it felt like she was talking to pretty much everything. Everything is fair. Doing the best we can. Everything happens for a reason. The universe provides. What doesn't kill you makes you stronger. "You know I have to call your parents?" Sunday was now a different flavor of serious.

"No, you don't," Monroe said, not kidding. She looked straight at Sunday.

"I do. As soon as you walked through my door with clear signs of severe stress and anxiety, my hands were tied."

This totally didn't make sense to me. Tied hands can't dial a goddamn phone. And how were we supposed to trust this woman?

"I understand how you feel, Monroe."

"Really?" Monroe's eyes got crazy Ping-Pong ball big.

"Well—," Sunday started but got cut off.

"Really? You've had all this?" She pointed to her face with both hands. "You've had your parents give away all your pets?" Her laugh scared me. "And your stuffed pets too, because they are 'dust sponges'? People laughing at you at school or worse, pretending they don't see you even though you went over to their house to play Spice Girls records every day in third grade? You have arms like this? Weeks where you can't eat anything that has color? All this?"

"What I meant—"

"I know what you meant. I have another therapist too. And a whole rectal load of doctors. And a nutritionist. And a freaking energy healer who wants to feed me stem cells from a duck. And not one of them is stupid enough to tell me they know how I feel."

"Hey," I said.

"What?" She snapped to face me. "You brought me in here."

"Yeah, so you wouldn't get suspended or have Leapyear sic security on you."

She shot me her mad dog look, but I still said, "You don't need to be such a dick. She's just doing her job."

"Well, the job she's doing is lame." She pulled her sleeves back down and looked at me closer, like she was trying to read my mind. Have I told you about her eyes? As blue as menthol cough drops. Ice blue. Scandinavian villain blue. "And what exactly are you doing?" she asked me.

There was a weight in my chest, solid, unmoving. I picked a hair from my sleeve and let it float to the ground. Hanging my head in my hands, I thought about my so-called life. I didn't know what to say, so I said what came first: "I'm trying to be your friend. And it's getting harder by the minute."

"Well, isn't that special."

What Sunday said next I couldn't hear because my hands covered the sides of my cranium and I can do this thing where I bring my ears up using my muscles on the side of my face and all the blood rushes to them. It sounds like thunderheads rolling in, in waves, like there's a rainstorm. *"Rain rain rain rain rain,"* I sang softly to myself so I couldn't hear Sunday and her blah blah blah.

I stayed under the lyrics for a while. Then I resurfaced. Then Monroe said: "You're right. Bring it on."

19

Research Note: It is hard to believe that something as seemingly harmless as mold could have an effect on our brains, but it does. Exposure to toxic mold can have neurological effects, as spores enter the body and release toxins into the bloodstream. Common symptoms include chronic fatigue, hearing and memory loss, and mild symptoms of dementia. These are symptoms of the very advanced stages of toxic mold poisoning. These symptoms are elusive, and that is why you should make sure your house is mold-free.

"What's your project on?" Avree asked me from her usual seat to my right.

My binder was stuffed full of copies, notes, handouts, and doodles, starting with the platypussy and all the way to mycotoxicosis, which I hadn't had a chance to look up yet, so I drew a guy with sores all over his body riding a horse skeleton into a car wash made of fire. Shiny Happy People I know. Avree's hair had been highlighted recently, and my mom would say lowlighted too, swept back in a perfect ice cream swirl, dammed up off her face by her large Prada sunglasses. Strands ribboning from white to yellow then brown and red. It looked pretty cool. It was hard not to get lost, stare, I mean.

"I'm not really sure anymore, really," I said, looking at the mess expunging from my binder onto the desk, wondering why she was talking to me.

"Mine's the platypus." She chewed her gum on the right side of her mouth. "My sister had Beakman two years ago and said it's the easiest to get an A on."

"Great." She had one of the handbags all the Trees have— as big as a hippo's head (Monroe said that) with more buckles than a Pilgrim (I said that), the kind a woman three times her age would swing around in New York City, not this dusty crap town. Monroe carried a duct-tape wallet with the British flag on it, or a Ponyo pencil case or a vintage zip-up leather pouch made to hold soccer goalkeeper gloves. She used to, anyway. She said one of the Trees would fall in a lake and drown herself holding that dumbbell. Dumbbells with dumbbells, she called them.

Avree kept looking at me. I couldn't say "May I help you with something?" because that would sound like I fronted at a sporting goods store or the Gap (which we called the Gape or the Ape or the Gash or the Ghey), so I ran my finger along the lab table—someone had scrawled the word *ballsack* into the surface, what was it made of? The table, not the scrote. Plastic? Charcoal? I almost laughed. *Ballsack* is a pretty funny word, but that's the last thing I wanted to be: a loser guffawing at *ballsack* while a pretty Tree stared at him.

Avree checked Beakman and then leaned in. She smelled like caramel and flowers. I almost sighed. "That girl you hang with, Monroe something, did she really freak out on Ms. Liebner and get taken away in a straitjacket?"

It was only later that I realized that my *we* (me and Monroe) was everybody else's *they*.

There was a big moment after the initial shock of hearing Monroe's name come out of Avree's glossy lips where I realized I had a tiny cube of power at this flat school. I could say anything I wanted, all eyes on me. At least Avree's eyes. I could easily spread a rumor that would get everywhere by the end of the day, winding its way through the hallways, airwaves, teacher's lounge, and Internet. "It's sad, really," I said before I could power myself down. "Seeing her in that jacket and the cuffs scraping her wrists."

"Handcuffs too? Oh. My. God." She was dying to get on that cell phone and make the virus airborne. All junkie status.

"Totally." (I spoke Tree too.) I peered around the room. "Just to be on the safe side."

"Where'd they take her? Holbrook?"

"No, her parents wouldn't abide. They're kinda British, so they took her to this fancy place called El Dorado. Thirty miles away. Much nicer. More discreet." I couldn't believe what I was saying.

"It's still for crazies, though?" She didn't want her story to be ruined.

"I suppose so."

"What will they do to her?"

"I'm not sure. They usually start off with some sort of analysis, what's wrong with her, you know, and they'll have her go to meetings alone and then in a group when she gets more socialized." I could feel I was losing her here because she started doing that Tree thing of blankly nodding her head while looking over my shoulder for something shinier, like a clock or a mirror. So I ended with the money: "If she doesn't get better, they'll load on the meds, and if that doesn't work, they'll try shock treatment."

I had her back now, for reals. "They still do that? Like in *Cuckoo's Nest?*"

"You read that book?"

"Duh." Her eyes rattled in her skull. "I was in your English class."

I vaguely remembered staring at the back of her head now. And watching her whisper to this girl whose parents split up after the dad got cancer. What was her name? Harmony? "You never said much, so I didn't know," I said.

"You were no Elizabeth Buchanan either."

That made me smile. Maybe she wasn't 100 percent Tree. "So do—"

"Huh? Sudoku?" I thought I misheard. (I hate Sudoku. Like holding a menu in a café for losers.)

"No," she said with an arching eye roll. "Electric shock? So they still do it?"

"Electroshock, really electroconvulsive or ECT. Still do it, but in lower doses. . . Still do lobotomies too."

"Shut." She hit me on the arm, pretty hard too. Rings on her fingers. "Up."

"Believe. It helps some people. If people can't stop being violent, they sever certain brain fibers. Also, it can help stop seizures for epileptics."

Head shake, closed lips. "Wow. You sure know a lot about being crazy."

"Yeah, whatever. Takes one to know one, right?" So lame. I can't believe what I spew sometimes. I wasn't going to tell her all the research I did when my mom went away. TMI.

She started doodling on the front of her notebook. Little 3D boxes. I would have pegged her for hearts, her name in graffiti script, or long, thin model figures wearing triangular dresses. "I was thinking that maybe I'd like to be a psychiatrist or psychologist," she said a bit dreamily. "Help people reconstruct their scrambled brains. That or a CSI."

I felt like hitting her and saying "Little buckaroo" or "Babe" or something equally stupid because I was feeling fond of her all of a sudden. I know it's totally ghey, but I had the urge to go over to her house and watch *CSI* (Vegas only, my one rule), resting my head on her boobs and having her run her fingers through my hair. God, Monroe would crap herself if she knew I was lying about her and how I was feeling at that moment about a Poplar.

"I just saw this really small movie with my stepdad," I said, which was true.

"Small?"

"You know." I made that weird wavy "you know" gesture with my hands. "Not terrible, but not very good. Nothing really happened in it. Anyway, he always watches the special features, and this actor kept saying how much fun he had on the shoot and how he felt like he knew his costars all his life once he met them and even the writers and director were his great friends, and I thought how cool that would be, you know, meeting people like that and feeling like you knew them all your life."

I could tell by her scrunched-up face she wasn't following me. "You want to be an actor?"

"No. I could never stand up in front of people." I was talking way too fast now. "I'm sure I'd look stiff and probably freak out. Puke even. I'm just saying I'd like to be able to say all those things. On camera, I guess. Where someone was watching."

"What movie was it again?"

"I don't remember the name. My stepdad rented it."

"Oh."

I knew I had lost her with my dashboard confessional, but then Beaker swung by in his tie-dye lab coat holding his grade book like Wapshot's clipboard. Avree had a particularly creepy photo of the flat-billed furball on her screen.

"Platypus, I see. Nicely done."

Then he swung his gaze to me and eyed my mess. "You look, um, busy."

"I sure am," I said and shot him the thumbs up, making Avree snort, but she morphed it into a cough, waving off Beaker, who had turned toward her.

"Don't forget organization," he said, backing away. "It's a huge component of your presentation and your grade."

"I won't. I know what everything means," I said and patted my papers like a pet, if pets were thin, white, covered in ink, and not connected by organic tissue.

Avree was still smiling but started looking again at the DBP on her screen, and I knew if I didn't say something she'd go back to work and this might be our last conversation on this planet. My life at RRJH had basically been with

Monroe, my social life anyway (if you could call it that), and I had no idea what you say to girls. My only interactions had been over lost pens, answers on tests, and get-out-of-my-way kinda deals. All these lame song lyrics invaded my head mashed together (*Girls, boys, girls! . . . lonely heart, sad face, swift kick . . . talk stupid talk*) and got me all confused and led me back to the source of a lot of music in my house: "My stepdad." All I said. F-ing out loud. Let it be known: I am the world's biggest loser.

"What?"

"Um, my stepdad wanted me to do the platypus too."

"Okay." She snapped her gum. "Are your parents divorced?"

"Not exactly. I live with my stepdad, and my mom's away for a while but they're still married. She'll be back. Eventually."

"Okay." She thought I was lying. Squint + look away = skeptical.

"No, I mean—" What did I mean? Think quickly boy with a girl's name. "I mean I have loads of research, on the platypus, if you need any."

"That's sweet, but it's actually pretty easy." She pointed to the laptop. "It's like every kid in ninth grade in the country has done it, so it's really just cutting and pasting." She swept her palms across the sides of her head, an unnecessary act because there were no errant (vocab) hairs to smooth over. "What are you doing yours on again?"

It's hard for me to believe even now, but I told her. I started with my idea about nickel poisoning and a kid who swallowed a battery, through the subject of mold spores and aerial mold bombs that attach themselves to lung walls, until I was all lathered up like I had ADHD and Asperger's with OCD as a side dish. Then I paused. "The next part is kinda private."

"Okay."

"I mean, you can't really tell anyone."

"Okay."

"I have to ask." This was so hard, but I had to. "Okay like (a) you're playing me, or okay like (b) you won't say because you are not evil?"

"B."

"Good." I felt dizzy, so I actually, get this, secretly took one of Sunday's cleansing breaths. Then I spilled the beans about Monroe's guesthouse.

"Wow."

"I know what you're thinking. What's with the over share and how the hell is all that a project, well—"

"That's not what I'm thinking at all."

Can I say there was a sort of calm then? That all the kids around us, the ones huddled over Cooper's hawks and flamingos, joking about hippos and African elephants, trying to sleep under hoodies and texting behind the life-size human skeleton replica, all of them froze, and it was just me and her? Just us? Would you believe that?

"I was thinking that you must really care a lot about your friend."

Believe it because it's true.

20

Research Note: In April of 1997, two months after providing vocals for some lame Christian rock band, Foreigner lead singer Lou Gramm was diagnosed with a type of brain tumor called a craniopharyngioma. Although the tumor was benign, the resulting surgery damaged his pituitary gland. In addition, the recovery program had caused Gramm to gain weight (like a ton), and likewise affected his stamina and voice. Craniopharyngioma is a type of tumor derived from pituitary gland embryonic tissue that occurs in most commonly children but also in men and women in their fifties and sixties. It arises from nests of odontogenic epithelium within the suprasellar/ diencephalic region and contains the deposits of calcium which are evident on an x-ray. Histologically, craniopharyngiomas resemble adamantinomas (the most common tumors of the tooth). Patients may present with bitemporal hemianopia, as the tumor may compress the optic chiasm. Don't know what half that shite is but it sounds terrible. Poor Lou.

Dan busted in my room with a buttload of bags, including the obnoxiously bright one that holds his laptop. Slightly out of breath, he said, "Okay dude, let's motor."

"No Panda Poison tonight?"

He didn't flinch at what he would call my "lack of grace and appreciation." Weird. "Not tonight."

"Not tonight?"

"Echo in here?"

"What then?"

"Need-to-know only. Just get in the motor vehicle, sir."

"Okay, Ociffer," I said, humoring him since he was in such a Shiny Happy People mood. We left my mom's Honda alone in the garage, and Dan drove like he was off probation, one hand on the wheel, the other behind my headrest, which should have felt all fatherly but landed on the ghey side of the gheyme board. No talk radio, iPod hooked up to the stereo by way of this quaint little cord. The first song was "Juke Box Hero," blatantly a favorite of mine. Then we passed the car wash (which was packed like always), then the turnoff to the highway that led to Dorado. Another song came on, "Don't Stop Believin'," one we hadn't listened to since pre-Dorado because all three of us sang it together. It was what Dan would call our "sentimental favorite."

"Okay. That's it," I said, putting my foot down but not really. "What's this?"

"Whaddya mean?" I don't think the poser even knew he was whistling.

"Whaddya mean whaddya mean? The music, for starters."

"You don't like it?" The way he said it reminded me of Monroe when she did that crap Chinese accent and asked if I liked boobs.

"Please stop being cute and tell me." I can't say ghey to Dan. He says it's homophobic when it's really not, especially coming from a lesbro.

"It's just a little mix I put together for you." His smile hung onto his face like a long-legged spider with only two legs left.

"Does that mean we're going out now?"

"That's funny for you. I'll burn you the CD when we get home."

"I have all these songs, Dan."

"Not all, and not in this precise order. There are some covers and B-sides deeper in that I'm sure you don't have."

If I didn't know better, I would have sworn he was cooked, but none of the other clues were there. Turning my neck, I could barely make out the tip of the crane. We were headed in the opposite direction into the armpit of our metropolis. Hell, maybe the worst part of America: Applebee's, Macaroni Grill, Petco—all these chain stores, strip malls, and turning lanes that lead you into parking lots if you don't watch out. Mom did that plenty of times with me in the car. She hated driving in this part of town, and inevitably we'd end up in a drive-through lane for Wendy's with an SUV riding up behind us. I'd tell my mom it was cool, we didn't have to buy anything, but she felt so embarrassed (*Again, Coy, again!*) at getting stuck, all flustered, grabbing her purse from the car floor and then trying to find change or a dollar for fries off the value menu. Then there'd be tax and we'd root around under seats and in ashtrays that should have been clean but weren't, but I didn't say anything. I'd eat whatever she bought even if I wasn't hungry or it made me sick (Taco Bell). Once or twice I might have dropped a junior burger from my hand out the open window. But it wasn't over after we exited the drive-thru. We'd be in the middle of a parking-lot clustertuck, cars trying to turn sharply to get out or speeding across the intersection to get to Target or stuck behind those sad little islands built from concrete with little dying trees or bushes turned gray by the exhaust and trash rained on them. Trying to get back to where we were before has always been a mess for me and my mom.

"Where ARE we going, Dan?"

"That's a secret."

"Swell. You know me. I crave adventure." I rolled down the window and hung my face out like a slobbery mutt.

Dan stayed true and got us through the newer stores and to the older ones closer to Red Rock. The sun started dropping, looking almost purple under the red that burned like the rest of the world was on fire. Above that red was a peach-colored rumpled piece of paper sky with all the clouds and triangular shadows. One of the only cool things, living out here: the Fellini sky. I don't really know what a Fellini is, but REM sings about it, so it must be cool.

We pulled into this weak-looking parking lot with a few vacant fronts, cardboarded-up windows, a store called Vacuums & More!, and a Mexican grocery with a glass door plastered with phone card ads, in *español* of course. Then there was the bowling alley.

"Here we are," he said, switching off the ignition.

I didn't budge.

21

I hadn't been to Rio Lanes since I was ten.

When the three of us went back in the day, it was fine. Fun actually, but I was only ten and remembered the place smelling like that shake-on pizza cheese and foot odor and smoke. I also remembered a bar inside and a snack center, slices behind a greasy glass case that rotated so you could grab your own. "Home of the Easy Bake Oven pizza," my mom had said to Dan, not thinking I'd heard.

"Here we are," Dan said again.

I craned my neck all around like I was onstage. "Got ears, professor. Aren't we going to El Dorado today?"

"Not today, next week."

"So we won't see Mom?"

"It's hard to say."

I almost let myself get excited. I could feel the butterflies start to emerge, but I cocooned them again. This was too odd. Why would my mom meet us at a bowling alley? Mom would not meet us in a bowling alley. "WTF?"

"Coy, I know what that means."

"I didn't say it. Abbreviations don't count. Vowels do all the harm, or so my English teacher says."

"Clever."

The place hadn't changed. I'd forgotten about the colors, though. Old-school peach and pale yellow. The back wall had these ribbed panels that looked like drapes that alternated yellow, peach, yellow, peach. All the trim between the alleys was peach, all the plastic chairs were yellow. Time warp really. The only sign of the twenty-first century was one of those shiny banners advertising a margarine brand and the "I Can't Believe It's Not Gutter" singles bowling league.

I turned to Dan. "Why are we doing this?"

"Shoes first."

"Do we have to? I didn't know our little adventure would include a change of clothing."

"Don't be such a downer, bro."

"You're lucky I almost like you." One lane held only colored balls. A little blond girl in a ponytail and white dress was waving at everyone who went by, even the sketchy old men with nasty-smelling beards. I mean, I wasn't close enough to smell them, but they looked rank. You know what I'm saying?

We exchanged our dogs for the fruity bowling kind, and the washed-out-looking guy with a Sanchez mustache asked for Dan's license.

"Why do you need that?" I asked.

When he answered, "'Cause folks steal the shoes," he looked straight at me. Hard stare. "Some sort of fashion thing, I guess." Inarticulate assneck. As if I'd want those poser New Age Ally Sheedy thinsoles. "Don't get it myself personally, I don't, but that's just me."

We walked past the little kids rolling balls with two hands, their gutters filled with long tubes to avoid a miss, a Goth

couple who frenched after the trench-coat omega male managed a spare. Some buttoned-up guys straight outta Intel were
keeping strict score on the one lane that still had a scratched
overhead projector. This whole colony of people I never really
knew existed coming here week after week, throwing their
balls around, having conversations about love, TV, what to
eat, movies, books even. All the spheres even just in my town
where I lived now: Mom and Lindy in El Dorado, Monroe
in her bubble, Mack and his cubes, construction workers,
teachers. You could choose to visit them all or stay in one
forever. Then I saw it. "Oh god!" I yelled, kinda like a puss. I
might have squeaked. Sad.

HAPPYBIRTHDAYCOY!

in white copy paper across the peach and yellow wall, each
letter on a single sheet, taped over a long table on the other side
of a metal fence separating the bowling part of the show from
the snackage portion. A few balloons were fixed to the wall (tape
was showing), and the tablecloth had cartoon guitars all over
it. Plates, cups, and napkins too. Monroe and her mom were
sitting there like a sad photo I once saw in a museum or something. Depression-era status, I think. Monroe was not even in the
smiling area code and had on a white birthday hat like a French
clown who'd lost her way in a black-and-white movie. Her face
was the only colorful thing on her body: red as a traffic light.

"Um, my birthday isn't for two weeks, *Dan*." Stress crawled
all over that last word.

"I know, but they were booked the next month solid. Can
you believe that?" He put his bags down on one of the yellow
chairs. "Anyway, this is more of a surprise."

"Good thinking."

He turned to me. Open face. "I know, right?"

Ever have those moments where what stands before you tunnels away like you're on a treadmill just moving in place while the object in front of you fades into the background? Probably not. Monroe and her mom were at the last two seats against the wall, Monroe in all white and her mom in a shiny turquoise jumpsuit, guitar party hat string cutting a red slice into her family of chins. She clapped when she saw me, trying to muster up some festivity in a gray-aired place (*If the wind was colored, if the air could speak*) where drunk people hurled black balls down a slick runway to knock over pieces of wood. I went straight to Monroe.

"Hey."

She let loose an overacted movie yawn. "I tried to tell them it was a bad idea."

"Happy birthday, young man!" Her mom threw her arms around me, creating a feeling kinda like being smothered by a couch covered in plastic.

"Thanks, Mrs. Alpert. Nice hat, Roe."

"Made it me-self, Guv'nr. These too." She lifted up her leg and showed me the top of her slipper, painted to look like a bowling shoe. One side blue, the other red, with painted-on laces and little bowling-pin logos near the heel. Pretty sweet job. "I used organic dyes and some other stuff my mom picked up at the health freak store."

"Cool. My mom used to do that. Only not on sterilized fabric to emulate recreational sports attire. Thanks, though. For getting dressed up and coming and stuff."

"No worries, matey."

Dan was running around to the snack bar and back like he was on a game show. When he came close enough to grab, I asked him, "Who are all these chairs for?"

He put his hands on his hips and exhaled as if I didn't see him playing his own version of Frogger. "I called the guidance counselor, and she gave me the names of some of your friends."

"She what? You didn't. Really?" FML.

"Yeah, she said she'd call your teachers and see who you hang out with in class. Since you never tell me. Then she gave me their numbers, and I called their folks. How cool is that?"

"You didn't." Shut. "Please tell me you're kidding."

"I wonder if they all know where the bowling alley is." He glanced toward the door. "Some of them must. It's kind of retro, isn't it?"

"Who is *them*?"

"That is a surprise."

I looked to Monroe to have my back, but she had put a big cone cigarette in her flat smile. She'd made her own noisemaker.

"Nice touch with the noisemaker. Crafty even."

"Squeak. Squeak. Squeak," she said and surrendered a laugh.

Over the loudspeaker came "Kids in America," which Monroe and I agreed had to be the stupidest party song ever.

"I couldn't hook up my MP3 player, but they had this," Dan said. "I kinda like it. Kim Wilde, right? Anthemic? Thought Happy Birthday traditional was too lame anyway."

It's an iPod, Dan, I said to myself, and you can just say the song's name without the arrangement. And the three-eyed balls shot out from their underground canals on a rubber conveyer belt with a seam like a zipper, and I recognized the hum of the balls hitting the polished wood, the roar, and then the loud crack of pins. And the squeals of girls having a good time a few lanes down made me feel even worse.

Monroe propped up a smile between two baby-butt cheeks with bad diaper rash. She'd lost weight and looked older than even a high school kid. Our three lanes were silent and glowing yellow, the pins neatly still, midget pencils in their grooves on the stands, score sheets fresh from the copier. All ready.

Dan kept glancing at his watch, waiting for the other six or eight people he'd called, spoken to their parents or left his voice on their digitized info vault. But they wouldn't come, and I felt worse for Dan and Monroe than I did myself. I knew my situ. I was sure he thought I was all *Freaks and Geeks* (I finally watched it) with my little pack of nerds or potential clean-shaven hipsters that I just kept squirreled away at school because of the empty no-mom-in-the-house deal. Dan had dreamed up little scenarios about me: in the cafeteria ogling some girl with witty commentary, or in the locker room discovering pubes or getting wedgies. Hell's bells, I'd heard stories like that told by funny adults on the car radio on rides out to the Dor. Truth was that I was invisible to most people at school. Most times that was okay by me.

Dan was setting up his laptop on the snack bar counter next to the pizza zoo. I couldn't believe he put his precious baby near so much grease.

"What do you think he's doing?" I asked Monroe, who had a slight grin on her face.

"I don't want to ruin the surprise."

"Probably some ghey cutout movie or e-card, right?"

"Hmm mmm."

"Not a montage of me as a baby or something with 'What I Like About You' playing in the background? That would be awk-ward."

"It would, yes." She closed her eyes, all sensei status.

"You know, don't you?"

"I'd hate to spoil this roller coaster of fun."

"Hint? Phone a friend?"

"Okay." She sat up straight and held one gnawed-looking finger up. "Number one: It's not match-dot-com, though you could use it." Another finger resurrected "Number two. Not porn, though you could probably use that too."

"Thanks very little. That's all you got for me?"

"That's all. Present time is after this moment, or so I was told."

Monroe's mom got up and whispered something into Dan's ear as he hunched over his laptop, fingers fiddling all over the keyboard.

"How you feeling?" I asked Monroe. She seemed okay enough to get here, but I knew there was a lot going on. She hadn't been in school, and her e-mails were short but not happy short. Almost like code.

"Let's see." She poked her index finger against her white party hat. "Relevant to this situ you're in? I'm peachy."

I started humming the lyrics from "Kids in America."

"Shite. Are they playing that rotten suckfest song again?"

"Earworm anthem."

"Where are the Columbine kids when you really need them?"

"Almost there!" Dan yelled, his head still under the hood of his MacBook.

"Is it a slideshow of all our bromantic moments together?" I yelled back at him.

"Nope, but that would be fun for your friends to see. Come on, everybody gather 'round."

Everybody still included only me, Monroe, and Monroe's mom, whose jumpsuit squeaked when she moved. Snackage arena smelled like cheese, cotton candy, and something bitter, probably years of dust and foot powder never vacuumed up. I tried not to lean on the counter and kept an eye on Monroe. There was a blank screen on the laptop, with a little hand cursor quivering like it was waving at me. Dan messed with his cell phone and laptop at the same time. The roar of the ball sounded behind us, and then someone yelled, "Sweet Jesus!" I turned, and the little girl was still waving.

Dan: "Taa-daa!"

My mom's balloony face filled up the square. "Hello. Hello. Anybody out there?"

"Just nod if you can hear me," Monroe and I both said out loud.

"Is there anybody home?" I continued without my own permission slip.

"Coy, I can see you!"

"Hey." This was weird to the weirdest power. Houston, we have a mother.

"Happy birthday, sweetie. Isn't this neat?"

"Golly gee whiz, sure is, *mamacita*."

"You can thank Dan for all of it. He planned everything, right down to the folks here getting all hooked up to the—" She turned to her right, and we saw her profile come in and out of focus. "What's it called?"

"Skype," a voice said from off-screen.

"Skyped. Right." She nodded. "How are you, honey? Feeling older?"

"My birthday's not until the week after next."

"I know that. We just thought—" Mom's face fell, and her gaze moved from searching for Dan in the camera they'd installed for her video chat to whoever was offstage. Then the sound was muffled, and my mom turned to the camera again and perked up. "Let me see, who's there?"

Mrs. Alpert dragged Monroe in front of the screen. While they all said their hellos, I stared at my mom's lips quivering slightly. All that flickering and her pixilated face reminded me of *Blade Runner*, only bowling was such a crazy background for this new tech. I felt like I was trapped in the middle of two centuries: vidchat on one side, standing ashtrays on the other.

"Coy," my mom called. "What did you get?"

"We haven't opened gifts yet."

"Oh, okay." I could see the top edge of the notecard she was reading from in her hand. "What was your score?"

"Score?"

"Bowling. Remember when we went there?"

"Haven't done that, either."

"We just got here," Dan said, leaning into the frame like Mr. Bean.

"Oh, well. Let me meet the rest of your friends."

"This is it. Just us."

Dan piped in: "So far."

"Let me meet your friend behind you." When she pointed, the screen made her hands look big and manly, almost She-Hulk green.

"You already said hi to Mon—" I turned around, and there she was: Avree, looking even prettier than she did at school. I lost my breath. Her hair was slicked back, and sunglasses perched high on her clean hair. No gum. She had on a short black jacket made from that soft material that looked like it'd been through the wash a thousand times. That soft. Dryer-lint soft.

All of us just stood there staring at her, and then one of us would remember the linkup and look back at my mom, who was blinking, trying to figure out what was going on, why was everyone so quiet?

"Is the volume on?" she asked the off-screen ghost.

"I cannot believe this," Monroe said.

"I know. This is great, right?" Did Dan tell whatever parents he called that there'd be a linkup with the birthday boy's mom who, BTW, is locked in the funny farm? If so, how would he have put that? If by chance anyone would remotely want to come, how could he put that fact in a way that a teenager could not think it was super creepy? If they did come, how did Dan think it would go? Just one of those goofy things that happen at these kinds of parties? Same as, say, a jumpy castle or pony ride? What did he tell my mom? Kids in the miPod generation are totally used to these cyberchats, have

'em all the time, with teachers, friends overseas, reality television stars? Kids are so used to them that it would be like
Mom was standing there for reals in the grease-scented air,
downing a flat Fanta?

"Hi! I'm Avree," she said with a bonsai wave, short and mini.

"Nice to meet you, Avree. Sorry it's not in person, but . . .
I'm glad you can be here, there I mean. For Coy's birthday."

Monroe was eyeballing Avree, and so was everyone else, so
it was like show-and-tell: Avree had to talk to both my virtual
mom and the real folks standing around her. She handled it
better than I would have. Monroe would have pretended to go
to the bathroom and left the building for the next town over.

"I'm in science with Coy. He's helping me with my project."

"What did you choose?"

"Platypus."

"See!" Dan chirped like a goddamn game-show host.
"That's what I told you to do, but you had to resist. You had
to decide to buck the system and—"

"I don't know what I'm doing," I said, cutting him off.
"It's totally like me. Really."

He looked straight at Monroe. "But you said you—"

"I'm considering all options currently. Don't worry, my
teacher is cool with it. All about brainstorming, that guy, my
teacher, Beakman, is."

"Avree, now where do you live?" my mom asked.

With Avree verbally mapquesting, Monroe stared at me
like I just evacuated in her piehole, while her mom's jaw seemed
wired shut, as if opening her mouth would let piles of pain
out. All I could think about were those three lanes: three

blond wood runways like three bars in some dumb cell-phone commercial. People mobbed the Sanchez guy's shoe counter, pointing at our three quiet exclamation points at the end of the alley, even though the lanes are alleys, right? Can I say those stage-lit lines were beautiful without sounding ghey? Can I say I wanted to take off the thin leather fruity shoes and skate on my socks without sounding like I belong in Dor? Apple never falls far.

"Time's almost up," Dan said, looking at his watch. "I promised."

"Where's Coy?" the screen called.

"I think we should give up a few of our lanes," I said, but no one heard me.

Her huge hands pressed together like she was praying. "Happy birthday, sweet sweet boy. I wish I could be there."

"Okay. You're not much of a bowler."

"Ha! Right. Neither are you. And Coy."

"Yup."

"Try to enjoy yourself, will you? It's your birthday."

"I—" Then disconnect. Log off. Power down.

I picked at the edge of a Brunswick sticker on the counter while Dan packed up his laptop and slipped it in the neoprene sleeve and then into his padded messenger bag, which he secured with a little ghey silver lock.

"Wireless ain't so bad for a bowling alley, huh?"

"Wonders of technology," I said. "Welcome to the space age, Mr. Bond."

And then there was a colossal silence, and I felt like I was attached to one of those 360-degree cameras that swung from

Mrs. Alpert to Dan, Monroe, and Avree, who had this neat
little box all wrapped in her perfect hands. She was wearing
ironed jeans and a black sweater under her jacket with these
little braided pretzel patterns running up and down. She'd
spent some serious time on her hair. Monroe had taken off
her hat and stowed the noisemaker. I don't know how long
this silence was: coulda been six minutes or sixty, and I tried
to think of things people say at these awkward moments:

*Avree, how nice of you to come. Does anyone want to roll a
gutterball with me? Har har. Mrs. Alpert, did you lose weight?
You look great! Dan, thank you so much for putting this on, so
thoughtful of you.*

But nothing felt right, more like plastic trucks shooting
out of my mouth. Then it hit me: When will I stop thinking
about being a little kid? When will my memories be more
about sixth or seventh grade than six or seven years old?

Dan asked, "Should we do gifts?" Everyone nodded, almost
sighed from relief, except for Monroe, who closed her eyes and
shrugged. We went back to the cartoon guitar table.

"Open mine first. It's small. No big deal." Avree thrust the
parcel into my hands. She was a good wrapper; the Vs on the
back were tight and thick and sealed with good tape, the kind
that is the color of fogged windows. I slipped my index finger
under each fold at the same time and lifted so they popped.
Inside was a plain gray box, and inside that was a white tissue
that wasn't as neat. Inside that was a flash drive in the shape of
a platypus. Brown body, blue bill. The metal that you put into
the USB connector was hidden inside its head. You needed to
decapitate the mammal to make it work. *Très* cool.

"I thought it was funny." She checked her glasses on her head, then looked away. "Beakman's project, I don't know." She shrugged.

It's hard to tell you how much I loved that gift. Also couldn't tell her either, not yet, not there, not in that crowd.

Later she would say that part of the reason that she showed that day was because she was curious. I said, "Train wreck curious?" She laughed. But then she added that there was another part too, a part that actually wanted to celebrate my birthday with me. But that would be much later. Oh, and there would also be parks and photos by empty train cars in our future.

"It's great," I said, and it sounded sarcastic but it wasn't. It was the perfect gift because it showed that (a) she remembered our conversations, and (b) we had an inside joke, and maybe even (c) our own mascot.

Avree just watched me breathe through my mouth and saw Monroe roll her eyes and said, "It's stupid, I know, but . . ."

I wanted to go full heartthrob on her and say *No no no*, hold her hands and tell her why I loved it and how I'd use those six gigabytes—Colonial Studies, English essays, downloaded music—but I was too late.

"That was very thoughtful, dear," Monroe's mom said, which was true and the worst thing anyone could have said.

"And useful!" Dan piped in. "It's hard to find gifts that meet so many criteria."

I was shocked because Avree didn't leave. It didn't look like she won the lottery either.

"We're next." Monroe's mom handed me two packages in white paper.

The first was an "I Love 80s Movies" DVD box set with everything from *Pretty in Pink* to *Planes, Trains, and Automobiles*.

Next was Top 100 80s songs CD box set.

"These are so . . ." I was gonna lose my shite and say "badass," "killer," or at the least "awesome" (an overused word if there ever was one), but then Avree would feel bad, so I took a ghey cleansing breath and said, "So great."

"Great, yeah," Monroe said flatly, "if you could get those TPS reports by this afternoon, that would be great." She was quoting *Office Space*, one of our favorite movies, and insulting my monotone and lame thanks at the same time. She was good like that.

"Funny, Roe."

"Mon-roe to you, mister sister."

"Here's mine, bro." Dan's was thin and wrapped in slick pages from *Rolling Stone*. Even before I opened it, he blurted out, "It's a refurb. Nothing to look at on the outside, but I think you'll be pretty pleased with the inside . . ."

The laptop had a matte black cover with scratches, and you could tell not much was new—keys were worn and faded, and even the original manufacturer's plate had been scratched off.

"Perfect for you," Monroe pointed at the plate. "Says GAY." I guess they used a Gateway housing or whatever they call it and the G, A, and Y were the most visible silver letters. Never would have noticed if Monroe wasn't there to point it out.

"Super." When I booted it up, it was eye-blinking fast and the Internet connection (RioLanes2) was three bars strong. Just fiddled around, googled my name and saw the familiar stock exchange abbreviation for some finance company, then the definition in Middle English, Old French, and Vulgar Latin. Your mom is all Vulgar Latin, Monroe would say.

"One more thing," Dan said, handing me a small gift. "This one's from your mom. She wanted you to open it in front of her, but it got too crazy. Here ya go."

The package was flat, longer than a CD, and wrapped in gold paper. This one I tore. "Be careful," Dan warned.

And it was the picture.

"Guess you don't have a corrupted memory after all."

My dad holding my burrito-wrapped self up toward the camera, leaning against that Ford Galaxie 500.

"Your mom made me search through a crazy amount of boxes and pictures to find that."

He had longer sideburns than I remembered, and his hair was high, not bumpit high but like a wave rolling, about to crash on his forehead. Almost like the Romantics album cover, the one when they're all dressed in those red leather suits.

"I had to take a half day off work and go into the attic so you…"

The car was long and hefty, with its grill coming at the lens like a menacing wall of chrome. Closer to a fence or a gate, actually. Black-and-white photo, greenish in the shadows.

"Is that you?" Avree asked Dan.

"No, no." He shook his hands and backed away a little.

"Does it look like him?" Monroe hissed.

"Monroe!" WTF?

"She doesn't even know you! Not about your dad or your mom."

"She knows about my mom." *Especially now.* I glanced over at Avree. "Kinda."

"Oh, well, that's swell. . . . What else does she know about?"

I should have lied and said "Nothing," but the photo got the room tilting and those three lanes like little runways but no planes or supermodels anywhere nearby. Crowd noise and thunder and lightning bowling me over. I just stood there, and Monroe—

Have I ever said how smart she is with people? How once she pegged this sub as way off, worse than a creeper, turns out later that day he was canned for chasing the girls around the track in PE, kicking them on their shorts-covered backdoors. No shite. Monroe spotted him first, and so, in the bowling alley, Monroe spotted me. And then she was gone, a puff of white smoke fading into the beer-drinking crowd, her mother saying good bye and grabbing coats on her way out, not needing to explain since this was not an uncommon occurrence, them leaving events, hell, everything, unexpectedly. Me. Avree. Dan. Six pitchers of soda turning flat, untouched cake, new plastic silverware, and crisp, clean napkins. Three lanes.

22

"Not exactly the way I imagined this," Dan said.

"Guess not."

"Should we bowl?"

"Guess so."

Dan stood there waiting for us to invite him to play, and I didn't want him to. He tried to do something nice, but it ended up being a pathetic mess. What I did was look at him full frontal and then move my eyes to the left, not like I was giving him a tell to leave, more like it was awkward that I couldn't really stand to look at him at that point, only it's not as harsh as it sounds. I don't know exactly what he felt, but he understood. "I'll just go close out two of the lanes and then make some calls to the office. That cool with you guys?"

Nods all around.

"Bowl much?" Avree asked, walking slowly toward the last lane.

"Not quite."

"Me neither. My uncle does. He lives in New Mexico, and he's always trying to get me to pick it up. He says it's a very social game. Feeling very social?"

"Crazy social."

"Yeah, it's weird. He was stationed there and then retired and took over the bowling alley. It's on this missile range, White Sands."

"Missile range? Really?" I thought of bombs bursting all around this dump and it being the only building surviving. Just me and her. Dan would've already left, but he could be safely ensconced (vocab word). I can't bomb Dan.

"Hard to explain." Her eyes dropped to her sides. "You know that sandy place in the first *Star Wars* movie?"

"I think you mean episode four, the first one filmed?"

"Sorry, nerd police." Eye roll, side of rice.

"I'm not a nerd." I thought about it for a sec. "Not every day, anyway."

"Just kidding." Her smile! Can I say it made me feel better? "Anyway, that's where it is. Roadrunner Lanes. Mostly military dudes go there because there's a base. You can go sledding down the dunes, though."

"That's pretty cool."

"Yeah, but most of the time too hard to explain to people who haven't been there."

I grabbed a ball and rolled it down and hit a few pins. I heard somewhere that a bowling ball was supposed to be an extension of your arm, but it didn't feel that way to me. It felt like some sort of spell gone wrong where my hand was swollen and then amputated, but as Avree was going off on her *Star Wars* stuff I realized, if only for a second, that I was actually having a toothpick of fun. Sure, the music was now turned back to Lady Gag Me and the place still smelled like cheddar rotting under a hobo's armpit and Avree and I were all gutterball status with our rolls, but I laughed for the first time that day. I can't remember if it was the time my ball went into another lane or Avree's jumped off her hand when it was behind her body, but we were laughing pretty hard and joking that we needed those short bus tubes to cushion our patheticness, not the little runts. She snorted, and it made me think of Monroe and me before she was sick, before my mom went away, and then I felt bad.

"I need to tell you something," I said.

"You hate my gift."

"No, no, I really like it."

"It's okay." She smelled so good. Girls are so clean. "I still have the receipt."

"No, I really like it. I swear." I grabbed her hands and then dropped them just as quickly. My move startled us both, I think. "It has nothing to do with that."

"Okay."

"Some of the things I said about Monroe were a bit—"

"Personal?" She leaned in close enough for me to smell her shampoo: grapefruit. Maybe I lingered too long, because she said, "I can keep a secret—"

"Exaggerated."

Her grapefruit scent retreated as she leaned back. "I don't know if I should ask which ones or why first."

"Yeah." I tried to peel the carpet up with the toe of my circus shoe.

"Yeah, what?" She seemed a little pissed.

"I'd feel the same way." I told her there were no guys in white coats or straitjackets or even ambulances. But Monroe WAS poisoned and depressed and making frequent visits to an annex of the hospital. Her parents were building her a guesthouse though I called it a bubble and it could break them. For reals.

She said nothing. I've lived inside a lot of pauses and this one seemed as long as the longest train you've ever seen go by. Times two with a caboose. Only I wasn't in a car with my nose pressed against the glass with my mom in the driver's seat heading west.

"Why'd you lie? She's your bestie."

"My what?" I knew what it meant, but it sounded weird. "Best friend."

"Oh. 'Cause I'm a dick."

"No, really."

"No, really." I widened my eyes to show her.

She shook her head, all disappointed. "Too easy to say. I'm a bitch, you're a dick. Too easy."

I could see Dan near the entrance pressing a cell to his ear and pacing, no doubt calling his brochachoes and freaking out on how weird I am and the fact that I have one friend, maybe two if I survived this awkwardness with Avree. The photo was in its frame on the cartoon guitar table. I can't tell you how uncool this is, but what came to my mind? Foreigner. Yup. Lines about being a loner and danger zones. So inopportune.

"I wanna know why you lied to me about your friend."

There are times when these synapses go off in my head like birthday-candle-size bottle rockets, only the rockets hit each other in midair and careen off to hit other rockets also in the air. What I'm trying to say is that I lied to Avree because I was tired of carrying Roe's illness in me like wet cement in my bag, and I was tired of her illness reminding me that my mom was just a Friday visit and now a flickering image in a laptop in a greasy bowling alley, and then Dan and his pathetic attempt at a birthday that provided nothing but a full time vacancy in my friend department, and then back to my mom who is a conduit (Beaker's class vocab) to my father who is dead but now I see his photo and it hurts even more that it's not him trying and god knows if he didn't die then my mom coulda been okay (no guarantees I know, I know) and I coulda been an ath-a-lete with friends coming out of my butt like Skittles and everything would be different.

"Because I like you." I shrugged. And she almost seemed to accept that.

23

After a few nights of us talking on the phone (which made Dan far too giddy), Avree started coming over. She'd hop the bus with me and take the ride to my house. I didn't tell Monroe. She'd been in and out of school and mostly out of touch except for a few e-mails. They stopped work on her bubble because of a problem with the loan or something, and she was seeing another doctor after a few more trips to the hospital. She didn't want me to visit her there, she said. Too ghastly even for Chinese TV.

I know this sounds ghey, but I never met someone or really knew someone who was so, well, fun (lame word, I know). I have to say it was weird. Avree's whole deal was that life was one big adventure and that everything she came up against was for laughs or fun or both. It worked for her, obviously, but took a robotron like me a while to get used to. Me and Monroe, we didn't jump into things too fast, and we'd really grown used to the music and movies we liked, TV shows we didn't ("American Idolatry sucks 4ever!" written on our hands), food and clothes, all of it. Monroe once told a kid during break at school, "We are who we are, get over it!" when the douche said she looked like a freak when she dressed like Nurse Joy and I was a loser for being a friend to someone who didn't know that every day wasn't freaking Halloween. Monroe said some other choice things too after the dickhead was out of rimshot. I was happy I didn't get into a fight. My karate is not up to par just yet, Mr. Miyagi-san.

Dan would later joke that Avree had replaced Monroe, but that wasn't it at all, probably the same way he didn't replace my dad for my mom. As if. I'm sure my mom saw it the way I did: two very different roles in two very different movies. It would be like comparing Bill Murray and Will Ferrell. Or even Bill Murray in *Caddyshack* versus Bill Murray in *Lost in Translation*. It was stupid to even try.

"I've never really seen one of these before," Avree said when she first spotted my turntable. I was glad she didn't hit the closet. She ran her finger along the edge of the record, *Back in Black*, I think it was. "I mean, I've seen DJs play in clubs and on TV, but I've never seen one up close. Or how it's hooked up to your laptop."

She wore her hair down that day. First time I'd seen it like that. Lighter on top than at the ends, and the wave on the crown of her head poofed a little. I felt totally awkward, she and her amazing hair in my house, Dan still at work, stacks of albums on the floor (and some pretty rank clothes), posters of the Clash, *Stripes*, and *Better Off Dead* with little baby John Cusack hanging off big John Cusack's mirrored sunglasses. I thought she'd see the whole mess and think I'd end up my own version of the forty-five-year-old virgin.

"Why do you hook it up like this? Why not speakers?" She plopped herself down in my computer chair. I had to lean over her, which made my glandular areas overheat a little.

"This one is made to connect to a computer. I have that one over there that's all old-school with speakers." I pointed to the jumbled mess in the corner: wires, speakers, spare tweeters and woofers I bought at a garage sale, cables and a mike stand. "Then I had this hooked up to my PC, but the laptop Dan gave me is about a million times faster and with more memory, and this has to be the most boring conversation ever." I dragged my finger across the mouse pad, just for something to do. I wished I had gum or smoked crack.

"I think the word is boringest," she joked, "and I'm interested. Really." She smiled up at me as if she was in the running for the nicest person ever or playing an elaborate and cruel hoax that would end up with me handcuffed to my toilet with duct tape on my eyebrows.

"How could you be? Possibly? Come on, really?" How many similar questions could I ask in the same sentence?

"Shut." She hit me hard, giving me a dead-arm. I hadn't noticed the pencil-mark mole on her ear. "Show me more, DJ Apologetic."

"Fine." Reaching across her and praying my deodorant was long-lasting, I stripped a few beats from the opening riff of *Back in Black* and then isolated them, kept them on repeat, added the same beat slowed down but had it enter late into the loop. I added another in a lower register, on and on until I had a mess that sounded almost like part of a new song.

She nodded and crossed her arms. "That's pretty cool."

"Not really."

"Why do you say that?"

"No reason."

"Seriously." Her back went straight. "Why is that your default mode?"

"My default mode? Who's the nerd now?"

"Yeah, your fallback setting is always 'no big deal,' " she said in a mocking voice. Nice touch.

I thought of all the why-donkeys-don't-go-to-school answers I could have given, but she was here, wasn't she? "It's not cool to me because that kind of stuff, it's been done, and what I see in my head or hear in my head is beyond what I can actually do. You know. When I get to messing with it all, it becomes just that: a mess."

"Everybody feels that way about something."

"Rrr-eally," I said. Of course she would say something like that to someone like me.

"Take me."

"Take you?" Raised my brows. "Keep talking."

She shot Cusack a knowing glance. "Sad-boy moment. Try not to have too many more of those."

"I'll try. It won't be easy."

"Seriously, remember I told you that I wanted to be either a CSI or a vet? Working with animals?"

"Yeah." She didn't know this: I remember every word she ever said. Ever.

"What if I said I wanted to combine the two?"

"Vet by day, CSI by night?"

"Nope." She spun around on my chair, 360 degrees. "I mean really combine the two. Start an animal cruelty task force."

"Okay." I had no idea what the hell she was talking about, and it must have showed.

"Okay." She rolled up to me. Her face was at my chest level. If I had a chest. "Like where if a dog is killed in a dogfight or someone leaves their pet tied up in the sun all day, we investigate, prosecute, and save the animals. Bust on some crazy cat ladies too."

"Wow."

"Cool, right?"

Her smile floored me. "Would you wear superhero costumes when you knocked out false teeth and kicked their wheelchairs?"

"Yes and we would definitely wear them when kicking one hundred percent of your skinny white-boy ass."

"I'll be on the lookout."

She scanned my room: chest of drawers with comics and assorted crappage falling off it. Stand-up lamp, no bulb. Guitar never played. Trash can overflowing with tissues and one sock. Bed on the floor, covers in a knot. File cabinet inside my closet. Broken CD stand. "I see you don't have any animals."

"Is that a crime?"

"It could be."

"I had a fish named Angus once, but he died." Bubble bubble. I remember: blue pebbles, a phony pink shell shoe box casket, and a funeral under our apricot tree. That tree died too. Drought.

"Why didn't you get another?"

"I had a lot going on at the time."

She knew what I meant or at least made a decent guess, because she stopped talking, but not because she couldn't hold her own in our ridonkulous banter. Her eyes went sideways a bit, the way they do when you're watching a movie inside your head. Then she licked her lips almost like a kid, but Avree wasn't a kid really.

"My mom's had affairs." The words slipped out all quiet-like. Eyes were still stage left.

"Huh?"

"At least one. I found out when I was ten." She spun again, which kinda surprised me, given. "She went out a lot. At night. She was always real sweet to me and my sister, saying she loved us, sweet dreams, and all that, but she had to go to a late meeting or meet her boss or her girlfriends at Starry Night Yoga."

"Starry Night Yoga?"

"I know, right? But it does exist. Old chicks under the stars praying for chardonnay rain, my dad called it." She picked up the platypus flash drive she gave me and squinted like she'd never seen it before. Her nails were red but square on the ends, not pointed. Didn't go past her fingers. No overhang whatsoever. "I mean, I could tell my parents weren't happy, but I didn't think much of it. My dad always stayed home with us, made dinner, put on the CDs we listened to when me and my sister went to sleep."

"Sister's name again?"

"Delilah."

"Roger that." She couldn't be as pretty. No one could.

"So. Then one night we got a call. I answered it like always, excited to see who was calling. A big surprise. After that night, we got caller ID. No more surprises. On the phone anyway. It was a woman, but not my mom or aunt. She asked for my dad.

He took it in his bedroom and told us to get ready for bed."
She pressed her finger against the tip of her nose, flattening
it. I imagined her doing that for her sister, making her gig-
gle. "When I heard the screaming that night, I crawled into
bed with D and turned her CD back on and loud. *The Point.*
Harry Nilsson. Do you know it? It's sort of weird but really
amazing. There'd never been violence like that in our house.
And I'm told there won't be again. No matter what happens."

"Your folks said that?"

"And the therapist. And the sheriff. Even my sister." She
waited. "And the man's wife." Her face grabbed a faraway
stare like she heard something that wasn't close by and she
was trying to figure out if it was a hawk, a cat, or the wind
whipping off Red Rock.

"Are you okay?"

"Oh, yeah. No children have been physically harmed in
the making of this story."

I know I should have held her or something, but I'm not so
good at that stuff, so I did what we do at Dor: I patted her back.

"Thanks, Grandpa." She laughed, but her eyes (which are
as dark as a keyboard) had been moisturized.

"I'm sorry!" I said, embarrassed at my acting like
an Aspy-kid.

"It's okay. We're all still together. As of today. Dinner at
six-thirty."

Then there was the silence that follows shite like that.
I tried to figure out why she told me, and I bet she tried to
figure out if she did the right thing by leaking her family
secrets. We weren't like Monroe, who wore her secrets on the

outside. Avree could have hid hers from me for a really long time. Maybe forever.

Now this would be the part of the movie or Disney Channel series where they'd hurl into montage because what we did next: music video. Believe it. Somehow, after the pause, like we just woke up from a drug-induced nap, Avree asked if I'd seen some animated music video by Gorillaz (ancient almost) and I told her about the first video that really combined those elements: A-ha's *Take On Me*. How it starts with sketches and panels like a comic book and then it transforms. Everything transforms, right?

"Here. Found it on YouTube for you." I waited a second for it to load, then played her the real deal.

When the drum intro ended, she laughed, tilting back in the chair. "Whoa! Easy on the synthesizers."

"Hey now! Synthesizers aren't that bad. They'll be saying the same thing about all that autotune hip-hop crap now."

Looking back, we were so into performance mode. Flirting, I guess, but it was all so amplified. My heart was beating like crazy.

"Hip-hop is not crap." I liked the way her hair fell: straight waterfall. "This song's kind of fun actually."

We watched as the cartoon hand came out of the comic book and pulled the girl inside. "You're right. A bit synthy, but still holds up." I thought the video had it backward though. I was the nerdy one looking at the cool singer who was Avree. That whole two-world thing. I wasn't sure who the crazy tool-wielding dudes in numbered helmets were, though.

"We should make our own," Avree said, spinning again, feet in the air. Somewhere along the way, she'd slipped off her shoes. My mom would have said bare feet was not a bright idea given my cleaning-habit history, but hey.

"I know it's all primitive status, but a vid like this would still take a lot of time—"

"No, no, no." She put her hands on my shoulders and shook me. "Just something fun and easy."

I held back the mom joke. I can't believe I even thought of it. Damn Monroe.

"Just turn on the camera and leave that song."

I did as I was told and left A-ha rocking while I turned on the webcam and started recording video.

Shot 1: Me looking dead straight at the camera while Avree shadowboxes at me and the camera. Hair falling on her face like curtains.

Shot 2: Avree slamming her shoulder into mine in an attempt to get me to move. Nicely in sync with the lead singer of A-ha busting into the chick's room. I think his name is Morton. I know. TMI.

Shot 3: I move a little in a mocking way, like I'm being forced to, which I almost am. I have a slight smirk on my face. Avree big laughs—HA! (like Julia Roberts)—at my sad excuse for a smile. (FYI: not a big Julia Roberts fan, but seen enough with my mom to know she's famous for her HA! coming out of that big mouth.)

Shot 4: Avree shimmies and moves even quicker when the chorus comes on: *Take on me, take me on*, and this sounds the gheyest, but I can't help but really smile (she's in my room!) so I figure WTF and start matching her move for move. (I'm not as bad a dancer as you'd guess. I can do all the ones that are good for a white boy to have in his bag o' tricks: shopping cart, butter churn, sprinkler, credit card machine.)

Shot 5: We start this weird head-bob thing where my head goes by her right side, hers going by mine. Then I bob on the other side. It was weirdly birdlike but right before the song ends and the couple gets their own comic book (I think that's what they wanted), Avree kisses me. For reals. And after the rush, I think of the worst things. First, my mother. Would she be scared? Oh, could she be proud. Please? Then my dad and how he'll never see me now or the future version of me. Then the interrupted construction site, but I tell that image to go die. And then: Monroe, my friend in white. At home. So sick and getting sicker. "Monroe would die if she saw all this," I said, and breathed like I'd been underwater for a very long time.

"Then turn off the camera," Avree said.

24

What I brought to the table when Dan and I met Mom was an image stolen from the ride over. I had my eyes wide open this time—no reading, just looking. The construction site was still frozen, and the vicious heat we'd had lately made it look even worse than before. Worse. Worser. Worsest. Paint flaked off the trim of broken windows and a dust storm had hit pretty hard on that side of town. Everything was covered in a thin layer of brown grit. But that wasn't the image. Dan had driven us through a different kind of construction, the road kind—orange cones, bored fat guys limply waving flags, pulsing lights clipped to sawhorses. They also had one of those machines, speed monitors I think, you know, portable lifeguard chairs that give you the speed you're supposed to be going and the one you're actually doing. The limit was 25 mph, and I saw Dan doing 20 but the readout was YOUR SPEED IS 50. Never changed from car to car. It was stuck at YOUR SPEED IS 50. And the 5 kinda looked like an *R*. So it read RO to me. As in Mon-Roe.

"How is she?" my mom asked, and I said, "I don't know."

"What do you mean?" She checked Dan, who shrugged. "Dan says she's practically been living at our house."

She meant Avree.

True, I was pretty crazy about Avree, and we spent a buttload of time together. We met at the detectors in the morning, after homeroom for a quick minute before I went to Language Arts and she went to PE. Lunch, Beakman's. We traded smiling fist bumps in the hall when she was with her friends. Bus rides after school. Dor was the only place she'd hadn't been with me. But the truth of the matter, the truth of the truth inside the truth, is that I'd been ducking Monroe. I was behind about five or six, okay, maybe ten e-mails asking me about updates on school daze, if I'd hit the comic-book store lately to get the latest issue of *Priest*. She said she was pretty bored at home, slept a lot of the time when she wasn't getting tests done. She said the doctors were considering apheresis or something like that. Replacing all her blood with fresh blood. I don't know who from.

"Oh, she's great," I told my mom, meaning Avree but still thinking of Monroe in her white robe, face all swollen, hands the color of a skinned animal. Sick. Sicker. Sickest.

"They're making movies together." The way Dan said it made it sound all creeper status.

"Not exactly," I said like I was the adult here. "More like music videos and stuff."

"Now that sounds fun." My mom moved her over-smile around like there was a studio audience behind me. Monroe was all up in my head. My stomach hurt.

The worst of it had come in Colonial Studies class. Leapyear had handed out another tactile project, this one where you churn milk into butter. We didn't have no stinkin' butter churn, it was more about shaking. Each group had been handed a metal container that had been refrigerated and we took turns agitating it. We had to be aggressive, Leapyear said, or it wouldn't transform. No halfhearted shakes. I was still in the same group with Elizabeth and Flip, and we were kinda/almost/maybe having fun.

"I hear you have a girlfriend," Elizabeth said, handing me the container after her turn was up. Leapyear called time every five minutes. The metal was cold and wore a thin robe of condensation. We were all getting breathy and red, which was good timing, since I probably blushed like a baby girl when she mentioned my news.

"Who?" Flip said. He probably had to be reminded of my name; he wouldn't know any gossip even remotely related to me. I'm sure if he saw me outside of school, at the mall or wherever, he'd probably look right past me.

"Avree Sandoval." Elizabeth grinned, all excited, like she was the one who set us up or something.

"Pretty hot." Flip made a joke about me getting buff for my new girl and handed me the metal jug. Then he checked the phone in his hoodie for texts. Everybody in class was getting pretty ridiculous, dancing like the containers were oversize maracas or something. Some guys even pretended to hump theirs, riding them across the room like small metal horses. I looked over once, and a brown-skinned girl had hers perfectly balanced on her head like she grew up hauling water. She walked the room like it was a runway and didn't even have her arms out. Perfectly balanced. Even Leapyear didn't look totally miserable cutting up slices of homemade bread that another class had baked, but she still said no when someone asked if we could play music. To shake to, that is. This was the thing: school actually was getting kinda okay. People seemed to be looking at me differently, and I felt happy. If Monroe had been there, she would have wanted to take the piss out of the whole thing or not participate and ask me why I'd join in something so universally ghey. Or made some kind of Mormon or Amish horse-and-buggy joke. How now we can buy butter in the store for $1.59. After all, Monroe constantly reminded me, we were cursed. Colon Studies was the worst elective in the whole school. Maybe the universe. And we were chosen to be in it.

"Coy Carnoy," Leapyear said, which freaked me out 'cause I was totally immersed in a shaking zone. I could feel the liquid transform into something heavier, matter with substance. Some random kid who worked for the office had a message for me, so I handed the pot off to Elizabeth and scampered to the door pretty quickly, hoping it wasn't about my mom. I opened it on the way back to my group. Nurselor wanted to see me about Monroe by the end of the day. Not an emergency, it said. But she had something important to tell me.

"Everything okay?" Elizabeth asked like she really cared.

"Fine." And then I slipped it in my pocket and forgot all about it. "Not an emergency."

"Tell me more," my mom said, folding her arms underneath her chin. Room was really bright that day from the white sun streaming through the windows like bleached fog. My mom seemed almost backlit, like you see in movies or photographs. Dreamy. I had already given her my Mother's Day gifts: a CD I'd burned with a "Mother" theme (Beatles, Pink Floyd,

Mothers of Invention, Danzig, Willie Nelson [ew]) and a letter on how much I missed her. All she wanted, and all I was allowed to bring into Dorado. "I want to know all about her."

"She loves sunsets, walks on the beach, hates busy signals, Monday mornings, you know."

"You're not being fair. I can't call. It's not like we can get Skyped every day. I don't have a facepage." She sighed. "I'm missing your first girlfriend."

"Please don't say that."

"Say what?"

Say *Skyped* and *facepage*, but I didn't really care about that so much. "Say 'my first girlfriend.' "

"Why not? It's true, isn't it?"

"Yeah, I guess, but hearing you say it like that makes it sound so—"

"So what?"

So Disney Channel. So ghey. So Justin Bieber. So undropped nad. So pathetic. "So juvenile."

"But that's what makes it special. Did I ever tell you about my first boyfriend? Ted Thomas?" Her goofy flashback face was coming. I could feel it. "Everybody called him T-Bird."

"Are you kidding? Please say you are kidding."

"No, why?"

"T-Bird? Jesus, Mom."

"You just be quiet, mister." She patted my hand.

I could tell this was going to be one of her golden memories because her smile extended so I could see her row of straight white teeth (got them fixed before her wedding to Dan) and her neck stretched too, up, up toward the ceiling.

Half listening about T-Bird actually buying a T-Bird to fulfill his destiny once he was old enough to drive and taking young Joan to the drive-in to see *Grease*, I peeked over at the fish tank and saw the code-talking girl from before, the one with the pigtails but now her hair was cut short to her chin, roughly, like she'd done it herself. Her black-framed glasses were also gone, replaced by a cheaper drugstore pair. She was thinner-looking—all swallowed up in the orange Dor sweats. Skinny arms. It was like this place had been absorbing her, sucking the life from her blood and bones. My mom's weight had stayed pretty much the same. If anything, she'd added a few here and there (and there), though I'd never tell her that.

"Mr. Lindbergh wants to see you before you leave today."

That woke my ass up from my sunshine daydream. "Wait. What?"

"Aren't you listening? What's over there?" She turned around. All the shiny silk had vanished from her orange hair.

"Nothing. Wait. Mom. When did you talk to Mr. Lindbergh?"

"Why do you keep saying 'Wait'? I'm not going anywhere." She and Dan had a good kids-these-days laugh over that one. Har har har. Her trip down memory lane in a T-Bird sure got her all giddy.

"Can you just answer me, please? Jesus."

"You don't like a taste of your own medicine? And please stop saying 'Jesus.' Some people here might get offended by that." She lined up the salt and pepper shakers on the table so they were side by side. Sometimes I missed coming home to a straightened-up house. Dan was clean enough, made me take out the trash and recycling, but he wasn't like my mom, especially in the kitchen and bathrooms. Orderly is how she was. The counters always shiny wiped and things put in rows, columns, and categories. Lots of little wire baskets with compartments that organized all your crap. There was something nice about coming home to that, even if it is kinda anal. "After the last time you were here, Mr. Lindbergh told me how much he likes you and the time you spent together."

"His hawk attacked me."

"That was an accident. He says the bird has gotten a lot better. I might go see it. He's pretty much my only real friend here."

"Really?" My mom going out there to see a hawk that attacked her son was a good sign. "What happened to Martha?"

She turned away for a minute. "I'd rather not discuss it." Then she took a breath and recovered. "He asked if I would bring you by before you go. Is that okay?"

"Sure. Okay. I don't know." The table felt cool on my face.

"What's wrong with you? I thought you'd be over the moon. New girlfriend. Dan's been saying you've been pretty chipper around the house lately."

"I can testify to that, Your Honor." He held his palm up like he was swearing on a Bible. Un-be-lieve-a-ble. All the world's a stage, and some of us are idiots.

"If it's Mr. Lindbergh's past you're worried about, he's just trying to stay sober and get his life back on track."

"Sober?" The way I said it must have clued them in on what I had thought all along about this place and my mom: that they served only one kind of clientele, the crazy kind.

"El Dorado treats all kinds of people in distress, Coy." Her lips dropped curtain on her teeth, and whatever she'd grabbed, remembering T-Bird, she exhaled away. "Eating issues, drinking issues, all kind of issues related to just being a human being."

I shot a quick glance over to the fish tank, but the girl had gone. Probably to deal with issues related to being a human being.

"He didn't mean anything by it." Dan put his arm around her, and her face started to break.

"Can you get him over to Mr. Lindbergh's? I think he should head over there now." She turned away from us again, but this time she wasn't trying to see what I was staring at.

"Hey. Mom. Look."

"It's okay." It wasn't okay. Any idiot could see that, and as Beaker would say, I'm not just any idiot. She thought I'd just told her that she was nuts and a bad mother.

Dan walked me back to reception, where Daisy Death Star waited behind a bunker of blond wood. She had on a cream-colored top without a wrinkle, matching her porcelain face. I wanted to tell Dan to watch his nuts, but I didn't have the energy.

"Can you call Mr. Lindbergh for us? He's expecting Coy here." He put his hand on my head, which I hate.

"Expecting?" she asked, like she'd never heard that word used by oxygen-breathing humanoids in her darkened parallel universe.

"He requested that Coy stop by before we leave." Dan raised his voice to the tone people use when talking to the deaf or the ones who ride the short bus.

"I'll see if I can reach him." She picked up the phone, and even though I was only like four feet from her, I couldn't hear what she was saying. It sounded like "*Zub hazub zubba zub.*" I wanted to ask Dan if he could hear whatever the hell brand of Chinese or Vulcan she was speaking, but there was no way to do it without getting totally busted.

Lindy came out a bit slower than he had before. Maybe something had happened, but as he got closer, I tried to remember a vocab word. Sheepish, I think it was. Means, well, like a sheep. All meek status. His head was bowed, and he seemed almost twitchy saying hi to Dan, who then begged off to go see his wife, since my mom no longer occupied our table. She wasn't outside in the little green strip either. I knew they had other more private meeting places, and I couldn't remember if Dan was allowed in her room or not. I think not. They have had a few nights together at a hotel nearby, in case you were worried.

"How's it been going?" Lindy asked, and started walking.

"Fine."

"I've been having some nice chats with your mom. Nice lady."

"I know, she told me."

"She told you she was a nice lady?"

I let that one die on its own. Har har har. He led me through the double doors, back into the hallway with all the old-school black numbers. More people were around this time, coming in and out of rooms. A cleaning lady did a double take when she saw me. They probably don't have kids in the back much. She eyed me up and down like I was lost, but hell, I had an escort.

"Not really sure I want to see your bird again."

"You're in luck. It's too late in the day to see much of anything other than the reason I'm dragging you back here."

I figured why ask if he was leading me to whatever he wanted me to see.

"I've felt bad about the last time you were here. That's not how I wanted it to go. He misbehaved, and I was nosy that day. There was a black cloud over my head. The last thing a kid like you needs. Adults can be strange. What I'm saying is, I'm sorry, and I hope you'll forgive me."

"Sure." Whatevs.

"I'd like us to stay friends. I hope I can be someone you can talk to. Here or wherever."

I thought about what my mom said. "But you can leave, can't you? It's not like they're forcing you to stay, right?"

"No one is forcing me, but I don't think I'm ready just yet."

For some reason, I started getting pretty excited. "Don't you want to get out of here? Go where you want to? Live a normal life?"

"*Normal* is a tricky word. Everyone's version is different. Why a lot of folks don't get along, alone or together."

"What's your version?"

"Right now, it's what you see." He lifted his arm and sorta half-swung it. "A supportive place where I can make some friendships that are good for me, get help with some things I'm working on. A place that lets me keep my bird. A place that keeps me out of trouble."

"Maybe I should register with Daisy."

"I hope you never end up in a place like this. Not that it's so bad. But you have a lot of people who care about you—a good mom, stepdad."

"It's not exactly normal to have your mom here, even if she does love you."

"As I said, we all have to figure out our own definition of normal. Life is not a competitive sport. Not for me, anyway. That's why I have a bird, not a tennis racket."

Flash: all of us, each in our different places—me, Monroe, Avree, my mom, Dan, Lindy, everybody struggling to define their version of normal, and how it all kept shifting, all the forking time. Sometimes life seemed like playing Ping-Pong in an earthquake with a metal butter container balanced on your head.

"Here we are." Room 1704 looked exactly the way it had before: bed tight as a drum, tissue box, things neat and tidy. Not a hair out of place. I thought about what they say in cop shows after an accident has cleared: nothing to see here.

Lindy went over and slipped his hand under the cabin of the model plane. "Here you go." He handed it to me. It was so light. "I think it's better to give it to you than ship it off to the Smithsonian."

"Okay." Such a sweet plane.

"That was a joke."

"Okay."

"Besides, I can start making them again, if I feel the inclination."

"I can't accept it," I said, even though I hoped he'd say what he did say: "Of course you can."

"Thanks, Mr., um, I mean, Lindy."

"No problemo." He slipped his glasses off his face and rubbed the bridge of his nose. "Now what's this your mom tells me about a girlfriend?"

Research Note: On May 21, 1927, Charles A. Lindbergh completed the first solo nonstop transatlantic flight in history, flying his Ryan NYP "Spirit of St. Louis" 5,810 kilometers (3,610 miles) between Roosevelt Field on Long Island, New York, and Paris, France, in 33 hours, 30 minutes. With this flight, Lindbergh won the $25,000 prize offered by New York hotel owner Raymond Orteig to the first aviator to fly an aircraft directly across the Atlantic between New York and Paris. When he landed at Le Bourget Field in Paris, Lindbergh became a world hero who would remain in the public eye for decades.

The aftermath of the flight was the "Lindbergh boom" in aviation: aircraft industry stocks rose in value, and interest in flying skyrocketed. Lindbergh's subsequent U.S. tour in the "Spirit of St. Louis" demonstrated the potential of the airplane as a safe, reliable mode of transportation. Following the U.S. tour, Lindbergh took the aircraft on a goodwill flight to Central and South America, where flags of the countries he visited were painted on the cowling.

"Spirit of St. Louis" was named in honor of Lindbergh's supporters in St. Louis, Missouri, who paid for the aircraft. "NYP" is an acronym for "New York–Paris," the object of the flight.

I held the *Spirit of St. Louis* in my lap on the way home. It was pretty amazing. There wasn't any glue you could see where he'd connected the seams. I know if it was me, there'd be globs like the thing was a platypus secreting fluids. The plane was smooth all over. I ran my fingers over it with my eyes closed, trying to find a rough spot. I thought he'd at least skip the underside, but no, the guy was thorough, you had to give him that. Before I left, he said he hoped we could talk again soon. It was almost like he had something he needed to get off his chest.

"Do you think we'll ever get any rain?" Dan asked. It had been the hottest winter and spring on record, and I'd heard the newscaster say that if we didn't get rain soon, we'd have to go into some emergency status where people couldn't plant anything at all this summer. It would be major suckage for the plant stores and landscapers. We weren't supposed to water except at night twice a week, but I saw people on our street doing it anyway. No running fountains were allowed now, or any of those cheesy waterfalls old farts or hippies have in their backyards. They said they might have to shut down car washes too. Monroe would be bummed about that. The final step would to be halt all new construction, which Dan said would really throw the already crippled economy full-on into the low-flow toilet.

"Monsoon season's coming up," I said to make conversation, but I did hope for rain. I sometimes dreamed about it.

"That's not until summer."

Lindy had painted all the decals below the name of the plane: country flags, certificates, other official-looking stuff I couldn't figure out. "Hey, when do you think Mom's getting out?"

"It's hard to say, bro."

"Any way to estimate, bro? Might need a number sometime soon, bro."

"I'd hate to mislead you. I'm not her doctor."

"But you play one on TV."

He cracked a smile for just a second. "Yeah, right." His hands gripped the wheel tight and he ran them over the whole circumference. "The doctors say they see improvement, but as you saw today, your mom's still pretty delicate."

"Don't you ever get worried?"

"About what?"

"That she'll never get out."

He fake-laughed almost like it was a stupid question, but I knew it wasn't. "She'll get out. Don't you worry about that, mister."

We were stopped in that same construction, but there wasn't a speed monitor going this way. We'd been channeled into a single-lane chute that seemed too narrow for half the trucks and SUVs barreling through it. No margin for error that I could see.

"Don't you ever worry that your memories will boil down to driving once a week to see the person you married? Isn't that weird? Like a marriage you commute to?" I left out the part about the weird kid who kinda got dumped on him.

"It's certainly not the average."

The sun had set behind Red Rock, and there was a mustard color that seemed pretty unique lining the sky. Above that was a line of white and some blue still left over from the day.

Dan said, "My dad used to tell me that we all have our own little part of the sewer to swim in."

"That's sweet."

"I know, right? For a while I saw it that way, you know—life is suffering and all that. I'd guess your friend Monroe sees it that way. But after I met your mom"—he took his eyes off the road to check me—"and you, of course, I guess I saw things a bit differently."

"Explain, *por favor.*"

"It's not that simple. Life is more than just happy or sad, good or bad, pretty or ugly. It's bigger than any of those things. A marathon, not a sprint. It's a major production, not some small film with only one decent part."

A lot of cheese for me to swallow. "But your wife doesn't live with you."

"Not yet." Dan smiled like he was trying to reassure me or something. One of those smiles that held both sad and happy. I guess that's where the word *sappy* comes from.

"Not yet?" I thought about Monroe. Not yet? I thought about me. "Is that good enough?"

"It has to be," Dan said, and turned onto our street. Reaching over to his visor, I pressed the remote to open the garage where Mom's car waited for someone to come home and drive it.

25

I didn't want to get off the bus. I wished I'd faked sick with Dan, who was a pushover when it came to staying home, but I hardly ever took him up on it. He said he thought college was a royal waste of time and money, and most of high school too. Lots of other kids had to vomit gallons in their parents' bed to earn the right to miss classes. My mom was definitely from that camp. When I was little, the first thing we did after we moved was register for school. Before we even unpacked the freaking car. No one was making us rush, but my mom wanted me to start that day. She said I'd lost too much time already. All of the schools were public, so I could catch up pretty fast. I didn't cause trouble, and I was bright enough, or so they said. A quick study, one teacher wrote.

I could spot both girls through the bus window. Since it'd been so hot, they propped the school doors wide open with cinder blocks, and I could see all the way through to the detectors. There they were—Avree on the right, all in brown. Her hair was shiny wet and up in a tight swirl. She wore a loose-fitting soft brown shirt and a pair of jeans the color of desert sand. Amber bracelets on each wrist, and if I knew her like I thought I did, amber rings on the fingers of both hands, including one her dad gave her that actually had a fly caught in it. Older than old, she'd told me.

On the left was Monroe. I had no idea she was coming back, I swear. She wore her dad's white shirt, white pants, slippers, and all, but she'd bleached her hair the color of cotton balls. Flaming red face. I squinted to see if they'd noticed each other, and they had. Each had her body turned toward the lines of folks handing their bags to the guards and then streaming between the black frames. But both of them had their outside feet pointing away, like they were ready to flee if necessary. Avree thumbed her phone while Monroe stared straight ahead, all military status. She'd lost a ton of weight, her chipmunk cheeks had sunk in, and the redness in her skin had been over layered with white flaky stuff, almost like she'd just walked out of a snowstorm.

"Heya, kid, you need to get off now," Jesus said, running his hand over his shiny Elvis hair.

"Okay, Jesus."

All the kids called the bus driver the Bible pronunciation of his name (g-zuss) instead of the Hispanic way (hay-zeus), and he never seemed to give a *raton's culo*. He wore camouflage Carhartt all year round, even if it was like 110 degrees out. He didn't seem to care about much except that you didn't make him late for his next stop and that you got off at the end, which I wasn't currently doing. I pretended to look for stuff under the seats just to stall for time and then made sure to slap each seat as I went by. When I hit the front by the trash can, I felt like yelling, "Dead man walking!" even though it wouldn't have been funny to anyone but me. Maybe not even me. My throat got all twisted as I stepped down those deep rubber-lined school bus steps. Jesus pulled the door shut with a whoosh behind me as a song that my mom used to sing to me played inside my head:

Make new friends
But keep the old
One is silver
And the other gold

How stupid is that? Could I think of anything more lame at that moment? I don't know what gets in my cranial locker sometimes.

I could barely lift my feet. All the other kids moved by me like I was standing still: Juicy, American Eagle, Hollister, Volcom, DC, Billabong, Roxy, Quicksilver, Free People, Lulu-loser. Could smell them too: Axe body spray, grandma's perfume, something like grapefruit or orange, smoke, bad BO, doughnuts, sour milk, farts. All these images and scents swirling around in the bright sun. I had to keep it together. It was hard to keep it together. I'd skipped breakfast again that day too.

Monroe saw me first and gave me a little nod like she might be pissed, but let it be known: I had no idea she was coming back. Then again, I hadn't checked my e-mail lately. Just seeing her made me feel all guilt-trip status. Avree must have sensed the unspoken drama because she came up from her phone, smiled, and lifted her eyes to let me know that she knew Monroe was there. Usually Avree'd walk up and kick my Vans or Chuck Taylors, say "Hey," but today she just waited. I had to make a choice, and I wasn't the dude for it. My life was weird enough without this *HSM* crappage. I never should have gotten off that bus. I should've hid in the seats until Jesus took me back to his manger or bus depot or wherever they hide the buses until pickup. I drew a mental line between Monroe and Avree and walked it like I was trying to prove to a cop I was sober or something. It was the straightest line I could manage, peeking up at Avree, who was biting her bottom lip, and Monroe who was auditioning for the marines or something. I was now close enough to see the stars of blue smashing out from under Monroe's baby-powder lids. I tried to flash her the wait-one-minute with my finger but instead did something spastic, like she was deaf and I was trying to sign the Declaration of Independence to her. She looked at me like I was nuts as I walked crazy fast over to Avree.

"Monroe's back, obviously," I said. It was hard to look in her eyes. They are darker than oil.

"Yeah."

"Can I lunch you at meet?"

"What?"

"Sorry." I shook my head to clear the cobwebs. What's a cob? "Can I meet you at lunch?"

"Yeah, sure, whatever." She snapped her phone shut and jammed the thing halfway in her hip pocket.

"Don't be mad."

"Not mad." She turned and walked away.

Mad.

I did the ten-step walk of shame over to Monroe, who hadn't budged. "Welcome back, Kotter," I said. We loved that show. Watched it all the time. So stupid it was amazing. We were the Sweathogs.

"What's up, Tree?"

"Come on, Roe."

"It's Monroe to you, mister sister."

We handed our bags over to the guard dogs, who rifled through them, and then we stepped through the gates of what I imagined would be hell for me that day. Principal Pornstache gave Monroe a mad-dog look and whispered something into the ear of the vice, who nodded all serious, like we could read his mind and he needed to put up a wall.

When Monroe got her bag back, she said, "I guess that ghey Franken-laptop your dad built you is broken, huh?" She still hadn't really looked at me.

I knew what she was doing, calling Dan my dad and giving me shite about not e-mailing her back. I wasn't gonna fight her. She needed to be mad, so I was going to let her. I could take it. "You dyed your hair."

"I'm all about the matching. Should know that by now."

"Seriously, why did you?"

"Does it really matter?" Monroe was best at making you feel like the worst.

"Sorry I haven't e-mailed, been kind of busy, you know?" Now it was me not looking at her.

"The kind of busy that has you driving to the hospital all the time, that kind of busy?"

"Come on, you know." I could have said something about driving every week to see my mom, but I knew she had better cards to play.

"The kind that has your skin flaking off so you spend hours picking at it until it bleeds?"

I figured I just had to take whatever she'd throw at me and she'd be done, eventually. So I let her pelt me with blood tests, CAT scans, insurance forms, mounting (her word) credit card debt, dropping off dog leashes and cat bowls at the Salvation Army, steam-cleaning clothes every few days. I felt awful about it all, even though I hadn't meant any harm when I didn't reply. Walking with Monroe in the hall was like a scene out of some kung fu movie where the young monk has to walk the human gauntlet, getting kicks and chops and jabs and punches all the way and not being allowed to fight back.

"How come they let you come back?" I asked.

"Last time I checked, I am enrolled here, Officer."

"Seriously."

"It's in the e-mail you ignored."

"Come on, Roe."

She told me that the doctor or doctors want her to try to come anytime she's able. That they're doing everything they can otherwise. Something like that. The way she said it sounded like this might be a pattern that lasted a while. The way she said it sounded like she was scared.

"What the—," Monroe barked when we hit homeroom. I followed her gaze. They'd taken down all the old posters and replaced them with a new series on cyberbullying. One had two obvious mean girls snickering and pointing at a computer screen; another had a list of things you could do if people were talking smack online. There were more, but you get the picture. Monroe marched over to Mrs. Gross, who was grading a pile of quizzes with a red felt-tip pen. She corrected one problem per sheet and then shuffled to the next quiz, so all she did while I was watching her was problem number three. Three on one quiz, three on the next. I'd never seen it done that way.

"What happened?" Monroe asked with huge attitude. Gross scrunched up her face in a mix of confusion and annoyance. "To the posters?"

"Name?" Gross asked, grabbing a piece of paper.

Monroe told her and Gross ran her finger down a computerized printout. "You need a readmit."

"I was on medical leave. You can check the office."

Gross pushed back from her desk. "No, YOU can get a readmit or else I mark YOU absent AND unexcused."

"Whatever. Can you please tell me what happened to the posters that were here before?"

"Got rid of them." Gross's voice had a lot of *WTF?* in it. "They've been up here for years. I don't know if any of the info was still valid. We have a new directive now from the district."

Monroe stared in disbelief. "This late?" She meant in the year.

Gross shrugged and then went back to all the ungraded number-three problems. Kids started staring at Monroe staring at Gross, and then there was me acting like a tool with nothing to do but watch Monroe watch Gross watch her quizzes. I was going to drop my Mexican standoff line, but some boy said "Boo!" behind Monroe. She didn't even flinch. Another dork made a comment to a girl in basketball sweats that it must be Halloween. Monroe had now been deemed a ghost.

"I liked the other ones," she said, like it was her bedroom at home they'd redecorated, though she probably didn't have a bedroom yet. Everything was so messed up.

Gross didn't look. "Tell it to the office when you go get your readmit. I'm sure they'll value your input."

"Let's go to the office, Roe." I had to stop myself from grabbing her arm.

"Screw that." She walked over to our usual seats. Thank god's underpants no one was sitting there.

"You'll be absent again."

"Do Trees not have ears?"

Once you cause a scene like that in class, you can bet all eyes will be walking all over you the rest of the time. Sure Monroe didn't notice, but I did and hated it. Kids were whispering or laughing or pointing, rolling their eyes. Some were texting under their desks, sending messages that the psycho was back and in Gross's homeroom. Avree would tell me all about it later that day. One dickwad took a picture with his phone and posted it on Facebook and Instagram. Who knows what they would post that night online? About Monroe and her silent partner. FML. "What's going on with you?" I had to ask. "They're just stupid posters."

"Really?" Turned to face me. Eye to eye. Almost scary. "I come back after being sick, and look what happens. They take down the posters and replace them with lame bullshite and . . . And you."

"Me?"

"You ditch me for some Tree. A Poplar! You might as well be banging Lezzie Buchanan and her mom."

"Her mom?" I backed up.

"In for a penny, you know, might as well get jumped in all the way."

"That's not even funny. And you haven't really even met Avree. She's really cool."

"Really?" She cocked her head. "What makes her so ku-ewl?" That last word just corkscrewed itself out of her chapped mouth.

Flash on why Avree was cool: my birthday bowling, platypus, laughing in Beaker's class, making goofy videos to eighties bands like Thompson Twins and Bad Company, laughing, calling me to tell me something she'd seen on TV, saying those things about my eyes, things—gasp—only my mother had ever said. Any of those things, I realized, would just be bottles for Monroe to shoot down. *Ping ping ping.* "She just is. You just have to trust me."

"Trust is the one thing I can't have, especially after you not e-mailing or calling."

"You said your mom won't let you touch phones."

"You still could have left messages. I get messages on speakerphone." I didn't have the nuggets to ask who from. She glanced over at the spot where the half-jaw guy once hung like he'd crawl out of the computer screen in the picture Freddy Krueger style and scare the crap out of the two catalog models pretending to be that firecrotch, Lindsay Lohan. But I still didn't get why she was so freaked out about some posters.

"Do you want to know why?" She rubbed the inside of her sleeves, and I was scared to see what they looked like now.

"Yeah, I do."

"Really?" she asked, pulling her cuffs down with two pops.

"Yes."

"Because when my life at home is shite and each doctor says he knows what's wrong and makes me go through all these tests, taking buckets of my blood, which totally wipes me out, and does this—" When she rolled her cuffs up, I could see the black and blue marks, like someone had grabbed hold too hard and not let go. She was talking pretty loud now. "Pretty? And then put me on some treatment that makes me throw up so they give me pills that make me stop throwing up. Pills that make me sleep all the time so they wake me up to eat and I hate food now and then after all that, they say they still don't know what's wrong with me."

I wanted to tell her how much that sucked and how sorry I was, but I figured it was better if I kept my mouth shut. Besides, the virus was now airborne. A line of kids with bathroom passes marched back and forth in front of the door, slowing down to see if Monroe would have a freakout. They'd all gotten text messages alerting them to a possible riot.

"So maybe I want something to be the same, to come back to the same stupid posters in the same stupid room with the same ugly-ass teacher at the same stupid school. I want my posters where they were, my locker where it was, even if I never use it, the cafetorium ladies still standing there ladling liquid diarrhea, but most of all, know what I want?"

"Monroe, please keep it down," Gross called from her desk.

I could have guessed, but I said, "No."

"I want my friend where he was, not with some—"

"Ms. Monroe, didn't I tell you?" Gross called again, and she was pissed. She still didn't get up (she never gets up, famous for not getting up), but her voice was like flaming fiberglass shot out of a Nerf rifle.

Monroe turned away from me toward the front of the room: "Will you puh-lease shut up for once, you goddamn storm trooper."

"That's it. Office. Now. Or I'll call security." Gross made it plain with her outstretched arm where exactly the door was located. She still didn't get up, though.

"Let's go," I said, standing.

"Not you." Gross swung her arm over to point at me. "You sit. Just her."

Monroe marched out, but before she passed under the Exit sign, she shot me a look that said: *You would have left with that Tree.* And she was right. I dropped my head in my hands as she parted the crowd hovering in the hall, and the boos and jokes about spooks and Q-tips and Einstein's ghost started. School had changed back. I didn't know if I could take it. I pressed my fingers into my eyes and saw stars. Where was Dan's super amazing epic film, Lindy's version of normal?

The bell finally rang, and on the way out I saw Gross working through problem number five. I knew she was supposed to be the enemy, but I had to ask. "Mrs. Gross, why do you grade it like that? You know, instead of one whole quiz at a time?"

She gave me a look that could only spell D-U-H. "Consistency," she said.

26

In continuation of Pornstache's pretend-to-give-the-school-back-to-the-kids deal, the cast of *Cats*, the "highly anticipated" spring musical, were trying pretty hard to drum up business. The seven or so of them wore their painted-on whiskers, liver-colored lips, and clipped orange Afros, but not their costumes, so they kinda looked more like zombies from a ho hair salon than any flavor of feline. Then again, is it me, or is musical theater embarrassing even if you're not in the show or don't know the ones who are acting wildly with their hands all over the place? Especially when people really come to your "theater" to eat tuna sandwiches, share fries, and drink energy drinks, not watch freaks with names like Rumpleteaser and Mungocherry? Last year a professional theater company from England came to our school to do *A Midsummer Night's Dream*, and I felt embarrassed even for them, especially when Puck spoke to the audience. I'm sorry, but flame on, Pyro! I so wanted to make a Midsummer Night's Exit. His pants were megatight—you could probably have seen his franks and beans from the balcony without the aid of a spyglass.

The library was closed that day for makeup exams, so I had my laptop open to a site about enzyme therapy, and my notes and sketchbooks were spread all over the cafetorium table. Seeing Monroe's hair all white made me wonder if dye was safe for her. Avree handed me half a sandwich. Her dad always made the best sandwiches: seven-grain bread he sliced himself with lettuce, tomatoes, thick cuts of Swiss and roast beef from the more expensive Standard Market. Made it the morning of so it wouldn't get soggy and put the masterpiece in an insulated bag so it wouldn't dry out. She said the sandwiches were her dad's way to try to make it seem like they were a normal family. I didn't care: they were good. The man was a genius. Besides, Dan and I had gotten lazy about the whole lunch thing, so he left me a twenty each Monday to cover my week.

Today was Mexican Fiesta Party day in the cafetorium, and the lunch ladies had pinned little paper sombreros to their hairnets, hung a colorful banner behind the sink, and wore pins that said "Weather report: Chili today, hot tamale." The lunch ladies had other "specials," as they called them: Chinese New Year, Burger Barbecue Bonanza, Taste of Italiano. Each one had its own banner and little accessories the lunch ladies had to wear. Just like with the Cats, their lame pimping really didn't matter, though. Most kids just ate fries or pizza with a cookie and a sixteen-ounce can of Monster. Funyuns if they had 'em.

As we both chewed her sandwich, it was hard to ignore all those pussies stretching, hissing, and purring all over each other in a taped-off square by the bulletin board. I half expected them to start licking each other, the way they were getting into it. One of the zombie felines coughing up a hairball at this point would have been a total bonus.

"Do you think she's still in the office?" Avree asked. I had already filled her in about Roe's flameout in homeroom.

"I have no idea." Truth was, I had concerns, but I tried to act like I didn't. She hardly ever stepped into the lunchroom. We usually ate in an empty classroom or outside under a malnourished tree if it wasn't too hot. "You'll like this one," I said. "What is a cat's way of keeping law and order?"

"No idea."

"Claw enforcement."

"Lame," she said, but laughed anyway.

Monroe had been disappointed in me before for being awkward or embarrassing her by acting like a complete spaz in homeroom. But she'd never been really mad at me. Angry at her dad, yes. Her mom, absolutely. Even one of her cats when the thing pissed on her *Spinal Tap* DVD. Thought a cat pissing would be funny to Monroe, but it totally wasn't. Not when it happened to her. Things are less funny when you are the subject of the joke.

Don't think I've ever had anyone really mad at me. It felt strange, and I couldn't think about anything else during Language Arts or PE. Ms. J had handed out *The Book Thief* and had us all read the first chapter out loud. Usually I'm okay with books, and reading in class meant less homework, but I couldn't get the meaning at all. The words just floated on the page like I was dyslexic (I'm not). I felt the weight of Monroe's anger on my back like I was giving a piggyback ride to some porker. I couldn't concentrate.

"Hey," Monroe said, just as the kitties started some scene or skit about the bad cat, Macavity or something. She slipped in right beside me. "Watcha doing?" She'd pulled at her hair so it stood straight up like Einstein's. It was kinda freaky, even for Monroe. "What you two talking about?"

"Cats, mostly," I said, trying desperately to pack up my notebooks and shove them in my bag.

"Pussies?" She leaned over to see what was on my screen, but I shut the laptop. I think she might have seen the photos. Not clear.

"Sure." I paused. Awkward duty called. "You know Avree. You met her at my colossally successful birthday party."

"That was quite the celebration, wasn't it?" Monroe ran her fingers along the curved edge of the octotable.

"Acknowledged already in previous sentence," I said.

Avree tried to squeeze out a grin but barely landed a nod. Awk-ward was what she was thinking. Abso-awkward.

"Been teaching Avree about eighties music," I told Monroe, trying to make conversation that was like Sweden: neutral in the face of worldwide conflict.

"Best. Decade. Ever," Monroe said.

"What I said."

"Your little tutorials must be very special. For both of you." Monroe leaned in, wanting the juice.

Defuse, defuse. "She's really into A-ha."

"I think they're pretty funny," Avree said. No one was eating anymore.

"Funny as in?" Monroe's forehead wrinkled a bit, so some red color surfaced from under the white skin.

Avree shrugged. "I don't know, just funny I guess."

"So you guys are listening ironically?"

Avree shot me a confused look.

I explained to her that Monroe has this thing about the difference between being totally into a song or a band and listening ironically, like you're admitting the band sucks but you listen just to make fun.

Avree ran her palms along the side of her head. "I don't get it."

"Foreigner." Monroe sighed like she'd been in front of the rock and roll chalkboard all her life. "Foreigner is a band that moves effortlessly from arena rock to rock ballad. Great tempo. Heartfelt lyrics."

"Versus Kiss," I added, "who everyone knows is more spectacle than any hint of talent."

"What about Bad Company?" Avree liked *Run with the Pack,* and I'd never tell Monroe, even if I had car batteries hooked to my nipples, that we made a video off that one. The piece sorta combined somber and badass in a wholly unique way.

"Awesome." I agreed with Monroe on that one.

"Michael Jackson?" Avree asked.

"*Thriller* and before: awesome." Monroe tapped the table with her knuckles.

"After: ironic," I said.

"'Ebony and Ivory': anthem of ironic." Monroe gave me a kind look.

I nodded. Monroe and I had gone over this material many times before. "'Black or White' too."

It was at this point I thought things might go okay. Maybe she hadn't seen anything I was working on. As long as Avree

asked Monroe questions, things were cool. Monroe liked being
the expert and was happy to give thumbs up or thumbs down
to Stray Cats, Rush, Styx, and even the obscure Throwing
Muses (who I think are lesbians).

Avree seemed to relax. She took a bite of her sandwich,
chewed, let her face loosen, but then this: "What about music
that's just fun to listen to, you know, something that makes
you want to dance? You have to admit even Britney Spears
and Spice Girls can be fun if you're in the right mood. Right?"

Oh shit.

Monroe gave me the hairy eyeball that asked very clearly,
Who brought her *to this party?* There was this big silence. The
pussy patrol ended their performance with some kind of brawl,
but it was more like a tickle fight.

"I mean, isn't it just what people enjoy? Like someone may
really like, um . . ." Avree peered around the cafetorium, passing the tables of cheerleaders, video gamers, and the nameless.
"This stuff." She pointed to the cast, who were taking long
and deep bows, though no one seemed to notice.

"Well, maybe not that," I said, "but I get what . . ."

Monroe was so appalled that someone could have mistaken
her for a cadaver. Death mask.

"But seriously," Avree continued, "if a person likes something and has a good time and is happy, who is to say that
it sucks?"

"I get what you are saying. Like, life is not a competitive sport." *That's why I have a bird, not a tennis racket,* as
Lindy put it.

"Right?" Avree let her hand fall on my forearm.

"Riiiight." Monroe scanned the cafeteria like she was searching for someone else to sit with, though who could she be looking for? "Here's the thing, A-ver-ree."

"It's Avree."

"Sure." She put both hands on the table and moved her face too close to Avree's. "There's a difference between really listening to something and just background Muzak. Like the difference between sorta knowing someone and really knowing them." Her eyes fell on Avree's hand, which, as I said, had fallen on my arm. And stayed there. "You know, really trying to get the music versus having it on in the background while you do your nails or go shopping or whatever." Monroe edited out *girls like you.* "A lot more intense, you know?"

Maybe my life is one big Mexican standoff, but these two girls just stared at each other with the phony smiles you'd see on puppets. They were even worse than the cats' mouths. The silence was killing me, but what could I say?

Monroe rolled up her sleeves so we could see the dark bruises on the inside and white scabs on the outside. She was just showing off, but it still made me sad. "I just can't live all phony like that. I don't want a meaningless life."

"My life is not meaningless," Avree said. For some random reason, I thought of her mom and the no-faced man she went with and whether Avree ever wanted to know who he was or why she did it. What could that kind of info do to a family, or to her? Was it better just not knowing?

"Not saying it is." Monroe stood up after a long bit of nothing.

The cats were now sitting in orange chairs by the cash registers, taking off each other's makeup with moist white towelettes. One boy had half his face done and kept goofing with the girl who had wiped him, turning his head back and forth. You could tell by the girl's squeals and jazz hands that the half-and-half show was freaking her out. The lunch ladies were scurrying behind them, unclipping their sombreros and taking off their pins. The head lunch lady came around with one of those white clamshell to-go boxes, collecting the trinkets. The Mexican Fiesta Party banner had already been taken down. I had missed the fall of Mexico.

"Well, so, what is the dynamic duo doing this afternoon?" Monroe asked, having moved on to something else. The thing with her is that she seems to slash and burn, but something always lingers underneath.

Avree and I said, "Um, classes?" at the same time, but neither of us yelled *Jinx!* "You?"

"I'm not even here, remember?" Monroe said, then turned and walked away. The sunlight shot through the cafetorium's windows so she seemed to evaporate into rays that, when mixed with the steam coming off the kitchen, seemed a lot like mist.

"What just happened?" Avree asked, looking very tired all of a sudden.

I threw my hands up but knew that wouldn't do. "Monroe happened." I stopped. "Remember *The Odyssey*?"

"Yeah?" You should have seen the crazy look she gave me.

"I'm serious. You know how Odysseus has to go through all these, you know, the sirens and Cyclops and—"

"His obstacles?"

"Yeah." I actually liked that book. "Monroe likes to create obstacles."

"Why?"

"I don't know." Maybe to roll through them. Maybe to roll over them.

"Was she like that before she got—" Avree paused to find the right word. There was no right word. "Sick?"

I thought of Monroe and me spending hours at the comic-book store during their draw-your-own-comic day or going to bad action movies to laugh at the awfulness. At her house or my house. Her face pre. Her laugh, which you had to work for but was totally worth it. "She threw obstacles before to kids who tried to mess with us, but she wasn't as, um, harsh. Think she had it all inside her, had the possibility of being like she is now, and her getting sick just made it all come out, big and ferocious."

The cafetorium was almost empty now, and two maintenance guys in blue surgical gloves started clearing away the trash from the tables. One guy rolled the garbage along while the other threw the milk cartons, fry boxes, and hot dog wrappers into the bag that lined the can. Had a pretty good system, actually, the two of them.

"It couldn't have happened to a worse candidate," I said.

"Candidate?"

"Yeah. She was already kinda, you know, different, and her sickness, like, amplified it." The two maint guys made it over to our table and stared at us with their puffy, wrinkled faces. No one said anything. They didn't grab your stuff when

it was sitting right in front of you. School rule or something.
I wadded up some napkins. Avree wiped the table. We both
dropped our crap into their outstretched gloves because they
were blocking the rolling garbage can like they were defend-
ing a basketball hoop and there was no way they were going
to allow their opponents to score. The guys turned their big
backs to us and headed to the next table.

Avree turned to me like someone had died.

"What?" I asked. "I'm sorry she was so mean."

"Not that." Her head turned like someone was calling her
name. Then she eyed me hard. "She looked horrible. Someone
needs to do something."

I thought she meant me, but what could I do? But, I learned
later, it wasn't about me. Avree saw something I couldn't see
and it scared her. So much that she was speechless.

27

Research Note: On the day my parents were married, they had the party on a ship anchored in a harbor. It was either in New York or Boston, I can't remember which. My mom said it was one of those big ships, the kind we looked at in Colon Studies—tall masts and wide decks. Lights had been strung up on the lines that usually held the sails, and there was a live band and everyone danced like mad, she said. When I asked her why they didn't sail away on the boat, she told me it was docked permanently. As in forever. I said I thought that was kinda depressing. She said a person doesn't need a boat to sail.

We were in Beakman's class when we found out. Avree had pretty much finished her project early, just adding animation to her PowerPoint file—you know those tricks where the slides tumble into the frame or undulate (pretty sick vocab word) like they're on a wave. Splats, explosions, glass breaking, all those lame-oh effects that give teachers wood and fool them into believing you're actually saying something. She asked me what song should go on behind the breaks, and I suggested Dick Dale so the platypus would really be surfing.

I, on the other gland, was a hot mess, as Avree's uncle would have said. I had all my research notes on Monroe's menu of illnesses, musicians with ill illnesses, and other randomness.

One day, after a few Red Bulls Dan had left in the fridge, I went kinda nuts and started scanning photos of my dad in front of the car, my mom in various hairstyles, Dan trying to be cool, bands I love, singers I hate with red prohibition circles around them (Kenny Loggins, Milli Vanilli, Neil Diamond, Billy Ocean), drawings I've done of Monroe, Avree, Mack the cube guy, Lindy and his hawk; buildings I've designed; assignments from school; stained menus from Panda Pagoda. Even my crap Colon Studies project was lumped in there too.

"What am I going to do with all this?" I asked her Avree-ness. She scooted her stool close to me, which made a teeth-grinding screeching sound, so everybody turned. I dorkily waved them off, but I knew I was blushing like my fly was undone. It wasn't. I checked (I always check). Avree played a thirty-second movie I'd shot where I had all these cardboard cutout Puritans get their butts kicked by a Pee-wee Herman doll my mom gave me when I was little. I'd ripped some craggy sound from a few Godzilla movies, and it sounded like the Puritans were on the crumbling city streets in Tokyo, not my room in Red Rock. Avree laughed so hard that she snorted. It made me feel pretty good, seeing we were in class and all. I'd say cool, but I am def not that.

"Lolz. Really. How did you do it so we don't see your hands?" she asked after it finished. There were tons of kids around us, and Beakman was roaming around the Bunsen burners, but it felt like we were alone, you know, just the two of us.

"We?" I asked. "You are the only one who's seen it."

"Royal we."

"Word." Have I told you how clean her hands are? Scrubbed and rescrubbed, double and pre-scrubbed. Her nails! "Okay. Camera angles. All angles. Ask Paris Hilton. Oh, and double-sided tape. Trapdoors. You know."

"We should do a movie together. Move on from music videos."

I cupped my face in my hands to look all dreamy-like. I said, "I like this, keep talking."

"Shut up." She closed her fist and special-delivered a dead-arm. "Not that, you perv. Something funny or smart. Or both. We could write a script and everything."

"Got it. The one about the nerdass with the loco *mamacita* in the nuthouse who gets pity from the hot girl. It's got Academy Award written all over it."

She flicked something off the black Formica tabletop with her index finger. Each kid was on a metal stool at each work-station using a laptop. School can feel a little like a factory sometimes. It's almost better in black and white. "That's not funny," she said.

"My story. I can tell it. Own it."

"Really, you need to cut that selfish bullshit out." Her head started shaking.

"Selfish?"

"Yeah, selfish. Ever stop to think how your mom feels up there, all trapped and stuff. She can't leave." Her eyes showed she wasn't messing around.

Can I say that I try not to go there? That when I do, I don't want to get out of bed, that I start thinking back to all the places my mom and me lived and how hard it was for her.

Lots of spaghetti ("Not again!" I'd cry like a dickhead) and jelly jars of water; hell, soda was like champagne to us. All the way back to my dad's death, which I can't really remember so well (at all), and then, you know, to my own creation, which was probably a burden some (a lot) of the time.

"Do you ever think about next year?" Avree asked, all out of the blue.

There was no way to know then what she was up to, so I just chalked it up to her being all ADD.

"Not really, why?"

"I just think it'll be cool. More classes. New people to hang with." She scanned the class as if she was over all of it.

"You trying to get rid of me?"

"No. Not you, silly. I just think of all the cool things you could do in high school. You could start a band, take film classes, you know. Things to look forward to."

I just started imagining what high school would look like with me in it when there was this tap on my shoulder. "Look, Beakman, can you just give us a few more minutes, I mean?" I said. It wasn't Beakman. It was the Nurselor, not looking good at all. Her face was all wrinkled, like she'd slept facedown on a bed of faces. "You need to come with me, Coy," she said sternly. Beaker didn't even bother shrugging this time. I was on a list now, one of the tragic kids that always got pulled out of classes for forgotten lunches, asthma meds, talk therapy, backpack searches, drug testing, chronic bad news, mysterious doctor appointments, more bad news before disappearing for good to some NOLS course or boarding school no one's ever heard of in the middle of Utah.

"I do?" I tried to stall so I could scroll through all the things I could've been busted for. Nada surfaced. Shite, I realized, I'd been pretty good overall.

"You really do. Now." I half expected her to call me buster, as in *Right now, buster*. Her voice had all that 'tude inside it.

"Avree needs to come with," I said automatically.

"I'm not so sure that's a good idea."

Avree flashed her a store-counter smile. "I'm pretty much done with my project." Can I interest you in a free sample?

"She might be able to add a fresh perspective." Load it on, Coy. I could hardly believe what I was saying. I surprise even myself some days.

Everybody had stopped working, and even Beaker just leaned against his desk with his arms crossed. He knew when to surrender to spectacle. Nothing to see here? More like some-thang to see here. Everyone might as well enjoy it.

Sunday started getting agitated with all those eyebulbs burning holes in her uneventful blouse. "Fine," she said. "Let's go."

28

I'd never moved that quickly down the halls. I could tell
Avree hadn't either, 'cause she kept mouthing *WTF?* at me as
we struggled to keep up with Sunday's white shoes, which were
booking down the linoleum. She wore the kind that had the
springs embedded in the heels. *Boing boing boing.* Only hers
were faster, with longer strides, almost like she was walking
on the moon.

"Coy, why don't you sit here?" she said, pointing at the
clown ball when we all crammed into her office. "And Amy,
why don't—"

"It's Avree," I said, "and no thanks. I'll just stand."

"I don't mind." Avree slowly eased down on the thing. "It's
really good for your abs and back. Core workout. My mom
uses one." I could tell by the speaking-to-an-adult lift in her
voice that she was just being nice.

Sunday nodded. "I'm glad you like it."

Avree bounced up and down nervously.

Sunday turned my way and was all bidness. "You have
something you want to tell me?"

"You yanked me." I saw enough movies and *Law and
Order*s to know this was her meeting, not mine.

"I don't have time for games."

"Games?" I almost laughed at how corny she sounded. Why can't adults just say what they mean? Monroe would answer: "And mean what they say."

And then I saw it. Holy crap. "Where is she?" I asked, staring at the space where old Maya used to hang.

"That's what I'm wondering."

"No, really. Where are the posters? Is this some kind of conspiracy?" She'd replaced Maya and Albert and Gandhi (don't know if he has a first name) and MLK with quotes from whore-ribble bands like Air Supply, Peter Gabriel, and get this: the freaking Eagles. *Take it easy.* What the hell does that even mean? Next it will be "The Greeks Don't Want No Freaks."

"The district got some new ones for all the counselors. For the whole school, I believe. All departments," she said, irritated.

It sounds ghey, but it felt like a punch in the gut. "Why would you ditch them?"

I could tell by her lean-in move that she thought I was high. "Did you really like them that much?"

"Yes—no—I just liked things the way they were before." Now I was acting like freaking Monroe. I told myself to get a grip but couldn't stop. "And the Eagles? Really? Why didn't you pick Coldplay, for chrissakes?"

"Those aren't out yet. You like Coldplay too?"

Avree snorted.

"No, I don't like Coldplay." I turned my head toward Avree. "Totally not funny."

"C'mon." Her eyes widened. "They're just posters in a guidance counselor's office. Who cares? No offense, ma'am."

"That's okay." Sunday started looking at me all weird. She was piecing something together.

"Just like things the way they are, were, you know," I said. "It's not that sketch. Plenty of people would say the same thing. I don't like stuff changed around all the time."

"That's why I need to know where Monroe is," Nurselor said. "She's not well enough to pull this stunt."

"Wait," I said. Avree's scrunched-face-and-lean-back move told me that she was as confused as I was. "What?"

"Are you telling me you don't know? Because if you are lying to try to cover, I will—"

"I don't know anything."

"Her mother dropped her off at school today, and she never went to class."

"She was here," Avree said, a little out of breath. "All morning."

"We just saw her," I added. "At lunch. You can ask Mrs. Gross. She was in homeroom with me." Ask anyone by now. Sure it was all over school. The virus was definitely airborne.

"But Mrs. Gross marked her absent," Sunday said in that fake nice, robotic Matrix tone.

"That's because she didn't have a readmit. This is stupid." I rolled my eyes. Teacher arguing with a kid over a readmit like we invented the goddamn things. Like we invented any of this bullcrap. All of it made me pissed. "Go ask Gross."

Let it be known: Nurselor thought we were lying. Kids are always guilty until proven innocent. "She's not in her class now, I just checked."

"I hope she wasn't kidnapped," Avree said.

I shot her the glare: "Are you baked?"

"No." She wasn't, baked or kidding. "It happens to kids, you know."

"In the last half hour?"

"It could happen. That girl got kidnapped over in Cottonwood right off the bus. Remember?"

Sunday was getting impatient. I couldn't tell if it was more with me or Avree and her conspiracy kid-stealing theory. "You have no idea where she went?" she asked.

"Nope. I swear," I said, and it was true.

Then she rammed about a hundred million questions at me: last time I saw her (lunch with Cats), last time I spoke to her (same), friends in other schools (nope: slash and burn, long time gone), hobbies (music, being annoyed, being sick, hospital visits), favorite restaurants (Fu King Chinese and Soon Fatt Chinese, though she can't eat that shite anymore and only likes them because of the names). Did she text me or call me? (Even though I started using my phone again to call and text Avree, Monroe never used hers. Microwaves = cancer, ATM [according to Monroe]).

"Will you check anyway?" She nodded at my bag.

"Huh?"

"Your phone. Will you check?" She sounded all pissed.

"Whatever." I dug the thing out of my bag and saw that I did have one text. From Avree. A joke from a stupid movie we'd just seen. *What do you do with xtra bellybuttons? Send them to the Naval Academy.* It felt weird wanting to laugh at such a lame joke when Monroe was gone. And sick. There's a disease I read about in my research where if you feel emotion, your body thinks you are dreaming, so it paralyzes your body so you won't act out your dream. It's like narcolepsy, but triggered by joy. Joy! All those mixed emotions flying around in my body made me want to fall on the floor, paralyzed.

"Well?" Sunday asked after she saw me smile.

I shook my head. "Not her."

After it was clear that Nurselor Sunday was through with us, we had nothing for her, she said, all flustered, "I need to call the parents. You two can go."

Avree bounced up and reached for the door in one fluid motion. Pretty badass. Was she ever a cheerleader? I hoped so.

"Wait," I said, holding her back. "You need to give us notes."

"Right. Right." Sunday was all flustered. "Hold on." She grabbed a pad the size of an iPod and dashed off two quick ones. "Hold on," she said again, to Avree. "I need a minute with you alone." She looked at me. "You can wait outside."

I had no idea what the hell was going on. I hoped she wasn't telling Avree I was bad luck or something and that she should break it off with me. While I paced and hummed out of nervousness, I noticed something important about the notes.

"What was that all about?" I asked Avree when she came into the hall.

"Oh, nothing. She just wanted to thank me for helping out and all."

"For reals?"

She nodded and grabbed my hand.

"Look at these." I held the notes up like winning lottery tickets.

"What?"

"Like gold," I said to Avree and kissed the paper for effect. I could feel the heat coming off Avree's skin. She was a little breathless too. Shoot me now, I thought to my dirty self.

"I don't get it."

"She never wrote the time."

"So?" Shrug.

"So we have the rest of the day to look for Monroe." Who was the one who taught me all about notes and how to use them.

29

In our school the linoleum hallways are white except for two big tiles, one black and one red, every fifteen feet or so. Avree was on the red one, and I was on the black, and in this part of school the lockers were fire engine red. I looked at my watch. The bell was going to ring in a few minutes, and even though we had passes, I knew it would be easier to ride the crowd to the side door by the gym. Teachers sometimes saw you and "welcomed" you into their class. Not to mention Pornstache on patrol. It was better for us to go stealth status. I wasn't used to being in control of another person, calling the shots.

"I want you to go with me." I grabbed Avree's hands in mine. "We can be back by the end of the day and give these to the front office. They'll excuse all our absences."

"Dunno." She gripped my fingers tighter. "Your hands are warm."

"I'll take the fall if there is a fall." I checked my watch. Two minutes left. "When the bell rings, just come with me, okay?"

"Okay," she said. Her lips were like little pillows. Believe it.

I have this memory, I think it's a memory, when we lived back East, of swimming with a man I think is my dad, but I can't be sure. We're in the ocean, the water is chilly, and I'm treading. This man that could be my dad is teaching me about waves. It's clouded over, but I can still feel the sun stored in my skin so I'm not fully cold, not yet anyway. The water and sky and air have that eerie quiet that makes everything still, but I can see, even feel, the wave building in the distance. Waves have a stomach that churns and legs that shuffle and the power inside builds and builds well before the top has a curl like a pouty lip. Avree gripped my hands and I adjusted my messenger bag, fastening the strap across my chest. She did the same with her bag, following my lead. We both inhaled. I tingled a little inside. I checked my watch again: only seconds.

"Wait for it," I told her. The heavy silence was like church, or how I imagined church. I think I was baptized at least once, and it smelled like candles.

The bell still made us jump, and there was that fat millisecond after the sound and before all the doors opening and everybody invading the halls with their clothes and stink and the noise. Remember that noise? Feet tapping, bodies rubbing—no, fabric on bodies rubbing—and voices all over the vocal register, all over the hallways, ricocheting back and forth like crazy headphones. Thousands of songs from hundreds of countries all playing at once. I double-checked my grip and then pulled Avree, staying inside the phalanx of the crowd, down the hall to the right past the cafetorium and toward the gym. All that animal energy—I forgot how powerful a force school was. Avree and me perfectly hidden and saying nothing, just drifting in the wake of black backpacks, ridonkulous green old-lady purses, orange and yellow messenger bags, gangsta belt buckles, superhero T-shirts, and so many different-size waists, until we landed at the side door by the gym. Whoosh! The door was easier to open than I'd guessed. The two of us were bathed in sunlight as bright as a border guard's floodlight.

"What do we do now?" she asked, like I had the *Spirit of St. Louis* idling nearby.

"We walk."

I led her behind the bleachers, down a dirt hill into the woods, along the path to the shrine place I'd passed with Monroe before. The three trees had been sprayed with pink and blue Silly String, and even though it was cooler in the shade, whatever it is they make that stuff from had started to drip over the foil, ribbon, and plastic that people had already tied to branches. The whole thing looked almost like wax, like the tree was melting.

"Pretty gross," Avree said. I wasn't sure which part she was referring to, since there was so much foul stuff to choose from in nature's garbage can: cigarette packs, candy wrappers, spent bottle rockets, torn-up photographs, abc gum.

I spotted them first: two guys dressed all in black, head to toe, standing close to each other, the embers in their cigarettes painting swirls in the shadows. *"It ain't what we're saying,"* one of them sang, well, kinda sang. More like talky talk. No Grammies in their future. Fer shizzle.

"No, we ain't playing," the other answered.

I wanted to laugh. The pair reminded me of the crows in *Dumbo*, one of my mom's favorite movies, only it wasn't all racist and shite. I half expected the next rhyme to be about elephants flying and how they did done seen 'bout everything.

Then they stopped. "School out already?" one of the voices called from the shadows. I could tell they were older when they stepped into the light. Seventeen or so. Maybe sixteen. One was big and thick with pretty bad skin, dark hair, and the other was thinner, blond, with a sharper chin. Both of them wore black baseball caps, gold stickers still shining on the brim, only the skinny guy had his on backward. I wasn't sure who'd talked, so I just stood there and waited.

"Aren't you worried about detention?" the skinny one asked, cigarette pinched between his fingers. The thick one had a laugh that sounded a lot like a sick dog coughing.

"Not really."

"Just looking for someone," Avree said, which kinda bugged me. I mean, I was the one handling the investigation.

"I'm right here."

I ignored the stupid joke. "Have you seen a girl?"

"We've seen lots of girls." The thick one stood up, wiping his hands on the front of his jeans.

Skinny laughed. "Your sisters don't count."

"Shut up."

I wanted to keep it moving, so I said, "It sounds kinda weird, but she's in all white, even her hair." These guys definitely didn't go to our school.

"*Get y'all dope tees on, all black, black cords, black cars, all black everyone,*" they sang on cue. They even grinned at each other about their timing. Skinny threw his hand out like he was scratching a record. He was pretty awful, but I figured my expert musical opinion was probably need-to-know basis.

Thick One laughed the way I would have if he were my friend, which he never would be, not in a million years. Light leaked through the trees above our heads, making all the foil in the limbs shine like it was Christmas, only it was daylight and it was only for an instant, since I then caught sight of all the colorful jizz melting and what Monroe would call the dog-ends scattered all over the ground.

"Have you seen her?" Avree asked impatiently, arms across her sweet chest. She was sports bra status that day. Not that I'm a creeper, I just noticed.

"Slow down, little sistah." Skinny One stood up too. Both tall, real tall. I thought *tall* then *Walking Tall* then *Deliverance* then *Deliverance, the hip-hop musical.* The refrain went through my mind: *Squeal piggy piggy, squeal. Word.* I laughed quietly. That's the way my mind works, corrupted memory and all. Full-on dork, I am. I am.

"Don't tell me to slow down, and I'm definitely not your sister." Avree shot a mad-dog look over at Thick One, whose arms had fallen to his sides.

"Avree?" There was no more laughter in these woods.

"What?" She turned at me, all pissed. "These stoners are just wasting our time. A girl is missing, and they sing hip-hop lyrics back at us. Screw them."

"You know they probably . . ." I had no idea what I was saying.

"No, she's right. Screw us," Skinny said, coming closer.

"Hey, listen, she didn't mean anything." I put my hands up in a way that I believe reads *No disrespect*, but I'm not sure everyone knows that. I started to get a little frightened.

"What are you guys doing here anyway?" Avree's voice was strong, angry even.

As I tried to think of a way to defuse the situation, I saw how much energy each side had. The two bakoids' fronting was based on pride or whatever or some stupid-guy crap programmed into them. Maybe their PlayStation had broken, or they'd killed all the cats they'd planned on torturing, but at least they had more chutzpah (my mom's word) than me. And Avree's feet were edging forward, not backward. Where was my gusto? Badassness? BrAvree? Where was my sword? My horse? My Gatling gun?

"What are we doing here?" He laughed. "Anything the hell we want." Still keeping an eye on Avree, I studied Thick Dude. He seemed nervous, the way he moved his hands. Not like he was ready to make a fist, more like these little flourishes that I'd seen somewhere before. These gestures didn't really fit with that Frankensteinian body.

"You talk big for a little girl."

Avree said some things that would definitely not be examples of polite in the dictionary. Skinny and Avree both stood in the light now, away from the dripping shadows of the melting tree. I knew I should step in somehow, but Thick One held my attention. I could tell everyone thought he was really cute when he was little, but growing had ruined that. I know this sounds ghey, but he had the sad eyes of someone all the girls once loved before puberty took a huge hairy dump on him. Now he had a big Abomination body, a fivehead, robot jaw, clown feet, and acne. I didn't look, but probably backne and neckne too. Avree and Skinny were almost in each other's faces. Almost, since he was a foot taller. Avree had her finger in the air and pointed at him. I could hear Thick start to hum as Skinny clenched his fist. It all made sense now.

"You guys went here," I said.

Skinny stopped and glared at me. So did Avree, kind of. "What?"

"To RRJH. You guys went here." The thick guy shuffled his feet behind me. I glanced at his back, since that was all he was showing. Over his head, a long piece of Silly String waved in the air like a pendulum that had lost its round thingy. "You probably—no—you definitely had Beaker and Gross and Ms. J and Liebner."

Skinny crossed his arms and threw us what Dan calls the white-man overbite. "So?"

"They probably remember you guys. What are your names? We'll tell them you said hey."

He made a noise like a leaky tire, like I was the stupidest kid on earth and he was the smartest. "We're not gonna tell you our names."

"That's okay. I can just describe you. You guys probably did all the things we do—sneaked out the side door near the gym, got sent to the principal or the Nurselor's, extra pushups in Wapshot's class." I thought of Monroe refusing to climb the rope and ring the bell. She said it was an action for circus monkeys, not humans. Choose your fate, she said, and shrugged. She was happier organizing the ball closet anyway. It made for better jokes, ATM (according to Monroe). "I bet you guys hung out a lot, so everyone kinda knows you as a pair." I could hear Thick One kicking leaves and pine needles, moving away from where we were, heading off in his own direction. "Bet they even gave you nicknames."

"You really need to learn to shut up," Skinny said, but he didn't have so much fire in his voice anymore. Thick's back was now just another shadow in a series of shadows in a town with very few shadows.

"Let's go, A," I said. "We should go," I repeated when I got nothing back. "Go means go."

She just stood there like the action movie she'd been watching had melted inside the mouth of the DVD player. I grabbed her hand and led her away from the crows and down the barely-a-path.

30

After we were a little ways away, well into the sun, she asked, "What just happened?" She blinked a bit and then slid her sunglasses down off her head and over her eyes.

"You ask that a lot."

"Only with you."

"I was going to ask you the same question."

"What do you mean?"

"Why did you go all gangsta status on that dude? You acted like Monroe was your beastie or something."

"It's bestie, and I know, right?" She turned and smiled at me like she'd even surprised her own bad self. I led her over some rocks covered by chicken wire and into a cul de sac, a word you cannot say in a ninth-grade class. Same with Balzac. Or "The cock crowed three times."

"I don't know," she said. "Even though Monroe's been a tit to me—"

"Tit?"

She shrugged. "I've been thinking about her more as a girl. I know this sounds all stupid, but . . ." Her eyes shot low and sideways as we stepped onto the curb. Thinking. Houses lining the street were all short and brown and newish, with one-car driveways and two windows in the front. Some had

white rocks as front lawn substitute, some had lava. A few
grew cacti like Monroe's. Ever since we moved to Red Rock,
I've often had to remind myself that I live in the desert. Heat
usually reminds me pretty quick. "It's hard to say, but I saw
this movie on TV, and we were reading this thing in Creative
Expressions . . ." Avree got all lucky and got CE as an elective,
while I got Colon Studies. Sweet.

"Which movie? What book?"

"Not saying."

"Huh?"

"You'll just make fun." She rubbed the crown of her head.
"Besides, it doesn't matter where you get ideas anyway. It just
matters if you have 'em, right?"

"Sure."

"I just started thinking of how Monroe only had you to
stick up for her, how low it is, all the kids being so mean for
so long. You know. Even I talked crap about her before I met
her." One house on the street was different, a holdout from
renewal or part of an old neighborhood. All choked with vines.
"Actually, before I met you."

I should have said thanks or something, but I felt embarrassed. I eye-held the choked house, all covered in ropy stuff.
Some of it was as thick as my arm. Vines twisting out of the
canales (Spanish: tongue-looking drains that shoot water off
the roof) like a mouth full of weeds. I could only make out
the windows by the change in texture or whatever, since they
were totally covered in live and dead leaves and live and dead
spiderwebs. Windows were sunk in, compared to the stucco,
and I guess the screens let the vines grab hold better 'cause

there was a whole mess of them concentrated there. I bet there were snakes crawling all over the place. Vermin too. Rats and mice and groundhogs and prairie dogs, probably all infected with plague or hantavirus or rabies or lice or maggots carrying lice. I started itching anyway. The place was too creepy for Monroe to hide in there.

Avree looked up into the old-music-video sky. "Where *are* we going?"

"Monroe's house."

"How do you know the way?"

"Toward Red Rock." Above the rooftops the top of the rock stuck out like a jagged tooth. To the right were a few radio and cell towers that I knew were planted just past downtown. "Besides, I've been this way before. With Monroe."

Then we turned the corner, and right then I knew what street we were on. I got nervous, looking for that guy Mack's house. Avree didn't know. I tried to keep cool, but not I'm sure what kinda job I did.

"What about you?"

"What?" I asked, far too loud.

"Back there. Using your Jedi Mind Tricks, isn't that what you call them? From *Star Trek* or whatever."

"Don't even." I hung and then shook my head, all funeral-like. "It's *Star Wars*."

"Fine. What were you doing back there, dumbass?"

We'd slowed down a lot because I didn't want to stumble on Mack's house by accident and get trapped again. We passed a vacant lot where no structure was built, all these midget pine trees in clusters and tall grass that had started to brown at the tips. The absence of a house made it easier to see the power cables across the sky, like those lines on a sheet of paper that you practice your cursive on. I never use cursive anymore. What a waste of time. We might as well have been learning how to spin flax into clothes like in Colon Studies.

"Hello? Anyway?"

"Sorry." I didn't tell Avree, but ever since Monroe stopped coming to school and Avree entered the picture—not as a replacement, remember—I've been thinking about this kind of metaphorical stuff. "Well, remember last year in English class when we had those vocab discussions?"

"What?"

"You know, we chose a big word from our vocab book, and we all went around guessing the definition or whatever?"

"Okay." She couldn't remember, I could tell. Her eyes darted around like fish.

"One time someone picked the word *disposition*, so we all went around naming each person's disposition. I think Elizabeth Buchanan's was bossy, which she didn't appreciate, and Teague was sleepy, and then someone said *laconic* was a better word—"

"Holy crap." She flipped the glasses off her face like she'd just said "Eureka!" in the bathtub. Her eyes got all crazy wide.

"Do you see her? Where?" I thought she'd spotted Monroe.

"No." She stopped and clamped her hands on her little hip bones. "How do *you remember* all this?"

"Oh, that." I took a deep breath. "I'm getting there. Anyway, everyone decided that you were all confidence, and Jakob was eccentric. Remember Jakob?"

"Yeah. Sorta." She was really working her mind now. It was easy to tell.

"Wool cap? Old-lady glasses? Always wore weird shirts like the Black Plague Death Tour one? Floods? He spoke mostly in sound effects?"

"Right. Smelled like BO." She did remember. "Does he still go to school with us?"

"Nope. Went away."

"Where?"

"Just away." I thought Jakob was funny. I might have been the only one. I laughed a lot when he was around, and then he disappeared. "The weird thing about that exercise is that I started listing the different descriptions I thought I was, in my mind, as kids were giving other people theirs—"

"What were they?"

"I'm not saying." In my corrupted memory I could see the class (heads and torsos above dull desks) and the Seven Deadly Sins of Writing posters in all different colors tacked to the bulletin board across the back wall. "I was like second or third to last, near the door, you know, and people were all laughing and joking, trying to mess and use big words if they could, dirty ones too if they could get away with it."

"I think I remember."

Some of the houses started to look familiar—satellite dishes the size of small pizzas nailed to the siding, spindly antennas on the roofs, withered butterfly bushes—but I wasn't exactly sure it was the same place I'd been that one day. A lot of our town looks like that, all tired and hot like a choked plant.

"When they got to my turn, everyone was dead silent. I'm talking dead. We had a sub that day, remember?"

"Not really."

"Yeah, you do," I said, though I knew she didn't. I lied because I could tell she was worried that this was a meaningful story for me, and she had no memory of it. Down the road, someone or something was just a small blur wavering on the sidewalk. "He had a few missing fingers, not the whole deal, just digits. You remember? The stubstitute?"

"I had him in other classes, I think."

"Yeah. He couldn't really save that moment because he didn't know me. He wanted to. Then I realized during those one or two big minutes that no one really knew me. I was a stranger to everyone in that room."

"But everybody feels—"

"Stop. Don't go all Nurselor on me." I was crazy nervous just then, cutting her off (did I tell you how hot she was?), and the boxy figure on the sidewalk was starting to take form as we got closer. "I just wanna say something." I did. "All that time, whenever I wasn't with Monroe, I was living in my head, but I was paying attention. I'm real good at paying attention. Not so good at talking or whatever, but—"

"You're good at talking now."

"Don't. I mean I have to say this, and then I'll be done, okay?" I reached out and touched her like a tard. Why can't I be cool just once? I stopped in front of a carport, thin ridgy metal arc over an old RV, the kind that looks like a spaceship. An old lady with a dome hat and bug sunglasses was pulling her mail out of a black box bolted to her house. "I just don't

know . . ." I looked left and saw that the figure was that guy
Mack in his chair, spray-painting one of his toy cubes. His
hand moved back and forth, spreading silver air, like he was
some sort of hunched ex-wizard.

"Don't know what?"

"I don't know if I . . ." I didn't want to go down that street,
and Avree totally noticed that I was acting all spastic. "Still
want to be that guy." We waited there a moment, and I was
worried I might say more, so I blurted out, "Let's go this way,"
grabbed Avree, and pulled her down the next alley. Our town
is full of them, alleys I mean, for garbage trucks to pick up
trash where people don't walk or drive their cars.

"You're acting all weird," she said. "And this alley smells
like rump."

"I know." As we walked and I steered her toward Monroe's
house (and away from stinky Dumpsters), I explained all about
Mack and his cubes, and of course she wanted to see them.
Any kid would. I told her I would take her someday when we
weren't looking for a runaway friend during school hours on
an illegal pass given to us by a hippie counselor.

"Not really illegal. You're being kinda dramatic."

I turned to face her. "You're not afraid of getting busted?"

"Not yet. I'm sure I will be later. I'm still trying to deal with
the sad story you just told me. And trying to find Monroe."

We used alleys when we could, but had to venture onto
main roads too. There were long patches of time where we just
walked, not saying much, houses and vacant lots going by one
by one in a depressing parade. I tried not to think of what my
mom would say if she saw me walking down a strange street

past guys working on their old Chevys in their driveways or just sitting on their porches drinking beer and smoking cigarettes. And watching. I was worried about Monroe, a little guilty too, but then I thought that if Monroe hadn't been sick, I never would've met Avree. I don't know if you call that karma or fate or just an accident, and I didn't really know how to feel about it all. Same thing when my dad died or my mom had to go to Dorado. It's hard to make sense of any of it, really, without feeling like the world is against you. But then I had Avree walking next to me, and Dan wasn't the worst stepdad I could have. When we crossed some train tracks, I knew we were close.

"Are we almost there?" Avree joke-whined, like she was a little kid on a long car ride, waking me from my thoughts.

"Yup."

"What's the plan?"

"Okay." We turned onto her street and I saw the cactuses, I mean cacti. "We spy," I said, which was kinda funny, since there was really no place to hide and it was as bright as a prison yard during a breakout. The whole block could probably spot us. "This way," I said, and took Avree's hand. I was happy to find hers almost as sweaty as mine. We went around the house, but the side gate was locked. We wiggled past the garbage cans and some old cardboard boxes marked for Salvation Army pickup. Construction materials too—boards, plastic sheets, paint buckets. Peering into the windows, we could see the living room through lace curtains.

"What's with all the flags?" Avree asked.

"Her mom's British and started feeling all patriotic lately."

"Weird."

I nodded, too tired to defend or explain Mrs. Alpert. "See anybody?"

"Nope. It doesn't smell so great back here. You take me to all the best places."

"I try." At our house, this kind of area was in the back near the barbecue grill, somewhere to pour the extra cooking oil into Coke cans, leave coffee grounds for the compost we never got around to starting, and load the recycling bins. It's also where we leave bicycles Dan says he wants to fix. Or try to. "Do you think all houses have a place like this?"

"Like what?"

"A dumping ground. The place where you put all the nasty crap that you don't want to look at? I know we do at my house. Smells worse than here."

Avree pressed her lips together. "We did. Now my dad spends all his spare time cleaning and making containers so we don't have these places anymore. You should see our garage. It looks like a church or something."

"Full of people praying?"

"Really really clean. Everything put away or hung on the wall. 'Could eat off the floor in here,' my mom says, but I know she thinks it's weird." We scooched back to the next window. "See anything? What's this room?"

"It was Monroe's?" I said, not as a question, more out of surprise. All the walls were finished, white and clean, but only half the floor. It was almost like if you closed one eye, you'd have a decent room. Switch eyes, and you'd have a demo site.

"Weird."

There was obviously no one home unless Monroe was hiding in a cabinet somewhere. "Where the hell is she?"

"Coy!" someone called from behind me. I wanted it to be Monroe, but it was definitely her mom's British baby-talk accent. "I spotted someone around the side of the house and thought it might be you and Monroe. You don't know where she is, do you now?"

I shook my head. "You remember Avree from my birthday party."

"Oh, yes. Hello, dear." I could see her take a breath to readjust what she expected to see. She filled her hot pink running suit with air. She wore pink running shoes too.

"The gate is locked because we're doing construction back there. Liability and such."

"Sure," Avree said.

"I thought you were fixing Monroe's room."

She exhaled in a huff. "What we realized, Coy, after considerable time and expense, is that there's really no way to get an old house truly clean. Clean enough for a person like Monroe, anyway."

"But you guys got rid of all the mold."

"That's just the beginning. Do you know what's inside the walls of a house you didn't build?" I had no time to answer before she blurted out: "I know I don't. Or didn't." Her hands were on her hips, and she was still breathing heavy. "Or under the floors? Subfloors?"

"What about school?" I should've thought of the crusty white stuff in labs or monkey meat in the cafetorium but flashed on that horrible moment in Colon Studies.

"Right. Obviously we can't clean a whole school, and Monroe simply refuses to wear the respirator we bought her. Or even discuss homeschooling. That's what I'm saying." She lowered her zipper. The only thing running in her suit was sweat.

"Did her doctor tell you to do all this?"

She reached into her bag and checked her phone. "Shouldn't you two be at school?"

"Our classes ended early," I lied. "All we had left were study halls. We wanted to look for Monroe. We have notes." True. Kinda.

"Let me just use the WC, and I'll run you home."

"WC?" Avree asked when Mrs. Alpert's pink suit was out of range.

"Means bathroom in British. Water closet."

"Okay." I could tell that Avree felt the same way I did when I first heard that term: grossed out, like the toilet gives you a shower. And that we were no closer to finding Monroe.

31

We promised Mrs. Alpert when she dropped us off that we would call her as soon as we heard from or saw Monroe. She made us put all her numbers and Mr. Alpert's too into both our phones, even though that seemed total overkill. The odds of Avree getting a call from Monroe were about a gazillion to one. On the ride over, I ran my brain through all the places that Monroe and I had ever been together from the time we first met in seventh grade: children's museum, movie theaters, a buttload of ice cream and frozen yogurt stores and shops and "shoppes," the mall, fairs and farmer's markets, the water park (shut down because of a lawsuit), teen center (where we took an animation class together), Blockbuster (also shut down), Borders Books (out of business), and the pet store, which she would never go to now, for a litter of reasons.

"What do we do now?" Avree asked. We were standing in my kitchen, just having downed a few glasses of Gatorade. Neither of us was hungry. And, looking back, I had my girlfriend and an empty house, but instead of doing what every boy dreams of, I was cooking up a very different mission.

"I know a place we should try."

"Yeah?"

"True Believers."

"Huh?"

"The comic-book store."

"We have a comic-book store?"

"Funny."

"No, seriously, I didn't know there was one in town."

"It's where I buy my calculators and pocket protectors."

"Shut up." She pushed me, and I loved it. "Where is it?"

"And Vulcan ears." Even though I felt like Optimus Nerdicus and was teasing Avree, I understood how a lot of people missed the place, jammed between a nail salon and a Cookie Bouquet, around the corner from a store that buys desperate people's gold and silver when they need money to score drugs or pay rent.

"How are we even going to get there?"

"That's the thing." I took her hand and led her into the laundry room.

"We're gonna ride the dryer?"

"Nah, too hot." Then I turned on the light and opened the door to the garage. My mom's silver Honda Accord looked almost brand-new. I thought of saying something like "Your chariot awaits, princess," but my gheylarm stopped me, thank god.

"No way," she said, but not angry, more like surprise! I'm-not-sure-how-I-feel-about-this.

"It's the only way. I cooked up the idea on the way over. Dan's let me drive before."

"How much?" She eyed the car like it could tell her.

"A bunch of times, but I've watched him drive for hours and hours, and listened over and over on how to do it." I didn't mention that I only drove in parking lots, empty ones.

"I dunno." She crossed her arms. "It's not the same thing."

"I'm good at racing games too. You should see me rule the go-kart track. You could say I was born to drive," I said, secretly referring to the picture of my dad holding burrito me in front of his Galaxie. Avree was nervous, and I was too, big-time, but I tried hard not to show it. "I'll take the fall if there is a fall."

"You keep saying that, and I've read enough books and seen enough movies to know that with stuff like this, there's always a fall."

"Then I'll take it. You in?"

She didn't say yes, but she didn't go back inside either.

The good thing about driving the Acorn was that it was an automatic, so I didn't have to shift. I had a hard time figuring out how hard to push the petal and brake, so after I got out of the driveway and Avree used the remote to close the garage door, we rocked back and forth all the way up my street, both freaking out. The car smelled like my mom, all flowery with a little bit of smoke and the tiny packet she threw under her seat to cover up the smell of secret cigarettes. Dan had detailed the thing a few times, when he was missing her bad or during a hangover, when he felt guilty about drinking too much. Once again, too, when he thought there was a possibility that she might come home this one time. Somehow her smell still hadn't disappeared. My mind was racing a thousand miles an hour, trying not to crash or slam Avree, trying to remember how to get to True Believers using mostly back roads, trying not to think of the major heart attack my mom would have if she could see me, trying to get there before Roe left, if she was there. I turned on the radio to distract us from what we were doing. What *I* was doing? *We* were doing? I wasn't so sure, besides driving really slowly.

"Please don't," Avree said.

"Sorry." I took my eyes off the street for just a second to kill the radio, which made me swerve toward the curb. Avree braced herself on the dash. "I'm okay, I'm okay," I said, trying not to blow it. My arms were as stiff as baseball bats. Near my house is this pretty big hill, and once there was this freak snowstorm that blew in, melted, then froze overnight, and cars pretty much slid back down into one another in the morning when I was on the bus. As I climbed the hill with Avree (who said nothing), I had this worry of slipping. Crazy, I know, hot as it was. There was more chance of the tires melting than slipping. I tried to time the light so I wouldn't have to stop and slip or stall, but just as we reached the crest of the hill, it turned red.

"Crap."

"What?" Avree asked, all worried like the car might explode. Her hand squeezed the bar thing on her door.

"It's fine." Should I put it in neutral? Park? Was it bad for the car if I left it in drive? Was I slipping?

"No, really. What?"

"Stupid."

"You wanna go back?"

"No, not that." I told her about the storm and the ice and my crazy fear of slipping.

She started laughing. "Maybe you shouldn't be behind the wheel."

"Yeah, maybe." I laughed, but my eyes stayed straight ahead.

Then she turned on the radio. All my preset stations were still there: classic rock, every one of them. Bad Company sang about running with the pack.

Later, after it was all over, Avree would tell me that she was terrified being in the Acorn with me when I first took it out, but she kept reminding herself of all those news stories of little kids—six or seven—driving cars when their dads or moms were drunk. One kid was even younger, I think, and took his parents' car out to buy some candy. Glad she didn't say at the time that she was comparing me to them, especially to that last kid, because he crashed into a tree.

Monroe had been at True Believers. We didn't even have to ask. As soon as we walked into the store, the guy who worked behind the counter, Stevie, said she'd been there like a half hour before and he had no idea where she was going.

"You guys are usually connected at the hip," he said, not exactly nicely.

"Not really," I said. Then I saw Avree on the other side of the store, where they keep the vintage movie posters. Her hands were all over an *Edward Scissorhands*. "Sorta."

"Who's the girl?" Stevie nodded toward Avree, who had moved on to *The Nightmare Before Christmas*. Stevie was sort of an upscale nerd: polo shirts with Comic-Con logos, gooey green eyeglasses ordered online, and black hair slicked back like Clark Kent. Never really saw his shoes. Bet they were white sneakers.

I shrugged. "My girlfriend."

"Right."

"Not lying, I swear," I said, then felt dirty for trying to convince him.

"Okay."

No, I kidnapped her, you assface, is what I wanted to say, but instead I asked, "What did she buy?" as if that would be a clue as to where she'd head next. "Monroe?"

"She said she didn't have any money. I have stuff on hold for her, but she told me it'd have to wait."

"Me too, both, I mean." I was making no sense. "I don't have any money, so my stuff will have to wait too."

Stevie called me a liar with the cock of his head.

"I have money," Avree said, coming up behind me. True Believers is pretty small, so it didn't take long for her to work through the different comics and memorabilia, sales racks, and the limited movie rentals they have on this cheap wood shelf. I thought she was still thumbing through some of the old back-issue Avengers.

"It's okay," I said.

"No, really. I have babysitting money." She reached into her jeans and pulled out a rumpled cash sandwich. "How much?"

Stevie turned around and found a thin paper bag with my name on it on a shelf with a whole bunch of bags with other people's names on them. I almost asked him to see Monroe's. "Let's see, you have a Moon Knight, King City, Phonogram, Joe the Barb—"

"You don't have to list them." I kicked the wood bar underneath the glass case. "It's not necessary," I said to Stevie, and then "Really, it's not" to Avree.

Stevie cocked his head again. He definitely thought I was acting all weird, which I was, but he couldn't really say too much since he was on one side of the counter, and I was on the other. And I was with a pretty girl he didn't know, and she was buying me comics.

"It's okay," Avree said, handing Stevie some bills. "No big deal. I want to do this."

"Whatever," I said as if I didn't care, but I did. I felt embarrassed, like I was on that show *Beauty and the Geek*, which I don't even have to see to understand.

"Whatever," Avree said, all Disney Channel, teasing me, but then Stevie laughed too, which totally pissed me off. First he thought I was lying about her being my girlfriend, and then he laughed along with her. As if. Douche canoe.

We sat in front of the Cookie Bouquet, my comics in the back seat, COY written in bold marker on the bag. "Where to next?" Avree asked.

"I'm thinking." I stared straight ahead at all the cars driving by on Red Rock Avenue, wondering where everyone was headed. Everyone else on the road def had a purpose.

"Could you think out loud, please?"

"Okay. Sorry." I took my hands off the steering wheel. "It has to be somewhere within walking distance, somewhere she'd want to go that's still open. There aren't that many places."

"Is there a record store or something?"

I shot her a sideways look. "How long have you lived here?"

"Sorry. I buy all my stuff online."

"Right." I remembered her in Beaker's class, pre-us, watching her smartphone. "Other side of town. Lou's Records. You need to go. Lots of really cool vinyl there."

She checked her watch. "We're running out of time."

"Right." I heaved a breath.

"Not yet, but soon."

I tried to draw a mental map of the area with RRJH as the center. Put me and Monroe on the map, little action figures, walking the area. I used my mental joystick to move us north, south, east, and west. "There's the vets' park where we used to go to read comics after we bought them."

"Better than eating them, I guess."

"Funny."

Slapped the dash in a goofy way. "Let's motor then."

It took me a few minutes to back up without hitting a pole or another parked car and then an extra few minutes until the road was really open for me to enter traffic. Really, really open. I'm sure Avree was thinking that I could have gone like a million times before, but I was nervous. Even though I told Avree that I was born to drive, I could have told her that my family has a history of car wrecks, and that would have been equally true.

As we were passing Burger King, I spotted the square lights mounted on top of a shiny black-and-white car moving up from behind. "Oh crap," I said, letting out a lot of air.

"What?"

"Don't turn around."

She turned around. "Oh no. Okay, let's not freak out."

"I'm totally freaking out."

She wiggled in her seat. "My friend Tina says cops don't have ESP, so just relax."

"ESP?"

"They're not able to read minds," she said, and I can't say I believed her 100 percent.

Then I remembered: "Tina who dresses all fashiony? She's your friend?" I thought about her getting all dramarama in the fake lockdown in those bone-white jeans. It seemed like a million years ago.

"You know her?"

"Not really." I decided we should wait on that conversation. "Do you think I can go right on red here?" We were at a stoplight between the Sage Hotel and a gas station. The sign on the hotel read: "If You Stayed Here, You'd Be Home by Now!"

"I think so." Avree shifted in her seat. "I'm not sure. You better not risk it."

"Yeah, but what if he can tell I don't have a license because I'm not turning when I should turn?"

"Do you have your blinker on?"

I checked, then checked again. "Yes."

"That's good, I think."

"You think?"

"Well, I hadn't really thought about the idea that the cop could get suspicious because you're not turning right on red."

Then the worst thing happened: the cop flashed his lights— not his top ones, his headlights. "What does that mean?"

"Go, Coy, it's green!" Avree said, all megaphone mouth.

I took my foot off the brake and accelerated a bit too fast, again almost hitting a curb, and the cop turned too. My heart was trying real hard to escape from my chest. "He's following us."

"We don't know that," Avree said, craning her neck to try to see the cop in her side mirror. "Can you adjust—"

"I can't adjust anything, Avree." It might be impossible, but I swear I said those words without breathing in or out. I couldn't read anything on the cop's face. His windows were tinted, and he wore sunglasses. No hat. "He's not talking on his radio or anything."

"That could be good." She nodded and spoke in a tone that I knew she meant to be reassuring, but the fact that I knew she meant to be that way on purpose stressed me out even more.

"We need to turn up here at the stop sign."

"That could be good too."

"What?" I sounded pissed. I guess I kinda was. Where the hell was Monroe?

Avree threw her hands in the air. "What do you want me to say?"

Like Dan on wife probation, I started slowing down about a mile before the sign and reached to turn my signal on and hit the wipers instead.

"Not funny," Avree said, all pouty.

"Not trying!" I yelled, and my voice cracked a little. I killed the wipers, got the signal blinking, made sure to stay still for three Mississippis, then made the turn. The cop kept going. I was so happy. "I am so happy," I said.

"Wow." Avree slumped down in her seat and put her bare feet up on the dash. "Wow," she said again.

"Good thing cops can't read minds, or we would be dead."

32

A pool supply store with fake palm trees clustered out front got behind us, then a car insurance place, then another stop sign, then crappy houses followed by less crappy houses with fresher paint jobs and not as many broken-down bikes and faded kids' toys dying in the front yards. I was a mix of nerves, having survived the stalking-by-police. I didn't know whether to feel paranoid or supervictorious as I struggled to keep the car straight. I knew some guys from gym class who would have had a high-five fest after they evaded five-oh-no. I felt no such impulse. Avree sat in a jumble next to me like she'd just finished a marathon or a few rounds in a boxing ring. Some of her hair had fallen, different color strands bisecting her cheek, barely missing her eye. I have to be honest: at that moment, I wondered why the hell we ever left my house. My freaking empty house. I wondered if, after this mission, we'd ever get an empty house again.

"They took the horses out," I told Avree after seeing square blocks of concrete lined up at the edge of the vets' park.

She sat up like I meant real ones.

"They had those back-and-forthy kind of metal horses before," I said. "Like on a spring. They kept the swings, though." A few adults rocked their kids on the baby buckets.·

The flat strips of tire rubber for the bigger kids were empty but swaying a little, as if a bunch of boys and girls had just jumped off. Parking sucked because the lot was tiny and filled with mostly vans and SUVs. I had to carefully wedge the Acorn in between a blue minivan and a really dirty Bronco missing a tailgate. On the back windshield someone had fingered the words "Wash Me!" in the dust.

"Look at her." Avree pointed to a black woman pushing a white baby with her left hand while talking on her cell with her right.

"Multitasker," I said, trying to be funny, but the joke was an epic fail.

The vets' park was bordered by cottonwood trees on three sides, with an arroyo running down the right. After the playground area, a football-field-size dirt patch opened up. Back in the day, before the drought, before the Water Wise campaign, before the budget cuts, these parks were all green grass. Now the vets' park is mostly dirt with some patches of brownish yellow, kinda like a bald head with clumps of dead hair here and there. The largest cottonwood stood tall in the middle of the dirt field like an exclamation point.

"What's that?" Avree pointed to this flash of white in a clump of trees on the west corner of the park. I squinted. A ghost. My eyes aren't the best. I probably need glasses. I know a lot of people who think spectacles are elegant and all, but I'd look like a dork, I know it. Some kids at Red Rock wore expensive frames without lenses like they ruled the catwalks in New York or L.A. Believe it. I squinted again. I know this sounds ghey, but I could tell it was Monroe by the way she moved: chin up as if she was in control of the situ even now. Broadish shoulders, as if her clothes had been put on a walking hanger. "Monroe!" I yelled, waving my arms.

"Hey!" When Avree screamed, all the parents on the swing looked at us like I'd been hitting her. I gave them a half wave. *Everything's okay. Nothing to see here.* The rag of white floated deeper into the trees.

It must have freaked the women out when I started tearing across the concrete, past the swings, and then—thud—onto the dirt. "Monroe!" I yelled as I pushed my legs harder, out of breath almost immediately. Never was much of a runner—ask Coach Wapshot. The large cottonwood came closer and closer, so I moved left to avoid it, trying to remember the exact place where the rag of white had been swallowed up by the woods.

I was booking pretty fast when my toe caught on a root and I flew forward, Superman-style, hitting the side of my head on the hard-packed dirt. I thought I was upside down in a car, saw flashes of Silly String, the dirty Bronco, and the bubbling fish tank at Dorad. Deep-sea diver waving good-bye next to his For Sale sign. My brain sloshed between wanting to stay down and throw up, and then a wave of embarrassment, and then spiking pain that said that the embarrassment needed to get in the backseat.

"Coy!" Someone was yelling a name somewhere. *Someone left the boy out in the rain,* my mom sang.

I touched my falcon cut that I thought was healed: wet. Damn. Mom. Dad?

"Coy!" The voice wavered and warbled in the air like corrupted audiotape. "Monroe!"

My mother said my dad's Galaxie ended end-up in a ditch, but later she said end-down in a dry gulch, and later, at a party one time, she said flipped into a ravine at a rapid speed to a bunch of fancy people drinking wine in plastic cups. I asked her about it a lot when I was younger. She said who he was in the world was more important than how he left it, though she couldn't help giving gory details once in a while to adults when she thought I wasn't in what she called earshot. Sometimes people asked her to please stop telling the story. Sometimes people asked her to leave.

"Oh my god. You all right?" I realized the voice was Avree's, and she was standing over me. "You're bleeding." I saw star blasts when I tried to stand, little clusters of white, heat moving through my head in waves. My mouth filled with salt. The wetness on my face and fingers reminded me of something. I took a minute, and then it came back to me. "I know where she's headed," I told Avree. "Let's get car."

"I don't know if you should be driving," she responded to my cave-man-speak. Her hand rested on my arm, sending waves through my skin. Warm ones.

She kept asking if I was okay to drive. Maybe I should have listened. Maybe if she'd driven that day, things would have been different. Certain things anyway. "I'm fine." I couldn't run, so I sort of fast-walked, which must have seemed super robotic. We had to pass by the line of child pushers, but I didn't look, since I knew the side of my face had gained zombie status and so had my shirt, since I'd been using the collar to wipe the blood out of my eye.

"You're freaking those—"

"I know."

"They might be calling—"

"I know."

"I'm not sure we should—"

"I know. Get in the car. Please."

Once I sat down, I saw through the windshield that all of the pushers were now on their phones, not just the original multitasker. Avree thought some might be calling the cops, so I jammed the car into reverse, but another car had come in after us and pinned me in. "Crap," I said. "Whose car is it?"

"You have enough room," Avree said, but then I eyeballed her and she changed her tune to: "I think it's theirs." She pointed to two older people in matching windbreakers near the jungle gym with what had to be their grandchild. The clock was really ticking inside me now. "Excuse me," I yelled. "Excuse me!" Everyone looked, but I tried to make it clear by finger pointing that I was only speaking to the grandparents. "Can you please move your car?" They put their heads closer and then stared back at me. I nodded. "I'm kinda in a hurry."

"They probably know that from the blood on your shirt and all the shouting," Avree said from shotgun.

"Okay," I said, but I didn't mean it. Not then anyway. All I wanted was for that car to get the hell out of my way.

"Sorry," the old guy said, fumbling for his keys inside his toast-colored jacket. "Is everything all right?"

"We're fine. Just need to go, thankyouverymuchsir."

"Breathe," Avree said, and I did so I wouldn't ram the cars next to me. I backed up way too far into the street while the old guy waited, blocking any traffic from behind. I waved, a really weird thing to do. I'm sure if things were different, Avree and I would have joked all over that goofy gesture. Goofed all over that jokey gesture.

I raced around the back side of the park, heading east toward this little warehousey area behind the stores and fast-food places on Red Rock Ave. I wanted to think out loud for Avree, really did, but I couldn't. The blood was still coming, I could feel it travel along my jaw and drip down my neck. I could even make out the blossom of red on my shirt without looking down. If the cop saw me now, he'd definitely pull us over. I was all over the road, but I didn't care.

"Where are we going?"

"Car wash."

"Now?"

"Not for that." I sped up a little and almost lost control. "There's this car wash by a gas station, Shell or something, and Monroe and me used to go there to watch it. This sounds like we were on drugs, but I swear we weren't."

"Just go on."

"Okay." I told myself: Be careful to stay away from curbs and continue breathing. Try to keep the car in a straight line. "We both agreed it was the best car wash ever because it was brand-new, and with every stage, water and soap and wax or whatever, lights would appear and then be replaced by different-colored lights. Words glowed like magic. We thought it was funny, saying the words together, all dramatic, exactly when they'd appear: ENTER, STOP, PRE-WASH, MOVE FORWARD, SOAP, ALMOST THERE, WAX, DRY, FINISHED, HAVE A NICE DAY! like there was deep meaning in those things, like it was our religion or something. Car after car for an hour or more. Goofy. Stupid. I'm embarrassed." I was speeding now, or what felt like speeding, and I don't know if she noticed but I blew through two yellow lights. She probably did.

"Still don't get why—"

"We even convinced our parents to get their cars washed there. But when I fell, I remembered what Monroe always said. It sounded like a joke, but she said it so often, I always knew she was partly serious. She always took the car wash a little more seriously than I did."

"What'd she say?"

I pulled what Dan called a California stop, but Avree ignored it because she wanted the story. At least I think that's why. "That if things ever got really bad, she'd walk through the car wash. Don't know if she saw it in a movie or whatever, but she said since the car wash was our religion, walking through it would be her baptism, and, no, but, but, but do you know what that shit'll do to her skin?"

"Take it easy. Slow down."

Imagining the soap foam and hot wax being sprayed all over Monroe's raw face made me push the pedal down even more. I heard the tires squeal as we turned the corner near Ojo Glass and the little Mexican grocery where my mom bought white corn tortillas by the pound. The line of cars waiting to get washed snaked out into the street.

"Holy crap. There she is!" Avree said, and she was right. Monroe was edging sideways along the cars toward the huge sloppy mouth of the car wash. I couldn't see her face, but no one could miss her clothes. It's amazing what a brain with a pair of eyes can handle at one time: a man in a wifebeater throwing trash in a metal bin by the robotic vacuum, the lights inside turning from red to green, and Monroe getting closer to entering the house of color, words, and water. Somewhere in the mist I saw my mom crying at Dorado and my dad ass up in a ditch, his face and shirt bloody like my own.

"Stop so I can get out and grab her." Avree shook the door handle.

"You won't make it. She's too far away." I blew past the line of cars to the handicapped spot right by the mouth of the wash. I slammed on the brakes and jammed the car in park with a jolt. I never closed the door. Since the car wash is automated, your ride goes through without a driver. The attendant vacuums it really fast and then gets the tires inside these tracks that propel it slowly through. Another attendant waits for it at the other end. Ghost wash, Monroe and I called it.

People waiting for their cars had no idea what we were doing, as we raced toward Monroe, who was already dripping, just from the initial rinse. Avree was crying now, and I yelled something to her that I won't share, and then I ran out and grabbed Monroe. I'd never grabbed Monroe. Not like that. People were screaming at this bleeding boy, waving their arms, as I pulled her into the backseat of a stranger's Ford Focus. I thought Avree would never speak to me again as I reached forward to yank the emergency brake. We were now immobile. With all the jets and brushes, it was like being in the middle of an intense rainstorm that paused every two minutes before starting up again. Neither of us said anything. We were both so shocked. I had my arm around a shuddering Monroe and tried not to let my tears come, but the Focus was crying too: drops ran off every part of its silvery body. Each noise sounded muffled inside the car: voices and gears and whooshing brushes, all followed by the spray of water, so when I heard the door open and all those noises go from lo-fi to hi, I thought it was all over. But that door slammed and another opened and then slammed too and then, almost like magic, Avree was sitting on the other side of Monroe.

Avree's knuckles brushed mine as she put her arm over Monroe's wet shoulders. I released the emergency brake. Even though Monroe would never say it like this, Avree showed something to us that day. Something to both me and Monroe, separate and together. If I put it in Roe's words, I'd say by moving into the backseat, Avree was in for a penny, in for a pound.

As we traveled toward sunlight, Avree asked quietly, "So what do we do now?"

"We wait," I said and reached for her hand. She let me rest my fingers on top of hers. She never pulled away.

33

It took the gas station about ten minutes of people yelling like crazy to realize they should hit the emergency shutoff valve, which stopped everything mid-cycle. The brushes, still covered in soap, ceased waving, and the water wands froze in place mid-rotation. All the lights and words died out with a groan. We heard the sirens in stereo through both open ends of the car wash, the wails growing louder and moving through our brains like we were wearing huge (but muffled) headphones. Surprisingly, we were calm. Maybe it was shock or maybe because we were all in it together or we realized we'd done something no one ever thought we were capable of, not even ourselves. For those waiting moments in the car, we were someone else, someone bigger maybe or more important or more . . . I don't know. Either way, we three were now veterans of what had just happened.

The cops were cautious at first, approaching the Focus with palms pressed to their guns, circling the vehicle to survey the situation: three teenagers—two girls and a boy. One of the girls was dressed in white and soaked to the bone, her face swollen and red. The boy had blood on his face, neck, and shirt. The second girl, nothing out of the ordinary. We didn't move until they asked us to please step outside the vehicle.

Even then, we all slid out on my side and stayed together as they steered us out of the dripping cave and into the blinding sun. I handed Monroe my sunglasses and Avree unscrewed a tube of watermelon lip gloss and offered it to Monroe before using it on herself. Everyone could smell the fruit.

34

We wouldn't let them separate us until our parents showed up. By then quite a crowd had gathered, and an ambulance dude had checked Monroe's vitals and cleaned and bandaged my cut. Avree's dad showed up first. I barely saw him before he hustled her away. She shot me a look over the hood of her dad's car that combined an *I'm in for it now* with an *Oh well*. She flashed me a brief smile. Monroe's mom was next, and when she started to freak out, trying to lay blame, that's when Monroe finally spoke. I was too far away to hear what Monroe was saying, but I could tell from the way her mom began dealing with the cops that Mrs. Alpert went from panic and anger to trying to get us off the hook. The way she moved her hands was a dead giveaway. All apologies and explanations. Probably could have used a whiteboard from Dan's office trying to explain it all. I tried to catch Monroe's eyes all that time but could only see her profile. I desperately wanted to sit down, but there was nowhere to rest in my little patch of painted gravel.

Dan arrived with a friend from work who immediately went to the Acorn and drove it off. After eyeballing me, Dan approached the head cop, who was talking to Monroe and her mom. Dan did a lot of nodding and then shook hands with the cop and said something while hugging Mrs. Alpert before she led Monroe away. Head down, hands in pockets, Dan started his walk toward me, obviously rehearsing what he'd say to his inherited kid who had finally gone too far. He now had his reason to let me have it, tell me how I had basically weighed him and his life down like a stone tied to his ankle. He'd never planned to have a kid like me, never asked for any of this. I'd feel the same way. But I heard nothing because right before Dan opened his mouth to begin, Monroe turned toward me with her lips pressed together and her eyes pushed up and to the right. A look I hadn't seen in a very long time.

"Take me home," I said. "I'll listen better in the car." I guess I was hanging my head because Dan lifted my chin with his finger. Dressed in his pressed khakis and white button-down shirt, phone clipped to his belt, he seemed more adultish.

"I don't want to lecture you."

I felt my face scrunch in confusion. Maybe, before all this, I would have said, "Then don't." But not today.

"I'm not condoning what you did. It was stupid and reckless and someone could have gotten hurt. We're obviously gonna have to start our driving lessons again, but I knew something had to give sometime with you." I started heading toward his car, and his hand locked on to my shoulder, turning me around. I'm sure the people watching us must have thought Dan was chewing me out, but he wasn't. "I know we don't have the perfect home situation, me and you, and you've had a rough time with Monroe, not to mention your mom. But I just want to say that I'm glad you're okay and I get it."

I dropped my head again because I had finally let out the breath I'd been holding and it triggered something behind my eyes that made them start pissing like rain inside a car wash.

Dan lifted my chin again. "Okay?"

"Okay," I said, staring him straight in the face. I didn't look away this time. For many Mississippis. Then he held out his arms to hug me. "Drugs, not hugs," I said, and we walked side by side to his car.

Research Note: The thing about Lindy is that he walks like a cowboy who once rode a horse a few sizes too small.

The thing about Monroe's mom is that she squints. She may need glasses.

The thing about Dan is that he always pulls down the cuffs of his shirt before he walks out the front door.

The thing about Mom is that she picks at these very small hairs at the crown of her head when she's nervous.

The thing about Avree is that she lightly tugs on her earlobes like she's checking to see if her earrings fell off. She's not checking for that, though (I asked her).

The thing about Monroe is that she is one of the smartest funny people I know. Or should that be funniest smart?

The thing about me is

35

Avree got grounded, I was told I wouldn't be able to drive until six months after my sixteenth birthday, and I had to face my mom at El Dorado (though Dan left out some of the more worrisome details). Avree and I didn't get into any textworthy trouble at school other than a one-day suspension. Everyone knew what had happened when we got back on that Tuesday, and most of the reviews from other kids were weirdly favorable. Funny the difference between a cool pointing from a kid you don't know (*You the man!*) and a freak pointing (*You a freak!*). I did get a lecture though from Pornstache about how we should never leave campus again without passes AND telling someone where we were headed. Or else. All lame gasbag talk, since we'd soon be leaving Red Rock Junior for RR High where, we were told, security is supposedly all fences and armed cops and dogs and closed parking lots. More security than Columbine, the paper said once.

It was the follow-up meeting with the Nurselor that was the hardest. She told me the same thing she'd told Avree, which was why Avree kept talking about the future and all the things that I (and we) could do in high school. I thought Avree was just being nice (she was), but there was another reason for this new thread of conversation, and it wasn't good

or pretty. Even now, it's hard for me to remember the day the
Nurselor broke the bad news about Monroe.

The other thing I did was make it so we all could give our
presentations together: Monroe and my Colon Studies and
Avree and my science dealy-oh all together at the same time
during presentation day. Almost like a band, but not really (I
thought it was, Monroe disagreed). I pimped the idea for a
lot of reasons. I wanted Monroe not to have to go to summer
school because she said she'd rather get her blood cleaned
again than sit with all the stoners and tards (her word, not
mine) for eight hours every day in a cleaned-out classroom.
It turns out that presentation day was the least of anyone's
worries, but at the time I thought it would mean something.
Maybe more than something.

Avree said she wanted the group presentation to happen
too, and at first Leapyear was all bent (*Not the way we do things
here*), but I had Dan, Monroe's mom, and Avree's dad all call
and squeaky-wheel her, saying after all we'd been through, it
would be therapeutic (Monroe's mom), educational (Avree's
dad), and highly super creative (Dan). After that chorus of
cranky voices, Leapyear had to give in. Beaker droned that he'd
be in the front row that day, but the way he said it sounded
more like *I'm tired of teaching kids like you, you take too much
energy*, not that he really wanted to see the three of us get
on risers and present our findings with video and music and
other spices.

One of the thousand hardest things for me during all this
(if you want to know) was visiting Monroe. This was like two
weeks after the car-wash catastrophe, and Dan dropped me

off at Monroe's house when her parents weren't there. I was nervous that she'd see right through me, know that I knew, and that would upset her. But she hadn't told me anything during those two weeks, so I figured . . . I don't know what I figured, except that my gut felt funny. Not butterflies, cannonballs. Dread.

Her mom had put their house back together mostly, though there was an empty new cabinet for some minor royal wedding that was going to happen in the summer. "Memorabilia will start flying in here any day now," Monroe said, unimpressed. She was dressed in a white kimono with Japanese symbols painted on the back. It looked like a bunch of circles got into a fight with a spider. Her arms had become twigs.

"Memorabilia?"

"Teacups, saucers, plates, trays, potholders, and a buttwad of other items." All going next to its twin, filled with Charles and Diana crappage. Her mom's voice rang in my head: *That poor Di-an-a.*

"Didn't Charles get married again?" I asked, trying to delay talking about why I'd come.

"Camilla Parker-Bowels is dead to my mom," Monroe said, breathing hard. "She can't even say her name out loud. I only mention her when I'm trying to piss her off."

I could tell by the no dog and cat hair situ that her animals were gone forever. No chew toys, rubber balls, and the lack of a buttload of other animal-related items and evidence. Water bowls, scratching post, litter-box smell. "Aren't you guys too broke for all this, I mean, more stuff?" The cabinet was so freaking new you could taste the glue.

"You'd think so," she said, walking slower than even two weeks before.

To my surprise, Monroe's room was done, and more like a wo-man cave than a bedroom. All white walls, nothing on them.

"When did they, um, finish the floor?"

"After my wandering." That's what she called it when she ran away, her wandering. "Freaked them out so much that they asked me what I wanted for once. I told them my stuff." She picked up a Hello Dead Kitty pencil case and rubbed the Xs over the eyes. "I said I wanted all my stuff back."

All her albums and CDs and books and manga and collectibles were encased (vocab) in modern steel cabinets. Everything was so clean. It felt weird, but it kinda reminded me of Christmas—gifts in boxes, only all spaceship status. Presents for robots or cyborgs. Metal frames, sliding doors, smoky glass so you could just make out the outlines of the books without seeing any of the titles. Her CD player and turntable were in a cabinet too, only taller, and looking at her, I knew I had to tell her something soon, before her parents came home, especially if she was going to go mental on me, which was a real possibility. She sat cross-legged on a hypoallergenic rug over acid-washed concrete. She said they had to tear out all the carpet. Something was missing, duh, a lot was missing from the time when her room was a shite show and we had all these albums out, dirty clothes in the corner, poster board on the carpet, glitter pens, and design-your-own-temporary tattoo kits. Maybe that's why Monroe said what she said: "Wanna see my room?"

"Um, Neo, we are in your room."

"My sleeping chamber."

"I thought that was off limits to us germies."

"No one will know."

In the movies, my line would be "I'll know," but that didn't make sense, and Monroe stood up and walked out to the back of the house, past the laundry room, which was really a hallway with a large closet, doors removed, where the high-tech machines lived. They had to have the bestest washers and dryers, all eco-friendly and gentle cycle. In the corner was a green oxygen tank with clear tubing snaking off the top. The back door opened up with a sucking whoosh onto a hallway that was built from plastic so it felt like we were in a tent or a very clean and long portapotty with no toilet. It had that weird orangey portapotty light that makes you feel sick and trapped. "When did they put this in?"

"Same time as my other room."

My eyes were straining to get outside. "It's kinda trippy."

She turned back to face me, her face all orange glow. "We're heading to another dimension." Her teeth turned orange when she smiled. "I have to shower before I go in at night and my pajamas need to be clean. I can't bring anything in."

I asked about books, even though her mom had already told me. I was only killing time.

"No books. No magazines. No nada. Like being teleported."

"Weird." I checked my pockets for things that might corrupt my DNA if we traveled through time and space. Reflex. Too many movies, I guess.

"I know, right? But you get used to it. It is kinda nice sleeping in a place that's clean, with no crap."

"No crap."

We were at the front of this egg-shaped mini-house with two circular windows and a door that opened up like a spaceship. The pre-yard used to be just a big patch of dirt for her three dogs to run around on. A mess really, holes and old colored rags the dogs chewed on. Poop. Now the dirt had been leveled and they'd staked down that meshy material that you use to kill weeds. It felt weird to walk on it even for a second, but weirder to see the building, if you could call it that. From the side it kinda looked like a big egg or, with the round window, an eyeball.

A metal box held a pile of stacked white slippers. All of a sudden I felt all dirty, kinda like I smoke but I don't. I hadn't showered that day, and I couldn't remember when I'd last washed my jeans. I didn't want to go in and spoil everything. Guess my face was all fatty sad or something because Monroe hit it: "Just take off your shoes and socks. No big deal." Monroe eyed my bottom third, scrunched her eyes, and scratched her temple. "Roll up your cuffs too."

Her sleeping room was much bigger than mine, but only had a bed and two machines: air conditioner-size one bolted to the wall to purify the air, control the temperature and humidity, and do something with ions. The other was a combo iPod deck, CD player, and noise machine that had like twenty presets with different sounds. Monroe played them all for me: waterfall, rainstorm, desert evening (crickets and coyotes), fire crackling, light summer breeze blowing through leaves. The lights were the new kind that "mimicked" natural light and used almost no energy. Monroe had a razor-thin remote to dim or set them on a timer. "Mod-pods, I think they call my new boudoir." She moved her index finger in an arc to cover the whole space. "Or Archipods, I think, like architecture. I prefer to think of it as my own Tardis."

Cheesy, I know, but I wanted my own time machine too. I always had.

There wasn't much to see in the place after she played DJ with all the fake sounds. My stomach started hurting. There were only a few times in my life it had hurt that bad. I'd spent all morning distracted, on the Internet, then off the Internet, turned on the TV, then off. Even Dan said I was acting as fidgety as a spaz when he made me my breakfast burrito, but then he said he was sorry he used the word. Overapology. And I knew this was the time to say something to Monroe because she had nothing left to show me. In this room anyway. At this time. In our lives. On this planet. In this universe.

"I need to tell you something." I ran my hand through my hair and then wiped it off on my jeans. Germs.

She smiled. "You are really a girl?" she asked, but she hardly had the energy to nail the joke anymore.

"You guessed it," I answered automatically.

She didn't comment again, so I knew it was my turn. It was hard not staring at the new floor. It was so clean. "Ever since you got sick, you know, I did research on, you know, what was happening to you. And I had that science project on the platypus, but I couldn't concentrate, so I switched it from that to heavy metal poisoning?" I'm not sure why I ended it in a question.

Her face went wet towel, so I knew she was scrambling to keep up with my babble, but I kept going. I don't know if

I breathed at all. "And then I kept changing it based on what your doctors were saying and then I added some musicians who got sick, added them in there too, kinda like a soup I guess, anything that crossed my mind really so it wasn't *totally* about you, and I'm sorry if you think I'm a creeper and a stalker but I'm really not, I swear, I just couldn't get my mind around . . ."

Silence: I could hear the whine of the air thingy and the crackle and pop of the digital fire. All the walls were white and uninterrupted and kinda shiny-sparkly. Sunlight shot through the porthole windows like laser beams, just missing me and Monroe. *Would I be lonely sleeping in a place like this?* I sang in my head. Then a mess of other lyrics flooded in too while Monroe filled her cheeks with air and then released. The slight white lines from when I saw her face last had thickened like dried-up veins.

My confession was another type of confession. It doesn't matter if no one but me understands that.

She shrugged. "Avree told me you'd been keeping tabs on me."

"She did?" It sounded just like Avree to use the word *tabs*. "When?"

"The subject of you came up, and she said you didn't show her much or anything and at first she thought you were all obsessed with me, but then she realized you were just an emo friend. Hella emo." I could tell she wanted to pull at her hair like she used to, but her mom was really trying to get her not to touch anything she didn't have to, especially her face and hair and skin. "Yeah. And then after you made out with her and put your hands all up her shirt—"

"She said all that? Jesus." I was so embarrassed I might've blushed.

"No, I made that last part up."

Then she didn't say how she felt about any of my research for a few awkward minutes and my pants got all tight and I worried that my germs were flying everywhere and we should get the hellboy out of there but I didn't want to seem chicken or guilty so I waited, squirming on my butt cheeks, trying not to exhale so my heavy breakfast burrito breath didn't infect her pillowcase or anything.

"Don't use my name or anything, even though people will guess." She looked away toward the porthole in a way that made me bet she did that a lot at night. We'd always talked about being at an even bigger school where we could avoid the Trees and the ath-e-letes and just roam on our own, unbothered, making jokes, busting missions. I looked closer, since her stare had locked onto something else: her eyes now had flecks of yellow in the white parts, and that pissed me off and made me sad at the same time.

"No pictures of me unless you blur the face." I knew she didn't want to, but she brushed her cheek while pretending to brush her hair. Who could blame her for wanting to touch her goddamn face? "Or maybe one of those cool black bars across my eyes like in the Sex Pistols poster."

I agreed but felt an unjust churning inside me, anger and rage, and I started cursing everything I'd ever known to be true or hopeful or sure.

"And hands, arms, you know, try to cover those up."

"Okay," I said. It was almost like she knew, like she'd jumped in her Tardis and gone into the near future and then come back again. And none of it made me feel any better about where everything was going.

"I get to pick the music."

"All of it?" I had to ask that. Otherwise, she would have broken apart. (I would've too.)

"Most."

And then the fire sounds clicked off—they were on a timer, so all we had to listen to was air hissing in surround sound.

"And one more thing."

"Okay," I said, as if I could handle one more thing of all the one more things in my so-called one brief life.

"Don't tell anyone my secrets."

"Which ones?" There were so many. That's what being a ninth-grader was all about.

"No matter what."

What would you have said? Remember, we're talking Monroe and me in a freaking Archipod at the end of our school year in the middle of nowhere Red Rock. And words had started to appear in the future that was once so unwritten. Words I can't even say now. So I said, "No matter what," because that is what she needed to hear.

36

"I'll wait out here," I said, opening the door. I shut the front and then opened the back.

I love the sound of slamming car doors. I stepped in the back where I hadn't ridden in a while. It felt, you know, younger-like.

"Don't be nervous," Dan called to me as he raced up the steps, his sport coat opening like wings.

I wasn't sure which thing he was telling me not to be nervous about. Maybe he meant everything that day. Through the middle seat I could see the little scratchy juniper bushes and dry grasses, red dirt, and a baby of a hill. Was that where the guests snuck off to tell secrets about what they're in for? I wondered. Smoking's allowed in the rhino cage, so they didn't need to go anywhere to puffa puffa. Maybe they came there to mess around. Crazy people makeout sessions or something. That would be wild to see.

Math's not my best subject, but three people walked out of those glass doors to go to Presentation Day with me, not two as I thought: Dan, Mom, and Lindy. He was dressed in a hat cabbies wear in movies and a tweed jacket, the kind with the cow's udders flattened on the elbows, but it was my

mom who freaked me out a little. She wore the same outfit
she had on when she entered El Dorado: I always said it was
yellow, but she said "canary," which I thought was funny at
the time 'cause I'd seen a Bugs Bunny cartoon where *canary*
meant a snitch or rat or tattletale. My mom was a snitch.
I'd sounded "canary" out loud just to see if I could do it like
Bugs. Her shirt was shiny, like a big yellow pearl. I scooched
over to let Lindy have some room. They both spoke at the
same time:

"Only thing I had," my mom said, like she could
read my mind.

"Okay if I tag along?" Lindy smiled and then wrestled
with his seat belt. Like me, he probably wasn't used to riding
in back. He would photograph more like a driver, not a pas-
senger, I thought. Dan slipped the car into gear and crawled
around the circular drive. All careful-like.

"Well, look at us." My mom turned around in her seat to
face me. I couldn't see before, but I noticed she had an actual
string of pearls on over her shirt. Pearls before pearls (English-
class joke). "Like them?" She caught me staring at her necklace,
so she hooked her thumb underneath and pushed the shiny
balls of sand formed by oyster spit toward me.

"Sure, why not?" I shrugged. Nothing better than a shrug.

"I think your mom looks great," Lindy said in a way that
wasn't as creepy as it sounds.

"Ditto from the driver!" Dan saluted in the rear-
view. DorKing (king of dorks), Dorkarama, Dorkagogo,
Dorkus Maximus.

"Please don't say 'ditto,' " I said quietly.

"Well, you nervous?" Mom asked. She twisted to see me, her Sunday clothes getting all wrinkled and bunched. "Did you eat?"

"If you turn back around, we can still talk, Mom. You look all twisted." Abso.

"I just want to look at you. I don't get to see you enough."

"Not much to look at," I said, almost without wanting to. So stupid. Gag reflex.

"Don't say that. Mr. Lindbergh, don't you think—"

Before my mom, Dan, and Lindy could start that horrid convincing thing that parents do—*You are, too, good at math. Getting better and better each day at soccer! You ride beautifully*—I cut them off: "Just kidding, guys, I'm fine." I put my hands in the air. *Nothing to hide here. Move your pity along to the nearest subway stop.*

We drove through the neighborhood you have to cut through to get to the highway, and all the driveways were empty, people at work and all. White tongues of cement or concrete or whatever unfurled between green cheeks of lawn. This neighborhood didn't do lava rock or pebbles or Astroturf. One of the few I'd seen that hadn't surrendered to the fact that we live in the freakin' desert, hello? I knew I could get Dan going if I mentioned it, go on a rant about how selfish people are. Water is a valuable resource. If he's really mad, he'll say how selfish *white* people are and go into the history of lawns and how the whole wasteful idea came from rich-ass British cake-eaters in powdered wigs or something. You couldn't even buy grass seed in the States before 1900, according to Dan. But today wasn't the day for that.

"Isn't it nice that Mr. Lindbergh joined us?" Mom asked. "Sure."

"I hope you don't mind," Lindy said, placing his palms flat on his khakis. He looked older outside of Dorado, rough around the edges. Tired. Grayer, like a fading photo. "I really want to see what you've done, and it doesn't hurt me to get out. Now and then." He adjusted his glasses, which were getting darker with the sun, so I could no longer see his eyes.

"It's fine." It was. I could tell by the way everyone in that car was eyeballing me, even Dan in the mouth-shaped mirror, that no one believed me. "Really. It's fine," I said again. "Everything's fine." I tried to find a place to rest my eyes.

By this time we had hit the highway, and I don't know, maybe I thought someone would come along and do something with the frozen construction site, like in chapter books or movies. In those candy-colored worlds, some rich former hippie would buy the place and turn it into a theme park or, now, probably an organic garden and recycling theme park or a skate park that harnessed power from the skateboards to charge electric cars or old-age homes or Archipods. But those shows aren't real, and life is.

"We're very excited to see what you've come up with," my mom said.

"I can vouch for him," Dan piped in. "This *brochacho* and his two *chicaricas* have been burning the midnight oil for weeks now. Mostly one *chica*, but you know."

"*Chicaricas*? Really?" Oh, Dan.

The crane was still paused over a half-finished building, though the yellow paint on the arm seemed brown now from the dust and sun. Must be the sun. Too dry for rust. *Ghost town is the toast town.*

"Two girls? Man, I knew you had one, but now two?" Lindy was being funny. "Wow."

"One is only his friend." My mom checked her face in the mirror that flops down from the sun visor thingy.

"But the other is more." Dan smirked to himself.

"Whatevs." I turned to Lindy. "How's your bird?"

"Oh, well, I've been meaning to tell you when I saw you again, that day when you met him, he wasn't in best form. He's much better now." He had taken off his hat and was turning it in his hands like a steering wheel.

I liked him for seeing how weird that day was for me. Him too. It wasn't like the adults at school who wouldn't blink if the whole class started snoring, who didn't notice when kids gave haircuts or got piercings at lunch over sloppy joes. Even cut themselves.

"I hope you can get the chance to see him again."

I'd like that too is what they'd say on TV, but that was far too ghey for me, so I said, "Cool." *Whatevs* would have been too mean, especially since I just played it with Dan for getting overstimulated. Somehow it felt as if it was Sunday and we were all heading to church, a place I hadn't been since I was little. Everyone was dressed and sat up all proper posture status. My mom had a handbag, and Lindy wore the kind of hat that would fit in fine with the other not-everyday hats. Dan was just Dan, but we were all together, and everyone seemed happy or excited, which is like happy or at least it can be seen that way by most people. We were all facing forward, and for

a minute I almost completely forgot about El Dorado, like
we would never have to return. Someday, I thought, running
my hands down pretty much the only tie I'd had my whole
life, someday I would grow myself the most badass mustache.

When we arrived at school, Lindy put his hand on my knee,
which was an awkward adult gesture that said *Don't get out of
the car just yet.* Confused, I looked to my mom, whose door
was being held open by Dan. Neither one looked back as they
started walking toward the front entrance of the school. If this
was a mob film, I would have been goners for sure.

"I've got something I need to tell you," Lindy said. He
folded up his glasses and put them carefully in his hat, which
was lined in silk. "It's about your mom."

I hum-grunted to let him know I was listening.

"Sometimes it takes a while for things to evolve. I just
didn't want you to get the wrong idea, and I didn't know if
we'd get a chance to check in after the event—"

"Can you please just tell me?"

When he let the air out with an exhale, he looked even
older. "Your mother will be in treatment for a while longer."

"How much longer?"

"I can't say."

I tried to decode. "You can't say like a month, or you can't
say like six months?"

He couldn't say, so he didn't say. Anything. Looking back,
I should have (a) seen the signs that she was still struggling,
or (b) seized the day all *Dead Poets Society* style, since we were
all together for a few hours. Almost all of us, anyway.

"Who died and made you the messenger?" I asked, kinda like a dick, even though I already knew the answer.

Then I got out of the car.

37

Presentation Day is carved up into subjects, and we were scheduled to go on between the electives and science in our own special slot. All the cast were there that day: Nurselor, Pornstache, Leapyear, Gross, Ms. J and T-Dubs, the Nelson, Ms. Hempl, and students. The only one missing was Beaker, who wouldn't be back at RRJH. No one could ever tell me why, and like a lot of other stuff, his exit faded into the back of all that happened during that year.

The maint men had set up the cafetorium in a U shape, with the octotables around the sad little stage where the lame bands, theater freaks, and unfunny standup kids from the comedy troupers had performed for the last month or so. Little white pads lay scattered on the table next to the copied programs and gold pencils "kindly" donated by Holes and Knolls Mini-Golf. The teachers had asked us to rate each presentation and make a compliment sandwich, but only the parents participated in that. Some of them anyways. I knew my mom would say that everyone was wonderful, every snowflake of a child was unique and special, having unique abilities and talents. The place swelled with all the dressed-up-like-they're-going-to-court crowd, and I felt Dan, my mom, and Lindy behind me, waiting for me to tell them where to go and what to do (for once). I felt a little panicky for a second, with all my millions of friends waving me down (sure, right), but then I saw Monroe's mom at a table near the bulletin board. She was in that blue crinkly weight-loss warm-up deal.

"Dahling!" Monroe's mom shouted a ways away, eyes wetting themselves. "Are you finally free?" She stood up and held out her arm like a needy stuffed animal.

Awk-ward.

My mom's back stiffened. "It's so nice to see you, Viv."

Mrs. Alpert shrink-wrapped my mom in her arms. When my mom finally broke free, she said, "This is Mr. Lindbergh," but Monroe's mom was only paying attention to mine, eyeing her up and down for who knows what. Incisions? Tubes? Wires? She corralled my *madre* over to the two seats on the octotable that were far too close together, peppering (spicy vocab verb) her with questions, all red in the face, while my mom just nodded politely and answered. Mrs. Alpert is the kind of parent who needs a project, and my mom was ripe.

"What are these pads for?" Dan nudged one with his fingertips.

"In case you want to make comments on the presentations. Nobody ever—" Before I said "does it," Dan chimed in: "Good idea. Accountability. It might keep me a bit more engaged, too." He threw his shoulders back like he was getting to work and settled in for the dog and pony.

Lindy pretended to admire the round columns with carpeting up the base and the bulletin board that had the week's menu: Pizza, Taco Tuesday, Sloppy José, Hamburger, and A

Special, which was us that day. Not enough room in the grid
for Event, as in A Special Event.

I scanned the 'torium. Elizabeth Buchanan had somehow
convinced Flip and another buff guy to dress like Pilgrims
in shiny black smocks from a hair salon and big belt buckles
and stovepipe hats snipped from black poster board. She'd
volunteered to go first, and no one objected. Flip fingered the
low neckline thingy and didn't seem too happy to be on Team
Lizzie. I was looking for (you know who by now), and for a
minute I was thinking she might not show. Who would have
blamed her? No great movie-star catch here, no life-changing
event. I checked each group claiming a different part of the
room: Trees posing, stoners dragging beat-up shoes, under-
the-stairs computer nerds speaking in sound effects, theater
geeks doing vocal warm-up a-e-i-o-u deals, some kid dressed
like Einstein doling out free key chains that read GENIUS!
I gave mine to Dan, who said the idea showed initiative. He
said that Einstein could have cut the lines cleaner. Straighter.
Then I saw her. Them. For some reason, I didn't expect Avree
to be a them. Everything and everyone were multiplying on
me that day. I never would have guessed that her parents
would come. Stiff, they were. Like sticks. Giant matchsticks.

Her dad wore a three-piece blue suit like he was going
to the prom. Cool mustache I hadn't really noticed when he
retrieved his daughter at the infamous car wash incident. Her
mom was in a dress that snapped all the way down, covered
in little black dots, with a collar. Old-timey but stylish, you
know? She moved like she had a straitjacket on underneath.
All stiff-legged and neck-erect.

Avree didn't see me. She was searching frantically, yet trying not to look frantic or touch her hair, which she had straightened to rock-star status (pretty f-bomb *fuego*). She bit her lower lip, my cue to wave like an idiot. Her eyes lit up, and the three of them turned like a trio of geese or school of fish, necks first and then bodies. We didn't have enough seats, so I grabbed the octo to the left and pulled it until the two circles touched. Planets colliding. Eight orbiting suns each. I stepped back so they wouldn't feel, you know, like castaways. My mom in the pre-days said that most adults got totally freaked out by going back to class because it brought back all the PTSD feelings from middle school. Smells of BO, meatloaf, chalk, chunder, cleaning supplies, and the claustrophobia of all those kids running around. I didn't want them to feel weird, so I took those two steps back. Sometimes all it takes, right? Then they were right there.

"I'm Coy," I said. Avree's parents said hello, and I introduced them all around best I could.

"So I finally get to meet you," Dan said, standing up. "You have a really cool daughter." Too much emphasis on *really*. "If I had a daughter I'd want her to be—"

"Easy, Dan," I said, trying to save him from himself.

His hands shot out like the loud guy on the car commercial. "Hey. What? I'm just being honest." *Low low prices!*

Avree's folks nodded politely. Her mom was younger than I thought, and her dad not so young, with his thick curly hair and mustache. Her mom was the afraid kind of pretty, like she bit her nails or something when no one was looking or had to wear a retainer at night. The way her eyes went, it was like she was waiting for me to say something to her, something I should have known about but didn't. Maybe a password or I don't know what. It was kinda weird actually, but she seemed nice—fragile but nice.

Dan chatted with Avree's dad about where everyone in the world lived and parked their cars and avoided traffic at this time of day and how hot it'd been for so long but he'd swear he saw a fat cloud on the way over. Dan even got her dad a pad and a dwarf pencil, which I thought was so lame (*Low low prices!*), but Avree whispered "Hey, bub" in my ear, and her mom smiled when Avree did that, like she taught her or something, which would have been creepy. And everyone was paired up but her mom, a watery pretty woman acting like the last one picked for dodgeball or something. Note: I need to stop saying the word *something*.

"We should all sit down," I said. This me-in-the-mom-daughter-middle was getting awkward, and Pornstache was onstage, staring out with his dingy white shirt and polyester pants, trying to get anyone to listen to his sad song. He tapped the mike on his pants leg.

"Students, faculty, parents, and other guests, welcome to Red Rock Junior High School. We are happy to welcome you to our annual presentation day. Students will present by discipline . . ."

Lindy chuckled at that word.

"And I hope you will join us for a special lunch reception after the presentations."

"If they don't cut the budget again," Dan joked, and Avree's dad's mustache curled up out of kindness.

"You okay?" I whispered to Avree.

"Yeah, you?"

"Yeah. Sister at school?"

"Yeah."

"This is a fascinating conversation."

"We should do this more often." She was looking at Monroe's mom's hands flying all around my mom's personal space. Elastic pinching the cuffs of her crinkle suit. "Your mom is much prettier in person."

"Yeah." I nodded. "The bowling alley is not her favorite place to be transmitted to. It doesn't do her justice."

I guess Avree caught my eyes darting over to her mom standing there in a twisty way that made Dan later label her a wallflower. He called me that back in the day. More than once.

"Hey Mom," Avree called over. "Why don't you go sit with Dad? There are plenty of seats." She whispered to me, "She doesn't like crowds," and ran her thumbnail over her front teeth, but not in a gross way. "Neither does my dad, but he fakes it better."

Sure enough, he was nodding along while Dan yadda yadda yaddaed, and my mom was nodding along while Monroe's mom blam-blam-blammered. In the middle was Avree's mom.

In cartoons, when a mouse or cat or Scooby-Doo doesn't know what to do, he turns his head back and forth blurry fast, and it sounds like dice being shaken in a leather cup. I don't know if my head made that sound, but Lindy picked up on my awkwardness, so he went over to Avree's mom, introduced himself, and asked her to sit down. Nicely. It's just the kind of guy he is, and I never understood (or maybe believed) how cool that was until that very minute.

We all heard applause and saw that Lizzie had unrolled a
backdrop of two painted trees and a brown log bench. Lindy
said something that made Avree's mom smile and turn toward
the stage. Lizzie had obviously memorized her lines, while the
boys had def not. Flip brought out a cardboard adze and mumbled something that no one could hear, so Lizzie basically said
his lines for him, saying "You mean" at the beginning of each
sentence but twisting it into a question. Like: "You mean this
is a tool we use for smoothing or carving rough-cut wood in
hand woodworking? You mean we call this an adze?" Leapyear
was to the right of the stage with Ms. Gross (who was seated,
of course), and the Leapster seemed fine until the other dude
started reading his lines from the cell phone he held inside the
folds of his dressing gown. People started laughing, and Leapyear
showed her disapproval by flashing a deep frown. Dan was
scribbling away, marking the dude way down in Dan's poser
grade book. I almost felt bad for Lizzie. She was up there trying
to do a good job, she obviously knew all her shite, but she had
two boneheads as partners. And I wondered what it would be
like to do better in school. I mean, my grades were fine, but I
could try to care more about a few classes or something. About
what I'd like to do in high school or whatever. Not like Lizzie,
but someday, what I'd like to be someday, you know? Someday?
Make music or movies. Write something. I'm not sure.

Avree squeezed my arm as we all sat through a YouTube
video on the fall of the Roman Empire using Disney action figures (*Who put the bad in gladiator?*); a demi-boring PowerPoint
on Greek gods, demi-gods, and goddesses; and a hand-raising
activity on the first alphabet. No one raised hands except for

the adults. Even my mom got tired of the whole stupid thing, sighed, and stopped. Dan never stopped.

And then there was a break, which meant it was our time to set up. Mrs. Alpert checked her phone and nodded no-go, so Avree and I walked over to the maint closet behind the stage and got the gear we had stowed there the day before. I started hooking up my laptop and my turntable and speakers while Avree grabbed all the props. I plugged my platypus jump drive in and saw Avree gently placing Lindy's *Spirit of St. Louis* on top of one speaker, and one of Mack's crazy toy sculptures on the other. Avree had surprised me in rehearsal when she brought out the thing. She told me she had her mom drive her over to Mack's and ask him to borrow one. He said they should buy one, dammit, but Avree convinced him that it was for a school project on outsider art or something. She might have called him a genius to seal the deal.

I started to sweat a little as I inserted USB cords. The show we'd put together was a little weird. More than a little. And now one part was missing. We'd combined all our projects, so on the screen people were going to see Avree's platypus followed by an X-ray of Monroe's lungs followed by a short video of Pee-wee Herman knocking over a Jamestown hut. We all had reports we were ready to read (and hand in for credit), but they were alternating bits with music in the background, songs chosen to comment on whatever we were reading or showing on the screen. Monroe said we all had to put family photos, videos, and recordings in, since I was focusing on her illness. So imagine Avree's shaky family vacation to New Mexico projected on a big screen while the sound track to *The*

Good, the Bad and the Ugly played behind it, and Avree read a paragraph about a mammal laying eggs. See what I mean? Putting it together was megafun, but it could all seem like crazy talk to everyone else.

I was tacking up a poster of David Bowie when Pornstache came over, pointed to his nerdy watch, and told us to move it along. I quickly moved the mikes over so mine was by my turntable, Avree's in the middle, at the podium, and Monroe's was to the side. Avree and I put on sunglasses, which felt stupid, but she liked the idea so I went with it. My heart was pounding, I was so nervous. Avree seemed totally fine onstage, and Monroe's empty microphone didn't look too weird with all that other stuff. Only our families would know what it was there for. Only our families knew that our backup plan was to Skype Monroe during this time, so she could still be a part of it all. Only our families would know that Monroe was too sick now to even sit up.

Maybe I was wrong when I thought that the only choices in school are to laugh or be bored to death.

I nodded at Avree and played the opening chimes of "Hells Bells."

"Listen up," Avree said, fist in the air, and there was a great boom that made it feel like Monroe was there, if only for a second. Then the power went out. I flipped my glasses up. There were no lights on my laptop, no lights in the cafetorium, no lights nowhere.

"Pornstache cut us off because we took too long setting up," Avree said, upset. "I knew it."

The crowd stood, and even though I couldn't see much, I could hear people murmuring about a blown circuit. Dan was first up to the stage. "Need help?" he asked, and quickly started messing with the cables and cords. Then my mom and Lindy and Avree's mom and dad were front row, all asking if we were all right, and could we please step away from the mikes? Then it was Pornstache wagging his finger, Leapyear in tow. The Nurselor advised all to keep calm. The maint men shrugged near their closet, which I guessed held the breaker box. Thinking about it now, seeing all those adults running around was pretty funny and it was too bad we couldn't have played some Journey as a soundtrack as we watched them scurry about. Too bad Monroe couldn't see it, or that my mom would be heading back to Dorado in just a few hours. I heard a shoelace of a whisper, and there was Avree, standing alone in a crowd, hair long and straight, center stage like an old Velvet Underground poster. God, she was so beautiful. I moved my eyes and ears around to hear her better.

"Listen," she whispered. Then I lost the rest of it. "Listen," she whispered again.

"Hey!" someone yelled. I swear it sounded like Monroe, but maybe I made that happen in my ears. Everyone quieted down.

"It's raining," Avree said. Pitter-patter on the roof, and heads all turned to the nearest window to catch the drops falling. That curtain of water totally changed the view. That, and an amazing silence that seemed to last longer than all of my life so far.

"Told you," Dan said.

A NOTE FROM ROBERT WILDER

This is a work of fiction only and describes a fictional medical situation. Do not rely on information in this novel as a substitute for sound medical advice, diagnosis, or treatment. I am not a doctor. I don't even play one on TV. If this is an emergency, please hang up and dial 911.

ACKNOWLEDGMENTS

A portion of the novel was first published in *Ohio Edit*, founded by Amy Fusselman.

Thanks to wonderful friends and great readers Christopher Schelling, Robert Boswell, Antonya Nelson, Kathleen Lee, Tony Hoagland, and Eddie Lewis.

Deep appreciation to Andy and Sarah at Leaf Storm Press for believing in this book.

Special thanks to those who supported the book and/or its author: Andy and Sue, Audra Genduso, Augusten and Christopher, Natalie Goldberg, Patience Skarsgard, William Clift, Phyllis Leavitt, Carola Kieve, Melissa Carl, Mark Bixby, Michael Schroeder, Edie and Jonah, Nouf and Peter, Jack and Marta, Marc and Megan, my three brothers and their families, Nora Geiss, and Eva Wilder Kramer.

This book is also in memory of my father, Ben Wilder (1929–2014), and my mother, Joan Wilder (1931–1983).

ABOUT THE AUTHOR

Robert Wilder is the author of two critically acclaimed essay collections, *Tales from the Teachers' Lounge* and *Daddy Needs a Drink*.

A teacher for twenty-five years, Wilder has earned numerous awards and fellowships, including the inaugural Innovations in Reading Prize by the National Book Foundation. He has published essays in *Newsweek, Details, Salon, Parenting, Creative Nonfiction*, plus numerous anthologies and has been a commentator for NPR's *Morning Edition*.

Wilder lives in Santa Fe, New Mexico.

Visit him at RobertWilder.com or Facebook.com/ RobertTWilder.

Follow him on Twitter @RobertTWilder.